MURDOCH'S
World

MURDOCH'S *World*

THE LAST OF THE OLD MEDIA EMPIRES

David Folkenflik

PublicAffairs
New York

For Nora—
who warned me never to be boring

And for Jesse and Viola—
who never are

Copyright © 2013 by David Folkenflik.

Published in the United States by PublicAffairs™,
a Member of the Perseus Books Group

Printed in Australia.

PublicAffairs books are available at special discounts for bulk
purchases in the U.S. by corporations, institutions, and other
organizations. For more information, please contact the Special
Markets Department at the Perseus Books Group, 2300 Chestnut
Street, Suite 200, Philadelphia, PA, 19103, call (800) 810-4145,
ext. 5000, or e-mail special.markets@perseusbooks.com.

Book Design by Pauline Brown
Typeset in Century Expanded Lt Std by the Perseus Books Group

Library of Congress Cataloging-in-Publication Data
Folkenflik, David.
    Murdoch's world : the last of the old media empires / David
Folkenflik.—First edition.
        pages cm
    Includes index.
    ISBN 978-1-61039-089-7 (hardback)—ISBN 978-1-61039-090-3
(electronic)—ISBN 978-1-61039-408-6 (international paperback)
1. Murdoch, Rupert, 1931-2. Mass media—Australia—
Biography. I. Title.

P92.5.M87F65 2013
070'.92—dc23
[B]
                                                        2013014186

First Edition
10   9   8   7   6   5   4   3   2

CONTENTS

AUTHOR'S NOTE

THE EVENTS DESCRIBED IN THIS book opened an unprece-
dented and broad window into the thinking of Rupert Murdoch, his
executives, and the culture at News Corporation (News Corp), the
company he has led for more than six decades. Many senior employees
have been forced to go on the public record in the United Kingdom as
a result of allegations of widespread criminality at News Corp's tabloids there. Yet it is hard to apprehend the context for those scandals
without mastering the history of the company, the dynamics of the
Murdoch family, and the world they inhabit. This book is an effort to
understand and explain what really happened.

News Corp and the Murdoch family made a conscious decision not
to cooperate directly in the preparation of this book and actively discouraged others from doing so. That said, I have always found the
company to be professional in my interactions with it and have en-
deavored to round out my reporting and understanding of the events
described here in other ways. In particular, I am deeply appreciative
of the many current and former News Corp executives and journalists
in three countries who have taken time to offer insight, details, and
guidance for this book.

As a consequence, however, I have had to rely at times on sources
that I cannot identify directly because they are not authorized to talk
publicly about News Corp and Murdoch family matters and do not
want to jeopardize their jobs or future livelihoods. Every remark or
statement presented in this book inside quotation marks is taken

directly from interviews, transcripts, public testimony, court records, contemporaneous notes, speeches, corporate or government documents, or as otherwise specifically noted. Quotations that are italicized were obtained from at least one source with direct knowledge where the import is clear, but the precise wording was not recorded in such a way as to be ironclad months or years later. Quotations taken from news articles, documents, or previous books are noted as such, either in the text or the notes that follow.

This book reflects the knowledge I have gained during my thirteen years covering the media, first for the *Baltimore Sun* and especially since joining NPR News in 2004. NPR News is both my employer and the subject of parts of two chapters of this book. To its credit, NPR has always allowed me to report on the network as my editor and I believe events warrant. Similarly, NPR has approved my decision to write this book but has not sought to influence its content.

1

TWO FAMILIES

THE MAN AT THE CENTER of the maelstrom sat across from the parents of a dead girl, his head cradled in his hands. He rocked slightly. *I'm sorry*, he kept saying. *I'm so sorry.*

He was tanned and reasonably fit, with closely cropped hair that he had allowed to assume its natural gray color. He wore a perfectly cut pinstripe suit and a sharp gray tie, befitting talismans of his status as a commanding corporate chieftain. The people gathered in an expansive suite at the luxury hotel One Aldwych in the heart of London, a five-star stop that catered equally to Saudi investors and Hollywood celebrities, were all fixed on Rupert Murdoch.

The billionaire was used to being the focus of attention among the powerful, whether they were asking for favors or complaining about the way he ran the English-speaking world's most important media empire. Some competitors could boast a greater market value than Murdoch's News Corp. None was more influential. Murdoch had become a man beyond states, someone who sliced Gordian knots rather than trying to untangle them, a self-styled buccaneer with little but contempt for self-satisfied establishment worthies or narrow-minded government regulators.

Like one of his own satellites floating above the earth, by 2012 Rupert Murdoch floated above the borders and limitations of the practices, laws, and folkways of mere nations. His company served millions of readers and viewers on five continents, with a strong presence in the English-language powers of Australia, the United Kingdom, and the United States, as well as in China, Europe, India, and Latin America.

Murdoch had long ago become one of Britain's most powerful figures and cast an even greater shadow in his native Australia. Through the *New York Post*, his company enforced a kind of discipline among politicians who hoped to operate in the largest city in the US. Through Fox News and the *Wall Street Journal*, his journalists shaped popular and elite currents within the Republican Party in the States. And with its movie studios and its broadcast, cable, and satellite TV ventures, News Corp had the financial muscle to ride out losses elsewhere in the empire.

He had used flattery, disdain, and even remoteness to handle presidents, prime ministers, and popes. He had granted audiences to the aspirants and pretenders seeking to join those ranks. To encounter the ordinary people his publications had wronged was a rare event.

Yet here Rupert Murdoch sat, human, even vulnerable. What else could he be, given the other people in the room? Bob Dowler was an IT consultant with a thin crown of white hair, an imposing presence, and an impassive expression. His wife, Sally, her face pinched and gaunt, was a teacher. They were in their fifties, roughly the same age as Murdoch's daughter from his first marriage. And they had endured unimaginable pain, partly because of one of his most famous properties.

The Dowlers' daughter Milly had been a thirteen-year-old with a quick smile. She was a saxophone fan who liked to gossip about boys with her older sister, Gemma. On March 21, 2002, dressed in classic

British school uniform—blazer, Oxford shirt, and skirt—she left her school in the Surrey countryside at seven minutes past three in the afternoon. Twenty minutes later, she was on a train home. She got off at her stop. A witness spotted her a hundred yards away at about six minutes past four. After that, Milly was never seen again.

For most of 2002, Milly's parents and sister had no idea what had happened to her. The disappearance became fodder for hundreds of headlines speculating on her fate. The police focused on exactly the wrong clues, poring through Milly's journal writings for proof of tension between the parents. They looked for evidence of conflict between the two sisters: Gemma was the favorite, Milly wrote. The absent girl was unhappy. Perhaps she had run away. Some investigators fixated on her father's claimed interest in pornography.

The outcome was as gruesome as any tabloid editor could imagine. Milly's bones were found months later, dumped in woodlands. It took until June 2011 for prosecutors to try and convict a man for her killing. Police had missed earlier clues tying Milly's death to the man, who had been found guilty in two previous deaths.

The Dowlers' pain and anger were heightened by the disclosure that people working for Murdoch's *News of the World* had hacked into Milly's cell phone voice mail messages to mine them for fodder. Even in death, her privacy had been violated. The Dowlers' phones had been targeted too.

They were not the only ones. In late 2005, aides to princes William and Harry had asked police to investigate whether their phones had been hacked. Two men working for the *News of the World*—the royals editor and a private investigator—were convicted and sent to jail. Celebrities, politicians, and sports stars were added to a growing list of people who had been targeted in the intervening years. But few in the United Kingdom and no one outside it cared until the Dowlers, an ordinary family who had faced a prolonged and extraordinary grief over their dead daughter, were shown to have been victimized as well.

The police swung into high gear, while politicians who had sought Murdoch's blessing lined up to denounce him in Parliament. Rival newspapers that had largely turned a blind eye to such behavior by the Murdoch press (and some of its rivals) turned on News Corp, which sold approximately two of every five national newspapers purchased by readers. The nation rose as one in revulsion.

THE PUBLIC fury struck at the heart of Murdoch's media empire— at some of his much-beloved newspaper properties that were the financial cornerstones of his print business and were supervised by some of his most trusted lieutenants and likely heirs. Britain had been the launching pad for Murdoch's international growth beyond his native Australia. The scandal-driven tabloids *News of the World* and the *Sun* served as his financial base to buy two of the nation's most respected papers, the *Times of London* and the *Sunday Times*, as well as to expand into the United States. His second son, James, his presumed successor and the company's third-ranking executive, held responsibility for the company's operations in the United Kingdom. Rupert ran News Corp like a family business, though its shares were publicly traded on NASDAQ. Together with his adult children, Murdoch controlled roughly 40 percent of News Corp's voting shares. He had made it clear that the next leader of the company (perhaps after a brief caretaker period) would be someone who shared his last name.

Those few days in July shattered many assumptions. How could *News of the World* function when police were treating its newsroom as a crime scene? What to do about the CEO of Murdoch's British properties, Rebekah Brooks, or her predecessor, Les Hinton, the man Murdoch had handpicked to publish the *Wall Street Journal* after decades of devoted service? Rupert Murdoch, although famous for his loyalty, could be ruthless when threatened.

Meanwhile, the company's $14 billion takeover of the United Kingdom's largest cable broadcaster had been cast deeply into doubt. And the standing of James Murdoch, the executive chairman of News Corp in Britain, Europe, and Asia, was imperiled as well. James's older brother—Lachlan—had once been the heir apparent, but he retreated to Australia in the face of vicious political fighting with some of Murdoch's senior executives. Amid the tabloid crisis Lachlan flew to New York and then London to be at his father's side for strategy meetings. But he did not want to rejoin the company, even in a senior role. He enjoyed the freedom of distance from his father and the ability to lead his own, smaller media company back in Sydney. The boys had never taken their sister Elisabeth seriously as a possible future CEO for the company, largely because their father didn't see her in that light. But her outsider status was looking stronger with each passing day, as James's failure to head off this crisis seemed increasingly disastrous for the company.

Murdoch was accompanied to the hotel by Will Lewis, a senior British News Corp executive who had previously been editor of the rival *Telegraph* newspaper. Everyone at that meeting with the Dowlers knew an out-of-court settlement would ultimately ensue. The logic was inescapable. The revelation that the paper had broken into the phone of a dead girl, barely a teenager, transformed the issue of cell phone hacking in the public's eye from a bit of naughtiness, a lark, to something that frightened the general public. If it could happen to Milly, it could happen to anyone, however innocent and removed from the crosshairs of gossip reporters chasing after celebrity fluff.

So some sort of deal made every sense. But at this meeting no one raised the question of money. The Dowlers' lawyer, Mark Lewis, gestured for people to sit down. (The two Lewises are not related.) Mark Lewis and the Murdoch camp shared a secret that was about to become public: executives for News International, the British wing of News Corp, had assigned journalists and private eyes to follow him in hopes of uncovering some personal transgression they could use against him and his clients. Murdoch's company was publicly contrite. But privately it had been playing rough.

I know about you, Mark Lewis told Murdoch. *I know your mother is still alive. She'd be ashamed of you for what you've done.*

Dame Elisabeth Murdoch was then 102, by concensus the conscience and chief patron of the Australian port city of Melbourne, Rupert's birthplace. The media baron assented but then changed the emphasis. *My father. He'd be ashamed.* Keith Murdoch had led one of Australia's most influential media companies. At his death his young son Rupert inherited a small paper in a forgotten city. Mention of his father seemed to change Rupert's mood. His shame melted and he found himself repeating a signature complaint that had motivated him throughout his career.

My father was a great newspaperman, Keith Murdoch's son said ruefully in the London hotel room. *The British never gave him his due.* It was absolutely irrelevant to the people in the room, a strange aside, an echo of old battles called to mind by his father's ghost that he had summoned unwittingly to the conference.

Although they lived in different worlds, the couple sitting in that hotel room and the billionaire shared one experience: parenthood. The Dowlers were still grieving, just days after the conviction of their girl's killer, and they were freshly wounded by learning of the tabloid's invasion of her privacy. Murdoch was attempting to salvage his son James's destiny.

Murdoch was tired, from flying and from the pressure he faced. New allegations claimed that his reporters sought to hack the phones of victims of the September 2001 terror attacks in New York City. If the scandal spread to the United States, it could prove catastrophic to his control of the company. The news magnate who was famously obsessive about details—down to headlines, story selection, and photo captions—appeared out of touch when it mattered most. James, far from being able to shield his father, had left him and News Corp vulnerable to shame and ridicule.

Gemma Dowler spoke directly to Murdoch on behalf of her parents and dead sister. When her sister disappeared, Gemma had been a round-faced sixteen-year-old studying for the standardized tests that would get her into college. In the intervening nine years she had received a rough education about the cruelties of crime, the justice system, and the press. She took the time to admonish the media mogul. *How would you have felt if it had happened to someone in your family?* He sat with his head in his hands.

In the space of a few days much of his record had come under assault, and Murdoch's character was also being questioned. Was his cowboy style a quirk, a key component of his success, or a fundamental defect that had led to this very moment? Was he guilty, complicit, or, as he suggested, a bystander to this raft of cruelties?

When he finally emerged blinking into the July sunlight on the marble steps of the hotel, Murdoch was confronted by a scrum of reporters and photographers and video camera operators, some of them his own. "As founder of the company, I was appalled to find out what had happened," Murdoch said. "I found that out, I apologized. I have nothing further to say." Later he would tell members of Parliament, his own reporters, and a judicial inquiry that he had been betrayed by those in whom he put his trust, as well as by the people they in turn had trusted.

But it was not clear whether those people, his reporters, editors, and lawyers, had betrayed the nature of the company he had engineered from his father's modest bequest. The uproar that ensued from the disclosure about the hacking of the voice mail messages of Milly Dowler and others arose from a creeping understanding of the culture of News Corp, based primarily on the qualities of one man.

Rupert Murdoch's company embraced a buccaneering spirit to create new fortunes, and it was built on personal and family ties more than most, with a clubbiness, or mateship, that was almost impossible for outsiders to penetrate. The scandals of 2011 revealed that culture had also become untethered from the well-being of the people it claimed to serve.

2

RUPERT IN OZ

———————

IN GREEK MYTHOLOGY, THE GIANT Antaeus was the son of Gaia, goddess of the earth, and Poseidon, king of the sea. The mighty Antaeus forced all passersby to wrestle him. The trick of his invincibility, as the story goes, was that he drew strength from any touch or contact with the ground—the earth of his mother.

For Rupert Murdoch, Australia, or at least the idea of Australia, serves as an analogous source of strength. In New York, London, and Los Angeles, Murdoch entrusted outposts to people who served him in his native land. Robert Thomson, born in a small town several hours north of Melbourne, led the *Times of London*, ran the *Wall Street Journal* and Dow Jones, and became the first CEO of the new News Corp publishing company when it split off on its own in June 2013. Col Allan, from the tiny agrarian town of Dubbo far outside Sydney, has been entrenched at the heart of the world's media capital for more than a decade as the editor of the *New York Post*. The British-born Les Hinton moved to Australia as a teenager and got his start as a gofer at Murdoch's *Adelaide News* in the late 1950s. He became CEO over Murdoch's British operations and then publisher of the *Wall Street Journal.* David Hill, an Aussie who ran sports for Murdoch in the United Kingdom and Australia, reinvented Fox Sports in the United States when it successfully bid for rights to broadcast NFL games in the early 1990s and returned to lead a new national Fox Sports network in 2013.

Whatever their relative skills, each man—and the overwhelming majority of senior Murdoch executives are men—also serves as a talisman from home. And the history of News Ltd (as Murdoch's holdings were known there) in Australia is instructive about the company's instincts in situations when it becomes dominant and its reflexes when challenged.

"The story of our company is the stuff of legend: from a small newspaper in Adelaide to a global corporation based in New York, with a market capitalization of about $44 billion," Murdoch told shareholders in October 2011.

Australians demur. "Adelaide is irrelevant," said Graeme Samuel, the former chairman of Australian Competition and Consumer Commission, the powerful agency that regulates antitrust and media issues. I met Samuel in Murdoch's true hometown of Melbourne, a city famed for hosting the Australian Open tennis tournament, trolley cars, and street buskers playing the didgeridoo, an Aboriginal instrument.

Melbourne is Australia's second-largest city, a melting pot on the country's southeastern coast. Samuel, currently a corporate investment consultant whose office enjoys a commanding view from thirty floors up, pointed out the many beneficiaries of the Murdochs' enormous enterprises along the sinuous Yarra River.

An infant born in Melbourne could be delivered at the Royal Children's Hospital, underwritten in part by the largesse of Rupert's mother, Dame Elisabeth Murdoch; the birth announcement, of course, could appear in his tabloid *Herald Sun,* whose predecessor papers were run by Murdoch's father, Sir Keith. The child could learn to read from books published by HarperCollins Australia, another News Corp offshoot; attend music and art classes at institutions subsidized by the family foundation; enroll at a high school named for Dame Elisabeth; amble with dates at the botanical gardens; attend shows at the major theater downtown; have a marriage notice published in the *Herald Sun;* work for one of the foundations sponsored by various Murdochs; buy tickets to movies from Fox Studios; down a pint at a pub while watching Australian rules football on Sky Sports; vote for politicians cast in favorable light by the company's papers; receive care at various hospitals underwritten by the family's contributions; and be commemorated at death, once more, in the pages of the *Herald Sun.*

Murdoch's grandfather Patrick was a Scottish clergyman who became influential after being posted to Melbourne. Rupert's father, Keith Arthur Murdoch, lived in the quarters at the back of the red brick church as a child.

Stephen Mayne, formerly an editor at Murdoch's two biggest Australian tabloids, the Melbourne *Herald Sun* and the Sydney *Daily Telegraph*, gave me an extended tour of Melbourne Murdochiana. He took me to Trinity Presbyterian Church on the corner of Riversdale Road and Waterloo Street in Toorak, a prosperous suburb a few miles southeast of Melbourne. "There was discussion at the time that [Keith] may pursue a religious career as well," Mayne said, "and he said no— journalism was his thing." As a teen, Keith Murdoch obtained a cadetship, or apprentice reporter's job, writing about suburban news for the *Age*, a prestigious Melbourne newspaper.

As a reporter during World War I, Keith Murdoch witnessed the doomed Allied assaults on Gallipoli and wrote an impassioned letter to the Australian prime minister denouncing the willingness of British commanders to endanger Australian soldiers. Decades later, Rupert Murdoch acknowledged to his biographer William Shawcross that much of what his father had written didn't stand up to scrutiny. Despite what the letter said about British commanders recklessly costing the lives of Aussies and Kiwis, British troops had also been in peril.

No matter. The letter made Keith Murdoch a hero to Australians. He had stood up to power. He rose to be top editor of the Melbourne *Herald* and a top executive of his employer's growing corporation. To make the profile complete, he needed only to establish a family. He had seen a picture of Elisabeth Greene in a magazine and, after inquiring, arranged to meet her at a Red Cross benefit dance. A swift courtship led to a quick wedding. Keith Murdoch was in his forties and much older than his wife—by twenty-four years. The knighted Sir Keith prospered and brought up their children in great comfort. The Murdochs lived in a mansion in Toorak and bought a cottage outside the city. They named the accompanying estate Cruden Farm, an echo of Patrick Murdoch's Scotland.

Rupert had a tough time at boarding school and never excelled at sports. He took an interest in the newspaper business, apprenticing in London for some of Keith Murdoch's friends there. The son adopted radical leftist politics at Oxford University, giving pride of place to a bust of Vladimir Lenin. On campus, he won election as publicity manager of the *Cherwell*, an independent student paper. Off campus, Murdoch absorbed the way the owners conducted themselves. London was already home to long-form newspapers filled with sober accounts and tabloids offering splashy and salacious headlines. Press barons could indeed become peers of the realm: Lord Northcliffe, Lord Rothermere, and Lord Beaverbrook actively and even bruisingly participated in the nation's political life and expected their beliefs to be reflected in their papers.

Sir Keith died in 1952, and twenty-one-year-old Rupert rushed home. The Toorak property was sold to pay off Keith Murdoch's outstanding debts and the taxes due on his estate. True, his mother, Dame Elisabeth, owned Cruden Farm outright. But the son was angered that his father was not able to bequeath greater media holdings. Keith

Murdoch had obtained a personal stake in papers owned by the Herald & Weekly Times Co. in Brisbane and several other properties, including the Adelaide *News*. Yet just before Keith died, former colleagues had reversed several of his maneuvers, depleting his fortune.

Rupert Murdoch went back to Oxford that year to finish his degree in philosophy, politics, and economics at Worcester College. Yet memory of that grievance helped to spur the son's return home and his ambition to expand his holdings beyond Adelaide, a city in which he had no emotional investment beyond newspapers, beyond news. He acquired major newspapers in every Australian state, often leveraging his properties to finance debts for succeeding acquisitions. Murdoch bought TV stations, acquired the rights to broadcast shows from the American ABC-TV network, and established the country's first truly national daily, the *Australian*.

These extraordinary moves, which often anticipated Australians' appetite for news and entertainment, seemed self-evident to Murdoch. "I don't know of any son of any prominent media family who hasn't wanted to follow in the footsteps of his forbears," Murdoch said in 2001. "It's just too good a life." And he hoped to create something for one of his own children. He married young and had a daughter, Prudence, by his first wife, a former airline attendant named Patricia Booker. They divorced in 1967, the same year he married an aspiring young reporter named Anna Torv, with whom Rupert had Elisabeth, Lachlan, and James.

It took three-and-a-half decades for Murdoch to acquire the company that his father had once run. Stephen Mayne, my guide around Melbourne, had been a successful business editor there at Murdoch's *Herald Sun* and held the same job at its sister paper in Sydney, the tabloid *Daily Telegraph*, by far the country's largest-circulation paper. He was later promoted to be chief of staff for the *Telegraph*. By Mayne's account, he wasn't up to the task of leading the newsroom in Sydney, a sprawling center of power, finance, and pop culture in which he had few nonbusiness contacts and no real roots.

Over time, Mayne became a leading Australian critic of Murdoch and News Corp. He sees present-day parallels between Rupert's arrangements and Sir Keith's efforts to win ownership of several titles while serving as a top executive at the publicly traded company he ran. "We've seen similar questions asked around the way Rupert Murdoch has run News Corp with his own family interests first versus the public shareholder interest," Mayne said: the sons installed as top executives; the daughter's film production company acquired for more than $670 billion.

In public, Murdoch defined a clear barometer by which he would judge himself: "The thrill of success is in how many people you get to watch your television programs—how many people you get to buy your newspapers. And if you're doing that well, the rest looks after itself," he once said. Dame Elisabeth subtly rebuked her son's view. "It's very satisfactory if you do very well and are so-called—this dreadful word—'rich.'" She would not allow Rupert to set the terms by which he could measure himself. Philanthropy was her pursuit but not in any major way her son's.

Politicians from both major Australian parties have granted Murdoch's company key concessions. In 1985 News Corp was granted waterfront property on Sydney Showground for its movie studio in exchange for a paltry figure by the federal government and the state of New South Wales. A state auditor later established that the deal may have benefited News Corp by more than $100 million. In 1995 News Ltd went into business with the state communications corporation Telstra and another private firm to create FoxTel, the country's leading pay-TV service. News Corp held a 25 percent stake but had full rights to control the management and direction of the company. Such deals showed how the corporation often operated.

Tony Blair flew to Hayman Island, on the Great Barrier Reef, to address News Corp's editors and directors in July 1995 after becoming leader of the British Labour Party. Murdoch took the visit as a signal of seriousness, which it was. Australian prime minister Paul Keating gave Blair some advice: "He's a big, bad bastard, and the only way you can deal with him is to make sure he thinks you can be a big, bad bastard too. You can do deals with him without ever saying a deal is done, but the only thing he cares about is his business. And the only language he respects is strength."

Murdoch started acquiring British media outlets in the late 1960s and then expanded into the US, ultimately becoming an American citizen to satisfy requirements of US television regulators. By 2004, he pulled News Corp from Australian exchanges and listed it in New York. By then the transformation from regional media executive to worldwide powerhouse was complete. "I don't want to pretend this is a guy who went from rags to riches, but he was gifted one newspaper in Adelaide, which is one of the smallest cities in this country," said Andrew Jaspan, former editor of Fairfax Media's Melbourne *Age*, who previously worked in senior positions for two Murdoch papers in the UK. "So he's perceived as a real success story—a guy who started with one paper and built a global empire. From that perspective, he's seen as a bit of a hero."

News Corp does not always achieve what it wants, even in Australia. Its cable TV division failed to win exclusive rights to broadcast rugby and Australian football. But it has always been prominent in the mix of broadcasters. And journalists say his national newspaper the *Australian* exacts a toll on those who oppose Murdoch's interests.

In summer 2011, when scandal overwhelmed its British sister company, executives for News Ltd in Australia scrambled to contain the damage. On July 14, John Hartigan, then CEO and chairman of News Ltd, was asked by the Australian Broadcasting Corp's Leigh Sales if Murdoch's newspapers had bullied politicians there, as she said they had in Britain.

Hartigan said that his journalists hold politicians accountable. "I don't believe that we ever overstep," Hartigan replied. "Yes, it's a love-hate relationship, and sometimes it's loving, and sometimes it's very hateful, but I don't think, generally speaking, that we exceed our authority."

Though Australians often feel slighted by his long absences, Murdoch still casts a long shadow there, as he proved when he informed Hartigan it was time to step down a few months later. The unit's print revenues were sagging. The Labor government had launched formal reviews of media behavior and ownership. Rupert Murdoch reclaimed the title of chairman for himself. The king had returned.

———

AUSTRALIA SERVES as an important test case of what happens when a strong media figure becomes an inescapable one. Step up to any newsstand in Australia, as I did in Melbourne's central business district, and ask about Rupert Murdoch, and you'll get an appraisal like this one from Tom Baxter, an officer with a local disability foundation: "Long time in newspapers, ruthless; dedicated to [his] craft; a global citizen."

In the beachside community of Albert Park, feelings toward him were equally complicated. At a bookstore I ducked into, a prominent display featured the best-selling memoir of former prime minister John Howard, a favorite Murdoch politician. I bought a popular children's book for my daughter Viola, called *Josephine Wants to Dance.* Josephine is a young kangaroo who aspires to be a ballerina. The Murdoch imprint HarperCollins Australia published both books.

There is admiration for the global success of a local boy, but cynicism too. "In Australia, there are a lot of cities that only have Murdoch press as their newspaper," said bookseller Kate MacFadyen, "so it just feels like his organization dominates the media in this country."

Until Dame Elisabeth's death in late 2012, Murdoch typically visited her once a year at the estate. Graeme Samuel said Dame Elisabeth's philanthropy bound the city of Melbourne to the family. "For Rupert, I think it's a combination of goodwill," Samuel said, with "fear that's being created by the sheer omnipresence of the Murdoch family and the Murdoch press."

News Corp owns the dominant papers in nearly all the country's major cities. The *Australian*, the only national general interest paper, has a modest circulation of approximately 130,000 but shapes elite opinion; it's the paper that gets chewed over by talk radio, television programs, and blogs. In addition, News Ltd owns popular news websites and the controlling stake in FoxTel, the nation's largest cable TV provider, in Fox Sports, and the cable Sky News Australia service. Murdoch's older son, Lachlan Murdoch, makes his home in Sydney and is a key investor and chairman of the ostensibly rival broadcast Network Ten while remaining a corporate director of News Corp in New York.

Between six and seven of every ten copies of national and metro papers sold in Australia are owned by News Ltd, according to government and trade figures. The papers are not monolithic in approach. But they tend to champion a strong military stance, a smaller government with fewer regulatory powers, and restrictive policies toward immigrants. Murdoch's tabloids exude a more populist sheen than the *Australian*.

Paul Barry, who has written periodically for Murdoch's *Daily Telegraph* in Sydney, pointed out that the livelihoods of an overwhelming number of Australian journalists depend on the whim of a single media conglomerate and the sensibility of a single mogul. "Ultimately, he's the bloke they have to please," Barry said. "And so, while they may not actually get an order coming down saying, 'You will run *this* headline, you will do *this* story, you will take *this* point of view,' they know what sort of things are going to play well."

The fact of that concentration is a notable element of two separate recent government reviews of the media in Australia. "It's a pretty clear stranglehold on the flow of information, which in itself might not be such a bad thing if you weren't open to claims that certain media organizations represent certain political interests," said Monica Attard, former foreign correspondent and media critic for the ABC. "I think it's very, very difficult to overcome those barriers."

Rupert Murdoch addressed the nature of media ownership decades ago as he sought his first foothold in the UK by taking over the tabloid *News of the World*. "I think the important thing is that there be plenty of newspapers, with plenty of different people controlling them, so that there are a variety of viewpoints, so there is a choice for the public," he reassured the British public in 1968. "This is the freedom of the press that is needed."

Murdoch's Australian editors insist that the country does enjoy a diversity of views. They point to the nation's public broadcaster, the ABC, and the rival Fairfax Media's holdings, including worldly daily papers in Sydney and Melbourne, as well as the national business daily *Australian Financial Review*.

The former media and antitrust regulator Graeme Samuel perceives real danger in the state trying to interfere with ownership: "News Ltd is powerful, but is it vulnerable? Yes, I think it is," Samuel said. "Like any traditional media organization, they're vulnerable to the whims and fancies of the reader." Samuel noted that paid newspaper circulation is declining in Australia, as it is elsewhere in the industrialized world. People read blogs and foreign newspapers online, or tune in to talk radio. Ahead, Samuel sees the promise of Internet TV. He dismisses the idea that a single media company can control anything in Australia, even if its myriad publications generally share an outlook.

Still, Australia is unlike other western countries in the extent to which one private company holds such a dominant position. "It's bad for a democracy when 70 percent of the newspapers in this country are pushing one line and pushing it so hard, whether it is right or whether it's wrong, frankly," the media critic Paul Barry said.

The gravitational pull is inescapable. Leaders of both major Australian political parties, whether favored by News Ltd newspapers or punished by them, routinely pay their respects at News Corp's global headquarters in midtown Manhattan when they visit the United Nations or have other official functions there.

"Most [Australian] Labor politicians hated Rupert," said one former senior executive who witnessed the parade of supplicants. "But they all came to New York City to kiss the ring. Prime Minister [Julia] Gillard among them."

<hr />

AUSTRALIA IS perhaps the most fully formed demonstration of the media strategy Murdoch has pursued in other markets. A look at the nature of Murdoch's Australian stable of papers proves revealing about his intentions elsewhere. The *Australian* is "by far the most detailed paper in regard to national politics," said Robert Manne, one of the country's leading public intellectuals. "And it's also at a higher level of analysis, in general, than the other papers."

The paper is "smarter, sharper" than the others, he said, with more resources and fewer profit demands to boot. "The *Australian* has the personal support of Rupert Murdoch. Everyone knows it. He created the paper. He's incredibly proud of it as one of his creations."

Indeed, Murdoch launched the paper in July 1964, with this mission statement printed prominently on the front page:

> Here is Australia's first truly national newspaper. It is produced today because you want it; because the nation needs it. In these pages you will find the impartial information and the independent thinking that are essential to the further advance of our country. This paper is tied to no party,

to no state, and has no chains of any kind. Its guide is faith in Australia and the country's future.

It will be our duty to inform Australians everywhere of what is really happening in their country; of what is really happening in the rest of the world; and how this affects our prosperity, our prospects, our national conscience and our public image.

We shall not hesitate to speak fearlessly. We shall criticise.

We will not be influenced when there is need to be outspoken.

We shall praise. We shall encourage those feelings and movement in public and private life which elevate the individual and advance the nation's welfare.

The world news service which appears in the *Australian* surpasses any yet assembled in the pages of one newspaper anywhere in the world.

The authoritative writers who will contribute regularly on topics ranging from the arts to aviation are acknowledged leaders in the subjects they will discuss. The business and financial section is organised and written by the shrewdest and best informed financial journalists in the nation.

Vigor, truth and information without dullness will be found day by day in these columns. We believe the people of Australia will welcome the new approach to national journalism.

This morning, we believe, we shall make thousands of friends, who as the thinking men and women of Australia will have a profound influence on the future. You are welcome to this company of progress.

But another component emerged from the pages of the paper, unstated but no less important: the *Australian* is not only a chronicler but also a player in national politics. It has no peer. The *Australian*, known as the *Oz*, did not always adopt a conservative course. In 1972, it had supported the candidacy of the centrist Labor Party leader Gough Whitlam. Murdoch believed that the avid backing of his papers had played "a substantial role" in Whitlam's win that year, as he later told the US ambassador to Australia. But along with many Australian business leaders, Murdoch grew disillusioned with Whitlam, and his papers, including the *Oz*, followed suit. The government's standing seemed shaky. The Queen's emissary to Australia, the governor general, dismissed Whitlam as prime minister, sparking a political crisis. In 1975, a group of journalists staged a strike to protest how openly the *Australian*'s coverage favored opposition leader Malcolm Fraser of the Liberal Party, who became prime minister.

Under Chris Mitchell, the paper's current editor for more than a decade, the *Australian* has favored smaller government with fewer regulations on business, vigorously supported the invasion of Iraq, treated increased immigration skeptically, and displayed active concern about issues affecting Australia's Aboriginal peoples. The paper's positions actively drive news coverage, not just editorials. And the *Australian* sets the tone not only for News Ltd's other papers but also for the debate on talk radio, blogs, and TV, including Sky News Australia.

James Chessell, a former business and media reporter for the *Australian*, is now deputy editor at Fairfax's *Australian Financial Review*. He expressed admiration for the clarity of the *Australian*'s stance under Mitchell and said critics are wrong to attribute its editorial choices to meddling by Murdoch. But, he said, it's accurate to say "someone's probably not going to edit the *Australian* or the *Daily Telegraph* in Sydney if they haven't risen up through News and aren't sort of enmeshed in the culture and probably don't have similar views to other people at News." ("News" is how many Australians refer to News Ltd.)

The papers do not always act in perfect lockstep. But that said, the Murdoch papers hammered away at then-Labor prime minister Gillard and her Green Party allies, and the *Australian* has taken the lead. Jaspan, the former editor in chief of the Melbourne *Age*, said aggrieved politicians never like tough coverage, but this time may have a point. "There is constant scrutiny of the Labor party by the *Australian*, which at times is not just forensic—it actually becomes quite caustic," Jaspan said. "It's quite corrosive."

The governing Labor Party has suffered over the past few years from infighting and policy reversals, and its popularity has dropped sharply in the polls. But Jaspan noted that Australia has fared better under its stewardship than just about any industrialized society during the global financial crisis. You'd never know that, he said, from the *Australian* or its sister papers.

The *Australian* is not strictly partisan. It supported the rise to power of Kevin Rudd, a centrist, before a falling out with Rudd and especially his successor, Gillard. The schism was taken as a renewed warning to other politicians: stay on the right side of the company. Previously, John Howard of the Liberal Party earned the strong support of News Ltd papers, especially on fiscal matters and the Australian involvement in the 2003 invasion of Iraq. In an earlier era the Labor Party's Paul Keating won support from the Murdochs. He had been integral to the Sydney Showground deal for Fox Studios.

The switches back and forth between parties made Murdoch an unpredictable and incomparable force in Australian journalism and politics.

Robert Manne was once a favorite of the political right, and hence the Murdoch press, as an anticommunist magazine editor. No more. In fall 2011, he took direct aim at the *Australian* with a lengthy critique in the periodical *Monthly*. He said the paper was intellectually dishonest and run by political bullies and climate change "denialists."

The paper commissioned a full book review of that critique. "What I would say is that on any given day, the *Australian* simultaneously produces some of the best and some of the worst journalism in this country," wrote Matthew Ricketson, a former *Australian* staffer who was subsequently media editor for the rival *Age*. "Reading it can be disorienting, like watching a driver with one foot on the accelerator, the other on the brake."

Ricketson even wrote that he found Manne's critique "persuasive overall" and encouraged readers to make up their own minds. But the newspaper fired back. Manne calculated that it published 40,000 words of response. The editor, Chris Mitchell, joined other senior editors in assailing Manne anew. "They essentially said I'd lost my mind, that I was insane," he said, "that I was a narcissist, that I had a series of personal agendas which were driving me on."

The message rang loud and clear: don't screw with the guy at the top. It is a template that Murdoch has perfected in his exploits around the globe, especially in the three English-language countries he calls home.

3

"THE GUTTER IS A GOOD PLACE TO BE"

KELVIN MACKENZIE, EDITOR OF THE *Sun* from 1981 to 1994, may have embodied Rupert Murdoch's newspaper instincts most faithfully of anyone on earth. Lacerating, clever, populist, punchy, and joyful, MacKenzie knew where the big boss wanted to go—and often got there first, sometimes so pungently he had to be reined in.

In 1982, Argentina invaded the tiny Falkland Islands, held by the UK but standing just a few hundred miles off the coast of South America, and British battleships steamed to the Southern Hemisphere. The crisis unfolded like a feverish dream for MacKenzie. Roy Greenslade, an assistant *Sun* editor whose politics lay elsewhere, later wrote that MacKenzie's approach to the war was "xenophobic, bloody-minded, ruthless, often reckless, black-humoured and ultimately triumphalist." One headline taunted Argentina's military leaders, who had taken power a few years before in a coup: "Stick it Up Your Junta!" When news broke that British torpedoes had struck an Argentine cruiser, a features editor shouted "Gotcha!" MacKenzie slapped that onto the next morning's first editions, but misgivings soon mounted in the newsroom as it became clear that hundreds of lives would be lost. He swapped it out for another headline, asking whether 1,200 Argentinians ("Argies") had drowned. Murdoch, patrolling the newsroom as he often did during news events of major moment, told MacKenzie the first headline should stick.

MacKenzie was also editor when the paper made its most egregious mistake. In 1989, stands in the Hillsborough soccer stadium in Sheffield collapsed. Ninety-six people ultimately died. Police said fans at the stadium had picked the pockets of victims who had been killed or badly injured in the disaster. Police officials leaked stories to a news agency serving papers in London that fans had urinated on police responding to the emergency call and alleging that others had beaten a policeman trying to give a victim mouth-to-mouth resuscitation. McKenzie wrapped these accounts in a front-page headline: "The Truth." It proved untrue.

The reporter on the story, Harry Arnold, later admitted he was aghast at the headline. "That wasn't what I'd written. I'd never used the words 'the truth,'" he said. "So I said to Kelvin MacKenzie, 'You can't say that.' And he said 'Why not?' and I said, 'because we don't know that it's the truth. This is a version of 'the truth.'" Arnold said MacKenzie brushed him aside: "'Oh, don't worry. I'm going to make it clear that this is what some people are saying.'"

MacKenzie did not apologize for more than two decades. Even then, his concession seemed grudging. He said the *Sun* simply based its conclusions on what the regional news agency had learned from its police sources.

MacKenzie once wrote a huge front-page headline claiming that a comedian had eaten a woman's hamster. He hadn't. As the comic's press agent acknowledged, the negative publicity only aided the comic's career. MacKenzie contended editors merely met readers' expectations in creating the tabloid sensibility. "It's always been in the gutter—and it's quite a good place to be, actually," MacKenzie explained. "Ordinary people are not high-minded. They basically want a bit of entertainment. They want a bit of sport. They want a bit of crime. They want a bit of expenses fiddling" by members of Parliament.

MacKenzie boasted that the stories he published were too good to confirm. He once told me that the only story he ever double-checked involved Elton John, not yet out of the closet, paying for sex with a male prostitute. Even so, it wasn't true. The paper had to apologize and pay damages of £1 million. Double-check? MacKenzie sputtered: Never again!

Under Murdoch, the *Sun* tabloid thrived, shedding its tenuous finances of the past to become the nation's best-selling daily paper, which it remains to this day. Its corporate sibling *News of the World*, the leading Sunday paper, earned the nickname *News of the Screws* from the satirical publication *Private Eye* for its emphasis on revealing affairs of the famous. Murdoch also owned two of the nation's elite papers: the *Times of London* and the *Sunday Times*, which he acquired in 1981. But no one underestimated the importance of the tabloids, not just to the company's bottom line but to the chairman as a reflection of his psyche. Asked under oath about his contacts with public officials, Murdoch answered: "If any politician wanted my opinion on a major matter they only had to read the editorials in *The Sun*."

Prestigious UK broadsheet newspapers—the *Guardian*, the *Financial Times* (not a true general-interest newspaper), the *Independent*, the *Observer*, the *Sunday Times*, the *Telegraph*, and the *Times of London*—are printed on sheets of paper about forty-eight inches across, give or take, folded in two to make pages with six columns apiece. These days, the *Times of London*, the *Guardian*, and others actually print in "compact" size, a smaller edition that's easier for commuters to carry and read on the packed cars of London Underground trains. The size of the broadsheets signaled to readers they could expect distinguished, reasoned journalism, literate writing, thoughtful political analysis, in-depth foreign coverage, and cultural criticism, much more than they could find elsewhere.

In the US, several leading newspaper families—the Sulzbergers of the *New York Times*, the Grahams of the *Washington Post*, and, in a previous generation, the Taylors of the *Boston Globe* and the Binghams of the Louisville *Courier-Journal*—articulated that they were stewards of a "public trust," who stood for something beyond the bottom line. As competition waned city by city and as the reportorial core became professionalized, papers typically shed overt partisan ties on their news pages as their publishers sought to appeal to the broadest possible audiences. In recent decades, talk radio and cable news channels have taken up ideological banners.

Heavily regulated by the government as to content, British broadcasters adhered to nonideological programming and saw news shows as a public service, not a profit center. The newspapers were fractious, contentious, and opinionated. British newspaper journalists often argued that their American cousins lost something vital in the process of shedding partisanship from the news.

"I find American newspapers boring—and biblical," said Simon Jenkins, the former editor in chief of Murdoch's center-right *Times of London* who now writes columns for the liberal *Guardian*. "These are news sheets for a genre of readers who want vast slabs of information and get entertainment in a different way. And they are micro-monopolies, all of them."

Murdoch's editors call these papers the "unpopular" press. His heart has always been with the scrappier tabloids—the "popular press" for which Fleet Street is perhaps better known. The midmarket daily tabloid newspaper is a peculiarly London invention that, depending on the particular title, mixes elements of TMZ.com, the *Economist*, ESPN, the *National Enquirer*, *Maxim*, the Huffington Post, *Time*, the *Weekly Standard*, and *Politico*. The ensuing coverage sounds much as though Capitol Hill, the Garment District, Hollywood, K Street, Madison Avenue, and Wall Street all met for drinks, got soused, and started to dish.

The papers are locally produced, nationally distributed, and wildly competitive. In most American cities, the majority of those who read printed papers are subscribers, providing a guaranteed audience to publishers and, more importantly, to advertisers. By contrast, many UK readers pick up papers at newsstands, which helps explain why the front pages of tabloids rely on sensationalism, scandal, sex, violence, shock, rough-edged political satire, and celebrity watching.

In 1989 Murdoch sketched out his philosophy: "Anybody who, within the law of the land, provides a service which the public wants at a price it can afford is providing a public service." The immediate context for Murdoch's remark involved British television programming, specifically the BBC, which he argued failed to satisfy viewers. But he had articulated his approach to publishing: let the people decide with their pocketbooks.

———————

IN DECEMBER 1989, Prince Charles, by then married to Princess Diana, telephoned his girlfriend, Camilla Parker Bowles. He expressed his desire to live eternally in her trousers, as a tampon if necessary. The conversation became infamous after the adulterous talk was published several years later, first in a Murdoch-owned celebrity magazine in Australia, later in British tabloids. The *Sun* initially held off, then asked readers to call in to say whether they wanted to see the transcript in print. They did. At least some of the public clearly wanted the service that Murdoch's paper provided.

It was never exactly clear how an Australian publication—though, as part of the Murdoch stable, one with strong British ties—had first obtained and published the conversation. Former *News of the World* reporter Paul McMullan said the prince's sexual banter was captured from his portable phone by reporters sitting a few blocks away from Buckingham Palace in a converted London taxicab kitted out with a police scanner and recording devices. Portable phones at that time were not manufactured with encryption.

For all the rapacious hunger of the tabloids, the British press faces tight regulations from the government and its own industry that its American counterparts do not. British newspapers cannot report about the details of ongoing court proceedings. An official secrets act allows the government to outlaw the publication of certain documents. Until recent years, private individuals could obtain so-called super-injunctions—effectively, gag orders preventing news organizations from publishing information they do not want to come to light. The Press Complaints Commission, set up by the industry itself, judges public challenges to coverage. And should that fail to satisfy, British libel law favors plaintiffs more strongly than does American law.

All of these restraints lend momentum to the impulse for mischief. McMullan, a wiry, twitchy man who keeps a camera with telephoto lenses stashed in the back of his van, now runs a pub in the town of Dover, by the English Channel. But previously he flourished as a reporter at the *News of the World*, becoming a senior features editor and for a time living fat on expense accounts.

McMullan snorted at the idea that the public only recently learned reporters relied on questionably obtained tapes of private exchanges. People paid money for the right to call a special line set up to listen to the peculiar flirtations of the next in line to the British throne. At the time it occurred, recording conversations from portable phones did not break the law. But even if it had, British courts have often set aside prosecution against illegal intrusions if news proprietors can convincingly argue a story they had published served the public interest.

McMullan argued judges and lawyers construe that protection too narrowly. "I think anything that the public is interested in is in the public interest," McMullan said, echoing Murdoch's views. "And who is anyone to say that you are not allowed to read that? Who is putting themselves in the position to restrict what the British public can read? It's people in power who don't want to get caught and thrown out of office."

"Privacy," he said, "is for paedos"—pedophiles. No one else needs to keep secrets.

He does not apologize for his former way of life. McMullan's words evoke American principles of freedom of the press, demanding, not requesting, freedom from government censorship or prudish meddling. And yet his ethical construct fails to account for the question of how the story is acquired. The *News of the World*, the *Sun*, and other papers routinely failed to inform their readers which sources they had paid for information and how they obtained other damaging material.

One of McMullan's infamous scoops involved the late British actor Denholm Elliott's daughter, who had become addicted to drugs. A policeman found her begging in a London Underground stop. Instead of helping the troubled young woman, he called the newspaper and pocketed a fee for the tip. "And then I went and chatted to her and did the story," McMullan said. "The tragedy is, a few years later she actually killed herself. So that's something I feel guilty about." The story never mentioned the payment.

McMullan showed undue modesty. In reality, the reporter actively set up Jennifer Elliott, playing on her desperation to convince her to come to an apartment to have sex with him for £50. He made sure the hidden cameras captured her face for the pictures that would be published in *News of the World*.

McMullan displayed something of a nihilist streak that blinded him to limits on his ability to intrude upon the private lives of others. If a receptionist at a medical clinic called in with a tip that an internationally known model had shown up pregnant at a doctor's office, McMullan said, he would have eagerly paid ten grand, even though the receptionist would have broken the law in violating her privacy. "Do you just stick your fingers in your ears and go, 'No, no, don't tell me?' No, you're a journalist." Celebrities relied on publicity from the tabloid to hawk their movies, albums, sports teams, and the like. This brutal treatment marked the unspoken other half of the bargain.

McMullan was one of the few who surfaced to acknowledge what life looked like on the news manufacturing production floor. Yet he did not operate that way in isolation. Former reporters for the *News of the World* said editors screamed at them, or worse, sacked them, if they failed to deliver three promising leads at each Tuesday's story meetings. One young reporter fainted under the pressure, according to the former *News of the World* reporter Graham Johnson. Johnson's account of his own time at the paper involved fabricating stories and sources, staging photographs, and manufacturing stings, not to mention major bouts of drug abuse and faked expenses.

Much of the time, reporters manipulated the subjects—targets—of their stories into talking. Johnson later claimed that he had "black-mailed" a soccer star, Steve McManaman, into admitting his mother's incurable cancer. Editors at *News of the World* frequently horse-traded with the PR handlers for the celebrities they intended to expose. If your soccer star admits he was sleeping with a stripper, we'll omit the part about cocaine that would kill his endorsement deals.

"When a story breaks, the editors start shouting," McMullan recalled. One editor at *News of the World* "used to ring up my phone and say, 'You fucking fuck, what the fuck are you doing?'"

"The tone was buccaneering, get the story, be rewarded for getting a headline that sounds good," whether or not it's true, said David Gordon, the chief executive of the *Economist* and the television news service ITN during the 1980s and 1990s.

One man set that tone. Murdoch's cadre of Australians imported what's called "mate culture"—or "mateship"—into his newsrooms in London and New York. The culture flourished at the tabloids but also made its presence felt at the prestige titles. The Australian novelist and historian Thomas Keneally traces the origins of mateship back to nineteenth-century bush life, particularly the life and legend of the bush ranger Ned Kelly, an Australian born of Irish parents in the mid-1850s. His petty crimes yielded to cattle rustling, bank robberies, and increasingly elaborate plots involving family and friends (the "Kelly Gang") against corrupt and brutal territorial police. His gang was loyal and fearless, if lawless, bound together against an outside authority considered unjust.

Mateship, Keneally said, continued in the carnage of Gallipoli during World War I, where Australian soldiers felt they had been subject to particularly hazardous duties by their British commanding officers. The ill-fated invasion was later depicted in the 1981 Peter Weir film, *Gallipoli,* starring Mel Gibson. It was financed by Associated R & R Films Pty Ltd, Murdoch's newly formed production company.

The defining element of the mate culture was a kinship infused with a sense of grievance that led Australian men to risk their careers, security, or lives for their brothers, as soldiers did defying officers' orders or helping one another survive prison camps during World War II. Mateship. "When most Australian men say, 'He's my mate,' they're speaking of a genuine fraternal solidarity," Keneally said. But mateship also serves as a double-edged sword: "It is an inclusive, fraternal virtue, and an excluding device."

Under Murdoch, those excluded from the circle of mates usually encompassed women, liberals, people of color, academics, environmentalists, union members, and government employees. Andrew Jaspan provided a translation of how mateship played out in Murdoch's newsrooms.

MATESHIP CAN TAKE THE FORM OF A FAVOR: "Mate, would you like a job?"

AN ADMONITION: "Mate, we don't do that."

A REQUEST: "Mate, give us a hand."

AN ORDER: "Mate, get the story—I don't fucking care how."

That culture, Jaspan said, allowed Murdoch and a small circle of trusted aides to "control the various entities because people know what's expected—and know their cushy livelihoods are dependent on it." Jaspan said mateship builds in its adherents a kind of self-constructed identity that proves tough to dispel: they believe themselves to be outsiders, rough-hewn, self-sufficient, distrustful or even contemptuous of authority. The establishment rules are not for them.

This outsider image was—and is—a preposterous confection. Murdoch and his crew became consummate and powerful insiders, creating their own establishment from which to operate. In 2000, Freya Petersen was a twenty-eight-year-old Australian journalist working at Murdoch's *Courier-Mail* tabloid in Brisbane. She had done a brief stint in New York City and was invited to spend a boozy night on the town with *New York Post* columnist Steve Dunleavy, an Australian, and some others from the paper. They started at Langan's, a favorite bar just a block from the *Post* newsroom, and ended at Elaine's, a restaurant patronized by the city's political, cultural, and media elites. The owner, Elaine Kaufman, stopped by the booth to greet Dunleavy warmly by name. Petersen, sitting next to the columnist after a few drinks, started haranguing him about working for Murdoch, who, she said, had done so much to tarnish the industry.

After a bit, Dunleavy stopped her cold and said, *So what you're telling me is that you never want to work for Rupert Murdoch again?*

"It was a little shocking," Petersen later said. "He'd distilled everything I'd said into a conclusion so simple, and one that demonstrated that he either didn't understand—or care about—my concerns."

She recalled trying to engage him again on the substance of her complaints, but was stopped anew.

What I'm hearing is that you never want to work for Rupert Murdoch again, Dunleavy repeated, pausing, and leaned in closer for effect. *You know, I can make that happen.* The bond between the two Australians had endured over decades. When Murdoch was en-meshed in a business feud with Warner Bros. chief Steve Ross, he tapped his mate Dunleavy to lead a team of *Post* reporters to dig up dirt on the man.

Petersen's eyes grew wide as she envisioned her professional life evaporating. She had placed herself outside the circle of "mates." She joined Australia's public broadcaster, the ABC, after working for a non-Murdoch paper in Brisbane, Queensland.

In London, Rebekah Brooks, initially editor of *News of the World*, then the *Sun*, similarly prized devotion in reporters above all. Brooks (back then, Rebekah Wade) always presented something of an enigma for those who followed her meteoric rise in London. In her entry in *Who's Who*, she was said to have studied at the prestigious French university, the Sorbonne. (The *Daily Mail* later reported with no small amount of snark that Brooks had only taken a short course there while working in Paris for an architecture magazine.) She had materialized at the *News of the World* as a secretary and occasional features writer in 1988 after a brief stint at a fledgling British tabloid called the *Post*. Little more than eleven years later she was the tabloid's editor in chief and, at thirty-two, the youngest editor in chief of any British national newspaper.

Her boldness, even impudence, tended to pay off. According to her peer, rival, friend, and predecessor at *News of the World*, Piers Morgan, Brooks had prepared particularly well for an interview with the presumed lover of Princess Diana at a fancy hotel room: she had arranged in advance for a team to "kit it out with secret tape devices in various flowerpots and cupboards." On another occasion, she stole a scoop from the *News of the World*'s upscale sister paper the *Sunday Times* by posing as a cleaning woman at the presses to grab an early copy of the paper and rewrite it for her own publication's editions.

Soon after Brooks took over *News of the World* in 2000, eight-year-old Sarah Payne was abducted and killed, her body left in a field. The tabloid dedicated giant headlines to the crime, but Brooks wanted to do more. It adopted a "name and shame" approach. Over a two-week period, it published the names, addresses, and photographs of eighty-three convicted sex offenders, a figure all the more impressive given that it appeared in print only once a week—on Sundays.

On one day, the front-page headline, "Sign Here for Sarah," kicked off a campaign for what Brooks called "Sarah's Law." Brooks wanted legislation requiring authorities to allow parents access to the registry of criminal sex offenders living nearby. She became a confidante and champion of the girl's mother, handing over a mobile phone from the paper. *You can use it for anything—call me anytime,* the editor told her. The two women would stay in touch for years. Sara Payne, the mother, became an occasional columnist for the paper.

The tabloid's "name and shame" approach won the attention of readers and some politicians but the decision proved controversial with civil libertarians, lawyers, and some police officials. Mobs showed up outside the homes of many people whose names were published. One sex offender identified in the paper committed suicide. At the height of the public frenzy, Dr. Yvette Cloete returned to her home in Wales to find the word "paedo" (for the British rendering, paedophile) scrawled in red paint on her front door. She was a pediatrician, not a pedophile, apparently the target of mistaken *and* misspelled identity.

A mob chased a family with no links to pedophiles from their home. Three hundred people appeared at the home of another man whose sole transgression was to sport a neck brace much like the one worn by a sex offender who lived nearby. And a full-scale riot broke out outside the apartment of a pedophile in the coastal city of Portsmouth. Under duress from officials, the paper backed down on "name and shame" but not on its campaign for "Sarah's Law." The disappearance and death of Milly Dowler in 2002 sparked similar concerns and fed the paper's crusade.

Over time, Brooks became known for her news judgment, at once calculating and impulsive. But she became memorable for her ability to endear herself to those in positions of influence and power. Inside News Corp, she stood alone in her ability to ingratiate herself with not just Rupert but his adult children, too. In the testosterone-drenched alleys of Fleet Street, Brooks proved memorable for her wrath to those who challenged her.

Labour MP Chris Bryant never forgot what happened to him in the months after he asked her unwelcome questions at parliamentary hearings in 2003. A few months later, pictures surfaced of Bryant clad only in briefs from a gay online dating site. The *Mail on Sunday*, a tabloid rival to the *News of the World* and the *Sun* owned by Associated Newspapers, broke the story. But Bryant contended the *Sunday Times* and *Sun* feasted on it, quoting from his randy messages to other men in consensual private exchanges through the site. At a moment when online dating was just starting to seep into the public consciousness, the exposure of Bryant's pseudonymous cyber come-on provided rich material for the British tabloids. But it lacked a public policy component or even the reliable hook of hypocrisy: Bryant was unmarried, openly gay, and had pushed for the government to relax laws cracking down against sexual activity by gays in public places. The coverage from News International's titles felt like payback time.

The payback arrived in person as well. Bryant felt the sting of Wade's casual cruelty at a party thrown by News International at the Labour Party conference a few years later.

"She came up to me and said, 'Oh, Mr. Bryant, it's after dark. Shouldn't you be on Clapham Common?'" Bryant recalled. The park in south London served as a pickup spot for gay men. According to Bryant, the news editor's then-husband, the actor Ross Kemp, snapped back, "Shut up, you homophobic cow."

Brooks had been ambitious, a more public presence than her successor, Andrew Coulson, mixing with the powerful and glamorous as she pinged from one top News International job to the next until she became head of the whole British wing of News Corp.

Her own reporters feared her and her peers. Some of the older reporters hired private investigators because they no longer wanted to stay in a van from dusk to dawn, urinating into plastic jars, on the off-chance they might catch a married soccer star or reality show contestant sneaking out of someone's apartment. Other reporters skipped out to a bar for a drink or home for a nap. But editors kept tabs on bylines and scoops. Pressure on reporters became more pronounced as newspaper circulations declined and websites emerged as rivals. The need to slake the public thirst for scandal would lead the tabloids to take even more daring measures.

4

"THE WORLD THROUGH RUPERT'S EYES"

ON A SUBFREEZING MORNING IN March 2013, the *New York Post* decided to take its headlines to the streets, introducing a two-and-a-half hour bus tour of Manhattan to point out the sites of incidents that inspired some of its frothiest front pages. The double-decker bus, wrapped with reproductions of its nameplate and some of its more lurid headlines, became a rolling advertisement for the paper.

Seated at the front of the open-air top deck with a small clutch of hardy visitors, the guide for the tour company, Dennis Lynch, took cues from a script written by *Post* staffers, his voice slipping into and out of a throwback Brooklyn accent that would have suited a minor mug in *Guys and Dolls*.

Less than a minute in, Lynch announced an enduring classic of the form: "Headless Body in Topless Bar." Few newspapers carry such laconic punch, such an efficient mix of knowing humor and casual cruelty. Of course, the paper's artistry in that particular form often cloaked the grittiness and brutality of the news it covered and, in fact, of the way in which the news was covered. As a paper of crime, sex, and corruption, the *New York Post* played on racial fears but proved far more likely to cover stories of triumph and tears in Queens, Staten Island, and the Bronx than the *New York Times.*

The "headless body" murder had taken place three decades earlier in Queens, an outer borough that the tourist-friendly bus did not visit. The hilarious headline trivialized a gruesome story: a twenty-three-year-old man hopped up on cocaine got into an argument with the owner of a bar in Jamaica, Queens, shot him, cut off his head, took four women hostage, and raped one of them. Upon learning one of the hostages was a mortician, the killer demanded she fish the bullet that had killed the bar owner out of his skull. The shooter thought its absence might confuse the cops. It was perfect copy for the *Post.*

On the south edge of Central Park, instead of marveling over the brilliance of Frederick Law Olmsted and Calvert Vaux, Lynch pointed across the street to the Helmsley Park Lane Hotel. When hotelier Leona Helmsley died, the will of the woman the tabloid dubbed "The Queen of Mean" left $12 million to her dog. The tabloid commemorated the bequest to the Maltese with a front-page headline: "Rich Bitch." A bar in the Meatpacking District where golfer Tiger Woods met one of his mistresses triggered another page-one tribute: "Tiger Admits: I'm a Cheetah."

Lynch omitted some headlines from the tour, however. Rock and roll legend Ike Turner predeceased his wife, whom he had abused physically. The *Post*'s headline was "Ike 'Beats' Tina to Death." Assuredly few outside the paper found that funny. Another, showing a photograph of a man who fell onto the subway tracks taken moments before his death, simply said: "Doomed."

Murdoch had broken into the American market in 1973 by purchasing the *San Antonio Express-News*, the only daily he could acquire; the next year he created the *National Star* to compete against the more established supermarket tabloid, the *National Enquirer*.

Murdoch had circled the *Post* (started by Alexander Hamilton in 1801) in the mid-1970s at a time when New York City had skirted bankruptcy, drug dealing occurred openly in public parks, and Times Square earned renown for pornographic movie houses. This world welcomed Ken Chandler when he arrived in the US for the first time in 1974 after a brief stint working at Murdoch's *Sun* in the UK. In London, Chandler had been assigned to the copy desk, where he wrote the captions for the pictures of topless models, the Page Three girls, following this daily edict: "Forty-five words. If possible, at least two puns." He volunteered to come to America in response to a posting on a bulletin board for British staffers to join Murdoch's new *Star* tabloid.

When Murdoch offered to buy the *Post* from longtime owner Dorothy Schiff, he promised in writing that he would keep faith with its liberal and midmarket past, not pull it down-market by replicating his British scandal sheets. Schiff was charmed by Murdoch and heard what she wanted or needed to hear, selling it for $31 million—a bit more than $120 million today.

Once the deal went through, Murdoch inevitably, and swiftly, recast the *New York Post* in his image. The *Post* became punchy, with front-page headlines that were crass, if provocative and amusing. The *Post* did not offer topless models—but did feature bathing beauties on excuses as flimsy as their garb. And it sold papers through the introduction of Wingo, a numbers-based game, a bit like bingo and a lottery, promising riches to lucky readers, as Murdoch had in Australia and the UK. Chandler joined the paper as an editor. "He'd worry about *Star* magazine in the morning, and in the afternoon he'd be on the phone to Australia—the sun never set," Chandler recalled. The paper cultivated two generations of conservative writers on its opinion pages to allow them to refine their voices and shout down liberal pieties.

Throughout the years, the media executive remained hands-on—in Britain, Australia, and New York. Murdoch loathed public holidays—when a federal or bank holiday approached in the US, he would fly to London the night before so he would not squander a day's work. For good measure, Murdoch added the influential *New York* magazine, which catalogued the fights, finances, and fears of the moneyed class of Manhattan, and bought the left-of-center, establishment-loathing *Village Voice*. He later would pick up and, under regulatory duress, discard two more big-city tabloids: the *Chicago Sun-Times* and the *Boston Herald*.

Murdoch deployed his tabloids' pages—in both the news and editorial sections—to help those candidates he favored. The *New York Post* plucked Congressman Ed Koch from relative obscurity in the Democratic primary for the New York City mayor's race. The endorsement (and favorable coverage in the news pages) helped propel Koch to victory over future governor Mario Cuomo, among others.

In 1984 *New York Post* columnist Steve Dunleavy, a Murdoch favorite from Australia, wrote an internal memo about how to take down Geraldine Ferraro. The Democratic congresswoman from Queens was the first woman to run on a national ticket, as Walter Mondale's vice presidential running mate. The unwillingness of Ferraro, a Catholic, to oppose abortion firmly angered Murdoch. The Scottish Presbyterian faith in which his grandfather held such prominence took a stance similar to the Vatican on the issue. The paper reflected his negative views toward the candidate despite her local ties.

Murdoch didn't think much of a woman as possible VP, a belief reinforced, surprisingly, by Margaret Thatcher's performance as British prime minister. Though he squarely supported Thatcher, Murdoch held a "conviction that women were emotionally ill-equipped to hold high office," according to Thomas Kiernan, an early Murdoch biographer.

Over time, Chandler held various senior roles at the *Post* and at the *Boston Herald* for Murdoch. He remains a political conservative and currently serves as the editor in chief of the news site and magazine Newsmax, created by former *New York Post* reporter Christopher Ruddy. Chandler said the *Post*, when he first joined, proved a product of its times but also its leadership, covering the news but not itself in glory.

"When I look back at some of the stuff we did, I cringe," Chandler said. "There was no question it was homophobic." The paper singled out AIDS victims for particular scorn, he said, and treated people of color poorly. "The only time you had a picture of a black person was when they'd been arrested or done something horrible," he said. "The pictures of the celebrities were almost all white. The only blacks were in the sports section. There was that attitude—that people don't want to see pictures of black people."

Forced to sell the *Post* in 1988 by regulators, Murdoch swooped back in as a savior five years later when the paper's subsequent proprietors collapsed financially. Political figures in both parties agreed to set aside, for a while, the restrictions under laws limiting ownership of newspapers and television stations in the same markets to ensure the paper would continue to publish.

Chandler became editor and later publisher of the *Post* once again in the 1990s. "I was the editor, so I was in charge of the day-to-day operation, but he treated the *Post* like a favorite child. The *New York Post* and the London *Sun*—no question they were his favorite children," Chandler told me. At that time, Chandler said, the *Post* focused anew on the obsessions of Manhattan: media, fashion, crime, Broadway, TV, politics, sport, and gossip.

Murdoch would call Chandler at least three to four times a week—often three to four times a day. In days before email and cell phones, most News Corp editors maintained separate phone lines, whose numbers were known only to Murdoch. *Murdoch here*, he'd say. *What's happening?*

Murdoch tended not to issue orders. "You'd tell him what you were planning," Chandler said. "He wouldn't interfere." After the fact,

Murdoch might well criticize a front-page headline, or a photograph, or the angle on a story. Ahead of time, however, he rarely interfered with coverage in the works. But Murdoch loved to gossip. "He might well say, well I was at a party last night, talking to Ed Koch, and Ed told me, and he'd tell me a delicious story, that you could use on Page Six," which delivered scandal, gossip, and celebrity items every day. "You'd have to check. Sometimes he exaggerated, and sometimes they turned out not to be true."

The chairman's voice and sensibility would materialize unsummoned even when he did not call. "In my head was, this guy is losing a million dollars a week on the *New York Post*. He's providing work for two hundred journalists who, in any kind of rational economic situation, wouldn't be having a job here. There's probably eight hundred people at the company in total, including the pressmen and the ad people who are working there. So, yeah, I want to produce the sort of paper that he would like," Chandler said.

"That doesn't mean printing stories that you think aren't true. But it does mean printing stories that you think he'd be interested in. Avoiding stories that he might not want to see in the paper," Chandler said. "Definitely, there's self-censorship." Former London *Sun* editor David Yelland said much the same took place elsewhere. "Most Murdoch editors wake up in the morning, switch on the radio, hear that something has happened and think: 'What would Rupert think about this?'" Yelland said. "It's like a mantra inside your head, it's like a prism. You look at the world through Rupert's eyes."

Murdoch believed it was important to take out Iraq's Saddam Hussein in 2003. Pundits making the conservative case for war in Murdoch's *Weekly Standard* and *New York Post* were often reproduced in the *Times of London*, the *Sun*, the *Australian*, or his Aussie tabloids. A headline in the *Post* characterized the French as "cheese-eating surrender monkeys" for voting against the US position at the United Nations (the reference came from *The Simpsons*). Another headline called France part of the "Axis of Weasels." Murdoch called British prime minister Tony Blair three times in the week leading up to a House of Commons vote to deploy UK troops to Iraq, promising the support of News International's newspapers. And the fervor was shared throughout Murdoch's other titles as well, including Fox News. Murdoch told *Fortune* magazine the time was ripe: "The whole world will benefit from cheaper oil."

Whenever Murdoch came to New York, he'd duck into the newsroom, and always make a beeline for the business department. *What have you heard?* Murdoch would ask. Every now and then he'd invite a reporter up, as he did when he beckoned a young Tim Arango, a media reporter for the *Post* in the early 2000s, to eavesdrop as he talked shop with another corporate titan on speaker phone.

He saw the *Post* as one of the chief proving grounds for his older son, Lachlan Murdoch, then enjoying uneven luck in Sydney. Lachlan became deputy chief operating officer of News Corp in 2000, under president and COO Peter Chernin. His father put him in charge of the Fox Television Group, the HarperCollins publishing house, and the *Post* as well as the company's Australian division. Suddenly Chandler witnessed the ejection of top officials at the *Post* around him. Col Allan of the Sydney *Daily Telegraph* became editor in chief. He had been infamous for periodically urinating in a sink in a corner of his office during editorial meetings as a way of underscoring his authority. Allan protested to a reporter that the sink was actually behind a door. But the mind games worked. The general manager left too, in favor of an Aussie. Chandler's turn followed.

Under Col Allan, the Page Six gossip section developed into the tail that wagged the dog, brought to heel only by FBI intervention. One of the section's lead reporters, Jared Paul Stern, sought to extort a billionaire buddy of former president Bill Clinton, promising to keep negative items out of the paper if he paid $100,000 upfront and $10,000 a month subsequently. Another former reporter for the gossip section wrote in a sworn affidavit that many writers accepted freebies from those they wrote about, or didn't write about, to influence coverage, and that Allan was among the worst offenders. The *Post* had to get out ahead of the story; Page Six acknowledged that Richard Johnson, the gossip section's editor, had accepted $1,000 from a restaurateur he was writing about. Johnson's four-day, $30,000 bachelor party in Mexico had been underwritten by Joe Francis, the founder of the soft-core pornography site Girls Gone Wild and a frequent subject of gossip reports.

But Johnson was not the only figure at the paper accused of such coziness with those he covered. In 2007 it emerged in the Aussie press that Allan had taken future Australian prime minister Kevin Rudd to Scores, a popular New York strip club during a visit to New York a few years earlier; the incident briefly clouded Rudd's career. Allan seemed amused by the disclosure, until some of his former colleagues accused him of accepting free drinks, lap dances, and sexual services at the club. He denied those accusations.

Under Allan, the Australian culture of mateship allowed a frat house aura to flourish at the *New York Post*. Sandra Guzman, a Latina journalist who had been fired as editor of a *Post* magazine section, accused Allan of sidling up to her and several other female employees to show them pictures of a man displaying his penis on his cell phone; she also alleged he rubbed himself lewdly against a female colleague, and that she herself was serenaded with "I Want to Be in America"—an allusion to the Puerto Rican character who sang the musical number of that name in the musical *West Side Story*.

The paper contested her charges. Yet under oath, *Post* editors admitted that Dunleavy had called conservative black columnist Robert George "a token nigger," saying he would never have his job at the paper if not for his race. The city editor, James Murdoch's closest childhood friend Jesse Angelo, chastised Dunleavy. No other punishment was meted out.

THE *POST* was rigidly ideological, reflecting a conservative populism, except when it chose to diverge from that path. The tabloid had endorsed GOP congressman Rick Lazio in the 2000 race to represent New York in the US Senate, but it did not complicate life unduly for Democrat Hillary Clinton, who ultimately won. Murdoch personally hosted fund-raising events for her fellow Democrat, Senator Charles Schumer, in 2003. The press baron helped her raise money at a dinner three years later as she ran for reelection and the *Post* endorsed her for Senate that time around, well aware she would win handily and was laying the groundwork for a White House bid of her own.

The Clintons had found ways to make peace with those who had been adversaries. Former president Bill Clinton broke bread with Chris Ruddy despite the former *Post* reporter's seminal role in questioning the official version of the suicide of White House aide (and Clinton friend) Vince Foster. Ruddy's long articles suggested Foster had been murdered and inspired congressional hearings from Clinton's Republican foes. By 2007, Ruddy was speaking warmly of both Clintons. The Clintons and their surrogates had publicly praised Fox News for what they characterized as its fair-minded coverage of Hillary's historic bid; MSNBC hosts, with a lineup almost entirely male and increasingly dominated by liberals, had favored Barack Obama.

And yet the *New York Post* endorsed Barack Obama in the Democratic primary. Senator Clinton's election would presage, the paper held, "a return to the opportunistic, scandal-scarred, morally muddled years of the almost infinitely self-indulgent Clinton co-presidency." Obama, the paper wrote, was an intelligent man with a record as a conciliator with whom it rarely agreed on substance, but he still appeared the better choice.

Fox News chairman Roger Ailes interceded with Murdoch, fearful that his boss's more liberal children would convince the News Corp patriarch to endorse Obama in November. Elisabeth Murdoch and her husband, the British public relations executive Matthew Freud, had raised money for Obama from expatriate Americans living in London. James Murdoch had given money to Hillary Clinton's campaign and his wife was a committed environmentalist.

In early September, for the general election, the *Post* reverted to form. It tepidly endorsed John McCain, an antitax campaigner, national security hawk, and relative social moderate (on many issues such as gay rights) whose positions meshed decently with the outlook of the paper's readership, if not its own record. The paper cited Obama's intelligence but invoked his "tissue paper thin resume."

In her lawsuit, Sandra Guzman asserted the paper intentionally sought to undermine Obama after he won. She claimed the agenda was permeated with racial overtones. In February 2009, after Congress had passed a $787 billion stimulus legislation championed by the new president, *Post* cartoonist Sean Delonas drew a chimpanzee shot dead by a policeman. The caption showed another officer saying, "They'll have to find someone else to write the next stimulus bill."

In an editorial headlined "That Cartoon," the paper insisted it was not racist. "To those who were offended by the image, we apologize," the paper wrote. "It was meant to mock an ineptly written federal stimulus bill. Period."

Allan also released a statement: "The cartoon is a clear parody of a current news event, to wit the shooting of a violent chimpanzee in Connecticut. It broadly mocks Washington's efforts to revive the economy." He dug in his heels, dismissing the flap as a stunt driven by activists such as Al Sharpton.

The controversy came at an inopportune time. News Corp had been operating WWOR, a New York City station based on New Jersey soil, without a renewed license. Federal regulators appeared skeptical, if only because Murdoch already owned a station and two newspapers in the New York market. The company had won the support of many black groups for license renewals at other stations, but some challenged it.

Black journalists protested. Days later, as the NAACP and others called for Delonas's firing, Murdoch issued his own apology "to any reader who felt offended, and even insulted." He added: "I promise you that we will seek to be more attuned to the sensitivities of our community."

Allan then said he would personally be offended by a caricature of Obama as a monkey even though he claimed ignorance of the demeaning depiction of blacks in the US or Australia as monkeys and apes in the nineteenth and twentieth centuries. "I don't understand the history of the affiliation of black people and primates," Allan said. "I am not aware of that."

He could not be racist, Allan insisted. His wife was half Australian Aboriginal.

———

AMONG ALLAN'S critics in early 2009 was Michael Wolff, author of *The Man Who Owns the News*, a book about Murdoch. Wolff was a writer for *Vanity Fair* magazine, a digital news entrepreneur and media savant who had conducted dozens of hours of taped interviews with the man himself and many more with his family and friends. An advance copy obtained by the Murdochs had caused friction as it betrayed the unease with which the younger generation viewed Roger Ailes of Fox News. Other elements irked various Murdochs as well. According to Wolff, Gary Ginsberg, Murdoch's top adviser on publicity and other strategic matters, told him that they would allow such concerns to pass if he were to do one favor: change the date when Murdoch met his third wife, Wendi Deng.

Deng's story was one of astonishing ambition and opportunism, first chronicled by the *Wall Street Journal* in 2000 (seven years before the paper joined the News Corp fold). Deng had moved to the US with the help of an American couple, then had an affair with the husband. She married the husband, Jake Cherry, roughly three decades her elder. They stayed married for two years and seven months—as the *Journal* noted, seven months longer than needed to obtain the green card necessary for her to stay and work in the US as a legal resident. Cherry told the paper that they lived together "four to five months, at the most." While working for an Asian satellite television venture of News Corp, she caught Murdoch's eye by confronting him with sharp-edged questions during a staff meeting on one of his trips to China. (A leading Australian newsmagazine termed Deng a Chinese Becky Sharp, after the conniving antihero of William Makepeace Thackeray's *Vanity Fair*.) A relationship ensued and Rupert and Wendi were married just weeks after his divorce from his second wife, Anna Torv Murdoch, was finalized. The divorce settlement was reported to have cost $1.7 billion, but in reality she settled for a nine-figure payout, valued between $100 million and $200 million, to lock in the fortunes of the adult children. (She had raised Murdoch's daughter Prudence, by his first wife, since the girl was nine.)

As Wolff tells the story, Murdoch wanted the timing of his involvement with Deng out of the book, but it stayed in. *The Man Who Owns the News* received scant coverage in any News Corp properties. And Wolff also criticized Allan by name on cable television for the racially charged cartoon. Soon an article appeared on the gossip website City-File, and then another surfaced on the better-known Gawker, alleging that Wolff was having an affair with a younger colleague—a woman just a year older than his daughter. The *Post* pounced, citing, of course, the reporting of others. Over the course of the month, the *Post* published seven pieces invoking the affair and publishing another cartoon by Delonas, unfairly depicting the couple, in the words of Wolff's girlfriend Victoria Floethe, as "a thirteen-year-old girl in bed with an eighty-year-old." By the end of the coverage, Wolff had moved out of the apartment he shared with his wife and the tabloid was running pieces about a legal fight the soon-to-be divorced couple were having with Wolff's mother-in-law.

Wolff still had the tapes of his conversations with Murdoch. According to Wolff, he called Ginsberg and reminded him of the interest websites expressed in putting the chairman's unguarded musings online. Murdoch typically spoke indistinctly, making reproduction of the tapes of less than clear value. But the *Post*'s articles stopped cold at the end of the month.

5

FAIR AND BALANCED

TABLOID BLOOD WOULD CIRCULATE THROUGH the arteries of what would become a new American television network, breaking the monopoly of the big three. In 1985 Rupert Murdoch acquired six television stations in the nation's largest ten markets, including New York, Los Angeles, Dallas, and Washington, DC, from John Kluge's Metromedia conglomerate. The deal, constructed before Murdoch had acquired 20th Century Fox, put the creation of a fourth network within reach. When Murdoch bought out Marvin Davis's stake in both Fox studios and the stations that year, the Australian newspaper king was suddenly America's newest multimedia mogul—with major holdings in print, movies, and television.

At its debut in 1986, the Fox network broadcast but a night or two a week. Even when Fox became full-fledged, it provided just two hours of nightly prime-time programming. It offered magazine shows inspired more by the *New York Post* and daytime television than nightly news programs. In fact, Fox had built no indigenous news division to cover the news.

A Current Affair was a syndicated scandal and entertainment TV show that originated in 1986 from News Corp's flagship local TV station WNYW Channel 5 in New York City. One of its stars was Steve Dunleavy. He wore a trench coat, chain-smoked like Bogart, and cut a memorable figure with a jutting chin and unavoidable pompadour. And he chased just about anything with two X chromosomes. The oft-recycled claim was that he had been in coital vigor with a Scandinavian heiress late one snowy night outside a bar when a city snowplow ran over—and broke—his foot. Dunleavy was said to be so soused that he continued his aerobic affections unabated.

The tabloid columnist Pete Hamill joked, "I hope it wasn't his writing foot."

Dunleavy shone as a reporter for Murdoch's tabloid *Mirror* in Sydney before breaking stories for the *National Star*. He headed to greater glories on the *Post*. During the height of the scare over the Son of Sam serial killings in the New York City boroughs of Queens and Brooklyn, Dunleavy wrote a florid front-page piece advertised by the headline "Gunman Sparks Son of Sam Chase." Readers learned right before the article's conclusion that the gunman was not the Son of Sam at all.

After helping to launch *A Current Affair*, Dunleavy surfaced yet again for Murdoch on the early Fox weekend show *The Reporters*, another hour of gossip and crime. "In its first couple of years, television was considered a foul little business that no self-respecting journalist wanted anything to do with," *Washington Post* TV critic Tom Shales wrote at its debut in 1988. "Fox Broadcasting is trying to bring those days back."

The Reporters didn't last long, but Dunleavy never lost his luster with Murdoch. Fox did not need to develop refined taste. The early reality Fox show *Cops*, an exceptionally cost-effective production that taped raids by patrolling police officers on low-level criminals, frequently beat its competition in the ratings. *The Simpsons*, a spin-off of

Tracey Ullman's comedy show, became a breakaway hit. *Married with Children,* coarse by anyone's definition, helped brand the network as edgier and younger than its network elders and prefigured some of its recent successes, such as Seth MacFarlane's animated *Family Guy.*

Meanwhile, local Fox stations conjured up newscasts with a brisker, more tabloidy feel. By 1992 Murdoch decided that the local stations Fox owned and ran itself would no longer carry CNN's feed (which he had obtained from CNN founder Ted Turner at a dear cost). In 1995 Murdoch brought to New York one of his foremost British executives, Andrew Neil. To be precise, Neil was a Scot, like Murdoch's grandfather, but not stereotypically dour. The mirthful former reporter and editor for the *Economist* had served for nearly a dozen years as editor of Murdoch's *Sunday Times*; he was also the founding chairman of Sky TV, later merged into BSkyB, today one of the most important holdings that News Corp and the Murdochs control. Neil came to the US to help guide the creation of Fox News.

The birth of Fox News sprang from Murdoch's decision to create a television empire around sports, as he had previously in Australia and the UK. In 1993 Fox bought the rights to broadcast the games of the NFL's then dominant NFC division, swiping football from CBS for nearly $1.6 billion. "We're a network now. Like no other sport will do, the NFL will make us into a real network," Murdoch exulted to *Sports Illustrated.* "In the future there will be 400 or 500 channels on cable, and ratings will be fragmented. But football on Sunday will have the same ratings, regardless of the number of channels. Football will not fragment."

He was right. And he wanted a winning weekly bookend for football to strike at another top-rated CBS program. "At that stage, Rupert Murdoch had in mind to set up a Fox News answer to *60 Minutes,*" Neil told me. "It was to be an hour-long news show going out after the NFL football program on Fox." His costar was to be Judith Regan, a young woman who had sliced her way to the top-selling echelons of the book publishing business. Smart, and possessed of finely sharpened elbows, Regan had by this point been rewarded with her own imprint, ReganBooks, at Murdoch's HarperCollins publishing house. Neil started getting uneasy as Murdoch brought in a consultant to help punch up the concept of what news would look and sound like on Fox. The idea of creating a show yielded to the idea of creating an entire cable network—a niche news channel.

The new network would speak to viewers who felt the rest of the press was too liberal, like the *New York Times*, even *60 Minutes* itself. The consultant had been a political strategist for Presidents Richard Nixon and George H.W. Bush, the executive producer of a TV show starring Rush Limbaugh, and the head of financial news channel CNBC.

His name was Roger Ailes.

MSNBC LAUNCHED at about the same time. It was a partnership of Microsoft and the giant manufacturing and finance conglomerate GE's NBC division. In short, its executives had very little idea of what they were doing other than amortizing NBC News's costs across an additional channel. A parade of executives came and left in the ensuing decade.

Under Ailes, Fox's vision was clear and pure. Its cultural sensibility offered a modern version of a *Mad Men* world, where opinions were declarative: men were confident; professional women smart, young, and sleek. And it chased stories of dysfunction in Bill Clinton's America.

"I'll tell you what television didn't do at the time," Ailes later told *Esquire* magazine. "It didn't reflect what people really thought. I mean, they're sitting there saying, 'Wait a minute, New York's going broke, Los Angeles is broke, the United States is broke, everything the government has run is broke, Social Security is broke, Medicare is broke, the military is broke, why do we want these guys making all these decisions for us?'"

The American news consumer of just fifteen years ago would not have been able to recognize the country's current media landscape—the range of choices, the technological innovations, and in particular the cacophony. And no other news organization has done more in recent years to reshape that terrain than Fox. Just about every news organization either mimics or reacts against the way Fox presents the news and the values it represents.

That's not because Fox News breaks many big stories. It doesn't. (Part of the brilliance of its financial model is to have a lean reporting staff.) That's not because the channel draws the biggest audiences in news. Nor does it do so in television news, with some exceptions, though it is a dominant force in cable television.

What Fox News does, instead, is to determine what it believes should be the story of the day. It is a choice intended not just to select its own coverage, but to force others to pay attention—day after day. Fox News does so with an eye for episodes overlooked by other major news outlets. It particularly seeks storylines and themes that reflect and further stoke a sense of grievance among cultural conservatives against coastal elites.

"Cable news punches above its weight, if you look at its influence," former Fox News vice president David Rhodes once told me. "How many people are actually watching it, from moment to moment?" The highest-rated shows draw between 2.5 and 3.3 million viewers on any given night, at most a bit more than 1 percent of the US population.

When not inflamed, the channel's anchors often look as though they're having fun. And the network's news staff includes some professionals whose work could appear on any number of outlets.

At the outset, Ailes made a couple of key moves on the news side to shore up its credibility on the air. He hired John Moody, a veteran of *Time* magazine and United Press International (UPI), as a senior news executive. Fox's first reporters included Jon Scott and Gary Matsumoto of NBC. Catherine Crier of CNN and Court TV became an early anchor. Tammy Haddad, the executive producer and creator of CNN's *Larry King Live*, was briefly employed to develop a Sunday public affairs interview show carried on both the Fox network and on the cable channel. As perhaps Washington's premier booker of top-shelf guests, Haddad also helped to plot the show's launch more generally. The first day, anchors interviewed Israeli prime minister Benjamin Netanyahu, Nation of Islam leader Louis Farrakhan, and GOP presidential candidate Bob Dole. For the desired core audience, the channel offered someone to root for, someone to root against, and someone to vote for.

On the first day, Bill O'Reilly, formerly of ABC, CBS, and the tabloid television show *Inside Edition*, appeared on his new program the *O'Reilly Report* (later rechristened the *O'Reilly Factor*). "How did television news become so predictable and in some cases so boring?" O'Reilly asked viewers. "Few broadcasts take any chances these days and most are very politically correct. Well, we're going to try to be different—stimulating and a bit daring, but at the same time, responsible and fair."

Those remarks sounded much more temperate than O'Reilly proved to be. He had a calibrated sense of rights and wrongs, and a hair-trigger temper. With O'Reilly, Sean Hannity, a forceful conservative paired with a relatively weak liberal, Alan Colmes, and Bill Shine, who oversaw the opinion hosts, the new network was defined at least in part from its earliest days by three Irish Catholics from Long Island who liked a good rumble.

One of the most important new faces of Fox was Brit Hume. He had been a political reporter for the *Baltimore Evening Sun* and did legwork and writing for Jack Anderson's investigative column. (The CIA had briefly put Hume under surveillance after the column featured some scoops involving the agency.) He had risen to become the chief White House correspondent for ABC News. Tall and courtly, his suits often accompanied by a pocket square with a printed pattern complementing his ties, Hume bestowed credibility and class on the brash new network. His wife, Kim Hume, had left ABC to become Fox's first Washington bureau chief before he arrived.

Brit Hume was a hardworking reporter with a textured understanding of political combat and a sly appreciation for irony. He had been the one to make the considered case for the journalistic soundness of the Fox way. Most reporters and editors, he argued, approached their jobs with professionalism but could not escape a culturally liberal outlook. Reporters covered gay rights and environmental activists through this prism, Hume said, seeing parallels to the civil rights movement, and failed to subject them to the same scrutiny social and religious conservatives faced.

"A very large percentage of readers and viewers out there were really insulted and found their sensibilities offended," Hume told me some years later. "I had always had the feeling that if somebody built a broadcast network that challenged that, that there would be a tremendous market for it." Stories not being told by the other news outlets represented "low-hanging fruit," the kinds of pieces that could be reported evenhandedly by anyone but were not selected for broadcast or publication elsewhere.

A push for new EPA rules might strike the *Washington Post* or CBS News as a story about the debate over cleaner water. Fox might frame the same story around small business owners struggling to keep pace with red tape from Washington.

Perhaps most important, Ailes instinctively recognized good television and understood how to create it—defining "good" as something viewers would want to watch and keep watching. It was close to Murdoch's definition of the public interest. In this case, Ailes knew that Fox's defining feature would require a highly cultivated resentment toward other news organizations. The "fair and balanced" slogan alone was an increasingly explicit assertion that mainstream press organizations were not fair or balanced. "We report. You decide," provoked the same reaction in viewers and the competition. On Fox, the news programs served to get out the mission statement: the other news organizations look down on you and your beliefs. Here, you're home.

Fox initially had to fight to force cable system providers to carry the network. Luckily for Ailes, he had a powerful friend in the nation's most populous metropolitan region. Time Warner's refusal to welcome Fox in New York City caused Mayor Rudolph Giuliani to threaten to carry the channel (along with Bloomberg TV) on the city's public access station. Giuliani also implied he would revoke Time Warner's lucrative cable franchise for the city. His brass-knuckled tactics showed a preference for one for-profit over another. He argued that Time Warner was favoring its own station, CNN.

Murdoch had been angered by Time Warner's roadblocks. Ailes had run Giuliani's first, unsuccessful bid for the mayoralty in 1989, and they remained close. Top Murdoch executives (including Ailes) had spoken more than two dozen times with aides at City Hall to co-ordinate a strategy in a two-month period. The coordination was too cozy for the federal judge ruling on the case. "The city's purpose in acting to compel Time Warner to give Fox one of its commercial chan-nels was to reward a friend and to further a particular viewpoint. As a consequence, Fox was the recipient of special advocacy," wrote federal judge Denise Cote. "The city has engaged in a pattern of conduct with the purpose of compelling Time Warner to alter its constitutionally protected editorial decision not to carry Fox News. The city's actions violated longstanding First Amendment principles that are the foun-dation of our democracy."

Yet Time Warner yielded. And Fox took advantage to build a greater audience. It covered the Clinton impeachment as ABC built *Nightline* on coverage of the Iranian hostage drama—an ongoing crisis with an uncertain outcome of national import. Only Fox News would tell the full truth, its tenor implied.

The pacing was fast, the graphics crisp and lively. Fox's Ailes wanted viewers to enjoy what they saw. And he made enough liberals part of the mix to ensure some ideological clashes. Ailes hired people he had battled during earlier political campaigns, including Geraldine Ferraro and Bob Beckel, Walter Mondale's campaign manager. Children of such prominent Democratic families as the Kennedys and the Jacksons found work at Republicans' new favorite place to watch TV.

In 2000, Fox News covered the political conventions for the first time. In news from the Middle East, Fox won favor with many Jewish viewers by employing the term "homicide bomber," rather than the more common "suicide bomber," to keep the emphasis on the deaths of innocents, not the perpetrators. Fox painted those who did not climb on board its various campaigns as opposed to the country's well-being.

6

THE
"FOG OF WAR"

ROGER AILES DEVELOPED HIS PHILOSOPHY as he shaped the media efforts of two presidential campaigns—Richard Nixon and George H.W. Bush. Ailes knows how to make a candidate look presidential. And he also knows how to throw a punch. Ailes is not just more conservative than Murdoch but more steeped in the world of politics than his boss, who still thinks of himself as running a journalistic outfit. Ailes's key insight is defining opponents before they define themselves. And Ailes finds opponents all over.

Fox's PR shop, led by Ailes's longtime executives Brian Lewis and Irena Briganti, wears its reputation as a badge of honor. The two senior aides consider their performance a key component of their channel's ratings dominance and the billion dollars a year it generates for News Corp. There are moments when the essence of Fox News can be discerned most clearly in the maneuvers of its public relations department, not on the airwaves.

Whatever the story, reporters calling Fox News on a regular basis become inured to the onslaught of questions from Fox's public relations staff: What's the precise focus of the piece? What quotes are you using? Who else are you talking to? Why aren't you making these other points? These questions are intended to steer coverage, glean intelligence, head off unflattering conclusions, and even intimidate reporters from interviewing people at other cable outlets.

The deluge of queries can crop up at just about any network. But Fox's creativity far surpasses such controlling techniques, as it believes its bargaining position has solidified with its ratings lead.

My own early encounters with Fox's public relations representatives when I was a reporter and media critic at the *Baltimore Sun* showed them to be sharp and contentious. On Election Day 2000, television networks announced and withdrew calls awarding the White House first to Al Gore and then to George W. Bush. The *Baltimore Sun* had arranged to have a young freelancer, a former intern for the paper, spend the night inside Fox's New York City studios. John Ellis, one of the top analysts on Fox's decision desk, helped Fox become the first network to call Bush the winner at 2:17 AM. He was also in contact with his cousins, George W. Bush and Florida governor Jeb Bush. (Jeb's given name is John Ellis Bush.) When their consultations were revealed by Jeffrey Toobin of the *New Yorker* magazine, Fox spokesman Rob Zimmerman pressured me to convince our freelancer to get on a conference call with other reporters to refute the story. Zimmerman said Ellis was barely involved at all.

When I talked with our freelancer, she said Ellis had actually bragged to her that night that he would greatly influence the network's call. Furthermore, though she had remained late into the night, she left before the Bush decision played out in full, as she had to show up early the next morning for her day job at a financial trade publication. I called Fox back, saying the editors had decided against putting the freelancer on the spot to defend the network. What's more, I said, even if she were to speak out, she wouldn't confirm Fox's version of events. Zimmerman told me it was clear the *Baltimore Sun*'s fairness was in doubt.

The inconclusive election results—"RECOUNT" in the inevitable on-screen caption—did not damage Fox and served as one of the episodes the channel used to cement the loyalty of its viewers. One of the secrets of Fox's success lies in its ability to draw viewers who stay tuned to the one channel for much longer than other cable stations. The aftermath of the September 11, 2001, terror attacks marked another such opportunity. Fox News proudly flew a graphic flag in the corner of its screen. Anchors wore flags in their lapel pins. MSNBC and CNN rushed to catch up.

Little more than year after the election, early one morning in December 2001, I called Fox in trying to sort out the basis of a story by the network's new chief war correspondent, Geraldo Rivera. He had been a swashbuckling investigative reporter, then a network news magazine star, a tabloid talk show host, and finally a political talk show host under Ailes at CNBC. Still under contract to CNBC in the fall of 2001, he had bristled at the idea of staying behind a desk while a war raged elsewhere, quit his CNBC talk show, and rejoined Ailes at Fox. Rivera soon traveled to the mountains of Tora Bora in eastern Afghanistan.

He was, Rivera announced, on a quest to track down "the dastardly one" (his personal term for Osama bin Laden). On an early December day, he showed footage from Afghanistan, twice in a twenty-four-hour period, in which he prayed over the site where he said three American soldiers and numerous allied Afghan fighters had been killed by a US bombing raid in what was euphemistically called a "friendly fire" incident. He said he had seen their tattered uniforms and showed himself, on video, reciting the Lord's Prayer.

There was, however, a problem: Rivera filed his report less than a day later from Tora Bora, a cave complex in the White Mountains roughly three hundred miles northeast of the site where the bombs actually fell in Kandahar. I talked to reporters in Afghanistan, people who handled logistics at rival networks, senior staffers with international relief agencies and human rights groups active there, and US military officials. None of them thought the journey from Tora Bora to Kandahar and back was feasible by road in less than twenty-four hours, while an official at the Pentagon said Rivera certainly had not hitched a ride with US forces or aircraft.

When I asked how he could have made the round trip down and back in a single day, given the bombed-out roads, the rival warlords, and the highway bandits patrolling what routes were functioning, a Fox News spokeswoman angrily asked whether I was saying he made it up. By the time the network consented to an interview, deadlines approached. Because of the nine-and-a-half-hour time-zone difference in Afghanistan, they said, Rivera was asleep and unreachable. *Wait a day, and we'll give you Geraldo.* By that point, we could have run a story without speaking to him. But my section's editors and I agreed it would make the story much stronger to talk to Rivera. I imposed one condition: that he would talk to no other reporters that day. Fox News agreed.

The next day, Rivera gave me a vivid and livid interview by satellite phone. But he interspersed his anger toward what he clearly saw as my impertinence with a fascinatingly self-aware account of the various twists and turns in his career. Finally Rivera said he had been confused by another, similar friendly-fire incident that killed a group of Afghan rebels: "The fog of war," he said. As contemporary newspaper reports and accounts by human rights groups subsequently demonstrated, that separate incident involving only Afghans did not happen until the following week.

The Fox PR people had taken some protective steps. Despite their promise, Rivera also spoke to Associated Press television reporter David Bauder. In this interview, Rivera boasted that he carried a gun despite journalistic conventions advising against it. Such bravado created the fear that armed reporters might appear to Al Qaida fighters little different from combatants, and then all journalists in war zones would become targets. The AP's global reach ensured that Rivera's tale of packing heat drained the appetite for any other controversies he might have engendered. Hundreds of newspapers published Bauder's story. Fox's Irena Briganti left a message on my voice mail, suggesting only minor media outlets paid attention: "Reuters and MarketWatch? Pretty pathetic placement, my friend."

I wrote a second article, a few days later, weighing whether a television news network had an obligation to acknowledge and correct an error such as the one Rivera had made. The Drudge Report picked that one up—and the second story ricocheted around the world. Fox put out a tepid statement to the Associated Press between Christmas and New Year's Eve—a media dead zone—stating that Rivera had made an "honest mistake." No formal correction appeared on air. All this landed me on Fox's blacklist. I later learned that internally staffers called it "Irena's doghouse": the constantly changing catalog of offenders that PR staffers review on a regular basis.

After about fifteen months, Zimmerman called me to say Fox was wiping the slate clean. I continued to work with the public relations department on what I consider to be a professional basis—profiling such Fox anchors and hosts as Shepard Smith, Brit Hume, Bret Baier, John Stossel, and Glenn Beck. The PR department's retribution was meant to punish me and to warn others. But it was not personal.

A year or two after I broke the Rivera story, Fox News invited me as a guest to the White House correspondent's dinner. It was a deeply inside joke for the amusement of its publicity department and the small world of media reporters who took any note. The *Baltimore Sun* paid the cost of my $135 ticket. And I had a good time, dining and drinking, without guilt, among the same Fox News staffers who had been told not to talk to me for more than a year. Years later, when my wife and

I married, the Fox News PR team sent over an exquisite bottle of champagne from a 2002 vintage—specifically picked by Brian Lewis, Briganti pointed out, to honor a prize I won for the Rivera story. Nice touch. It was a shame to have to return it.

As the campaign against Al Qaida and its Taliban allies in Afghanistan yielded to the drive to invade Iraq in 2003, Fox News adopted a pro-war tenor that overrode that of many of the reports of their reporters in the field. Anchor Neil Cavuto mocked a professor he deemed an "obnoxious, pontificating jerk," a "self-absorbed, condescending imbecile," and an "Ivy League intellectual Lilliputian," for criticizing his broadcast as setting aside journalistic traditions of objectivity for outright nationalism.

"Am I slanted and biased? You damn well bet I am, professor. I'm more in favor of a system that lets me say what I'm saying here rather than one who would be killing me for doing the same thing over there," Cavuto said. "You say I wear my biases on my sleeve? Better that than pretend you have none, but show them clearly in your work." As if to prove his point, during an antiwar protest in Manhattan, the Fox News ticker that wrapped around the front of the News Corp headquarters switched from headlines to jeers against the demonstrators.

At times the network's publicity staffers turned their sights on their own former colleagues. When Fox host Paula Zahn moved to CNN, Zimmerman said it was like "putting a fresh coat of paint on an outhouse." Ailes himself told the *New York Times*, "I could have put a dead raccoon on the air and gotten a better rating."

At another point, I noticed that Fox News had fallen into the habit of wishing people well in ways that conveyed the precise opposite. In 2004, then MSNBC host (and former ESPN and Fox Sports anchor) Keith Olbermann criticized Bill O'Reilly, drawing this retort from Brian Lewis: "Since he stopped reading sports scores, Keith has attracted fewer viewers than a test pattern, and his career has been nothing short of a train wreck. We pity his tortured soul *and wish him all the best.*" (All italics mine.) In 2005, when CNN experienced a mild ratings boost under a new president, Jonathan Klein, Fox's Briganti replied: "Our focus is on beating the broadcast networks. *We wish Jon well* in his battle for second place with MSNBC." That same year, Ted Turner denounced Fox, triggering this: "Ted is understandably bitter, having lost his ratings, his network, and now his mind. *We wish him well.*"

The steady stream of cruelty had become funny by sheer force of repetition. Ailes sometimes took part in crafting the put-downs.

On occasion, Fox News's PR team aimed its jabs at current colleagues. Laurie Dhue, a Fox anchor who had complained she was not receiving sufficient press coverage, mistook a junior Fox publicity assistant for a young fan seeking an autograph at a black tie event in Washington. Dhue would be taught a lesson. Among Fox's guests at that radio and TV correspondents' dinner was Anne Schroeder, a reporter who wrote gossip features for the *Washington Post*. She sat at a table that included John Moody, a senior news executive, and Chris Wallace, the host of the Sunday political talk show *Fox News Sunday*. At an after-party, Schroeder witnessed Dhue dancing energetically— and raising some eyebrows among Fox executives.

Schroeder's later story for the *Post* reported that "the Fox News babes were in high spirits—especially Laurie Dhue." The item mentioned Dhue's misunderstanding over the autograph and continued: "The sultry anchor boogied the night away on the dance floor, bumping into numerous people in the packed house. Partygoers were overheard hissing (but barely, thanks to the loud music): 'Laurie don't, Laurie don't!'"

An accompanying photo showed Dhue, glass of champagne in hand, mouth agape in a wide smile—much wider than that of her three colleagues. A Fox News spokesman was quoted in the piece: "Laurie had a good time. Everyone had a good time." Readers could only draw the clear implication that Dhue had been inebriated. Years later, after leaving the network, Dhue acknowledged publicly that she had been an alcoholic. But this leak was intended to bring her to heel. Fox's staffers had picked the specific photograph to forward to the *Post*. And no one shouted "Laurie don't!" as a pun on her last name. That had been entirely concocted by Fox.

In a variety of ways, Fox engaged in a pitched public relations battle to dominate the narrative about the cable news business. Fox PR staffers were expected to win every news cycle, on every platform imaginable. When reporters printed quotations from Fox News officials in articles that did not focus exclusively on the network, Briganti upbraided her employees. *Why would you embarrass me like this?* she would ask.

For all of Briganti's tough cop bravado, she was not doing anything that her boss, Brian Lewis, didn't want done. Lewis was one of Ailes's closest advisers. Often Ailes was involved in planning in publicity tactics himself. Lewis and Briganti believed that such intensity would be the subject of admiring profiles in the *Washington Post* or Politico if it surfaced on a political campaign. They thought it was hypocritical for reporters to complain just because it came from a media company.

On the blogs, the fight was particularly fierce. Fox PR staffers were expected to counter not just negative and even neutral blog postings but the anti-Fox comments beneath them. One former staffer recalled using twenty different aliases to post pro-Fox rants. Another had one hundred. Several employees had to acquire a cell phone thumb drive to provide a wireless broadband connection that could not be traced back to a Fox News or News Corp account. Another used an AOL dial-up connection, even in the age of widespread broadband access, on the rationale it would be harder to pinpoint its origins. Old laptops were distributed for these cyber operations. Even blogs with minor followings were reviewed to ensure no claim went unchecked.

I HAVE spoken with Roger Ailes only a few times in person. One encounter took place in October 2007, several years after I joined NPR, when I reintroduced myself to him at an event staged by his own company. With suddenly blazing eyes turned on my face he said: *Oh, I remember who you are*, as he gripped my hand firmly. *You tried to fuck us.*

We were standing a few yards away from a stone temple with intricately carved depictions of Isis, the ancient Egyptian goddess of magic and fertility, and Osiris, the ruler of the underworld.

At that moment we were also surrounded by powerful forces and shimmering stars from the present-day worlds of media, entertainment, and high finance, including Hollywood producer Harvey Weinstein, former GE chief Jack Welch, and the comic actor and screenwriter Mel Brooks.

To get there, they entered the Metropolitan Museum of Art on the eastern edge of Manhattan's Central Park, walked past the votive candles spelling out Fox on the main marble staircase, slowed on the red carpet to be immortalized by the paparazzi, and ducked through the rooms with smaller antiquities from Assyria and Babylon, to the glass-encased Sackler Wing that houses the Temple of Dendur. Despite its Egyptian roots, the temple was constructed and dedicated to the honor of a foreign-born conqueror, the Roman emperor Caesar Augustus, as was the evening itself, a point not lost on Ailes, who jovially referred to Augustus as the "Rupert Murdoch of his day" as he toasted the launch of a new sister channel that he would also run, the Fox Business Network.

But at that moment, Ailes was busy erasing my awareness of all that. The man with the increasingly forbidding countenance had been brooding over the Geraldo Rivera story I had written six years earlier.

You fucked us, Ailes repeated.

It was all true, I replied. *I reported the facts.*

The facts, he spat out. *People like you always say that.*

People like what? Reporters? Didn't he have a bunch on his payroll?

A photographer popped up and offered to snap our picture, breaking the tension and making us both smile as we pressed closer for the shot.

Ailes brightened as he shared a thought: *Won't this upset all those left-wing friends of yours at the parties you go to?*

I laughed too, impressed and amused by his audacity, and as I replied, I gestured to the Egyptian temple, the servers circling with chilled champagne glasses filled near the brim, and the hundreds of guests—his guests, and Murdoch's—who were milling about. *You mean, like this one?*

———————————

THE 2008 presidential campaign brought new challenges to the cable news ratings front-runner for the first time in years. In the early weeks of that year, Fox's audiences sagged. Signs appeared to point the Democrats' way; they had retaken the Congress in 2006; the fallout from the Iraq War attached to Republicans. Nor did candidates John McCain, Mitt Romney, and Mike Huckabee stir passion in most voters.

On the Democratic side, however, the primary had quickly narrowed to two heavyweights—senators Hillary Clinton and Barack Obama. Getting viewers to tune in when the headlines focused on Democrats proved a tougher sale. So in February 2008, Fox's claim of ratings dominance appeared shaky. CNN's estimated ratings in the highly desired set of twenty-five to fifty-four-year-olds (the demographic most television advertisers paid to reach) rose 150 percent above the previous year's levels. That meant CNN actually beat Fox News for the month in prime time for the demographic in which bragging rights were won and lost.

MSNBC, then a distant third, enjoyed a jump of 71 percent and some nights beat Fox in the demographic. Fox's loss of that key demographic in prime time for the first time in six years caught the attention of several media reporters. Two reporters were punished for pursuing their interest in the topic.

A reporter for *Crain's New York Business*, Matthew Flamm, was sandbagged when he decided to turn a relatively quick story on CNN's ratings successes that month. He called officials at the three big cable channels and hit a brick wall at Fox News. Yet a producer for Bill O'Reilly's show shot Flamm an email from a private Hotmail account, saying she had heard he was asking questions about the ratings. The producer wrote that she could not talk in person but that he should know top Fox executives were indeed worried and had decided on a shift: *They want to copy the success that MSNBC has had with [Keith] Olbermann and [Chris] Matthews anchoring their coverage.*

For those who closely followed the vagaries of cable news, this was a big deal. Fox News winked at the notion of journalistic objectivity with its "fair and balanced" slogan, its carefully chosen story lists, and its list of commentators weighted to the right. But it had always handed major news events to its news anchors, such as Brit Hume, Chris Wallace, and Shepard Smith, although such coverage often gave way to special broadcasts of the big opinion shows. To ask O'Reilly to handle actual anchoring duties would be to erase that clear line of separation. MSNBC had headed in that direction, out-Foxing Fox. Flamm made sure the producer who had emailed him actually existed. But he could not get a second source. His editors split the difference. Don't write it for the print edition, they said, but post it online. It'll draw plenty of clicks.

Splitting the difference turned out to be a mistake. On the morning of February 29, Flamm's story was posted online. He cited CNN's good fortunes and said that a chastened Fox wanted to "spice up its coverage" and that Hume would be "relegated to a senior news analyst role." Fox pounced. The industry website TVNewser was a widely read bulletin board for the industry. It had been started by *New York*

Times television reporter Brian Stelter as Cable Newser when he was just a college student at Towson University outside Baltimore, and remained a clearinghouse for industry information after he sold the site. Within a few hours of Flamm's online article, TVNewser posted a punishing item. Brit Hume would anchor for Fox News, as always. O'Reilly never figured into the plan as an anchor.

"The notion that O'Reilly would ANCHOR election coverage of any kind is beyond absurd and wildly inaccurate," Briganti told TVNewser in an email. "If Flamm is so off base with this 'fact,' you'd have to question all of his other 'reporting' when it comes to Fox News."

A second-tier site, Big Head DC, channeled Fox without quoting anyone at the network by name, reciting its financial and ratings successes. "In light of all this, we hear Flamm is being referred to as Matthew Flailing in some media circles today," the site claimed. "The bigger question remains: how did such a woefully inaccurate story make it to print? Some insiders are even wondering whether Flamm will even have a job come Monday."

What the hell had happened? Flamm called the producer at Fox who had given him the errant tip. She was incredulous when he finally reached her. *Who are you?* she asked him coldly. *I have no idea what you're talking about.* Panicked, the reporter sent an email to the Hotmail account from which he had received the original scoop. It bounced back. The account had been shut down. As Flamm and his editors conceded to associates, they should have treated the email as a tip rather than a confirmation. A former Fox News staffer knowledgeable about the incident confirmed to me they had been set up.

To salt the wound, the posting at Big Head DC was accompanied by a photo-shopped picture of Flamm, with a bulbous nose, inflated ears, yellowed teeth, and enhanced rings under his eyes. The alterations were obvious when compared with the original photograph on TVNewser.

Timothy Arango, then a media reporter on the business desk of the *New York Times,* told me he called Fox, more as a courtesy than to conduct a probing interview, as he prepared a story on CNN's good fortunes. He received in reply an email containing the network's internal ratings analyses designed to knock the story down. That's a common response from many networks in such circumstances.

As Arango pressed on, Briganti emailed an entire statement and said he could only use it if he printed it verbatim. "It was very vitriolic against CNN," Arango told me. "I said, 'I'm not running a full statement.' Nobody has the right to make that demand." He called her back to read the part of the statement that the *Times* would print. Arango had written from 2002 to 2006 for another News Corp property, the *New York Post.* He had developed warm relations with the parent company's public affairs department and he believed he had a professional rapport with Fox.

This time, he said, Briganti warned him: *They're going to go after you personally.* On March 5, 2008, Arango's story, headlined "Back in the Game," ran on the front page of the *Times* business section, and it was featured prominently on the paper's website. That morning, he received a call from a blogger with Jossip, a now-defunct gossip site. Arango knew what lay in store but did not return the call.

The unbylined story on Jossip said Arango had just returned from a two-month medical leave that "many allege may have been a stint in rehab." The Jossip posting utilized every element of Arango's past coverage at the *Post* and *Fortune* magazine to draw a portrait of a craven reporter in unsuccessful pursuit of on-air reporting jobs at cable channels. It referred to "blowjob pieces about CNBC execs" written, the blog claimed, when Arango was hustling for a job at the network.

Arango braced for the slam about rehab because he had indeed returned a few days earlier from an extended medical leave to address his substance abuse. Arango kept silent, expecting a wave of disgust from his own newsroom. It never materialized. Bill Keller, then the executive editor at the *Times*, emailed Arango a note of encouragement: *We don't take that kind of bullshit seriously. Keep your head up.*

A few months later, on June 28, 2008, another *Times* media reporter, Jacques Steinberg, wrote an article on "an ominous trend" in ratings for Fox News: its cable news rivals appeared to be closing the ratings gap. On July 2, Steve Doocy and Brian Kilmeade of *Fox & Friends* went after Steinberg and a *Times* editor, Stephen Reddicliffe, calling the article a "hit piece." Doocy offered a backstory: "Mr. Reddicliffe actually used to work for this company—he got fired."

Reddicliffe had in fact left more than five years earlier as editor in chief of *TV Guide*, which Murdoch had sold in late 2007. *Fox & Friends* broadcast distorted photographs of both Reddicliffe and Steinberg that appeared on the screen as Doocy and Kilmeade spoke. Reddicliffe's forehead was elongated, his teeth yellowed, his eyes blackened; Steinberg's ears and chin were inflated, his nose greatly enlarged, his hairline lowered to collapse his brow, and his eyes blackened as well. The effect evoked what was done to Flamm's picture. No disclaimer told viewers that the picture had been altered. A number of people, especially colleagues at the *Times*, regarded the images as anti-Semitic.

In early July 2008, *New York Times* media columnist David Carr accused Fox News of targeting the reporters, citing the Steinberg episode and alluding vaguely to Arango's run-in, though not by name. The episode involving Flamm largely escaped public attention. In the glare of attention, Fox pulled back on some of its most aggressive tactics.

For Arango, there was a coda to the story. He later collaborated with Carr on an extensive profile of Roger Ailes. Fox regained a strong ratings lead. But its brass worried about what their piece might say. Brian Lewis called Bruce Headlam, the media editor of the *Times*, arguing that Arango should be taken off the story.

There was no cause for anxiety. The resulting front-page story painted Ailes as one of the most dominant media executives in the country, operating from the intersection of television, politics, and commerce. He had done so in part by deploying all of the weapons available to him—including his programs and a muscular political operation that happens to work for a cable news channel.

7

THE VOICE OF
OPPOSITION

———————

IN 2007, DEMOCRATIC CANDIDATES HAD refused, one by one, to take part in a planned early primary debate on Fox, complaining of unfair coverage of their party. As Barack Obama's bid for the White House picked up momentum, the candidate endured a drubbing from Fox News. In one case, *Fox & Friends* had cited a report based on unnamed Clinton operatives to assert that Obama had studied at a Wahhabist madrassa while a child in Indonesia—just the kind of school at which a young Islamic jihadist would have been indoctrinated. Such segments continued after reporting from CNN and the Associated Press found the school Obama had attended was not Wahhabist nor did it preach violent struggle against the West. A drumbeat of speculation questioned whether Obama had been born in Kenya, the land of his father, and was ineligible for the White House.

Others on the network suggested Obama had radical sympathies, citing ties to William Ayres, an antiwar revolutionary in the 1960s and

1970s, a founder of the Weather Underground, who set makeshift bombs to protest the Vietnam War. Over the years, improbably, Ayres had become a well-regarded educator; Obama had attended an event at Ayres's Chicago home in 1995 when starting his bid to become a state senator. Amid criticism from Fox's Sean Hannity, Republican candidate John McCain, and others, Obama denounced Ayres's revolutionary record and said the two had no sustained relationship.

Rupert Murdoch was fighting a rear-guard movement among his immediate family members, some of whom favored the young senator. His daughter Elisabeth and son-in-law, British PR executive Matthew Freud, had raised money for the Obamas in the UK from American expatriates, while Murdoch's wife, Wendi Deng, participated in a fund-raising dinner held for Obama in Los Angeles. He also liked to build rapport with people who gave off a winning aura. So Murdoch brokered a meeting between Fox's Roger Ailes and the candidate in June 2008 to smooth the waters.

They met in a secluded area at the lobby of the Waldorf Astoria. Murdoch offered the advice that a new president had six months to prove how he would lead the nation. And then Murdoch beckoned the Fox News chief to join. Ailes and Obama sat close, knees grazing, the older man jowly, unyielding, the other trim, intense.

Obama's demeanor shifted from solicitous to aggrieved. He asked Ailes whether he could expect to get fair treatment for the rest of the campaign. Obama had been livid at how he had been portrayed—as some kind of foreigner with suspect motives. Ailes challenged Obama to appear on Fox's programs more often instead of rejecting or ignoring its requests for interviews. Don't use Fox as a rallying cry at campaign rallies, Ailes retorted.

As the Republican convention started in St. Paul in August, Obama sat down for an interview with Fox's top-rated figure, Bill O'Reilly. It was a mix of contention and charm. O'Reilly visibly eased the intensity of his attacks. Obama had played ball.

November 2008 would mark the end of the run for Brit Hume as the network's Washington managing editor and chief political anchor. Hume told me he had lost his enthusiasm for the "poisonous atmosphere in Washington over the last fourteen or fifteen years."

"Sparks are what make news," he said. "There's dissent and disagreement, intense feelings and so on, which all contribute to an untidy, and at times ugly, but nonetheless newsworthy, atmosphere." As I could not help pointing out, Fox News had been a home for all kinds of rancor. Did Fox bear any responsibility for that "poisonous," "untidy and at times ugly" atmosphere? "We've certainly been a forum, as everybody else has, for the arguments of the day," Hume replied. "We are more a reflection of it, I think, than a cause."

As Obama cruised to a win on Election Day, liberals, at least for a time, became ascendant, controlling both houses of Congress, a majority of governors' mansions and, of course, the White House. Liberal commentators triumphantly wrote about the marginalizing of Fox in a progressive era. Andrew O'Hehir of *Salon* wrote that Fox "seemed a weak and piteous thing . . . staring mortality in the face."

Yet Fox News mapped out a strategy to ensure that times would be fatter than ever, as Bill Shine, Fox News senior vice president for programming, later told me. "With this particular group of people in power right now," Shine observed, "and the honeymoon they've had from other members of the media, does it make it a little bit easier for us to be the voice of opposition on some issues?" It did. The Fox News audience grew so much after the election that ratings estimates placed it among the highest-rated of all basic cable channels, above the usual strata of cable news. Fox journalists attributed the ratings boost to the skeptical eye they focused on the new administration.

Hume's job was divided between two people. Bill Sammon, a conservative columnist and author who had previously written for the *Washington Times* and the *Washington Examiner*, took responsibility for directing political coverage as the network's Washington managing editor. But tension emerged between Fox's Washington and New York shops over the tenor of its coverage. Other news executives wanted to protect the reputation of the news shows from what they believed was a heavy hand.

During the campaign, Sammon to varying degrees had tied Obama to socialist and Marxist thought—often by connecting him to the charged rhetoric of the president's fiery former pastor, Jeremiah Wright. Wright's radical rhetoric, replete with anti-American and anti-white overtones, was first disclosed on a national level by ABC News. The Obama camp could not ignore it. In early 2008 in Philadelphia, Obama delivered what was perhaps the most memorable speech of his campaign. Sammon repeatedly raised the specter that Obama nursed anger over matters of race—one reflected in the younger Obama's writings about his hurt over his reception as a racially mixed youth and his complicated feelings about his father.

"Candidate Barack Obama stood on a sidewalk in Toledo, Ohio, and first let it slip to Joe the Plumber that he wanted to, quote, 'spread the wealth around,'" Sammon later told patrons of a 2009 fund-raising cruise in the Mediterranean for Hillsdale College, a conservative school. "At that time, I have to admit that I went on TV on Fox News and publicly engaged in what I guess was some rather mischievous speculation about whether Barack Obama really advocated socialism, a premise that privately I found rather far-fetched."

Sammon went on, however, to justify that speculation, telling the Hillsdale crowd that it proved well founded after the government bailed out banks and car manufacturers: "The debate over whether America was headed for socialism seemed anything but far-fetched."

Amid those bailouts and stimulus spending, Bill O'Reilly could be found in full-fledged populist dudgeon against the liberal social engineering government bureaucrats he said were favored by the new president. Hannity had been newly unshackled from liberal cohost Alan Colmes and hammered the White House. And most outraged and outrageous was Glenn Beck, recently arrived from CNN Headline News, who quickly doubled the audience of Fox's 5:00 PM time slot.

In those early days of 2009, I marveled as I watched Beck on set at Fox News in Manhattan and interviewed him in a waiting room off his studios. In person, Beck was self-deprecating and often buoyant. On Fox, he depicted a bleak country run by shadowy forces. Beck brooded about whether FEMA was setting up concentration camps. He would later take credit for doing the heavy lifting to disprove the theory to which he had given so much airtime. Beck did not simply hammer away at the idea that Marxist thinkers had mentored Obama throughout his life. Only partially in jest, Beck also repeatedly invoked Stalinist imagery in characterizing the administration's proposals.

As for his own politics, Beck invoked an affinity for a group of politicians from an earlier era. "I have become more and more libertarian every day—more and more against both of these parties," Beck said, adding, "I have just become much more like the Founding Fathers. I just wanted to be in a place that understood that." Presenting himself as a modern-day Patrick Henry—give me liberty or give me death— Beck played the role of a scholar sorrowfully unearthing sad truths. Beck was a masterful broadcaster, keenly conscious of every element of his performance. And he was self-aware enough occasionally to wink at its ridiculousness. For the moment, Fox was just fine with the whole package: the divisive conspiracy theories, the flights of fancy, the grandiose self-aggrandizement, all of it. He was the network's newest star.

On the news side, Fox worked hard to win recognition for its anchors. The network's primary news anchor was Shepard Smith, a maverick figure in the basement studios of Fox News in Manhattan. Deeply tanned, truly mischievous, proud of his red state roots in Mississippi, and fit to the point of being gaunt—he would puncture pomposity wherever he encountered it yet struck appropriately respectful tones without lapsing into sentimentality during sensitive moments on the air. Smith was equally capable of apparently spontaneous takes on torture, gay marriage, and even the news business itself.

On several occasions, according to several colleagues, he refused to promote themes that recurred on other Fox shows. He liked to rattle O'Reilly in the hallway and openly mocked Beck on the air. His occasional shouting matches with high-ranking colleagues over stories made fewer headlines. Smith was cheered for saying what he thought, especially by non-Fox journalists, and Fox kept rewarding him with new contracts in the high seven figures. His ratings were strong, and publicly executives cited his unexpected sallies as part of Fox's claim that it let employees say what they thought while reporting the news straight. Behind the scenes, executives would occasionally argue that Smith was cheered for saying opinionated things that fell on the left side of the political ledger. More proof, they claimed, of the mainstream media's ingrained bias.

Bret Baier, a competent reporter who had covered the White House and Pentagon, took over Hume's responsibilities as the chief political anchor. A genial presence with a million-watt smile, Baier had a show that was often the second-highest rated in cable news, behind Fox's *O'Reilly Factor*, with roughly 2 million viewers a night. While Baier's *Special Report* relied heavily on reported segments, fully one-third of the show was consumed by a discussion he moderated among pundits dubbed the "Fox News All-Stars."

I reviewed six months' worth of Baier's panels and found a consistent formula: two clear-cut conservatives and another analyst. That other person was sometimes a Democrat or liberal—say, former Democratic strategist Kirsten Powers. But often that third slot was filled by a reporter from a news outlet that strives not to adopt ideological outlook in its reporting, such as Politico or the *Washington Post*. As I told Baier, his panels' blend of personalities seemed to underrepresent the left and also to cast nonideological reporters as liberals. The pattern suggested Fox defined balance as a counterbalance to other media outlets rather than a program that in itself was fully balanced as the network's executives pledged.

In the months that followed the inauguration, the relationship between Obama's camp and Fox News curdled. On September 9, 2009, Beck described Cass Sunstein, a Harvard law professor picked to lead the White House Office of Information and Regulatory Affairs, as "a man that believes that you should not be able to remove rats from your home if it causes them any pain." Sunstein had indeed written about animal rights for a law review article and explored the trade-offs in putting a primacy on human priorities and impulses, though he hadn't really made the argument Beck ascribed to him.

The next hour, on Baier's program, Fox News correspondent James Rosen told viewers: "Rats could attack us in the sewer and court systems if all of Cass Sunstein's writings became law." The relevant passage from Sunstein's article was not quoted even in significant part to viewers. "If rats are able to suffer—and no one really doubts that they are—then their interests are relevant to the question of how, and perhaps even whether, they can be expelled from houses," Sunstein wrote. "At the very least, people should kill rats in a way that minimizes suffering. And if possible, people should try to expel rats in a way that does not harm them at all."

Sunstein, the author and editor of several dozen books, is an unconventional liberal who has written provocatively about regulation but was often defended by conservative colleagues for his intellectual rigor. He was an advocate of "opt out" versus "opt in" strategies, for example, advising companies to adopt a policy that assumed employees would contribute several percent of their annual salaries to retirement funds, unless they affirmatively chose not to. Studies showed people were more likely to save money for retirement if the choice was presented as an expectation.

Obama soon gave interviews on the same Sunday to five political talk shows, but pointedly not to Fox. *Fox News Sunday* host Chris

Wallace vocally objected on air. The Obama administration, he said, was made up of "the biggest bunch of crybabies I have dealt with in my thirty years in Washington."

IN FALL 2009, a delicate task confronted Treasury official Kenneth Feinberg, the special master overseeing the American corporations that received billions of dollars in bailout money. The surge in unemployment and mortgage defaults stoked anger toward corporate chieftains who received huge compensation packages, further fueled by the taxpayer dollars funneled to their companies. Even so, a backlash was already building among many conservatives against government intervention in the private sector, though many economists backed the bailouts. Much of that fury was reflected in the comments of hosts and guests on Fox News.

On October 22, 2009, Feinberg announced that salaries for the top executives at those seven big companies would be cut by 90 percent for the following year. Treasury public relations staffers scheduled a session to lay out the plans for reporters for newspaper and wire services in what is called a "pad and pen" session (meaning no officials would comment on tape). White House and Treasury press officials conferred over email how best to get their message out over the airwaves. At first, Treasury aide Jenni LeCompte said, the White House would invite reporters for big legacy TV networks, ABC, CBS, NBC, plus NPR. They'd keep it brisk: logistics allowed for eight minutes apiece. Then CNN and Bloomberg TV were added. But the bureau chiefs for the other TV networks asked, *Why not Fox News?*

Unknown to them, Dag Vega, the White House director of broadcast media, had earlier emailed to LeCompte: "We'd prefer if you'd skip Fox please." (The emails came to light only later, when obtained by a conservative legal activist group.) The administration's move backfired. Ailes pointed out to executives at other networks that Fox shared the costs of the joint television pool for White House coverage and questioned whether it raised First Amendment questions to exclude only one outlet. The bureau chiefs not only hung together, they started talking about it to the *New York Times*. Other publications and sites pounced. Fox, naturally, treated the story to unrelenting coverage.

White House deputy communications director Jen Psaki emailed a colleague: "brett [sic] baier just did a stupid piece on it—but he is a lunatic." The next day, Psaki sent out a barbed joke to Treasury's LeCompte: "I am putting some dead fish in the fox cubby—just cause." Thin skin and trash talk were saved for posterity on White House email servers. As the pool of networks involved expanded, Fox's White House correspondent was actively courted to come in to talk to Feinberg as well. Fox executed, and broadcast, as much of an interview on the subject as any of its competitors.

Publicly, administration officials denied intentionally blocking Fox. Yet an internal email from deputy White House press secretary Josh Earnest contradicted these denials, as he urged press staffers to hang tough: "We've demonstrated our willingness and ability to exclude Fox News from significant interviews." Within a day, White House officials admitted they had intentionally kept Fox away from Feinberg. And not just Feinberg: Fox should not expect Obama or top-level officials back on its airwaves anytime soon.

"We see Fox right now as the source and the outlet for Republican Party talking points," Anita Dunn, then the White House communications director, told me. She wasn't simply taking issue with the big-name opinion hosts. Dunn argued the supposed wall between Fox News programs and the sprawling opinion shows had proved utterly porous. The network, she said, had decided to infuse the ideology of its opinion hosts into their news shows to deliver exactly what its audience craved. "It's fine if that's how they want to build their business model. We understand that. And it's working for them and we understand that, as well. But we don't think we need to treat them as though they are a news organization the way other news organizations here are treated."

Michael Clemente, Fox's most senior hard news executive, joined Fox after decades at ABC News. He argued that other news outlets had bathed the president in a positive glow. Fox News alone asked the tough questions, Clemente said. His team would continue to do its job despite the rebuke from Obama's White House, he said, drawing on sports for metaphors: "You know, Michael Jordan used to do the same thing. He'd yell at the refs a bunch at the beginning of the game on a simple foul . . . and it just sort of brushed [the ref] back a little bit. That's fine."

THE BREAKOUT star on the news side, however, was clearly Megyn Kelly, who made a quick ascent from legal correspondent to anchor, with her good looks often blinding Fox viewers to the fact she was smart and tough.

University of Pennsylvania students serving as Republican monitors on Election Day in November 2008 took footage with handheld digital cameras that captured Kelly's imagination. They taped several members of the New Black Panthers swaggering outside a polling station in a heavily black part of Philadelphia.

One of the New Black Panthers brandished a nightstick as prospective voters appeared. The video prompted coverage from the Fox News Channel and others that day. In late 2008—during the waning weeks of the Bush administration—the Justice Department filed voter intimidation charges against the New Black Panther Party and several of its members, but charges against the group itself were dropped in May 2009. In the end, only one person was actually sanctioned.

Then, in June 2010, former Justice Department civil rights attorney and Bush political appointee J. Christian Adams rekindled the story by suggesting that under President Obama, the department had become unwilling to prosecute blacks for civil rights violations. "As I have said under oath, this is the easiest case," Adams told NPR's Michel Martin. "There's plenty of evidence that this was a violation of federal law. And don't forget—this is also important—federal law bans the attempt to intimidate."

The New Black Panthers are a "distinctly anti-white, anti-gay, anti-Jewish organization," said Mark Potok, director of the Intelligence Project for the Southern Poverty Law Center, a liberal civil rights outfit. "Some of its leaders have said things like, 'We ought to kill all white people, then bury them in the ground, and then dig them up and kill them again.'" Potok's organization had been listing the New Black Panthers as a hate group for about a decade. He believed the federal investigation and the charges were warranted. But Potok also considered the November 2008 incident to be relatively minor.

Fox's Kelly did not. In the ensuing two weeks, she devoted forty-five segments exceeding three and one-half hours to the New Black Panthers and Adams's allegations. Kelly also assailed others for failing to cover the story. She won fans at the network for her tough talk. Conservatives argued the episode fit a pattern in which the press sought to protect the Obama administration from embarrassing stories. "These stories kept building, building, building in this under-media," the late conservative blogger Andrew Breitbart said. "You can call it Fox News; you can call it the Breitbart sites; you can call it the Drudge Report; you can call it whatever you like—but this under-media builds up stories."

Still, Linda Chavez, the former staff director of the US Commission on Civil Rights under former president Ronald Reagan, and Abigail Thernstrom, that commission's Republican vice chairwoman, said the New Black Panther story was overblown. When Fox Democratic analyst Kirsten Powers disagreed with Kelly over the significance of the New Black Panther story, the anchor sought to shut her down. Kelly told Powers more than once, "You don't know what you're talking about," and threatened three times to cut off her guest's microphone. She would later apologize privately.

Yet Kelly was capable of reflecting a more liberal face of Fox to the world as well. On returning from maternity leave, she invited Mike Gallagher, a conservative talk show host, onto her show to defend calling such leave "a racket." "Now I happen to work for a nice employer that gave me paid leave," Kelly told him. "But the United States is the only advanced country that doesn't require paid leave. If anything, the United States is in the dark ages when it comes to maternity leave."

Kelly also stood up for the right of Chaz Bono—the transgender child of the musician Cher and the late singer and congressman Sonny Bono—to participate in the prime-time show *Dancing with the Stars*. Kelly contradicted her guest, a physician and Fox News commentator who claimed that children watching might be led astray, and she cited leading psychiatric authorities' assertions that there was no evidence for his claims.

In April 2010 Kelly promoted her coverage of Obama's trip to Prague to sign a new pact with Russia to reduce nuclear weapons with this question: "Now, critics are asking: Will the new deal leave the US defenseless until it's too late?" Her words were followed by archival footage from Fox Movietone News of a billowing atomic mushroom cloud accompanied by the rumbling sound of the explosion.

Jay Wallace, the vice president for news at the Fox News Channel, was rueful if not contrite about the suggestion that the Obama administration's deal could lead to a nuclear holocaust. "It wasn't wrong," Wallace told me, "but we failed to provide an appropriate context for the footage." In the absence of an explicit discussion of past political rhetoric using nuclear imagery, Wallace said, the footage of the atomic blast should not have been used.

IN OCTOBER 2010, one of Breitbart's websites accused Shirley Sherrod, an African American regional agriculture official, of reverse racism. The website posted a video clip of her speaking before a conference organized by the NAACP about an incident that occurred years before her federal service. She spoke of her antipathy toward a white farmer and her disinclination to help him. The Obama administration swiftly fired her.

Sherrod later told CNN that her bosses didn't care about Breitbart. But they did care about Fox. Bill O'Reilly had already blasted her as a textbook example of black racism against whites. Sherrod said she was told she was about to be featured on Glenn Beck's program. The administration just wanted her to go away.

Breitbart had a policy objection to a class action lawsuit settlement for black farmers, from which Sherrod benefited. But the video clip he used, which took her down, cut Sherrod off before the redeeming resolution of her anecdote involving her later tireless advocacy for, and friendship with, that same white farmer. Fox News executives issued a new policy instructing staffers to verify every video used from an outside source, especially those with an ideological cast. One Fox News producer told me the policy was observed for little more than a week before falling into disuse.

The Pew Research Center released a poll that year showing that 31 percent of registered Republicans wrongly believed that President Obama is a Muslim. (*Time* magazine released a competing poll that found that 46 percent of Republicans did.) Sixty percent of those who believed that untrue claim told Pew that they learned it "from the media." Fully 41 percent of registered Republicans polled by CNN wrongly said the president "definitely or probably" was born outside the United States, though state records and contemporaneous newspaper birth announcements show Obama was born in Hawaii. Fox News was not the only source of such misinformation. But its tolerance for such topics kept it part of mainstream conservative conversation. For CNN, Lou Dobbs's refusal to relinquish the subject of Obama's birth became an irreparable breach. He found sanctuary, and a nightly show, at Fox Business in November 2010.

8

THE GREENING
OF RUPERT

WITH FOX NEWS, MURDOCH FINALLY had a national platform
with a suitable reach in the US, though he gave Ailes great and unusual autonomy. Through a series of News Corp's interlocking properties and their allies, Rupert Murdoch could help shape public opinion,
help influence public policy, and help determine who held political
power on an international scale. However, global climate change confronted the global newsman with an issue he could not avoid.

In his native country, Murdoch's journalistic progeny were held
responsible, in some quarters, for blocking a meaningful response.
In 2006 Clive Hamilton, then executive director of a liberal think
tank based in the Australian capital of Canberra, identified twelve
figures in public life to whom he assigned culpability for thwarting
the Australian government's movement toward a policy that acknowledged global warming concerns by curbing carbon consumption. Hamilton named Chris Mitchell, editor in chief of the nation's

most prestigious paper, Murdoch's national daily the *Australian*, among his "dirty dozen."

"Mitchell has adopted an aggressive stance against anyone arguing that climate change is a problem," Hamilton said, shooting noisily across the bow of News Ltd. "Not only have the opinion pages of the *Australian* provided unlimited space for all of the anti-greenhouse crazies but the news pages have regularly been turned over to anti-greenhouse propaganda."

The treatment of climate change by News Ltd properties in Australia, and, for that matter, by News Corp properties in the US, provides a case study in how Murdoch's journalism differs from its rivals and how it shapes political discourse.

In the early 1990s, the governing Liberal Party, the leading conservative force in the country, had called for government action to stir significant cuts in carbon consumption. By 2007, however, the Liberal Party of Prime Minister John Howard had cast its lot with the mining, coal, and other energy and resource industries, which actively opposed any such taxes. Coal was and is particularly important to the country's economy; only one country in the world, Indonesia, exports more coal than Australia does.

A tax was by no means the only possibility. Others suggested instead the licensing and trading of permits for emissions of greenhouse gases, much as the US had done to great effect with acid rain. Some prominent Australians, such as Bob Brown, leader of the Green Party, called for curbs in the production and export of coal from Australia's domestic industry. Although scientists readily conceded none of the Australian proposals on its own would achieve any notable shift in global temperatures, advocates considered some such plan a vital component of any larger effort across borders. A carbon tax seemed the most effective approach to many policymakers and politicians on the political left and in the center.

The *Australian*, nicknamed the *Oz*, presented itself as a sober-minded arbiter of political fights. But Clive Hamilton argued that the paper turned its pages over to "anti-greenhouse propaganda." One episode stood out. On January 14, 2006, a story in the news section of the *Oz* written by an unnamed "special correspondent" argued that a rational approach to global warming would demand, above all else, careful deliberation.

"The public and political debate has tended to be dominated by the convenient but highly political argument that blames industry and industrial activity for its emissions of carbon dioxide," the article stated.

"To add tension to complexity, some of the science supporting this case suggests the need for relatively urgent remedial action now if serious adverse impacts are to be avoided in the immediate future, in particular rapid rises in sea levels and temperature change. . . . While recent, measured rises in temperature change are real, the cause of this change is still unproven, only assumed."

At the end of the article was appended the disclosure that the correspondent worked for a "resources company," or, as Hamilton more explicitly put it, an unnamed person directly employed by an unnamed firm in the fossil fuels, such as coal or oil.

It is an irony of Australian life and the primacy of the Murdoch family's role there that the environmentally-minded institute led by Hamilton that criticized Rupert Murdoch's prized creation received significant funding from the family of his younger sister, Anne Murdoch Kantor. Rupert had bought out her shares of News Corp in the 1990s along with those of his other siblings for hundreds of millions of dollars. Over time, Kantor's branch of the family gave more than $70 million toward environmental foundations and causes. "One of the reasons we do this," said Mark Wootton, husband to a Murdoch niece, "is because of some of the things the Murdoch papers have done."

Yet just a few months after Hamilton's speech, in May 2007, Rupert Murdoch appeared to make a striking reversal. At the Beacon Theater in New York City, he addressed his nearly 50,000-strong workforce in person and by satellite and made a pledge that delighted many of his liberal critics and astonished many of his fellow conservatives.

Murdoch cited the markedly below average rainfall in his hometown of Melbourne and drought in his native Australia. He promised his company would, on balance, emit no carbon within five years. The plan would combine energy efficiencies, the use of renewable energy sources, purchase of carbon offsets, and other strategies.

James Murdoch and his allies within the company, such as News International CEO Rebekah Brooks, saw the initiative as a genuine good, a means of forcing environmentally-driven cost savings on the company, and a way to connect News Corp to the concerns of the next generation of consumers. James Murdoch's wife, Kathryn, had worked for several years for the Clinton Foundation's climate initiative and would later join the board of directors of the Environmental Defense Fund.

The elder Murdoch had been won over at a session during a corporate retreat at Pebble Beach led by former vice president Al Gore, who screened his documentary *An Inconvenient Truth* sketching out the case for the existence of global warming and the threat it posed. Other attendees included then California governor Arnold Schwarzenegger, himself branded as an eco-friendly Republican, and British prime minister Tony Blair. The lively conversation that ensued led to studies on how improvements could be made. Murdoch described his son as a major influence on his thinking.

The chairman's Beacon Theater speech promised real action. "Now, I realize we can't take just one year in one city or even one continent as proof that something unusual is happening. And I am no scientist. But there are signs around the world, and I do know how to assess a risk," Rupert Murdoch told employees. "Climate change poses clear, catastrophic threats. We may not agree on the extent, but we certainly can't afford the risk of inaction."

Each of the company's various divisions vied to prove its loyalty to the program, though many of the journalistic outlets had built up a record of casting doubt on such fears. The *Sun* ran a picture of a newly anointed Page Three girl photographed wearing nothing above the waist but a coat of green paint. The *Sun* and the satellite TV service BSkyB gave subscribers energy efficient lightbulbs. Fox Studios embedded environmental messages into hit movies such as *Ice Age* and *Avatar.* "Global warming is a crime for which we are all guilty," Kiefer Sutherland, the star of Fox TV's antiterrorism thriller series *24*, told viewers at the start of a corporation-wide public service announcement. "We are all releasing carbon dioxide into the atmosphere, thus raising the temperature of the planet."

Articles in some News Corp publications subsequently wrote sympathetically of the need for action to stem global warming. While the *Sun* published the tagline "S.O.S. Planet Earth" over a story about rain forests, the *New York Post* ran a headline, "Go Green." All that environmental activism required significant intellectual backpedaling by publications on the record with their skepticism toward climate change.

Clive Hamilton was right: the *Australian* aggressively opposed the Green Party's agenda of addressing climate change through greater regulation and taxation of pollution. Indeed, the paper vowed in an editorial that it would seek to destroy the party at the ballot box. But one reporter for the paper claimed it happened in the news pages as well. At an academic conference in fall 2010, a former environmental reporter at the *Australian*, Asa Wahlquist, said she fought with editors routinely over the extent and nature of her coverage until she decided to depart from the paper.

Covering climate change, she said, "was absolutely excruciating. It was torture. There's no other way to put it." Julie Posetti, an academic at the 2010 conference, tweeted much of the talk, including the claim that Chris Mitchell had dictated his paper's coverage ahead of national elections in which Labor formed a government with the Green Party, and that he had adopted an "eco-fascist" line on carbon use policies. Mitchell denounced Posetti, even after audiotapes appeared to confirm the accuracy of her tweets. The editor said he had not spoken to Wahlquist in eight years and threatened to sue the tweeting scholar.

He never did sue. But the simmering tension about climate change coverage was apparent to outside journalists as well. In 2011 the longtime reporter and professor of journalism Wendy Bacon of the University of Technology in Sydney released a study examining how her country's newspapers handled the contentious issue.

Once in office in a coalition with the environmental Green Party, the Labor Party had adopted a series of policies designed to reduce greenhouse gas emissions by 60 percent over more than four decades. Over time, as support for the initiative waned, the proposals were whittled down. Bacon commissioned researchers and graduate students to review six months' worth of every article, feature piece, editorial, and column in ten leading Australian papers in regard to the governing Labor Party's plans to tax carbon emissions.

Researchers were told to classify stories as neutral if any doubt lingered about their thrust, and many were characterized that way. Still, negative articles about the proposed carbon emissions tax in Murdoch's newspapers outweighed positive ones, 82 percent to 18 percent. During my visit to Australia, journalists broadly affirmed Bacon's assessment: to varying degrees, they said, the Murdoch papers were keenly receptive to those who question the science underlying projections of climate change. Each year after the start of the new millennium it became harder to report credibly that there was uncertainty that humans were playing a key role in driving up the earth's temperature.

How much did Murdoch really believe in global warming? There is no evidence he was insincere in making his sweeping pronouncement on the need for carbon neutrality. Murdoch projected messages of personal and corporate responsibility. Yet he also watched as his journalists provided readers and viewers with coverage that often cast significant doubt on the very crisis he described.

Murdoch's belief in the need to contain climate change was pitted against his hatred for central government regulation. So he set a corporate example but refused to endorse a mandate. The dissonance revealed his blend of cynicism and self-regard. Murdoch is convinced that he has a nearly unerring sense for what his readers will want to see in print, whether in a tabloid or a leading national paper. Instinctively, he sees the environmental movement littered with alarmists, a cadre of managerial elitists who snatch away power and property and wealth from his working- and middle-class tabloid readers (not to mention upscale subscribers to the *Times of London*, the *Wall Street Journal*, and the *Australian*).

Murdoch comes by that contempt for government intervention by way of personal experience. He is a man whose very history tells him that regulations are designed to trip him up. He is an executive who built up his own empire after seeing his family's holdings shrink from the taxes levied on his father's estate. He is an entrepreneur who repeatedly had to win permission to buy television and newspaper properties in all three major English-speaking countries in which he became a dominant presence. He even switched his citizenship in order to satisfy American regulators.

Professor Bacon argued that the environmental policies of the government of Kevin Rudd and his successor, Julia Gillard, never got a fair shake. Seven of the ten titles studied by Bacon's team belong to News Ltd, a result of the concentration of media ownership there. And the Murdoch papers put their collective thumb on the scale, Bacon and her team found. That held true from the populist tabloids to the *Australian*—even though the *Oz* offers more nuanced and extensive coverage than its sister publications. The lone exception was the *Mercury*, the News Ltd paper in the Tasmanian state capital of Hobart. The island off the southeastern tip of the continent is considered a stronghold of the ecologically minded Green Party, the minority partner of the governing Labor Party.

The non-Murdoch papers were viewed as more balanced, with the two papers from rival Fairfax Media offering coverage deemed slightly sympathetic toward the need for carbon consumption policies overall. Bacon said the results showed a campaign by the Murdoch press against the governing Labor Party's climate change policies rather than tough-minded scrutiny of them. "If that's happening on that one issue, well, it's certainly happening on other issues," Bacon said. "Given that Murdoch is so dominant, we have to at least recognize the very big influence, a big potential influence, on public opinion wielded by one company."

During the speech on carbon neutrality, Rupert Murdoch indicated he wanted to use his influence to lead by example. In disclosures to an environmental group, News Corp cited operations in fifty-six companies where it had a direct carbon footprint. Murdoch's company would incorporate a green mind-set to do what it could to improve the environment worldwide, achieve savings that such investments could bring, and prove that corporate responsibility was an attainable goal to News Corp's competitors and peers among the world's top conglomerates.

"This is about changing the DNA of our business," Rupert Murdoch declared. Fox News dutifully contributed a half-dozen muted stories. Ailes appeared in that same corporate video as Kiefer Sutherland, the Simpsons, and the Murdochs. "I was very clear," Ailes said soberly, looking at the camera, "that energy was gonna be one of the things that was going to determine leadership for countries in the future."

In the context of the corporate video, Ailes's remarks functioned as an endorsement of Murdoch's initiative. More carefully parsed, however, the statement was devoid of meaning. It could have come from an environmentalist, an investment analyst, or a Tea Party protester who just finished chanting "drill, baby, drill." More charitably, Ailes struck an ambiguous note, perhaps indulging his corporate chief's impulses in a seemingly charged arena while protecting his own news organization's journalistic prerogative to pursue stories wherever they might lead.

Bacon's findings about Murdoch's Australian publications dovetailed with those of a pair of studies of the coverage of climate change by Ailes's team at Fox. The first, presented in 2008 by Sol Hart, a professor at American University in Washington, DC, looked at reports on Fox News and CNN from 1998 to 2004. Hart found Fox far more likely than its competitors to stress the uncertainty involved in climate change science.

A second study, conducted by researchers affiliated with George Mason University in Virginia, found Fox was far more likely to cover global warming in 2007 and 2008 than cable news rivals CNN or MSNBC. Amid that coverage, however, Fox News journalists, commentators, and guests, however, frequently derided the idea that a valid scientific consensus existed on global warming.

Murdoch's muse from the Pebble Beach retreat, Al Gore, won an Oscar for *An Inconvenient Truth* in 2007. As a bête noire of the political right, Gore's presence in the policy debates led to belittling treatment by many of Fox's more ideological figures. Prime-time talk show host Sean Hannity called Gore "unhinged." Fox News analyst Fred Barnes said Gore was "hysterical." Gore had to admit some errors in his documentary, including his characterization of the plight of polar bears. But scientists in the field said Gore's argument, while marred by the occasional overreach, remains valid.

In December 2009, the liberal press watchdog group Media Matters, which scrutinizes Fox for factual and ideological bias, obtained an internal memo sent by Bill Sammon, the network's managing editor for Washington news. The memo noted the publication of emails hacked from the computers and accounts of faculty members at East Anglia University in the UK, emails which reflected the frustration of some climate researchers that some raw data did not fully conform to expectations. The hacker's identity was not revealed, but conservative critics called the episode "Climategate." Cable news, led by Fox, stoked the debate.

"Given the controversy over the veracity of climate change data," Sammon wrote, "we should refrain from asserting that the planet has warmed (or cooled) in any given period without IMMEDIATELY pointing out that such theories are based upon data that critics have called into question. It is not our place as journalists to assert such notions as facts, especially as this debate intensifies." Many ensuing reports on Fox adhered faithfully to his suggested language.

In a review released in fall 2012, the Union of Concerned Scientists found an overwhelming imbalance in Fox's coverage. During a six-month period, it found, 93 percent of Fox News representations of climate science surveyed were off the mark—thirty-seven of forty segments. In ten cases, people interviewed accurately conveyed scientific understanding of climate change only to be drowned out by other participants or hosts.

The *Wall Street Journal*'s editorial pages were receptive to climate change skeptics well before 2007, when Murdoch took ownership. Its news coverage was measured, if modest. But opinion writers from industry interests and ideological groups were given prime real estate to cast doubts on the efficacy of major government action through taxation, regulation, or other intervention and to question whether any remedies were even needed.

The day before I met Professor Bacon at her home in Sydney, the *Journal* published an opinion piece entitled "No Need to Panic About Global Warming" signed by "sixteen concerned scientists." It argued that there was "no compelling scientific argument for drastic action," citing what it saw as the intellectual dishonesty revealed in the Climategate flap, and said a growing number of dissidents were speaking up despite the threat to their careers.

Bacon's study of the *Australian* (and other dailies) focused primarily on the news pages of the papers, not their opinion content. Murdoch's Australian arm, however, savaged the professor. Greg Baxter, then the director of corporate affairs for News Ltd, asserted she lacked credibility and further deplored that she was allowed to teach students. Baxter offered that the *Australian* "believes that humans are warming the planet—but obviously there is doubt among those who claim otherwise"—and explained the paper favored a market-based solution. "The fact that Wendy Bacon produces a piece of research that is negative about this company is no surprise to anybody," he told the *Conversation* news site. "She's been doing it for 25 years."

Bacon is a recipient of the Walkley Award, the Australian equivalent of the Pulitzer Prize, for her work exposing police corruption. Bacon's work made the cut when Murdoch's *Australian* published a list of the country's top 100 stories of the twentieth century. Bacon and her husband, Chris Nash, live in an eggshell-blue house in Newtown, a neighborhood made up of a jumble of working-class, bohemian, and academic streets on the west side of Sydney. She might well not fit in their profile of a desired demographic for the *Australian*. But as we sat on the interior brick courtyard of her home, lined by Australasian trees and blooms, Bacon said she was dumbstruck by News Ltd's reply. She had published little previously on the Murdoch press.

Robert Manne wrote a lengthy critique of the *Australian* for the *Quarterly Essay* in which he, too, devoted a section to reviewing the newspaper's climate change coverage. His conclusions echoed those of Bacon. "On balance, the opinion pieces and the news coverage in the paper was on the side of those who were against the climate scientists," Manne told me. "And that might be playing into the hands of the group I call the 'denialists' because all they have to do is create doubt in the public mind to make it much more difficult for politicians to take action."

The top editors and executives at the *Australian* took umbrage at that specific characterization, with its echoes of Holocaust deniers. They responded, correctly, that their paper had been open to a free-flowing debate. But Bacon argued the paper embarked on an intentional and insurmountable effort to tilt debate against any carbon consumption tax, a position consistent with the paper's long-held views on economics.

She had found the most negative coverage in the country's top-selling Murdoch tabloids—the Melbourne *Herald Sun* and the Sydney *Daily Telegraph*. The *Herald Sun*'s Andrew Bolt is by common assent the top-read columnist in Australia. He presents as an outright skeptic of climate change, at one point calling competing newspapers that treat it as settled science "propagandists." The clash over climate change is a frequent subject of Bolt's program on Lachlan Murdoch's Ten network.

"Everybody was rather taken aback and it seemed to change the editorial tone of climate change coverage for a very short period of time—but not very long. I think it lasted a year, perhaps less," said Monica Attard, a former foreign correspondent, media critic, and host for the ABC, Australia's public broadcasting network. "And then we were all left scratching our heads as to what Rupert's missive that News Ltd was to become a 'green' company was actually all about. Nobody quite understood. Perhaps they turned the lights off at night. We weren't really sure."

In 2012 tensions within various Murdoch factions in Australia surfaced once again. The Labor-led governing alliance sought modest remedies to contain carbon emissions. But public support had eroded. Murdoch's mother, the centenarian Dame Elisabeth Murdoch, signed a letter sent to the *Age*, the up-market Fairfax Media paper in her hometown of Melbourne, calling for a price to be put on the use of carbon. Americans would call that a carbon tax.

Columnist Piers Akerman of News Corp's Sydney *Daily Telegraph*, the nation's top-selling paper, expressed esteem toward the Murdoch matriarch but told fellow panelists on the TV program *ABC Insiders* that she had been used: "The very elderly, no matter how cogent they are, should not be out fronting a campaign." The national editor of the rival Melbourne *Age*, Michael Gordon, wrote that "Dame Elisabeth's stand is consistent with the stated position on climate change of her son Rupert, but out of step with coverage in his newspapers." That observation occasioned a sharp slap at Gordon in the *Australian* the next day.

In March 2012, Akerman's column in Murdoch's *Daily Telegraph* carried a provocative headline: "Greens and their crazy cronies are holding a gun to our head." Akerman called global warming "a bogeyman" foisted on the general public by environmental activists at the International Panel on Climate Change (IPCC).

In July 2012 Murdoch tweeted encouragement about the great promise shown in new technologies used to extract natural gas from shale. But he now warned against government moves to take drastic action on global warming. "Climate change very slow but real," he tweeted. "So far all cures worse than disease."

A message to his hundreds of thousands of followers—and his hundreds of newspaper editors and television news executives, economically conveyed in less than 140 characters: No need to get people worked up about it. We'll handle this one at our own pace. No need for the government to get involved.

9

THE
FLYING MUSLIMS

———————

MURDOCH ALWAYS RESENTED GOVERNMENT REGULATION
of for-profit news outlets and financial support for the public media
sector. That opposition stemmed from both philosophical and competitive reasons, and it was often reflected in the commentaries of
his journalists. In the fall of 2010, NPR's decision to sever ties with
Juan Williams because of remarks he made on the Fox News Channel
became more than just a professional cataclysm for the journalist and
a public relations debacle for the public radio broadcaster. The episode
served as a singularly telling moment about two distinctive journalistic cultures.

In the summer of 1995, I was a reporter on the metro desk for
the *Baltimore Sun* covering campus life and higher education. One
of the most contested issues in the state involved legal challenges to
a scholarship program at the University of Maryland set aside for
African Americans and other minority students. The university had

filed briefs defending the scholarships by invoking the state's racist past. At the outset of the Great Depression, it was widely believed that the university's law school, based in Baltimore, had denied admission to hometown native Thurgood Marshall, who eventually became the chief lawyer for the NAACP, the nation's solicitor general, and the first black jurist to sit on the Supreme Court.

The story had been told many times, including repeatedly in the pages of the *Sun*, but most notably by the late syndicated columnist and civil rights champion Carl T. Rowan. In his 1993 biography of Marshall, Rowan wrote the sting never eased: Marshall's treatment by Maryland fueled his quest for justice, including a landmark case in which he successfully represented a black Amherst College graduate seeking to overturn his rejection from the University of Maryland law school. Marshall also refused to attend the ceremony naming the school library in his honor.

An administrator tipped me off to a law review article suggesting the facts did not match the legend. There was little evidence that Marshall had ever applied to the University of Maryland law school, because he knew his race would preclude his admission.

I reviewed documents at the Library of Congress and conferred with Marshall's former law clerks and his widow. I found the rejection letter with the language cited by Rowan—but it was in response to an application by a client of Marshall's, not Marshall himself.

Finally I called Williams, then a columnist at the *Washington Post* who was working on his own Marshall biography. While I was in college I had read and admired his book on the American civil rights movement, *Eyes on the Prize*, a companion volume to the PBS documentary television series of the same name.

Williams had also concluded Marshall had not applied. Rowan, though indignant at the suggestion, by all indications misunderstood this seminal episode about Marshall. "He and every other young black person in Baltimore in this time period, in 1930, knew that the

University of Maryland law school did not accept black students," Williams told me. "At best, it would be defying the state and simply registering your refusal to accept this racist system."

"In that sense, it doesn't make much difference," Williams said. But he proved willing to report what he had learned, despite the power of the legend. Several years earlier, Williams had embroiled himself in controversy by defending the Supreme Court nomination of Clarence Thomas; women at the *Washington Post* denounced him for failing to disclose that he—like Thomas—had been accused of verbal sexual harassment by female colleagues. A lengthy apology helped to dispel that flap.

Williams signed up to be a commentator on Fox News in 1997, and in 2000 he left the *Post* to become host of NPR's afternoon public affairs interview and call-in show *Talk of the Nation*. The combination was striking. When I became the *Baltimore Sun*'s media columnist, I profiled Williams: "During the week, Williams acts as the reasonable arbiter, led by common sense to tease out greater truths. Sundays, he's the sparring partner of anchor Brit Hume, perhaps the toniest embodiment of Fox News' often-acerbic style."

Williams said NPR allowed him to avoid the cable catnip of controversy for its own sake. He was popular and affable, and became more visible than ever for his work on the air. In addition, Williams proved to be one of the network's most highly sought-after public speakers.

But controversy would shadow his time at the radio network.

Williams was eased out of the *Talk of the Nation* job after just a year. Senior producers and executives at NPR concluded—with almost no dissenting voices—that the role wasn't a great fit for him. He became a senior correspondent, tapped to do political coverage and some high-profile interviews.

But some of those colleagues and some of his listeners did not always appreciate how he subsequently handled himself. One minor element involved a cultural matter, internal to the network. He showed little interest in mastering how to record interviews on his own, and therefore frequently required a producer to accompany him on assignments. The practice is commonplace in network television, but less frequent at NPR.

Second, and more important, his performance on the air occasioned periodic heartburn. In large part because of his prominence on Fox News, Williams had a line to officials at the Bush White House that was hard for some of his NPR colleagues to match. That was at once envied and believed to be a good thing. He landed interviews with Vice President Cheney, Bush's chief political adviser Karl Rove, Secretary of State Colin Powell, and, in January 2007, President Bush himself.

It was the network's only interview with Bush during his eight-year presidency. By then the public had soured on the invasion and occupation of Iraq. Republicans had been tossed from majorities in both chambers of Congress. As he did during most of his interviews, Williams sought to connect with the person sitting across from him. This time, Williams seemed at his most empathetic, seeking a way to give Bush a chance to explain himself. "You know, people are praying for you," Williams said. "The American people want to be with you, Mr. President, but you just spoke about the polls and they indicate the public—and you know about what's going up on Capitol Hill with the Congress, some in the military. Even many Iraqis, according to the polls, don't like the idea of sending more troops into Iraq. So I wonder if you could give us something to go on, give us something— say, you know, this is a reason to get behind the president right now." Many listeners, including some of Williams's colleagues, believed he had veered dangerously into apologia, even as he broached an uncomfortable truth for the president.

Additionally, Williams had antagonized bosses by continuing to write opinion pieces in major papers such as the *Washington Post*, the *New York Times*, and *USA Today* without getting NPR's approval. He was not the only major NPR figure to write such pieces. *Weekend Edition Saturday* host Scott Simon occasionally weighed in, backing President Bush's war on terror in late 2001 in a piece for the *Wall Street Journal,* for example. But Simon tended to run his columns by his editors first. Williams did not.

After one such instance in late June 2007, I encountered Williams by chance, as he sat, looking stunned, on the steps of the J. Crew store in Georgetown. He had just concluded a phone call with NPR's top news official, senior vice president Ellen Weiss. In an op-ed in the *New York Times,* Williams backed the Bush administration's stance against considering race in assigning children to schools. It carried a provocative headline, referring to the historic 1954 US Supreme Court ruling that desegregated American schools: "Don't Mourn Brown v. Board of Education." Weiss had been surprised and angered.

Do you think I did anything wrong, David? he asked, as his wife stood nearby.

I told Williams, truthfully, that I personally didn't have a problem that he wrote what he wrote. But I said that I didn't create the company's newsroom policies, nor did I sign its paychecks. *Let them know ahead of time,* I suggested. *It's best never to surprise top editors.*

A few months later, White House aides offered him a one-on-one interview with President Bush to explore the legacy of the integration of Little Rock High School on the occasion of its fiftieth anniversary. NPR turned down the offer: "We're grateful for the opportunity to talk to the president," Weiss told the *Washington Post,* "but we wanted to determine who did the interview."

Williams was incredulous and took the interview to Fox News. Most other news organizations in that situation would offer an anodyne comment about the circumstances in which the interview was obtained. Not Fox. Fox spokeswoman Irena Briganti took the opportunity to berate and belittle the public radio broadcaster: "NPR's lack of news judgment is astonishing, and their treatment of a respected journalist like Juan Williams is appalling."

By 2008, Williams was just a contract employee at NPR. His time on the air had been diminished, although as an analyst Williams had a little more breathing room to offer his personal thoughts. While there is an expectation among many of NPR's liberal listeners that the network's mission is to reflect their beliefs and aspirations, most NPR journalists perceive their responsibility is reporting on unfolding news, providing crucial context and watchdog journalism, and offering a civil discussion of public events.

That notion of civility conflicted with Williams's role as a commentator on Fox, which requires clarity, forcefulness, even hyperbole. During the 2008 campaign, other Fox commentators had raised rumors that a video would show Michelle Obama referring to "whitey" in an unspecified rant on tape. The video never materialized, but months later, in early 2009, Williams gave the thrust of that charge credence. He told Bill O'Reilly that Michelle Obama could be a drag on her husband's White House.

"Michelle Obama, you know, she's got this Stokely Carmichael in a designer dress thing going," Williams said on the *O'Reilly Factor*. "Her instinct is to start with this blame America, you know, I'm the victim. If that stuff starts coming out, people will go bananas and she'll go from being the new Jackie O to being something of an albatross."

Called on the carpet again by NPR news executives, Williams apologized. In the heat of the moment on a charged cable show such as the *O'Reilly Factor*, Williams conceded, his analysis of Michelle Obama's press coverage was easily mistaken for an attack. "What I said about Michelle Obama is not out of the realm of mainstream political discourse," Williams told NPR's ombudsman. "The point is that NPR has a much more deliberative, slow-paced form with more time to explain what you meant."

NPR had repeatedly asked Fox to stop identifying Williams as an NPR analyst. Fox would cease for a while and then go right back to putting NPR in the identifying chyron, the on-screen caption. He could not believe the angst over the other gig, which he had started before joining NPR. And the radio network's decision to kill his interview with a sitting president dismayed him.

NPR executives had their own concerns. Williams's handling of the Bush interview concerned some of NPR's hard news veterans. Additionally, the network did not want to allow the Bush White House, or any other administration, to dictate who could interview the president.

Then came the flying Muslims. It was October 2010, and Bill O'Reilly was looking for some moral support. On an episode of ABC's chat show *The View*, he had blamed Muslims for the September 11, 2001, attacks— seemingly not just the plotters, but Muslim people more generally. The hosts swiftly turned on him and two of them walked off the set.

Back in Fox News studios, O'Reilly sought affirmation and received an attaboy from Williams: "Look, Bill, I'm not a bigot. You know the kind of books I've written about the civil rights movement in this country. But when I get on the plane, I got to tell you, if I see people who are in Muslim garb and I think, you know, they are identifying themselves first and foremost as Muslims, I get worried. I get nervous."

A few minutes later, Williams circled back, warning O'Reilly against mistaking all Muslims for "extremists," saying Christians shouldn't be blamed for Oklahoma City bomber Timothy McVeigh.

It was too late.

Complaints poured in. The common thread: Williams had demeaned people simply by their faith and affect. NPR news chief Ellen Weiss consulted with other editors and CEO Vivian Schiller. And then Weiss terminated Williams's contract early amid a sharp exchange by cell phone. She said Williams's remarks "were inconsistent with our editorial standards and practices, and undermined his credibility as a news analyst with NPR."

I spoke briefly to Williams that night. He was baffled, genuinely uncomprehending of what he could have done to offend. He would later say repeatedly on Fox News that he made a point of telling O'Reilly that it was wrong to blame all Muslims for one's own suspicions and fears. I am convinced that was the point he believed he was making.

NPR's brass decided he had proved a very different point: Juan Williams, they felt, could no longer be trusted in front of a microphone. And over at Fox, among its programming and corporate executives, a very different conclusion had been drawn: it was go time.

10

A TOTEBAG TO A
KNIFE FIGHT

AN EDITOR NOT INVOLVED IN terminating Williams's contract
suggested I might need to track it down and file a "spot"—a short
item about a minute long. And so the games began. Along with Brian
Stelter of the *New York Times,* I broke the story online late the night
of October 18 and early the next morning; the news about Williams
appeared in the *Times* in print on October 19 and instantly drew a
drumbeat of heavy and overwhelmingly negative coverage on Twitter,
on blogs, in print, and on the air.

On October 21, things just got worse for NPR. Few people, even
internally, would defend the way in which Williams was dropped—
by cell phone, not in person. And CEO Vivian Schiller, speaking to
the Atlanta Press Club at a previously arranged event, was asked by
reporters *why* it had happened. (His contract was set to expire the
following March.) She had been consulted on terminating him, in a
series of quick telephone conversations, and had backed Weiss on the

call. In Atlanta, Schiller attempted to explain that NPR was paying him for insight, not opinions, and added that he should confide his own beliefs to a psychoanalyst or his PR agent. She was attempting, she said later, to imply these were personal beliefs, and should be shared only with people who would keep his confidence.

But Williams took Schiller's remarks to mean she was suggesting he was crazy. And in the hours that followed, Fox News unleashed its arsenal. It started with interviews during news shows, surged in the late afternoon and early evening, and crested in the prime-time opinion shows.

Glenn Beck used Williams's termination by NPR as the cornerstone of an hour-long focus on free speech. "America, you're smart enough. You know what this is all about. You see what all of this is about. It's not about the truth. It's not about setting anything right. It's about intimidation, bullying, tearing down."

The next hour, Bret Baier announced that Fox News chairman Ailes had just awarded Williams a beefed-up contract with a bigger role at the network. The newscast's second story focused on calls for an investigation into NPR and the elimination of federal funding for its operations and shows, notably from Congressman Peter King, a Long Island Republican who had routinely been critical of Muslim groups in the US for what he characterized as sympathy for terrorist operations. Baier returned to the Williams firing anew with his panel of analysts—two conservative columnists and a political reporter for the *Washington Post*.

On the *O'Reilly Factor*, Bill O'Reilly called Schiller a pinhead within moments of its opening. (O'Reilly routinely sorts people into baskets of pinheads and patriots, which renders that decision even less surprising.) NPR, he said, was "a totalitarian outfit functioning as an arm of the far left."

Williams came on and told his side, fleshing out details of the indignity of being fired by cell phone. "I don't fit in their box. I'm not a predictable black liberal," Williams said. "They were looking for a reason to get rid of me because I appear on Fox News. They don't want me talking to you." O'Reilly promised he would have Williams's back—and that Williams would guest host his program the next night.

Williams was followed by Fox News analyst Karl Rove, George W. Bush's former top political adviser, who said NPR and public radio should be stripped of federal funding. Then Laura Ingraham inveighed against NPR. Fox News anchor Megyn Kelly, a former lawyer, appeared to suggest Williams might have a lawsuit against the network. Glenn Beck rehearsed his grievances one more time.

At 9:00 PM, Sean Hannity declared "a good man has been smeared." His guests uniformly blasted NPR. Frank Luntz convened a focus group whose members, he said, gave him a clear message: "You got to tell Juan, hang in there, because Republicans and Democrats alike want him to fight for his job."

Ailes wrapped himself around Williams with a three-year, $2 million contract. The maneuver allowed him to brand Fox as the champion of free speech and to delight a sizable segment of its audience by criticizing NPR as something valued only by liberals.

Other journalists had been fired over controversial remarks in other settings without such a muscular backlash. CNN had dismissed two figures in the months leading up to the Williams imbroglio. Longtime CNN Mideast expert and senior editor Octavia Nasr was forced out for a tweet that expressed sadness over the death of a prominent Hezbollah figure. Nasr had seen him as a bridge between the terrorist group and a more constructive future, but he had also been designated a terrorist by the US government. The network announced that her standing had been compromised. CNN daytime anchor Rick Sanchez also had been dumped by the network. Sanchez had complained on a satellite radio show that the *Daily Show*'s Jon Stewart, who frequently mocked him, was a bigot. Sanchez couldn't win, he argued, because Jews (like Stewart) controlled the media. Sanchez was gone within hours.

In Williams's case, people directly questioned the nature of the definitions separating different categories of journalists. "When is somebody giving his or her opinion?" ABC's Barbara Walters asked on her talk show, *The View*. "If you are a 'journalist,' where you're supposed to be straight and narrow and not give opinions—you know how careful I am, because I'm wearing two hats—sometimes that's one thing. But if you are someone who's giving your opinion, then you're allowed to give your opinion!"

The conservative media criticism group NewsBusters revived comments made by NPR's legal affairs correspondent Nina Totenberg fifteen years earlier, in which she appeared to wish harm to befall Republican senator Jesse Helms of North Carolina. In arguing against new funding for AIDS research in 1995, Helms had said, "We've got to have common sense about a disease transmitted by people deliberately engaging in unnatural acts." He was talking about sex between gay men.

Totenberg said on the syndicated political television program *Inside Washington*: "I think he ought to be worried about the—about what's going on in the good Lord's mind, because if there's retributive justice, he'll get AIDS from a transfusion or one of his grandchildren will get it." At the time, others on the show also reacted strongly against Helms, including conservatives; Krauthammer called Helms's remarks "bigoted and cruel." But Totenberg's comments became relevant once more. Jesse Watters, a producer for Fox's *O'Reilly Factor*, confronted Schiller on her way to an appointment to challenge her, on tape, about the disparities between the handling of Totenberg and Williams.

The entire story played out during the home stretch of the 2010 elections, in which Republicans would take back the US House of Representatives. News Corp had become a participant in the 2010 election cycle, with a $1 million contribution to the Republican Governors Association and another $1 million to the US Chamber of Commerce to defeat Congressional Democrats. The timing for Fox was propitious. In the US in 2010, the Tea Party protests strengthened, borne aloft by fear over the imploding economy and anger over the greater role of the government in health care. Much of the mainstream press was nonplussed at how to gauge this phenomenon. Fox News saw the development as a wave to ride. "Roger [Ailes] may not have given the Tea Party life," said Chris Ruddy, the CEO of NewsMax. "But he gave it oxygen to breathe."

Juan Williams's firing transformed a dormant rallying cry from GOP backbenchers to eviscerate funds for public broadcasting into a central rhetorical element of their appeal to the members of their diehard base. And officials at some NPR member stations were apoplectic. Complaining calls swamped volunteers and staffers answering phones during their seasonal fund-raising drives. (Donations went up at most stations but stayed flat at others. But local station officials wouldn't know that until later.)

Some of the complaints to public radio stations came from their own listeners. But many callers were fans of conservative radio shows on commercial stations or viewers of Fox News programs that were also stoking the flames. The Fox reflex was to rally behind a colleague. Chris Wallace told me in a hallway in Fox's Washington bureau that he "will never forgive NPR for what they did to Juan." But it was also the execution of a marketing ploy. "Are you kidding me, NPR?" Jon Stewart asked incredulously on his show. "You're picking a fight with Fox News? They gave Juan Williams a $2 million contract just for you firing him. NPR, you just brought a tote bag full of David Sedaris books to a knife fight."

Ailes's outrage was surely calculated to a degree. Nine months earlier, Ailes condemned Murdoch's son-in-law, Matthew Freud, for comments in the *New York Times* critical of Fox News. Freud, the great-grandson of the father of psychoanalysis, Sigmund Freud, was believed to be speaking for several of the Murdoch children. Roger

Ailes shot back that Freud "needs to see a psychiatrist." Schiller blundered by invoking the same word about Williams. Ailes knew exactly what he was doing.

A few weeks after NPR terminated Williams's contract, Ailes attacked once again in an interview with a favorite reporter, Howard Kurtz of the *Daily Beast* and, somewhat bizarrely, of Fox's cable news rival CNN. "They are, of course, Nazis. They have a kind of Nazi attitude," Ailes told Kurtz. "They are the left wing of Nazism. These guys don't want any other point of view. They don't even feel guilty using tax dollars to spout their propaganda."

Ailes's vitriol fit neatly with the extreme rhetoric being served up at that time by Glenn Beck. On one occasion, he offered listeners to his radio show a mind-set that would help them endure the Obama years: "You have to think like a German Jew [in] 1934." The month we spoke, Beck used Nazi allusions to assail Al Gore's environmental activism. "The government and their friends are indoctrinating our children for the control of their minds, your freedom, our choice and our future," Beck said on his show. "This is what Nazi Joseph Goebbels said about the Hitler Youth."

When I pressed Beck to say whether he actually believed Gore sought a dictatorial or fascistic society, the Fox host replied, "I don't think Al Gore is going to put anybody in gas chambers. I don't think we're actually going down that road."

"But when I heard him say, 'Well, you know, your parents don't understand the things you instinctively know,' you've got to be kidding me, right? Next—why don't you have them report on me if they're not recycling as well?"

Beck spoke of Israel with glowing reverence. But he often pivoted, warning viewers as well about a shadowy government in a way that some of his critics said evoked elements of anti-Semitic slurs. During an extended riff about the liberal billionaire financier George Soros, Beck called him "the puppet master."

"He's known as the man who broke the Bank of England. The prime minister of Malaysia called Soros an unscrupulous profiteer. In Thailand he was branded the economic war criminal," Beck said on Fox early in November 2010. "They also said he sucks the blood of people."

Soros is a Jewish survivor of the Holocaust. Deborah Lipstadt, professor of Holocaust studies at Emory University and perhaps the leading American authority on Nazi rhetoric, noted that the Malaysian prime minister cited by Beck had also ranted that Jews were behind his economy's instability. Beck shockingly even claimed Soros as a young teen collaborated with the Nazis in his native Hungary. Soros had passed as the young Christian godson of a government official who was acting to save his life; at that time he witnessed the cataloguing of a Jewish family's belongings for confiscation. Holocaust experts agreed this anecdote did not constitute evidence of any fair notion of collaboration. "I haven't heard anything like this on television or radio," Lipstadt told me, "and I've been in the sewers of anti-Semitism and Holocaust denial more often than I've wanted."

Beck also tied Soros to a variety of philanthropies and media groups, including NPR, which received a $1.8 million grant lasting several years from a Soros foundation to help train reporters for local member stations to cover state governments around the country. The age of blogging and tweeting has fomented a culture in which people blithely call one another Nazis online and on cable TV and talk radio. But Fox News stood out amid mainstream media outlets for its ferocity and frequency in doing so. The *Washington Post*'s Dana Milbank found Beck had referred to Hitler or Nazis on his Fox News program hundreds of times.

The example was set at the top when Ailes accused NPR leaders of engaging in Nazi-like behavior. Ailes ultimately apologized, but intentionally not to NPR. Instead, in a letter to the Anti-Defamation League of B'nai B'rith, a Jewish civil rights organization, he said he should have instead called the NPR officials "nasty inflexible bigot[s]"—

not Nazis. The ADL's Abraham Foxman has served as a public excul-pator for both Ailes and Rupert Murdoch, who has been a donor to the group. Murdoch received an international leadership award from the ADL the same month Williams was dismissed.

In a subsequent book, *Muzzled*, Williams argued that the termina-tion of his contract was part of a larger pattern of the suppression of unwelcome opinions. I suggested to him that it was a complicated case to make amid the cacophony of the blogosphere and the explosion of new social media sites such as Twitter and Tumblr.

"There are lots of platforms and lots of points of view out there. It's like going to a New York City street," Williams responded. "You hear the cabs honking, the kids screaming, the ice cream truck. You can hear everything out here. But I think to myself . . . the experience that most Americans have is that they bite their tongue on a regular basis."

Williams's termination by NPR took an emotional toll, leading to fears his career would be hurt and that he would be considered a bigot. Williams wrote that his editors at NPR were unhappy with his previous book—*Enough*—in which he criticized liberal black leaders. Williams said he was told by an NPR executive (whom he would not identify to me) that his thinking and his book were not in sync with the kind of African Americans valued by the network.

The record tends to belie his perception. NPR's *Morning Edition*, one of the network's most highly rated programs and one of the most listened-to radio shows in the country, devoted nearly eight minutes to an interview with Williams about *Enough*, a notably lengthy dura-tion for the program. The conversation was used to kick off a week of stories about leadership among African Americans.

The muzzled Williams was allowed to make his case in print inter-views, on Fox News, on the *Daily Show* with Jon Stewart, on NPR's *Diane Rehm Show*, and on other public radio programs as well.

In early January 2011, NPR's board of directors released a report from a law firm that found Williams's contract had been terminated lawfully but that there were managerial failings in how it was carried out. Weiss resigned after it was clear she was no longer welcome at the network for which she had worked a quarter century. Schiller was ousted a few months later. Her top fund-raising executive was taped in a stunt by young conservative activists posing as Muslim donors eager to trash Jews in the media. He had been captured making remarks deeply dismissive of conservatives and Tea Party members. That the thirteen-minute version of the tape initially posted online badly distorted what occurred at the lunch didn't matter. Nor did the fact that Vivian Schiller was not present.

It was April 2011. Ailes was riding high. But across the Atlantic, at another vital outpost of Murdoch's World, carefully constructed defenses were starting to fall.

11

"AS BAD AS WE FEARED"

BACK IN NOVEMBER 2005, THE *News of the World* had published a brief item about a royal limb out of joint. Prince William had to put off a mountain rescue course after pulling a tendon in a soccer practice with schoolchildren. He had been "crocked by a ten-year-old," the paper's royals editor, Clive Goodman, reported.

"He has to wear a knee brace if he wants to do anything other than walk, to stop it getting any worse," one friend of the prince had "confided." The economical, 156-word article detailed the injury, the circumstances, the location, the hospital, the course of treatment, and the inside joke from a friend about Prince Harry's nickname ("Sicknote").

Aides to the princes complained to police that someone was accessing their phones. Many of these remarks—such as Harry's nickname—had been uttered in voice mails, not conversation.

Goodman's reporting drew on the help of an athletic man with an eager-to-please affect named Glenn Mulcaire. In his early twenties,

Mulcaire had sought to work for military intelligence. Those who interviewed him said Mulcaire wasn't military intelligence material—but encouraged him to set up his own business one day. He dabbled in private investigation, scouring through records on behalf of insurance companies and doing some work protecting clients from unwanted media attention. That helped him pick up work around the margins for *News of the World.*

Mulcaire had been a soccer player too, known as "Trigger" for his quick-whip left foot. When opportunity presented itself, he joined the roster of a new lower-rank professional team, AFC Wimbledon, and scored its very first goal in 2002, a shot taken from beyond the penalty box that whistled past the diving goalie. "You don't get better than that in this sport," Mulcaire told a sideline reporter after the game. "It's still hard to take in, really." But he added, "to be honest, we should have scored a lot earlier." AFC Wimbledon lost to Bromley, 2–1. "Trigger had his moment of glory," his coach said later. "Talk about his five minutes of fame. He had his five minutes of fame, and he loved it."

Mulcaire could never beat that opening shot. He did not possess the talent, drive, or luck to make it to elite levels of the game in the UK or even star in the lower ranks. He left AFC Wimbledon the following year after an injury. He was thirty-three. With a dead end, the time was right to return to a private investigator's life. Soon he had steady work from *News of the World.* By 2006, Mulcaire had a signed annual contract with the tabloid that exceeded £100,000. The tabloid's editors had adopted a bit of cloak and dagger to hide payments to Mulcaire—itemizing his bills with receipts for "Alexander" and "Paul Williams."

Hacking someone's cell phone messages turned out to be a surprisingly easy task. It required two people, or at least two phones. On the first, a hacker called someone on his or her mobile phone. On the second, he dialed again, but because the line was tied up, the call would be sent straight to voice mail. Callers were given the option of leaving a message or retrieving voice mail messages. In almost all cases, mobile phone service providers had left the default setting for the code to gain access to voice mail messages as "0000" or "1234," trusting cell phone users to set up their own. Most did not. Of those who did, most users selected their birthdays. Private detectives like Mulcaire could readily acquire those, too.

In an August 2006 raid on Mulcaire's home, police turned up more than 11,000 pages of documents with several thousand names of potential targets. The documents showed the tabloid's reporting relied heavily on Mulcaire's investigations, as well as other private investigators, and that many reporters commissioned his work, not just Goodman.

In January 2007 Mulcaire pleaded guilty to hacking the phones of aides to the princes, as well as five other prominent people, and was sent to jail. Goodman was headed to jail too. Andrew Coulson, *News of the World* editor, resigned, saying he had no knowledge of their activity but accepted responsibility for what occurred on his watch. The case seemed to write a new but brief chapter in the eternal chase of the royals by the tabloid press. News International brought in Colin Myler, a British editor who was Col Allan's deputy at the *New York Post*, to run *News of the World* and to set new newsroom policies to assure such things would not happen again.

Goodman pleaded guilty to conspiracy to intercept the private mobile phone messages of three members of the princes' inner circle. A month later, in February 2007, Goodman was fired for gross misconduct by Les Hinton, then the executive chairman of News International. But privately Goodman wrote a letter to Hinton; Stuart Kuttner, the managing editor of the paper; and the company's chief human resources executive saying he had done nothing wrong.

"The decision is perverse in that the actions leading to this criminal charge were carried out with the full knowledge and support" of several executives at the paper, Goodman wrote. He added that others had approved his payments to the private investigator, Mulcaire, for the precise purpose of hacking into the phones of the princes' aides. The firing was "inconsistent," Goodman contended, because "other members of the staff were carrying out the same illegal procedures."

His next sentence gathered up the combustible material at hand and lit it: "This practice was widely discussed in the daily editorial conference, until explicit reference to it was banned by the Editor. As far as I am aware, no other member of staff has faced disciplinary action, much less dismissal." Throughout the trial, he had been suspended but remained employed, though the paper's top lawyer, Tom Crone, had attended his defense preparations and knew he would plead guilty. Crone and editor Coulson "promised on many occasions that I could come back to a job if I did not implicate the paper or any of its staff in my mitigation plea."

Within a month, Hinton had authorized the first in a pair of payments to Goodman that totaled more than £253,000 ($382,000). Only £13,000 of the payment went toward legal fees. Hinton wrote in a letter that the money was only being paid out of respect for his past service to the company.

In May 2007, News International announced that respected outside lawyers had done an extensive review and found no executives who had any knowledge or involvement in the conspiracy to break the law. The company would stick with that formulation for more than four years. Andy Coulson found new life as the chief communications director of the head of the Tory Party, David Cameron.

NEWS CORP'S executives have always defined themselves by its enemies—unions, liberal elites, the *New York Times*, the BBC, the *Guardian,* and the Australian Broadcasting Corp; self-satisfied politicians, red tape–happy government regulators, the leftist university professoriate.

Leaders throughout the corporate empire embrace the conflict. "We like being pirates," said *New York Post* editor in chief Col Allan. "We're like a pirate ship," a senior news executive at the *Wall Street Journal* told me, oblivious to the echo of Allan—or how remarkable it sounded coming from the mouth of someone leading one of the most prestigious newspapers in the world.

Murdoch's men (and women) insisted they didn't get the invites to high society parties, which is hard to credit, given their social calendars in New York, Hollywood, London, and Sydney. In the UK, Rupert Murdoch had not been knighted by the Queen—as had his father and many of his rivals. Once Murdoch took American citizenship in order to consummate a major television deal in 1985, of course, he could not actually accept a knightship anyhow. But Conrad Black, the former owner of the *Telegraph*, gave up his Canadian citizenship to accept a peerage. Murdoch still could have been offered it. (Then again, he may console himself with his papal knighthood.)

In turn, top News Corp executives convinced themselves the establishment loathed the corporation. This declaration would be repeated despite the fact that Murdoch père and fils and their top lieutenants were courted by prime ministers, and their top executives were often culled from the establishment's ranks. In the US, former US assistant attorney general and New York City Schools chancellor Joel Klein became a top aide to Rupert Murdoch; in the UK, Andrew Knight, former editor of the *Economist* and chairman and CEO of the Telegraph Group became chairman of News International in the 1990s and later a corporate director of News Corp.

On the parent corporation's board sat the former prime minister of Spain and a second former assistant US attorney general, Viet Dinh. (In classic corporate mode, both sides were covered: Klein was a Democrat, Dinh a Republican.) When David Cameron took office as prime minister, the very first private citizen to pay a call in person was Rupert Murdoch. Cameron welcomed Murdoch warmly—but the media magnate had been asked to arrive by the back door, unobserved by the press. It is the defining contradiction of Rupert Murdoch's corporation that it has accumulated more influence than any other media company in the world and yet remains convinced of its status as an outsider.

Often those characterized as enemies by News Corp would be more fairly classified as competitors or critics or even punching bags rather than pure foes. In the phone hacking saga, two avengers stood out. None of what followed would likely have occurred had either of these two men adopted a conventional concern for maintaining their status in British society—the conventions that Murdoch and his inner circle ascribed to their most threatening critics. They were the iconoclasts.

One of them operated far from the corridors of power in a historic town that sits a few miles from England's southern coast. Lewes provides a respite from London's traffic, grit, and crowds. At a fair on the day I visited, a Punch and Judy show enthralled toddlers, as it has for generations, at a schoolyard. Up a hill, past a battered Ford Fiesta in the driveway, a bit beyond a neatly tended garden with rhubarb and cabbages, a lean man with a thatch of almost-white hair sat in a converted garage, peering at an oversize computer screen.

"The view opens up, and it's like a sort of postcard of Old England," Nick Davies said, pointing to a stone church nearby, once he had looked up. "Beyond that, on a clear day, you can see the green hills rolling away in the distance, to the sea."

Davies was the relentless investigative journalist who broke a string of stories tying top executives at *News of the World* and News International to the hacking mess. But he was a bit of a renegade at the *Guardian*. The paper, denigrated as impossibly earnest by its competitors, is owned by not-for-profit Scott Trust with an identifiably left editorial page. Its annual losses are covered in large part by the trust's other, profitable holdings, especially AutoTrader, Europe's leading automobile classified advertising website and magazine. The

Guardian's journalism is on the whole serious, fearless, and thorough. But the politicians and business executives who dislike the paper's coverage point to its ideology to dismiss its findings.

Davies's scoops in the hacking case took time to build. "A blind man in a dark room could see that the official version of events didn't make sense," Davies told me. He had written an earlier book about the flaws of the British press, *Flat Earth News*. But hacking sounded worse. A source inside News International once told him mobile phone hacking was commonplace at its tabloids. At a dinner party, Davies asked an official from Scotland Yard: How many people were really targeted? Thousands, the policeman replied.

WORKING IN parallel to Nick Davies was a man who had been practicing law in the professional purgatory of Manchester. Mark Lewis had previously pursued cases involving defamation of character—in one instance, the controlling board of a professional soccer team that had smeared its fans. Lewis had a specialty in "reputation management" (what more typically is called defamation and libel) and had taken on a case involving Gordon Taylor, an official with the professional soccer players association. The *News of the World* was preparing an article that alleged Taylor had been involved in an extramarital affair. After some interventions by Lewis, the article was held, but he was told by the paper the reporting was "a proper journalistic inquiry."

Later, Lewis said, he saw Taylor's name and face flit by on a television screen during a story on the sentencing of *News of the World*'s Clive Goodman and his associate, Mulcaire. Taylor was one of a handful of people also named as targets. Others included Liberal Democrat MP Simon Hughes, actress and model Elle MacPherson, and high-end public relations executive Max Clifford. Lewis started inquiries and almost immediately received a very unusual visit from Tom Crone. Crone suggested the matter was a small one—worth only some thousands of pounds.

Lewis took the fact of the visit as proof the case was worth a lot more. News Corp mismeasured its mark. Lewis is a tall, slender man with a pronounced limp, a flair for dramatic rhetoric, and flashy garb. He was wearing a garish orange overcoat the day I met him. He grandiosely described his role in the case as akin to living inside a John Grisham novel. But then his was an extraordinary story.

Painstakingly annotated documents sat undisturbed for years deep in storage at Scotland Yard that detailed for any investigator who showed sufficient curiosity how Gordon Taylor's privacy had been illegally invaded.

As Crone later wrote in a confidential legal memo, a contract dated February 4, 2005, showed *News of the World* had agreed to pay Mulcaire £7,000 for information "on an affair being conducted by Gordon Taylor." Taylor's lawyer had also obtained a list of illegal privacy violations implicating many journalists at *News of the World* and its sister *Sun*. The most damaging blow came in the form of a single email from a junior reporter named Ross Hall (working at the paper under a pseudonym). On June 29, 2005, Hall sent a note to Mulcaire with the transcripts of fifteen messages from Taylor's mobile phone. Hall also transcribed another seventeen messages left by Taylor on the cell phone of his assistant, JoAnn Armstrong. Hall's note started: "This is the transcript for Neville." Neville, it was claimed, had to be Neville Thurlbeck, then the tabloid's chief reporter. His name would appear hundreds of times in the meticulous records taken from Mulcaire.

In 2008 Mark Lewis demanded documents explaining what had happened to his client, citing a provision of British law that compelled prosecutors and police to share any evidence they possessed.

"This evidence particularly the email from the *News of the World* is fatal to our case," Crone wrote on May 24, 2008. "Our position is very perilous. The damning email is genuine and proves we actively made use of a large number of extremely private voicemails from Taylor's telephone . . . pursuant to a February 2005 contract."

Crone recommended to Colin Myler, the editor, and the firm's outside lawyers that the company offer to pay Taylor £150,000, plus legal fees. On May 27, 2008, Myler met with James Murdoch, who was about to embark on a series of trips abroad. James Murdoch told Myler to wait for outside legal opinion. Myler wasn't happy—it was a mess. *Clive Goodman had sprayed around allegations against others. I can't ignore it,* Myler told Julian Pike, the firm's leading outside lawyer, who jotted down Myler's misgivings: *The new editor couldn't be seen to be dismissing these allegations. I had given assurances to the staff. Les Hinton had given evidence to a parliamentary committee. But Les is no longer here. James would say, get rid of them. Cut out the cancer.* Fire the people responsible.

This moment forced the first true corporate reckoning. Michael Silverleaf, a lawyer and a leading figure in British media circles, was asked to assess News International's prospects in court. He rendered his verdict on June 3, 2008: the disclosure could not "possibly justify the use of unlawful means to obtain information on it," Silverleaf wrote.

In the UK, judges and prosecutors tend to give much leeway to legal infractions by reporters who convincingly argue they broke the law in pursuit of the public interest. And even the bad consequences of a civil suit under British law are typically far less severe than in the US. But Silverleaf fretted it would be "almost inevitable that the court will wish to mark its disapproval of their activities by awarding an enhanced level of damages. The accessing of Mr Taylor's and [a woman's] voicemails was not only illegal but will be seen as immoral and repugnant by any judge who is likely to hear the action."

No precedents existed to guide estimates for the size of the judgment Taylor might win. Silverleaf advised Crone and News International to up the ante. Other implications came into play as well: disclosures of evidence in open court would show that prosecutors were wrong to accept *News of the World*'s continued assertion of the hacking as isolated. Damage to the company's reputation could far exceed any savings it would achieve in this single case.

Under British law, the loser in civil litigation pays all legal fees. That provided some leverage. A loss could cost Taylor hundreds of thousands of pounds out of his own pocket. Silverleaf suggested offering £250,000 plus legal fees.

Later that day, News International's chief outside attorney, Julian Pike, decided instead to offer £350,000 "on the basis that [it] drew a line in the sand and that the deal was confidential." Both elements were crucial to the defense: stop the damage and do so silently. Pike was in for a nasty surprise. Three days later, Mark Lewis informed Pike that Gordon Taylor "wanted to be vindicated or be rich." It would cost *News of the World*, "seven figures not to open his mouth." The price was £1 million plus £200,000 in legal fees, plus taxes owed to Her Majesty's Revenue and Customs.

On Saturday, June 7, Myler asked James Murdoch for five minutes of his time on the following Tuesday for a meeting with Crone. In the email, the editor warned Murdoch, "Unfortunately, it is as bad as we feared." Below his email, Myler had forwarded gloomy summaries from both Crone and Pike. James Murdoch sent off a chipper reply—"no worries"—just two-and-a-half minutes later, and offered to talk that night or the next day. Did James read the whole email trail? That remains a matter of dispute.

On the afternoon of June 10, James Murdoch waved Crone and Myler into his office at News International's Wapping headquarters for a meeting that lasted about fifteen minutes. The two men briefed Murdoch, who said he wanted to think through his options. *I'm sick of the drip, drip, drip,* Myler told one of the lawyers later. *Let's tell Taylor to fuck off.* Frustration reached a peak. The men feared that if

Taylor's suit against Mulcaire succeeded, the paper could face liability there as well.

One month later, on July 10, 2008, Murdoch approved payments hitting £425,000 (about $635,000) plus legal fees for both sides. The total cost exceeded £1 million. The settlement specified that the terms would remain secret—as would the very existence of the deal.

———————

IT TOOK Nick Davies until July 2009 to document the scope of the tabloid's hacking for public consumption. It focuses on the same private investigator as the story about the princes does, a man whom the *Guardian* sought to link to Coulson and Rebekah Brooks Coulson and Rebekah Brooks, by this time editor of the sister *Sun* tabloid. James Murdoch, then the executive chairman over the British wing of News Corp, had personally approved the secret settlement.

The story Davies wrote in July 2009 revealing that payment, he said, "provoked a kind of blizzard of dishonesty."

Assistant police commissioner John Yates announced he had conducted a review of the previous investigation—in less than a day—and that the *Guardian* had no new evidence to contradict the earlier conclusion of police that hacking had been limited at *News of the World*. Within forty-eight hours, News International put out a slashing statement, accusing the *Guardian* of lying, and still the public seemed indifferent.

Davies said he heard it all. "People kept on saying that I was obsessive, and maybe that's true." He kept reporting, but nothing seemed to come of it. Davies had stayed largely in Lewes, away from the newsroom, calling sources, badgering people—periodically popping out to meet them in person.

Guardian editor Alan Rusbridger was one of a few at the newspaper who dealt with him directly. Under British law, the press cannot report on criminal trials beyond the proceedings while they are under way. In 2005, it was later reported, Coulson had hired Jonathan Rees, a private investigator who had done seven years in jail for planting cocaine on a woman to frame her for a crime she did not commit. In 2008 Rees was charged with murder. His business partner had been found in a parking lot outside a pub, an ax lodged securely in his head. But Rees could not yet be identified in print.

In the run-up to the 2010 elections, Rusbridger sent warnings about Coulson to future prime minister David Cameron through a deputy editor, Ian Katz. In early February 2010, Katz called Cameron's director of strategy, with the message: *Do not allow Coulson to follow you from party headquarters into 10 Downing Street.* Rusbridger had also reached out to Liberal Democratic Party leader Nick Clegg by email on April 5 with the same message. Clegg had been stunned, according to Rusbridger, and said he had also cautioned Cameron. The actor and frequent tabloid subject Hugh Grant, an Oxford classmate of Cameron's chief political ally George Osborne, also privately warned against Coulson.

The *Guardian* had endorsed Tony Blair's New Labour on its way to power but in 2010 switched to Clegg and the Liberal Democrats. Though Gordon Brown had lost the support of News International papers, the Labourites were too compromised, Rusbridger and his colleagues concluded, by their extensive entanglement with the Murdochs. Cameron took office in a coalition with Clegg and the Lib Dems and brought Coulson with him.

Seeing in the actions of *News of the World* signs of a greater corruption, Rusbridger urged Bill Keller, executive editor of the *New York Times*, to send his own reporters to investigate. The two newspapers had collaborated on a WikiLeaks project, divvying up thousands of diplomatic documents hacked and leaked by the outfit for further reporting.

In this instance, Rusbridger and the *Guardian* needed external validation. Most other British papers shied away from making too much of the Murdoch titles' misdeeds. Rusbridger shared tips and sources with the *New York Times*, whose reporters developed their own reporting. The resulting cover story in the *New York Times Sunday Magazine* in September 2010 offered former *News of the World* reporters talking on the record, for the first time, about criminal activities. News International editors were particularly incensed by what they saw as a pincer movement—the *Guardian* had called in the *New York Times* to deliver a blow from the west. The week the *Times* published its magazine piece, the *News of the World*'s managing editor filed a complaint against the New York paper under its ethics code, saying its reporting was clearly driven by the need to damage a rival company.

We know things we haven't been able to publish, the deputy *Guardian* editor Katz told Cameron's chief of staff on October 4, 2010. *There's a big murder trial coming involving one of* News of the World's *investigators. He had been linked by investigators to corrupt police years ago. There's no way an editor wouldn't have known.* Katz laid out the details.

Nothing ever came back from the prime minister.

LEWIS HAD lost his job in 2009. His law firm in Manchester didn't want the attention as adversaries of the Murdochs. But Lewis thought he had a case and a cause. "He is a dogged, lone figure," Rusbridger said. News International's efforts to scare him off "whetted his appetite." Lewis moved to London and a small firm called Taylor Hampton, across the street from the High Court.

The highly regarded British media lawyer David Hooper told me that he initially thought that Lewis and his clients had overstated their case. "I don't think one would think that now."

Lewis had testified to Parliament that he had been told by Detective Sergeant Mark Maberly of the Metropolitan Police that up to 6,000 people had been targets of phone hacking. However, Scotland Yard told the Press Complaints Commission that the detective had been "wrongly quoted" by Lewis. The police were sticking firm to the idea that hacking was limited to "a handful" of instances.

The chairwoman of the Press Complaints Commission, Baroness Buscombe, told an association of editors that she had warned the head of the parliamentary panel to which Lewis had testified that his sworn remarks had been refuted: "Any suggestion that a Parliamentary Inquiry has been misled is an extremely serious matter." Later disclosures vindicated Lewis. He sued her, the Metropolitan Police, and the complaints commission. Buscombe apologized the next year, and she and the complaints commission later paid Lewis £20,000 in damages.

Officials at News International clearly perceived a threat. According to documents later found in the files of Tom Crone, reporters and private eyes were assigned to follow Lewis and another lawyer, Charlotte Harris, representing different clients with hacking claims against the paper. News Corp's British lawyers argued in court that Lewis should be blocked from the case: he was romantically involved with Harris and must have engaged in professional misconduct. But no evidence of such misconduct existed, nor did any proof surface of the supposedly illicit liaison. Defense motions failed to find favor with judges. Investigators also spied on Lewis's teenage daughter while she shopped and watched Lewis's estranged wife through the window of her home.

Lewis's health was investigated too. He said he was told that Crone and other lawyers concluded he had embarked on a kamikaze mission against News Corp because he was dying. He does have multiple sclerosis, a degenerative disease that causes his limp. The disease prevents him from taking notes in real time, a point that News International's lawyers highlighted in seeking to undercut his recollection. His riposte: "I have a condition. It's called life. We're all dying—someday."

In fact, Lewis had decided to use the media against its owners. If he did not care about his reputation or what reporters printed or broadcast about his personal life, their proprietors could not intimidate him from pursuing his cases or giving interviews that raised embarrassing questions. So he spent several years shuttling from TV studios to courthouses to parliamentary hearings—piping up whenever he could get the chance.

"News International was so arrogant about everything," Lewis told me one day, as we lurched in a taxicab from a BBC studio on the banks of the Thames past Parliament to a meeting he had scheduled with the newest crop of press regulators. News International should have apologized instead of concluding he was "part of the left-wing plot to damage Rupert Murdoch and News International."

In April 2011, News International established a fund to settle with a small group of people including the actress Sienna Miller—the kind of people who had public stature and the wealth to pursue their grievances. The company conceded that they had been targeted for voice mail hacking. Those who knew Murdoch's world well nudged me to keep an eye on developments. Andrew Neil, the former editor of the *Sunday Times* and founding chairman of BSkyB, said the newest revelations raised the questions from Watergate: "Who knew, and when did you know it?"

He continued: "If it's now accepted the 'rogue reporter' defense has bitten the dust and was smashed to smithereens, if it's now accepted that it was going on all over the place in this newsroom, then it beggars belief that . . . they didn't know," Neil said. "It is frankly incredible."

FOR ALL THAT, on the surface, as June gave way to July 2011, things looked quite promising for the Murdochs.

Major investors were giving Rupert Murdoch's company their continued support, allowing him to indulge his love of newspapers. In decades past, Murdoch enjoyed sauntering through newsrooms to peer at his papers' flats, the pages with the stories laid out by men with exacto knives before they went to press. He would look over the front page and section fronts, pointing out a headline that he felt wasn't up to scratch, playing to a gathering crowd of editors by suggesting a catchier alternative. In more recent years the pages were displayed on giant computer monitors but the impulse was the same.

Regardless of who held what job title, regardless of what country, he was the publisher of every paper News Corp owned, and the editor in chief too, when he wanted to be. The papers reflected Murdoch's right-of-center populist touch, his recurring demand that the writing be concise, the issues clear-cut, the reporting timely, and the matters addressed accessible, important, or preferably both. In the tabloids the elites hated (he loved their success in significant part because the elites hated them), Murdoch found a way to connect with readers. And he appealed to the great and mighty by also owning respectable papers with a more literate and worldly flavor.

Investors who gambled on Murdoch's impulses knew they had to accept some of them would go awry. When they did misfire, News Corp would lose hundreds of millions or even billions of dollars in shareholder money. The company wrote down the value of the *Wall Street Journal* and Dow Jones by $2.8 billion—about half the cost of acquiring the paper in the first place. Its managing editor, Robert Thomson, had embarked on an effort to streamline costs by compelling the journalists inside the newsroom of the nation's premier financial daily to work more closely with its sister wire service, Dow Jones. Not too many *Journal* staffers wanted to blur the distinction. Earlier in the year, Murdoch had paid $675 million for a boutique TV and film production company called Shine, founded a decade earlier by Elisabeth Murdoch. It had created some TV hits and some well-received smaller films. Analysts contended Murdoch had paid his daughter's company two to three times its worth. Elisabeth Murdoch walked off with more than $200 million from the transaction—as well as full payment for her legal costs, worth tens of millions more.

At the end of June 2011, News Corp sold the social media website MySpace for $35 million—about 6 percent of the cost he had paid for it in 2005. That purchase was, as Murdoch readily admitted, a debacle. Its primary competitor, Facebook, would soon be valued at $104 billion in its initial public offering.

Some good governance groups and pension and labor fund investors in News Corp called for the Murdochs to stop running the company as a family concern. The board waved through the Shine deal without serious reservations. Directors had approved a side investment for one of their own as well. Kenneth Cowley had led News Ltd in Australia and remained on the board afterward. Rupert Murdoch wanted to invest $28 million of the company's money in R.M. Williams, an agricultural company of which Cowley was the chairman. The idea was to convert cattle and chicken farmlands to the world's largest "carbon farm," enabling the company to trade credits for reducing carbon emissions through an initiative from the Australian government under Prime Minister Gillard. The corporation did not disclose the board's approval of the 2009 investment among its list of transactions for "related parties" in documents filed with federal regulators. The carbon farm did not materialize in a meaningful way.

But as the Murdochs controlled so much of the voting stock, and had fostered so many profitable elements for the company, those concerns were easily drowned out. The entertainment side of the ledger, especially cable and satellite television, was thick with cash.

Murdoch had expanded across countries and continents and industries. Most of those parts of News Corp, apart from the press, were outside his creative zone; he indulged *The Simpsons* and watched it become the longest running franchise in television history; despite little technical expertise or inclination he ran circles around competitors with computerized card technology for his satellite TV subscribers; his daughter Elisabeth suggested Fox import a now iconic show from the UK; called *American Idol* in the US, it helped lead the network to one ratings coup after another; he built up newspapers and television empires based on the loyalty of sports fans who would reliably return for more without particularly caring for sports himself.

Fox News kept on drawing in viewers, its profits standing at roughly $900 million a year. If News Corp could take over full ownership of the British TV giant BSkyB, it would gain access to all of the $1.6 billion in annual profit the company threw off. Hence News Corp's obsessive desire to complete the purchase of the remaining 60 percent in shares it did not already own.

FOR BRITS, the Milly Dowler story had been a sensation from nearly the moment she disappeared in 2002. She was a thirteen-year-old schoolgirl from Walton-on-Thames, a city of 25,000 about forty-five minutes outside London. She took a walk after writing despairingly in her journal article that her parents cared far more for her elder sister. She called her father to say she'd be home in about a half hour. Her bones were found six months later, a hundred miles away. It took nine years for police to track down her killer and for prosecutors to bring him to trial. On June 23, 2011, jurors took just seven hours to convict the man, who was already serving time for killing several others. He was sentenced to another life term in prison.

On July 4, 2011, the *Guardian* carried a sprawling front-page headline that could not have been more damning: "News of the World Hacked Milly Dowler's Phone During Police Hunt."

The *Guardian*'s blockbuster story alleged a series of grievous wrongs: her voice mail messages had been hacked by a private investigator working for the paper; those messages had been deleted by the same PI because her in-box had filled and he wanted others to leave juicy nuggets to mine for stories; the activity involving her messages gave her parents false hope and impeded the ability of police to track her down; the police in Surrey were aware of this hacking and did nothing.

"It is distress heaped upon tragedy to learn that the *News of the World* had no humanity at such a terrible time," said Mark Lewis, who had become the Dowlers' private lawyer too. "The fact that they were prepared to act in such a heinous way that could have jeopardized the police investigation and give [her family] false hope is despicable."

The nation convulsed. *News of the World* had plundered an innocent dead girl's private messages from relatives and friends, some of whom were desperately seeking confirmation she was still alive, simply in pursuit of an edge on stories against their tabloid competitors.

Labour MP Tom Watson, a frequent critic of the Murdoch press, seized the moment, calling the hacking "a despicable and evil act."

———

ON THE day Davies and his *Guardian* colleague Amelia Hill broke the Dowler story, Prime Minister David Cameron stood behind a lectern at the Arg, the Afghan presidential palace, in Kabul, a few feet from President Hamid Karzai. A delicate task dominated Cameron's agenda for the trip: continuing his country's military and diplomatic presence while scaling back the number of troops deployed there. But the death of a young Brit had cast a shadow over the visit. The soldier had wandered, inexplicably, off the military base and was soon abducted, apparently by Taliban sympathizers. His recovered body had been mutilated, and reports claimed it had been paraded in front of insurgents as a trophy.

The two leaders spoke of their shared commitment to stability for Afghans amid the continued threat of Taliban violence. They spoke soberly of the family of the eighteen-year-old infantryman, a member of a Scottish regiment. Then they took questions.

First up, a British reporter asked whether the UK should offer more civilian aid to Afghanistan and then added: "And, Prime Minister, if I could ask you a specific question: What is your reaction to the allegations that a *News of the World* investigator hacked into the phone of the missing girl, Milly Dowler? And in light of those allegations, do you think that the owners of the *News of the World* are a fit and proper company to take over BSkyB?"

The reporter had distilled a blockbuster story into a vexing and overarching question for both News Corp and the British government. No longer could the *Guardian* reporting be credibly dismissed as the hyperventilating of a competitor.

Former home secretary Alan Johnson, an MP for the Labour Party, stood to speak in the House of Commons. "The public mood, the mood in Parliament, the mood elsewhere, was this was an obsession of one newspaper," Johnson told his fellow lawmakers. "Let's praise the *Guardian* for doggedly staying on this case."

Revelations about victims of violence who had been hacked poured forth in the coming days: those killed and wounded in the July 7, 2005, bus and subway bombings in London and their families; British soldiers killed in Afghanistan and Iraq; the families of other victims of high-profile murders.

Even personal ties to the Murdochs or their associates offered little protection from the electronic sweep of the private eyes and their newsroom clients. Nor did political pull. Among those worthies whose mobile phones were believed to have been targeted for hacking:

- The daughter-in-law of a prime minister whom Murdoch and his papers initially supported (Emma Noble, daughter-in-law of John Major)
- The deputy to a prime minister Murdoch's papers supported for election three times (John Prescott)
- The wife of a prime minister Murdoch's papers supported at elections three times; the wife of the godfather of Murdoch's young daughter Grace (both Cherie Blair)
- The mayor of London, who did not pursue a claim against the company (Boris Johnson)
- The pop star who sang at Rupert Murdoch's third wedding without charge (Charlotte Church)
- The priest of the pop star who sang at Murdoch's third wedding (Father Richard Reardon of Cardiff)
- The former star of a Fox broadcast network prime-time show in the US (Sienna Miller)
- The former star of a Fox Studios movie (Hugh Grant)
- The brightest star of British soccer leagues, to which Murdoch's BSkyB held broadcasting rights worth billions of pounds (Wayne Rooney of Manchester United and the English national team)
- The grieving mother of a slain schoolgirl who had been given the mobile phone in question by Rebekah Brooks (Sarah Payne)

In an Escherian touch, among the hacking targets were at least two former Murdoch news executives. Tony Blair remained close to the Murdochs, even after the revelations. Cherie Blair sued News International. The logic held: everyone is fair game. The comedian Steve Coogan understood. "Strangely, I don't think it was a malicious personal vendetta against me. My feeling is that it was a dispassionate sociopathic act by those who operate in an amoral universe where they are never accountable. It has become a mind-set of those who work in tabloids, as a result of the environment and working culture that has been created."

In 2005—six years before the summer of scandal—Coogan learned from his cell phone provider that his messages had been compromised. News International would later pay approximately $66,000 to settle the case out of court. (Judgments in British courts are typically far lower than they would be if brought in the US.) Infuriated that his privacy had been invaded, Coogan testified against the Murdochs, but in commerce he accepted the rules. Coogan appeared in five movies produced by Fox-owned studios after discovering that his phone had been hacked. His comedic hit TV shows featuring him in the role of Alan Partridge ran on a Sky cable channel in the UK. And his book, *I, Partridge: We Need to Talk About Alan* was published in the UK, Canada, and Australia by Murdoch's HarperCollins publishing house. Its British publication date was in September 2011, less than three months after the Dowler revelation. It was hard to do business without the Murdochs.

12

SKY'S THE LIMIT

IN ENGLAND, RUPERT MURDOCH HAD been seeking to achieve in television the kind of inescapable presence that he had earlier attained in newspapers. To do that, he sought to compete against the BBC on what he considered to be a more equal footing. He had always resented the government subsidy it received.

The BBC had been the dominant UK broadcaster since its first radio transmission in 1922 from Marconi House in the Strand, at the center of London, just blocks from the seat of government and Piccadilly's theater district. The first words: "This is 2-L-O, the London station of the British Broadcasting Company calling. 2-L-O calling." Fifty-odd years later, the satellite television industry had evolved to the point where it envisaged dishes that were affordable enough and small enough for individual consumers to mount on their roofs. The Brits received five satellite channels. British officials allocated two satellite channels to the BBC and invited private broadcasters to submit plans to control and program the other three. Murdoch's News International joined a consortium to bid.

One catch: the plans required launching a satellite. A rival alliance of investors that proposed the British Satellite Broadcasting system won the channels. The investors included Richard Branson's Virgin and Pearson, the owner of the *Financial Times* and Penguin Books.

Murdoch had been shut out, but he already had a modest Sky channel in Europe. So he set up his British TV business in Luxembourg, outside the reach of UK regulators, though he kept studios in an industrial suburb of London. He contracted to broadcast a multichannel service from a midsize satellite called Astra based in the tiny European principality. Thanks to those small dishes, the television programs could be beamed into British homes with no meaningful intervention by the British government. Murdoch had taken a buccaneer's path—circumvention as innovation.

The BBC had set the industry standard in so many ways, first in radio, then television. It created a superstore of television and radio programming, offering news, soap operas, serious theater and music, and children's and educational shows. The BBC was home to the world's leading news service, soccer coverage, Monty Python, *Brideshead Revisited* and more. But it had run for years without serious competition. Murdoch considered it sclerotic.

Murdoch's Sky TV made its debut in 1989, but dish sales and revenues lagged badly behind projections. Yet British Satellite Broadcasting struggled too, launching its actual service more than a year after Murdoch's Sky TV. Sky was counting on lower costs—no need to launch its own satellite and no spending on the pricier movies and sporting events.

"He basically stole a march on them, the way that Murdoch has often operated," said David Gordon, the former CEO of the independent television news service ITN and of the Economist Newspaper Ltd. "Entrepreneurially, courageously, breaking the rules and just plugging along."

But both sides were losing millions of pounds a week. Increasing debt loomed with little likelihood of relief.

Sky and British Satellite Broadcasting merged just seven months after the latter's debut in late 1990. Renamed BSkyB, the satellite TV service achieved financial stability after a few shaky years, making strategic investments in sports, premium TV shows, and movies. Sky (as the blended company became known) served as the driving force behind the creation of the English Premier League in 1992, broadcasting the games of the nation's leading soccer teams. Murdoch had to issue and publicly trade shares in BSkyB to pay off debt accrued for the costs of satellites and everything else—hence his share dropped to just under 40 percent. But he operated as though it was his own.

Newspapers remained Rupert Murdoch's joy. But as the first decade of the 2000s came to a close, the people leading the British part of News Corp—from Rupert to James to Rebekah Brooks on down—focused on one priority above all: to swallow Sky whole.

Rupert Murdoch likes to portray himself as a creative corporate force who seizes opportunities where others cannot perceive them, and in the case of Sky that is certainly true. But his most recent effort to build on that record at Sky proves both the drive to succeed under Murdoch and the important role government officials play in aiding or frustrating his ambitions. In this case, the cabinet minister ultimately assigned to assess the merits of News Corp's drive to acquire Sky was the same person who most avidly lobbied inside the government for its success.

Sky served as a proving ground for the succession games Rupert Murdoch played. He had four adult children. Prudence, his only child by his first wife, wanted little direct part of corporate intrigue, though her husband held senior executive positions in Australia in News Ltd for many years. Rupert's sons Lachlan and James were as competitive with each other in their careers as they were in sports, no doubt, but at no point did it appear as though they were vying for the crown at the same time.

In 2000, Lachlan, the oldest son, was the anointed one, then the head of News Ltd, the corporation's Australian wing. He moved to

New York City to oversee News Corp's American television and newspaper holdings, a springboard to the top. He resigned five years later amid Machiavellian machinations, unconvinced that his father would protect him against the power plays of News Corp president Peter Chernin and Fox News chief Roger Ailes.

Lachlan's father saw the son's retreat as a sign of weakness. Dame Elisabeth had tossed the five-year-old Rupert into the deep end of a pool on an ocean liner pitching back to and fro to force him to learn how to swim. She would not allow anyone to rescue him, even though he was screaming for help, he recalled as an adult. Rupert effectively repeated the lesson with his son Lachlan at the headquarters in New York: sink or swim. Lachlan did not want to play anymore; he returned to Australia to set up his own media company there.

The boys didn't seriously entertain the idea that their older sister Elisabeth posed any threat. She was a girl, after all, and proved an ambivalent figure from the outset, alternately dipping in and out of careers within the company. She had married (much against her father's wishes) the son of a Ghanaian investor she met at Vassar. Elisabeth Murdoch worked at News Corp's basic cable channel FX in Hollywood, and then the couple briefly bought and ran two NBC stations in central California, with a loan secured by Rupert Murdoch. The stations were sold at a profit less than two years later.

Elisabeth Murdoch moved to London in the mid-1990s to work for BSkyB, rising to become the number two to Sam Chisholm. Chisholm referred derisively to Elisabeth in private as "the management trainee." Rupert Murdoch made clear his daughter would not succeed Chisholm at Sky, and while she won credit for several ventures, her handling of the broadcaster's failed bid to acquire Manchester United, the most famous soccer team in the world, counted against her.

"She's ambitious, she's aggressive, but she's simply not as good as she would like to be, and she's not as good as Rupert would like her to be," Jim Hytner, a former BSkyB marketing director, said in 1999.

"She wants to impress her father. I don't blame her, everybody has those desires. . . . The more she doesn't impress him, the more she wants to impress him." Elisabeth Murdoch left her husband for public relations executive Matthew Freud, who would become her second spouse and greatest champion.

The younger boy, James, had grown up on New York City's Upper East Side, though he spent long stretches in his parents' homes in California, Australia, and the UK. He had been a gawky youth, awkward with girls and trying fitfully to connect with his father. As a teenage intern for his father's papers in Australia, he famously fell asleep at a press conference, camera in his lap. (A photographer for the rival *Sydney Morning Herald* immortalized that moment by snapping a picture that ran in the next day's paper.)

James found a circuitous path to his acceptance. He dropped out of Harvard (kicked out, according to the wedding toast of his college friend and later *New York Post* publisher Jesse Angelo), got two tattoos and an earring, and in the mid-1990s provided the funding to establish a rap label, Rawkus Records. Initially seen as the dilettante move of a billionaire's son, Rawkus earned street cred by cultivating Mos Def and other emerging hip-hop stars. Rupert Murdoch awarded him oversight of News Corp's fledgling Internet operations.

James had lost the earring and adopted a highly managerial mien, with closely tailored suits and thin-rimmed glasses. Over time he perfected a bureaucratic techno-speak that suggested a more professional generation of the family was on the rise. More than one News Corp executive described him to me as the Murdoch most likely to have made an excellent consultant for McKinsey & Company.

Others believed the younger Murdoch had much to learn. At one of the annual conferences convened by Rupert Murdoch, a News Corp newspaper editor found James insultingly dismissive. Conversation turned to how the newspapers would come to terms with the implications of the Web—by this point, functionally two years old as a widespread consumer convenience. The walled-off email and content service AOL was cresting in its popularity but beginning to face challenges from free search engines and other sites.

Newspapers had to give away their articles for free, James told the assembled editors. It was the only way to ensure the continued loyalty of their readers. His family's editors argued back that giving away articles priced their value at zero, they said. It was a bad precedent.

You simply don't understand people's relationship to their computers, James responded. *You don't get it.*

"He did not seem to realize people only put such weight on his judgments and pronouncements because of who he was," the editor recalled.

James was running News Corp's Asian operation and earning praise for his work steering its endeavors away from China, and toward India. His father had been consistently blocked by China's ruling classes from expanding the reach of Star TV within China, despite the elder Murdoch's efforts to win their favor. At one point, Rupert Murdoch dropped the BBC there after a documentary about Chairman Mao offended the Chinese authorities; at another, News Corp's Harper-Collins withdrew from publishing the memoirs of Chris Patten, the last British governor general of Hong Kong. Patten's blunt account of the transfer to China appeared certain to ruffle powerful government figures. When Murdoch married Wendi Deng in 1999, it was seen by some as, in part, yet another way to ingratiate himself with the Chinese and to better comprehend their culture.

But the attempted appeasements had limited effect. The Chinese struck partnerships but held tight to control. The outsider could not work his magic—even with his younger Chinese wife at his side. India would prove to be more profitable. News Corp's satellite service Star India was on course to become that most populous nation's leading pay-TV service.

In 2003, at the age of thirty, James Murdoch had become the CEO of BSkyB. And soon enough, with Lachlan's departure, James abruptly supplanted his brother as his father's successor in the making. Later, as executive chairman of News International—the company's British newspaper wing—and News Corp's top executive over Europe and Asia, he became the nonexecutive chairman of the company.

James made his peace with Wendi Deng amid his work on the company's ventures in China. But all three children of Rupert and Anna Torv Murdoch felt burned by Rupert Murdoch's divorce from their mother. Lachlan took it particularly hard; former colleagues in New York said it colored his emotions about the company and his father. Anna had sat on the board of News Corp; now Wendi was pushing for formal recognition of her daughters. In 2006, during an interview on the *Charlie Rose Show*, Rupert Murdoch announced young Grace and Chloe would share the fortune in the family trust with their four siblings, but not have the right to select the trustees who held the shares' voting powers over the corporation. It caused strife with Wendi Deng Murdoch. The next year, Rupert gave each of the six children $160 million; the money gave Elisabeth the capital to run her own production company and Lachlan the seed money for his own Australian investments, most notably in non–News Corp media. James, however, sought to create a self-fulfilling destiny as the next Murdoch to lead News Corp.

It was with that ascending stature that James Murdoch traveled to Edinburgh in 2009 to deliver the MacTaggart Lecture, the UK's signature annual address on media and especially television. It had become a venue for industry heavyweights—top-tier writers, anchors, producers, thought leaders, and, especially, broadcast executives—to sketch out their sense of where the business was headed.

He started with more than a trace of humor: "Does this finally mark my invitation to join the British broadcasting establishment? While that thought does terrify me, I am comforted in the knowledge that after my remarks my membership will have been a brief one."

There it was again, "the establishment" against which generations of Murdochs had consistently campaigned. Ironically, the James

MacTaggart for whom the event had been named produced dramas for theater and television; the lecture was first delivered in 1975 by a socialist colleague at the end of a retrospective honoring his controversialist spirit. It became part of "a wee gabfest" for TV programmers with radical and often explicitly political agendas until the organizers realized that, as the *Guardian* later noted, "the suits started to come." The MacTaggart speaker had often been a top BBC official and occasionally a severe critic, such as the playwright and screenwriter Dennis Potter, who called the BBC and its programming "ponderously anodyne." (He also named his terminal tumor "Rupert.")

In 1989 the real Rupert Murdoch cemented the speech's status with his own appearance. He spoke presciently of the age of digital innovation ahead and warned of the country's centuries-long history of warring impulses between expression and censorship. "For fifty years," the elder Murdoch said, "British television has operated on the assumption that the people could not be trusted to watch what they wanted to watch, so that it had to be controlled by like-minded people who knew what was good for us."

And indeed, by statute, news programs had to be rigorously balanced; advertising, children's programming, and dramatic shows were all subject to limiting regulations.

No more, he announced in Edinburgh, invoking the free markets championed by that famous Scot Adam Smith. Thanks to satellites and other digital technologies, the elites would lose their grip. Murdoch thought so highly of his address that his aides distributed copies of it to leading public officials, not only in the UK but in President George H.W. Bush's White House. Like his father two decades earlier, James Murdoch used his address at MacTaggart to single out two establishment players that required challenge: the BBC and the regulators who constricted its private sector competitors.

Where the elder Murdoch had cited Adam Smith, the younger Murdoch chose Charles Darwin's *Origin of Species*. "It argued that the most dramatic evolutionary changes can occur through an entirely natural process," James Murdoch said. "Darwin proved that evolution is unmanaged." Broadcasters cling to a kind of technological and information creationism, he argued: "It threatens significant damage to important spheres of human enterprise and endeavor—the provision of independent news, investment in professional journalism, and the innovation and growth of the creative industries."

James assailed what he called unaccountable institutions, especially the BBC and OfCom, the independent government regulator. And he attacked the regressive taxes of the licensing fee—the £145 a year ($230)—levied on every home with a color TV. The fee underwrote the only true competitor to the Murdochs' growing television powerhouse in Britain.

Chase Carey, the chief operating officer who effectively ran the company, had been a News Corp exec before leaving to run the American satellite television provider DIRECTV; on his return, Murdoch said, Carey demanded they try to find a way to get BSkyB back for themselves. "In hindsight, I regret I ever agreed to an IPO," Rupert Murdoch said.

The younger Murdoch's campaign to win BSkyB was months in the making. Although News Corp owned nearly 40 percent of the company and its executives dominated the firm's board, a full takeover would enable News Corp to recapture more of BSkyB's profits and to distance News International from its past in newspapers. By the end of the first decade of the twenty-first century, BSkyB generated revenues exceeding $10 billion a year and a pretax profit of $1.37 billion. It was at once the UK's dominant satellite television and broadband Internet provider and a creator of content. Sky blended high-end digital TV shows and movies with some of the most desirable sports programming and premium channels available in the country.

The takeover was to be an audacious stroke. But James Murdoch would need to rely on a new generation of political allies to execute his plans. His father had supported Margaret Thatcher's Conservatives with gusto but had such severe reservations about her successor, John Major, that he switched to Labour's Tony Blair. Under Blair, the Labour media policies that could have threatened Murdoch with heightened regulatory scrutiny soon withered.

By the time of his speech in Edinburgh in 2009, James Murdoch concluded that his father should pivot back toward a new breed of forward-looking, business-friendly Tories. James and Rebekah Brooks convinced Rupert Murdoch to shift his support to David Cameron, a center-right Tory, despite the media mogul's affinity for Blair, and for that matter despite Brooks's friendship with Gordon Brown's wife, Sarah. Brooks had helped stage a pajama party for Sarah Brown's fortieth birthday.

Gordon Brown took the reversal hard. The *Sun* announced it to the world on its front page at the Labour Party's annual conference in late September 2009, just weeks after the MacTaggart speech.

Brown might not have been so surprised if he had known all the details of the courtship on both sides building up to that day.

———————

AS DAVID Cameron plotted to take command of the Conservative Party, George Osborne served as his chief political strategist. The two rising Tory stars embodied British privilege. They were young, wealthy, ambitious, and had belonged to the same exclusive club at Oxford University a few years apart. Cameron was a direct descendant of King William IV, while Osborne's father held an aristocratic title that dated back nearly four centuries.

Osborne's prospects could have been shattered in 2005. The *News of the World* and the rival, liberal *Sunday Mirror* obtained a photograph of a young Osborne from the early 1990s, his arm around an escort, seated at a restaurant table before what the papers suggested was a dish of powdered cocaine. He attributed its presence to a friend who became an addict.

The tabloids feasted. The *News of the World* ran a headline that said the politician "parties with a cocaine-snorting dominatrix" and quoted the woman saying she had witnessed Osborne consuming the drug with friends. Osborne and Cameron had adopted a hard line against illegal drugs as they devised policy platforms for the party. The charge of hypocrisy, a favorite of the tabloids, could have stuck.

But the *News of the World* published an accompanying editorial with a sympathetic tone. Though Osborne and Cameron faced questions about drug use, the paper, known for twisting the knife, wrote instead: "Osborne was a young man when he was caught up in this murky world." In its judgment, the Conservative Party leadership was still "Cameron's for the taking."

Cameron refused to answer questions about *his* possible youthful drug use. Thanks in part to the *News of the World*, Osborne and Cameron endured the headlines that week.

They looked for ways to build stronger ties to the media. Once firmly in place as leaders of their party, the two men discussed "politics and policy" over lunch one afternoon in January 2006 with Rupert Murdoch, Les Hinton, Rebekah Brooks, and Trevor Kavanagh, the *Sun*'s associate editor and chief political columnist.

When Andrew Coulson resigned from *News of the World* in early 2007, Osborne told Cameron that they wanted this man on their team. Coulson would be a conduit to Rebekah Brooks, his friend and mentor who was then editor of the *Sun*; and he would be their interpreter for all things Murdoch. The Conservatives had ignored warnings from the *Guardian* and elsewhere. A News International man stood inside Cameron's inner circle.

In June 2009, as she became CEO of News International, Rebekah Brooks emailed Coulson: "Have we any Tories coming to KRM party?" The initials stood for Keith Rupert Murdoch. Ten minutes later, Coulson replied: "I will encourage."

By July Cameron, the leader of the opposition, declared his hostility to the nation's media regulator, OfCom. It had recently angered News Corp executives by suggesting that Sky had too much control over movies and sport in the country. His social circle appreciated his stand. The Camerons and Brookses and Elisabeth Murdoch and her husband, Matthew Freud, all lived within fifteen miles of one another, in a particularly rustic corner of the Cotswolds called Chipping Norton. They dined, partied, and socialized together.

That August, Cameron dispatched Jeremy Hunt, the shadow minister of culture, media, and sport, to New York City to meet with executives at News Corp headquarters, including Rupert Murdoch. Hunt later maintained that the fate of BSkyB never came up during those meetings. A few weeks later, just days after his Edinburgh address, James Murdoch invited Cameron to drinks at the George, a private club in one of London's most exclusive neighborhoods. He revealed that Cameron could rely on News International's uniform and vigorous support.

So, in fancy restaurants, private clubs, corporate boardrooms and retreats, quiet dinners and boisterous garden parties, did Gordon Brown's hopes of retaining Murdoch's backing come undone.

THE SWITCH from Labour to Tory inspired a widespread conviction that Murdoch insisted on an act of fealty from his new political allies. "The perception is that, in return for Rupert Murdoch's support for David Cameron before the last election and subsequently . . . his Conservative government would pass through his bid for BSkyB," the *Independent*'s then editor in chief, Simon Kelner, told me later, though suspicions surfaced even at the time.

Murdoch biographer Michael Wolff said News International had additionally extracted promises to strip the BBC of some of its subsidy and to rein in regulators. Officials inside the company say there was never any such deal, merely an understanding that the government and the country's most powerful media company were philosophically aligned.

As the 2010 elections approached, Kelner's *Independent* ran a marketing campaign to underscore its identity supposedly free of outside influence. In its first full-page ad, the paper singled out the News Corp chairman: "Rupert Murdoch won't decide this election—you will." After a meeting in the same office complex, James Murdoch strode unbidden into the paper's offices with Brooks by his side, sought out Kelner and berated him as a "fucking fuckwit." As it happened, Elisabeth Murdoch's husband, Matthew Freud, one of Britain's leading PR executives, had advised the liberal paper on the campaign.

On May 6, 2010, Cameron and the Tories won the largest share of seats in Parliament but not an outright majority. They took office five days later after forging a coalition government with the Liberal Democrat Party. The following month, News Corp declared its intention to take over BSkyB. The business minister, Vince Cable, a Liberal Democrat not especially sympathetic to News Corp, had the role of determining the merits of its proposal to take over BSkyB.

Cable's assignment involved a decision in what was oddly called a "quasi-judicial" role that charged him to act more like a judge ruling on the merits of the case than a politician balancing competing public interests. He did not socialize with the Murdochs, as so many of his new colleagues in the Cabinet did. The company had plenty of other friends in government however. Education minister Michael Gove was a former *Times* editorialist. And James Murdoch's aides sought to mint new ones as they hoped to counter Cable's influence.

On September 15, 2010, four months after Cameron's camp took power, News Corp's chief lobbyist in the UK and Europe, Frederic

Michel, sent a text to the culture minister, Jeremy Hunt, about a story carried by the BBC. Sixteen minutes later Hunt wrote back that he hadn't seen the report.

The BSkyB deal was the most pressing priority for Michel. Inside News Corp, the project was code-named Rubicon, a fitting designation given how markedly it would remake the company's British operations. Hunt and his team adopted the nickname, too. An array of competitors, including the parent companies of the liberal *Guardian* and the conservative *Telegraph* newspapers, weighed in against the takeover. The BBC's director general, Mark Thompson, joined other media executives in opposition, though he was later criticized by the board overseeing the public broadcaster for getting involved.

Cable had referred the case to the independent regulator OfCom and commissioned an independent analysis from Claire Enders, a highly respected media industry analyst. She concluded that any takeover would lead to shared newsroom operations between Sky and the newspapers. She argued the combination would undermine, perhaps fatally, the continued existence of ITN, the third national television news operation after the BBC and Sky. (BSkyB also held an 18 percent stake in ITV, the network that was ITN's chief client.) And, Enders concluded, the unified company would control 22 percent of the nation's entire news market in print, television, and radio. This deal would create a risk, she wrote, "of a reduction in media plurality to an unacceptably low level."

News Corp officials countered that the digital age had ushered in rafts of new voices previously unheard to readers, listeners, and viewers throughout the UK. OfCom consisted of professional meddlers, the Murdoch camp felt. Even worse, the decision could be handed to the Competition Commission and reviewed anew on antitrust grounds too. In 1998 the Labour government had referred BSkyB's £623 million bid for the legendary football club Manchester

United to the commission, where it ultimately foundered. Rupert Murdoch had been livid.

It was time for Michel, James Murdoch's top European lobbyist, to ramp up his efforts.

Lobbyists traffic in information, ingratiation, and intimidation. Michel's emails and text messages suggest he focused on the first two. By chance, Hunt's child was born in the same hospital ward as Michel's baby; Michel sent Hunt notes that were nearly flirtatious in their solicitousness, playing on their mutual fatherhood.

In public, Hunt was alternately wary and eager toward the Murdochs; he praised News Corp effusively on his parliamentary website, yet hid behind a tree from a *Telegraph* reporter who spotted him ducking into a private dinner with James Murdoch.

In private, however, Hunt gossiped readily with Murdoch's top lobbyist. Hunt and Michel kibbitzed back and forth after the BBC's Mark Thompson defended the BBC's big government subsidy and criticized the Murdoch media. Hunt texted Michel not to worry: "because trained his guns on u he failed to make his case to me!"

On October 5, Michel and News International CEO Rebekah Brooks sat down with the media minister, with Michel recording that it was "a very useful meeting."

Michel also lined up government officials to attend various functions involving News International executives, playing to their interests and weaknesses. Sometimes his largess involved invitations to major sporting events such as Wimbledon, sometimes parties, sometimes policy, as in the case of deputy prime minister Nick Clegg, the Liberal Democrat leader who was invited to participate in an environmental summit convened by James Murdoch.

Michel constantly offered help to government officials. In October 2010, for example, he wrote to a prime minister's aide to send a letter circulated among CEOs that supported the new government's proposed budget cuts. "I would like to be able to show it to James asap for him to consider," Michel wrote on October 7.

But not everything was smooth sailing. That same week in October Michel wrote a worried note to Matthew Anderson, one of James Murdoch's top advisers, after meeting a senior aide to Cable. The aide had tied the company's predicament on BSkyB to the long-simmering questions over phone hacking. "There is real unease in Libdem ranks over Coulson and the relationship to NI [News International]. Simon Hughes, [the Liberal Democrats' deputy leader] is on a mission to make this an NI issue." The more the takeover is linked to *News of the World* and Murdoch's News International, Michel concluded, the more "toxic" it would become.

In November concern set in. On November 2, 2010, Cable asked OfCom to review the deal and set a December 31 deadline for the agency to forward its assessment. Cable's special assistant, Giles Wilkes, resisted Michel's entreaties. "What did you have in mind as an agenda?" Wilkes wrote back. "Obviously, there are huge risks to talking about anything to do with the OfCom business, which I would rule out; but I imagine that you chaps can think of little else right now, which leaves me puzzled."

On November 9, Michel texted an old friend. "Hi daddy!" he wrote to Hunt. "Can you meet James tomorrow morning for a catch-up? Would be good. Even early morning." Eventually they set a date for Hunt to meet with James Murdoch the following Monday. As it happened, Hunt then received direct legal advice that as the minister of culture, media, and sport, he should *not* meet with the chairman of a company that had major matters pending before a fellow cabinet official. He canceled.

When James Murdoch found out, he emailed his lobbyist: "You must be fucking joking. Fine. I will txt him and find a time." Hunt and Murdoch conducted their conversation by phone. Michel sent a thank-you text to Hunt the next day. But approval of Murdoch's BSkyB bid was far from guaranteed.

Inside government, Hunt channeled the News Corp cause and even lobbied the prime minister. "James Murdoch is pretty furious at Vince's referral [of the takeover] to OfCom," he started. "I am privately concerned about this because NewsCorp are very litigious and we could end up in the wrong place in terms of media policy."

Hunt invoked a historic moment for the media under the last heroic Tory prime minister. "Essentially what James Murdoch wants to do is to repeat what his father did with the move to Wapping and create the world's first multi-platform media operator, available from paper to web to TV to iPhone to iPad," he wrote, and added, "Isn't this what all media companies have to do ultimately?"

Rupert Murdoch's younger son was pushing to achieve what, in Secretary Hunt's description, anticipated an even further level of media domination. All the properties could integrate their content. Access to those properties could be tethered together, perhaps helping the newspapers to stabilize subscriptions after sustained and steep circulation losses. In that November 2010 memo, even as he envisioned this media bundling under a single roof, Hunt promised Cameron that safeguards could be put in place to ensure that a variety of voices would be audible in the media marketplace. He did so, however, by arguing that the market didn't have such distinct voices anyway. "I think it would be totally wrong to cave in to the Mark Thompson/Channel 4/*Guardian* line that this represents a substantial change of control," Hunt argued, "given that we all know Sky is controlled by News Corp now anyway."

The lobbied had become the lobbyist. Of course, Hunt wasn't the only one whose ear James Murdoch could bend. On November 7, James Murdoch and his family had joined the Camerons and other guests for a quiet lunch at Chequers, the prime minister's official countryside getaway.

In confidential memos to regulators and officials, lawyers for News Corp made seemingly contradictory arguments. On the one hand, a takeover would represent no big deal. "News and Sky are already deemed to be a single media voice for the purposes of plurality," lawyers for the company wrote, plurality being the shorthand of choice for concerns over concentration of ownership of news outlets. "UK Authorities have assumed that News exercises material influence over Sky."

News Corp held 39.1 percent of voting rights, but those votes enabled it to control the board. Its officials and allies sat as BSkyB's directors.

On the other hand, the company's lawyers were also arguing that there was no coordination between the agendas set in Sky's newsroom with those of the four News International papers, as a result of the two companies' separate corporate structures. British laws requiring impartiality by its television journalists would protect Sky's news judgment against any encroachment by corporate interests or the ideological leanings of its sibling newspaper editors.

Vince Cable was unmoved. "I am picking my fights, some of which you may have seen," Cable said in mid-December, speaking to two constituents, who were actually undercover reporters for the *Telegraph*. "You may wonder what is happening with the Murdoch press. I have declared war on Mr. Murdoch, and I think we're going to win."

Earlier that day, Hunt had been exchanging text messages with James Murdoch, congratulating him on winning approval from European regulators to acquire Sky outright. News Corp owned 45 percent of Sky Deutschland, the leading supplier of pay-TV services in Germany, and 100 percent of Sky Italia, which performed the same role in Italy.

"Just OfCom to go!" Hunt exulted.

The Cable recordings about Murdoch were posted and broadcast by the BBC on December 21, 2010. Peculiarly, the *Telegraph* posted its scoop second, in the middle of that afternoon. The *Telegraph* had published other remarks by Cable the day before but had not yet made the Murdoch comments public; internally, some *Telegraph* staffers wondered whether that was because their proprietors, the Barclay brothers, wanted the BSkyB bid to fail and so editors did not seek to damage Cable's standing.

Hunt and Murdoch already had a 4:00 PM call scheduled. Eight minutes later, Hunt texted Chancellor George Osborne: "Cld we chat about Murdoch Sky bid am seriously worried we are going to screw this up. Jeremy." Hunt then shot off another note: "Just been called by James M. His lawyers are meeting now and saying it calls into question legitimacy of whole process from beginning 'acute bias' etc."

The government scrambled to find a fair-minded person to take Cable's place. Who could fulfill the delicate role?

Within the hour, Osborne texted back to Hunt: "I hope you like our solution."

Cable was taken off the case; Prime Minister Cameron announced Hunt would judge the BSkyB deal himself.

Two days later, on December 23, the younger Murdoch dined with the Camerons and several other couples, an event arranged and hosted by Rebekah Brooks. Truly, the November and December meals were social affairs, Murdoch later testified.

———

CABLE CAME in for widespread condemnation. But he had been assigned an impossible task. His apparent prejudice against the Murdochs was matched by Hunt's advocacy. All government ministers are also elected members of Parliament, and are partisan political figures. Hunt was popular with rank-and-file Tory MPs, a telegenic former entrepreneur who had set up a charity to benefit Africans. He was exactly the fresh face Conservatives wanted to put forward under

Cameron. Yet he was also a child of privilege, the son of a knighted admiral, and a contemporary of the prime minister and London mayor Boris Johnson at Oxford. In the words of the British Press Association, he was considered a pair of safe hands.

This time around, however, those hands were not altogether steady. He came off as eager to a fault. (The playwright Alan Bennett wrote, "Jeremy Hunt has the look of an estate agent waiting to show someone a property.")

Hunt's team worked with Michel to make sure there were no surprises for either Murdoch or Hunt. One matter had to be resolved. Earlier the previous year, the *Guardian* had revealed that London's leading celebrity PR executive Max Clifford had been paid £1 million to drop his own phone hacking claim against *News of the World*. Lawyers signed up celebrities and other prominent figures who believed they had been targeted by the tabloid and demanded that police hand over information. By fall 2010, lawyers for the actress Sienna Miller had uncovered evidence that they said implicated the newspaper in widespread hacking. James Murdoch later said that was the first moment he learned of credible evidence of the practice's reach at his paper. Just before Christmas, the paper suspended its assistant editor for news, Ian Edmondson.

The public had yet again paid scant notice. But the presence of Andrew Coulson at 10 Downing Street underscored Prime Minister Cameron's links to Murdoch and the *News of the World*. That same day, James Murdoch, Michel, his adviser Matt Anderson, and another aide met with Hunt and his inner circle. According to Michel's minutes, Hunt flagged that he was likely to accept legal advice to refer the purchase of BSkyB to the Competition Commission. But he stressed that he could be swayed by evidence that any change in the number of independent news sources in the UK caused by the takeover would not materially affect the public interest. Hunt pushed Murdoch not to submit anew the arguments made to OfCom—but to make his case for why its conclusions were mistaken.

News Corp, in response, stressed that Hunt had the power to accept remedies before any such referral. The two sides were in sync, playing in tune and in tempo.

Pressure mounted on Coulson and Cameron. Michel texted Gabby Bertin, another press aide for the prime minister. "Good support for andy by the boss on R4 [Radio 4]. Good stuff. Keep the pressure guys! XX"

On January 23, Michel emailed James Murdoch, clearly informed about Hunt's intentions on BSkyB, though they were not yet public. The company had privately promised an "undertaking in lieu" (UIL in government jargon) to spin off Sky News, so judgment over news coverage for Sky would be handled by a different corporation than news coverage for News Corp's newspapers. That remedy could address concerns about media concentration and was an easy concession to make, given the modest size of Sky News (it had just 5 percent of the TV news audience) and modest financial importance. Hunt was moving to accept but would delay announcing any decision, allowing News Corp to arrange its ducks in a row.

Hunt "still wants to stick to the following plan," Michel wrote. "His view is that once he announces publicly he has a strong UIL, it's almost game over for the opposition. He very specifically said he was keen to get to the same outcome and wanted JRM [James Rupert (Jacob) Murdoch] to understand he needs to build some political cover on the process." Michel continued, "He [Hunt] said we would get there at the end and he shared our objectives."

Michel sent this MRI of Hunt's thinking forty-eight hours before the minister was supposed to reveal his position in the House of Commons. The next day, Michel followed with another email, this one even more breathless, to Murdoch.

"Confidential: Managed to get some infos on the plans for tomorrow (although absolutely illegal!). Press statement at 7.30am . . . Lots of legal issues around the statement so he has tried to get a version which helps us . . . JH will announce . . . that he wishes to look at any undertakings that have the potential to prevent the potential threats of media plurality."

As the *Guardian* later noted, Michel had provided his company's chairman with "the wording of Hunt's crucial, and market-sensitive, official statement, due to be delivered the next day." Hunt would later claim a top aide, Adam Smith, had shared the material without approval.

Hunt's formal announcement came on January 25, and it was a boon to the Murdochs.

The next day, Ian Edmondson's suspension, linked to hacking, was reported by rival papers. Coulson resigned from government, likewise reiterating his innocence, but adding, "When the spokesman needs a spokesman, it's time to move on." Murdoch critic and Labor MP Tom Watson got in a sharp dig: "This is the second job that Andy Coulson has resigned from for something he claims to know nothing about."

The hacking scandal had slipped inside 10 Downing Street.

———

HUNT AND his colleagues were constantly monitoring perceptions; one aide warned him against meeting with Andy Coulson for a drink: "Think it might be best to wait till news corp process is over," special adviser Sue Beeby wrote. "He's so closely linked to them that if you were seen it wouldn't look great. I'm sure he would understand."

David Cameron decided to keep links to the former PR aide and Murdoch editor, though he did not advertise them. Coulson dined with him at Chequers and stayed the night. But the prime minister's own advisers remained wary. On March 3, 2011, Craig Oliver, who replaced Coulson as Cameron's top PR official, sent Hunt a note: "View emerging that Murdoch will pull a fast one on selling Sky News—needs assurances that won't happen." Hunt told the press adviser he was confident the Murdochs would keep their word and he would convey that message in public.

Hunt had received the OfCom conclusions more than two months earlier, on New Year's Eve, the deadline initially requested by Cable.

But Hunt waited until March 3 to announce them. The independent media regulator OfCom had accepted News Corp's UIL as addressing the plurality of voices presenting news coverage, though not market concentration issues. But Hunt said a ruling of the European Commission had handled the concentration concerns back in December, and therefore no longer mattered. He spoke for twelve minutes on the floor of the House of Commons, and announced he had decided not to refer the decision to the British Competition Commission.

"You were great at the Commons today," Michel texted from his iPhone. A few days and texts later, Hunt responded, "Merci hopefully when consultation over we can have a coffee like the old days!"

The parties, the fund-raising, the dinners, the meetings, the personal blandishments, all the connections before the scandal would surely accrue to News Corp's benefit. But the regulatory review would take months. And the longer the process stretched out, the more it could trip up News Corp.

News of the World won a break when the murder case against its former investigator Jonathan Rees fell apart in March 2011. That was not due to a lack of evidence, but rather a surfeit: Rees's defense lawyers would be unable to review adequately 750,000 pages going back two dozen years to ensure a fair trial. (The *Guardian* hinted that the past corruption of police officers had compromised prosecutors' ability to get a conviction. Rees maintained his innocence throughout.)

But the next month incurred more damaging disclosures. News International admitted phone hacking at *News of the World* from 2004 through 2006 involved more people than previously had been believed. The company offered what it called "unreserved apologies" and money for a limited number of cases. They were the famous, wealthy, people. Labour MPs, who could have scored damaging points against News Corp and their Tory friends in government, held back in Parliament. Most were shackled or shamed by their own party's links to the Murdochs and News International. It was a land mine but did not trigger right away.

That came a few days later, when the Murdochs' leading Sunday tabloid was found to have hacked into the phone of a dead girl.

13

THE YARD

———————

THE EXPLOSIVE CHARGES UNLEASHED BY the blockbuster *Guardian* piece were not limited to hacking. They also placed Murdoch's tabloid papers at the center of a related corruption scandal that not only threatened his journalists but wreaked great damage at Scotland Yard.

Few of the illegal acts taken by the tabloids could have been accomplished without the active involvement of the police throughout the ranks. Similarly, the reporters and editors and their investigators practicing journalism in the shadows could never have gotten away with hacking "on an industrial scale" had senior police officials not decided that allegations of wrongdoing did not merit pursuit, sometimes as they were receiving gifts from News International executives.

Such concerns had surfaced years earlier. Back in 2003, when she was still editor of the *Sun*, Rebekah Brooks testified before a parliamentary committee holding hearings about the press and privacy. Labour MP Chris Bryant asked Brooks whether her newspaper—whether *she*—had ever paid the police for information. Brooks replied, "We have paid the police for information in the past, yes."

Asked whether she would do it again in the future, Brooks said, "It depends," prompting an interruption by her friend and fellow witness Andrew Coulson.

"We operate within the code and within the law, and if there's a clear public interest," Coulson said. "The same holds for private detectives, for subterfuge, for [hidden] video bags, whatever you want to talk about."

Bryant recognized the importance of the two editors' admission: "It's illegal for police officers to receive payments."

COULSON: "No, no, no. I just said—within the law."

Bryant was right. In paying police, the papers had acted outside the law. But under Prime Minister Tony Blair's leadership, there was little appetite to confront newspapers. Rather, as Blair would later testify, his government's officials sought to "manage" them, as best they could.

After that 2003 appearance before Bryant's committee, Brooks refused requests by MPs to answer more questions about paying police. Several lawmakers with the Commons Select Committee on Culture, Media, and Sport later told reporters they decided against compelling her testimony in significant part because its chairman had privately warned that her papers might retaliate by investigating their personal lives. (He denied warning lawmakers against such questions.)

Each subsequent installment of the tabloid scandals inspired more hearings, first in 2007, after the conviction of Goodman and Mulcaire, and again in 2009, after the *Guardian*'s piece on the Gordon Taylor settlement. In March 2011, Labour MP Jim Sheridan asked Assistant Police Commissioner John Yates: "Do you declare how much, if any, is paid by newspapers for stories that are given out by police?"

"As I think we all know, it is illegal to pay for stories from the police, and if we did have information about it, we would investigate it," Yates replied.

SHERIDAN: "So, that does not happen, then?"

YATES: "It has happened on very rare occasions, and where we have found out about it, we have caught them and they have gone to prison."

Not so very rare, it turned out. But rarely found out, and almost invariably unpunished. Time and time again, it was later alleged, police officers were paid for phone data and other information on databases that are by law confidential. The existence of payments had been a relatively common practice in the UK for decades. But it had started small, with a reporter buying a police officer or desk sergeant a beer (or three) at a pub, occasionally a fancy dinner, perhaps a free ticket to a soccer match. Reporters in cities across the globe routinely take sources out for a drink or a bite. In the UK, hard currency became a journalistic emollient. By American standards, such payments were considered both unethical and counterproductive.

From the *New York Times* ethics code: "We do not pay for interviews or unpublished documents: to do so would create an incentive for sources to falsify material and would cast into doubt the genuineness of much that we publish." Several leading news organizations, including the *Los Angeles Times* and NPR News, simply state they do not pay sources for information.

In the practice of British respectable media outlets, such actions are not entirely banned. The BBC, for example, cautions its reporters: "Payment or payment in kind to criminals, former criminals, their families or their associates (directly or indirectly) for interviews or other contributions relating to their crimes, must be referred to Director Editorial Policy and Standards." Similar warnings stand for other, analogous situations, but clearly envision circumstances that warrant or at least tolerate payments to sources for information. In 2009 the *Telegraph* paid the equivalent of $165,000 (£110,000) to obtain digital records of the expense accounts of members of Parliament from a government employee, arguably a violation of British law. However, the *Telegraph*'s coverage, generously ladled out in daily installments that rotated the focus of attention among the three major parties, led to an uproar over lawmakers who secured reimbursement for highly questionable personal expenses.

In the US, the professionalization of the news industry in the decades after Watergate and the relatively pristine codes of conduct that emerged tended to keep journalists at mainstream news organizations out of trouble. The spirit of such codes can be brushed aside, however, when a story turns out to be too tantalizing to resist.

ABC and NBC spent lavishly in pursuing interview subjects for their morning shows and their prime-time newsmagazines. Both networks had policies banning payments to people for participating in interviews. But producers would fly people to New York City and put them up at four- and five-star hotels. Occasionally a booker would be punished for paying for shopping sprees as well. (The hotel rooms, kept secret, had the added incentive of quarantining people from prying competitors.)

Networks evaded their own rules in other ways as well. In March 2010, Casey Anthony, a Florida woman accused of killing her two-year-old daughter Caylee, sought public support to pay fees for defense lawyers. The presiding judge asked how she had paid for the lawyers previously. Her lawyer disclosed that ABC News had paid her $200,000 for exclusive rights to use videotape footage and photographs of her then missing toddler for a story on *Good Morning America* and an hour-long treatment on the newsmagazine *20/20* later that night. No interview was granted, however, the shield behind which producers hid to justify the payment. ABC soon changed its policy.

American supermarket tabloids make no apologies for paying their sources and interview subjects. Iain Calder, editor in chief of the *National Enquirer*, once boasted that he had an impeccable source after comedian Tom Arnold angrily denounced the weekly tabloid for its coverage of his wedding and marriage to Roseanne Barr. Calder appeared on live television and held up a copy of a canceled check the *Enquirer* had given to Arnold. Arnold's signature was visible on the back.

In the UK, the home of freewheeling papers that combined serious news with a ferocious hunger for gossip, the law was actually much stricter than in the US. An official secrets act dictated what information news organizations could publish, post, or broadcast about national security. In addition, laws protecting privacy achieved their goal at the cost of the public's ability to gain information.

Reporters who considered such privacy strictures absurd thought little of payments or ruses to jump-start the flow of information. "It was almost industry standard," Paul McMullan, former deputy features editor for the *News of the World*, told me. The *News of the World* might not have been able to pinpoint the mobile numbers for Princes William and Harry had they not acquired the master manual for the royal family from several members of the royals' security detail, who, it was alleged, sold the phone numbers and contact information for the royal family, the princes, and their associates and friends.

Such information could yield the movements of Queen Elizabeth II. As head of state, the queen makes a ripe target for terrorists; her husband's uncle, Lord Mountbatten, was assassinated in a 1979 bombing by an offshoot of the IRA. Yet senior police officials overseeing the hacking investigation did not explore how the paper's investigator got his hands on the manual.

Perhaps editors at the two News International titles had cause for confidence because they had worked so closely over the years with the police. For two decades, another senior editor at *News of the World*, Alex Marunchak, had served as a paid translator for police investigations involving Ukrainian suspects. He stopped in 2000. In 2001 the paper's chief correspondent and former news editor, Neville Thurlbeck, had been an unpaid police informant, while still on the staff of the paper.

Thurlbeck had first joined the paper in 1988 and had held a number of posts, including chief investigations editor and news editor before settling back in as chief correspondent. A man who outwardly conveyed he held the high cards in almost any hand, Thurlbeck carried himself with élan and was not easily flustered. His targets included some of the nation's most famous names. His articles had proved that Lord Jeffrey Archer, a prominent Tory politician and best-selling author, had perjured himself in court testimony. Thurlbeck also landed a scandalous on-the-record interview with an Australian model who claimed to have had an affair with British soccer star David Beckham.

Some of his record was seedier than his manner might suggest. Thurlbeck had been caught on video pleasuring himself at a British nudist retreat after conducting a hidden camera investigation (earning the sobriquet "Onan the Barbarian"). For another story, he blackmailed women who had taken part in a sex party into giving interviews.

In 2001, a judge gave his blessing for Thurlbeck's arrangement with police to serve as a back-channel source for police in exchange for information from a secret intelligence database, terming it proper and declining to allow prosecution on corruption charges. A year later, at the height of the search for Milly Dowler, journalists from *News of the World* made no secret to police of the fact that the paper had been listening to her mobile voice mail messages—even though that might have reasonably led police to ask themselves whether the paper had broken the law.

Some of the messages to Milly Dowler simply vanished from her mobile mailbox. At the time, Detective Constable John Lyndon of the Surrey police wrote in a private note, "In light of the *News of the World* revelation that they or a third party has accessed the voicemail it is possible that the messages had previously been listened to by unknown persons and deleted." Indeed, reporters seeking to pry confirmations out of police offered an increasingly detailed glimpse of what they had heard on the girl's phone messages. Police knew of the voice mail hacking—the paper had all but boasted of it—and yet still they detected no crime.

On July 5, 2011, the day after the *Guardian* published its Milly Dowler hacking exposé, the *Times of London* reported police had been given evidence showing illegal payments to police officers by *News of the World* journalists between 2003 and 2007—which coincided almost precisely with Andy Coulson's editorship. The next morning, Sir Paul Stephenson, the commissioner of the Metropolitan Police, or Scotland Yard, indicated that lawyers for News International had passed along information disclosing the paper's illegal payments to what he termed "a small number" of officers. No evidence had emerged so far to implicate senior officials, he said.

Labour MP Tom Watson instantly charged the *Times of London* with doing the company's dirty work: hanging Coulson out to dry while seeking to distract attention from Rebekah Brooks, by then CEO. The *Times of London*, Murdoch's most prestigious UK title, had previously displayed little tolerance for those who took phone hacking seriously. But Coulson was incidental to Rupert Murdoch, and little more than a useful tool to James Murdoch. Rupert considered Brooks part of the family.

Others saw the accusation of corrupting police as a far more serious offense than phone hacking. In his statement, Stephenson acknowledged a second dimension to the police scandal: the coziness between top police officers and Murdoch's executives.

That first hacking investigation in 2005 had been badly botched. Assistant commissioner Andrew Hayman, who led the police's investigation, was, at the same time dining at pricey restaurants with senior British News Corp executives, with the company repeatedly footing the bill. (His former boss periodically also had meals with News International executives at expensive spots.)

On July 12, 2011, members of Parliament bluntly questioned Hayman, connecting the dots between the fifty quid slipped into the palm of a constable and the behavior of the police executives who oversaw the force. "Mr. Hayman, while a police officer, did you ever receive payment from any news organization?" one MP asked.

"Good God! Absolutely not!" Hayman replied. "I can't believe you suggested that."

"Lots of people did," the lawmaker countered.

"Oh, come on," Hayman said. "I'm not letting you get away with that. Absolutely no way."

He said he never discussed the hacking inquiry with his dining companions from News International, despite their direct interest in the outcome. Hayman left the force at the end of 2007 and fulfilled what he later said had been a lifetime ambition—becoming a paid columnist for Murdoch's *Times of London* in summer 2008. Roy Greenslade, former assistant editor of the *Sun*, recalled that reporters and police fraternized over drinks in his day, but said real money never changed hands. "If you think that senior policemen who were supposed to be investigating the *News of the World* were also enjoying dinners and meals with executives from the *News of the World*, you would have to say that is a corrupt or corrupting practice," said Greenslade, later a columnist for the *Evening Standard* and the *Guardian*, "even if, and this beggars belief, . . . when they sat down for hours at that meal they never once referred to that inquiry."

Hayman's deputy, Peter Clarke, took over responsibility for the hacking investigation at the time. But he was also overseeing the Met's antiterror operations in the UK, which he set as his chief priority. The man who replaced him two years later in that role—assistant commissioner John Yates—also said the force put greater priority on combating terrorism than casting a wide net on the hacking allegations. The memories of the bloody bus and Tube bombings that killed dozens and paralyzed London in July 2005 were all too fresh.

In July 2009, at the time the *Guardian* newspaper exposed News International's secret payment to Gordon Taylor and revealed the existence of hundreds of other potential instances of illegal voice mail hacking, Yates had little appetite for pursuing leads. After a review of the past inquiry that lasted not days but hours, Yates announced no further investigation was needed.

At the time, Andy Hayman chimed in with supportive columns that ran in the *Times of London* and the *News of the World.* "We put our best detectives on the case and left no stone unturned as officials breathed down our neck," Hayman wrote.

"As I recall the list of those targeted, which was put together from records kept by [the paper's private eye, Glenn] Mulcaire, ran to several hundred names. Of these, there was a small number—perhaps a handful—where there was evidence they had actually been tampered with," Hayman wrote. "Had there been evidence of tampering in the other cases, that would have been investigated, as would the slightest hint that others were involved." And then, in a coup de grâce, Hayman wrote, "Yet, as is so often the case, in the storm of allegation and denial the facts get lost. Well-known figures such as John Prescott are said to have been victims of the hacking without any clear evidence that their phones were in fact hacked into."

Lord Prescott's two-year affair with a secretary while serving as deputy prime minister had been disclosed by the tabloid and had badly damaged his public standing. Prescott had been repeatedly told by police he was not a target of phone hacking by *News of the World.* In January 2012, years after Hayman's column and months after the Dowler revelations, News International admitted it had in fact intercepted private messages and paid him £40,000 (about $66,000) in damages. Only then did the police apologize.

In New York, News Corp executives monitored the developments lightly and with relief. The declarations by police were good enough for them. The board did not formally review the matter—it was a local nuisance that could be handled in Britain.

Yates clung to the justification that a crime would have required proof that the person whose voice mail had been hacked had not listened to the violated message first. The Crown Prosecution Service later explicitly rejected that interpretation of the law.

Like Hayman, Yates of the Yard (as he was inevitably dubbed in coverage) repeatedly dined with editors of *News of the World* and executives from News International. In November 2009, he met with the tabloid's crime editor and the paper's new editor in chief, Colin Myler, at the Ivy, a restaurant known for its famous clientele and pricey fare. The Ivy charged about $125 per person, and $220 for a nice bottle of Bordeaux. Everything proper about it, Yates insisted in the moment: all such contacts were promptly disclosed online, per police guidelines.

Yates later admitted having at least ten meals with Neil Wallis between April 2009 and August 2010 that had not been disclosed publicly. Wallis was a public relations official who had just stepped down as the number two editor at *News of the World*. Those meals took place at restaurants that were among the most exclusive in the city. They also attended professional soccer games together, by Wallis's account. And none of those contacts was publicly disclosed.

In October 2010, a suspicious package was singled out at the UPS hangar at East Midlands Airport in England. The box contained a toner cartridge with wires sticking out. Initial testing detected the presence of explosive material. The package was sent from Yemen with a label designating a Chicago synagogue as its destination. President Obama and UK home secretary Teresa May issued statements registering their concern and dismay.

The *News of the World* felt it had an inside line to an international story with scary implications. An editor on the news desk emailed Lucy Panton, the crime editor. "John Yates could be crucial here. Have you spoken to him?" The news desk editor wrote he wanted a splashy headline for the front page: "so time to call in all those bottles of champagne."

Wallis's daughter also had a job on the force—a job that she got thanks to a plug from Yates. On January 29, 2009, Yates wrote to the head of Scotland Yard's human resources office: "Bit of advice, plse—the attached CV belongs to the daughter of Neil Wallis, the De-p[uty] Editor of the *News of the World*. You probably know that Neil has been a great friend (and occasional critic) of the Met in past years and has been a close advisor to Paul [Stephenson] on stuff/tactics in respect of the new Commissionership."

Stephenson had been elevated to police commissioner the day before. By October 2009, Wallis had left the paper and was on a £2,000 (about $3,200) monthly contract to the force, answering to PR chief Dick Fedorcio and Yates, newly head of antiterrorism efforts. The Wallis appointment was not formally vetted. Instead, Yates simply wrote Fedorcio: "Is there anything in the matters that [the *Guardian*'s] Nick Davies is still chasing and reporting on, that could at any stage embarrass you, Mr Wallis, me, the Commissioner or the Metropolitan police?" Yates said he received "categorical assurances" there was not.

At moments the membrane separating the two institutions seemed so porous as to be effectively absent. When I interviewed Paul McMullan, the former reporter and editor at *News of the World*, he made this casual slip of the tongue: "A few times, I was put on stories that came from police force employees—sorry—they weren't employees. Coppers we paid for good information."

The connections between the papers and the police were perhaps best personified by the *Sun*'s annual awards banquet, which recognized bravery and distinction among police officers. The decades-old practice enabled editors including Rebekah Brooks and her successor, Dominic Mohan, to cement their favored position with police and prominent politicians.

On the evening of July 7, despite the growing clamor about News International, Prime Minister David Cameron joined both at the *Sun*'s black tie affair at the five-star Savoy Hotel, featuring special appearances by the British soap opera star and victims' rights advocate Brooke Kinsella, among other luminaries. Cameron had also attended the dinner the year before. His predecessor, Gordon Brown, had done much the same when he was prime minister. But this was different: the phone hacking scandal had precipitated a crisis within the ranks of the country's top media and law enforcement echelons and denunciations from parliamentary benches front and back. Yet there was Cameron, outwardly in good cheer, circulating amid the nation's tabloid and police chieftains.

The next day, on the morning of July 8, his former communications director, onetime *News of the World* editor Andy Coulson, was arrested on charges related to the phone hacking and corruption of public officials, which he firmly denied.

Commissioner Stephenson found himself confronting prickly questions. Earlier that year, while on sick leave, he accepted hospitality worth £12,000 from Champneys, a luxury spa and retreat in the British countryside, as he recuperated from an illness. Champneys was one of Wallis's PR clients. It was run by one of Brooks's friends. Stephenson said he was unaware of such links. Later that month Stephenson and Yates resigned within a day of each other.

14

"GOODBYE,
CRUEL WORLD"

IN THE EARLY DAYS OF the summer of 2011 the Murdochs and News Corp's British executives were moving confidently to take ownership of BSkyB, the lawsuits seemed no more than an irritation and embarrassment, and the bombshell involving the Dowlers had yet to detonate. Prime Minister Cameron attended the News Corp annual garden party at which the Murdochs held court. (Labour leader Ed Miliband attended too.) "David [Cameron] was in great form," News Corp's top lobbyist for the UK and Europe, Frederic Michel, texted to Craig Oliver, the prime minister's communications director. Cameron saw Rupert Murdoch twice more that month: at a breakfast on the morning of June 20 and at a dinner for a summit of CEOs convened by the *Times of London* the same night.

On June 27 Rebekah Brooks had emailed Michel to ask when Jeremy Hunt would share his thinking on Rubicon—the acquisition. Michel replied that it would play out within days and that Hunt believed "phone-hacking has nothing to do with the media plurality issue." The secretary would extend a review of privacy concerns to all newspaper groups. In addition, Michel wrote, Hunt "has asked me to advise him privately in the coming weeks and guide his and No. 10's positioning."

By this point, Michel was puffing up his role; the lobbyist was in closer contact with Hunt's special adviser Adam Smith than Hunt himself. But the two sides—News Corp and media ministry—operated hand in glove. On July 3 Michel texted Hunt at the Wimbledon men's tennis finals and suggested a round of drinks. "Let's do that when all over," Hunt replied.

On July 4 the *Guardian* published the Milly Dowler story. For News International, time accelerated and yet stood still. All the suspicions, all the prejudices fueled a swelling chorus from defeated rivals, abandoned political allies, and targets of the company's coverage.

Blue chip companies withdrew their ads from *News of the World:* Sainsburys grocery chain, pharmacy giant Boots, Halifax bank, even Ford Motor's UK division. Others, such as T-Mobile, signaled they would tolerate only so much more scandal before jumping ship.

Brooks was among those who instantly registered the stakes. On July 5, 2011, as new accusations were mounting, she wrote a memo assuring staffers she'd stick around to lead the company to resolve this crisis. "I hope that you all realise it is inconceivable that I knew or worse, sanctioned these appalling allegations."

The accusations in the *Guardian* that her company—*her own newspaper*—had hacked into Milly Dowler's phone cut to the heart of Brooks's professional identity. "I am proud of the many successful newspaper campaigns at *The Sun* and the *News of the World* under my editorship," she wrote, citing her work against sexual offenders. "The battle for better protection of children from paedophiles and better rights for the families and the victims of these crimes defined my editorships. Although these difficult times will continue for many months ahead, I want you to know that News International will pursue the facts with vigour and integrity."

PRIME MINISTER David Cameron was fighting battles on several fronts, seeking to protect his shaky standing among political allies and fending off attacks from opponents. He did not yet frontally attack the Murdochs, his champions in the press, but by this point, restraint was a relative term. "What has taken place is absolutely disgusting, and I think everyone in this House, and indeed this country, will be revolted by what they have heard and seen on their television screens," Cameron told MPs in the House of Commons.

Cameron's opponents in the Labour Party ridiculed him. His Liberal Democrat partners in the governing coalition undermined him by demanding that a judge lead a wide-ranging inquiry. Cameron resisted those calls, instead urging police to follow the evidence wherever it might lead and promising that full inquiries into hacking and the press would follow, probably after criminal prosecutions had played out. He could not interfere, Cameron argued, in the BSkyB process, where his culture minister, Jeremy Hunt, was playing a "quasi-judicial role": "What we have done is follow, absolutely to the letter, the correct legal processes. That is what the Government have to do."

Hunt's department stopped accepting public comment on BSkyB Friday, July 8, and announced that its decision would come shortly. The juxtaposition of the BSkyB deal with the roiling scandal could not have been worse. Cameron's idea of an inquiry after criminal prosecutions—potentially hundreds of them—presupposed a delay of years, long after any verdict on BSkyB.

Even some of Cameron's fellow Conservatives stood up to object and directed their ire at the person they previously viewed as an untouchable power. "Rupert Murdoch is clearly a very, very talented businessman. He's possibly even a genius, but his organization has grown too powerful and it has abused that power," Tory MP Zac Goldsmith said on the floor of the House of Commons. "It has systematically corrupted the police and, in my view, it has gelded this Parliament, to our shame."

Rupert Murdoch had put out a statement late on July 6 in his own name that was meant to show his concern. He called the actions of *News of the World* "deplorable and unacceptable," but delivered a dissonant vote of support for Brooks. The message was meant to soothe public opinion but only served to inflame it. Many MPs had already called for Brooks's resignation and pressed for a hold on the BSkyB deal.

"These were not the actions of a 'rogue' individual or a 'rogue' reporter, but part of a wider, systematic pattern of abuses," said Labour leader Ed Miliband. "The public see a major news organization in this country where no one appears prepared to take responsibility for what happens. Nobody is denying that Milly Dowler's phone was hacked and nobody is denying that it happened on the watch of the current chief executive of News International, who was editor of the newspaper at the time." He concluded by asking Cameron to join him in calling for Brooks's resignation. Miliband also invoked Cameron's decision to hire Brooks's former deputy Andrew Coulson, who was now under police scrutiny.

"Is it not the case that if the public are to have confidence in him, he must do the thing that is most difficult and accept that he made a catastrophic judgment in bringing Andy Coulson into the heart of his Downing Street machine?"

After a few cautious days, Miliband declared Labour's independence from the Murdochs and News Corp. The scandal had inverted the formula of accommodation and courtship, as those politicians who recently had scurried for face time with Rupert and James Murdoch and their wives and executives now competed to denounce them most roundly.

But amid the deluge of scandal, News Corp lobbyist Fred Michel still labored behind the scenes—far behind the scenes—to maintain a sense of shared purpose between the government and the corporation. On the day after the *Guardian* piece, July 5, Michel wrote to Cameron's chief spokeswoman, Gabby Bertin, thanking her for her supportive messages to Brooks. Both Bertin and Michel ended their texts with multiple Xs—for kisses.

Michel texted Cameron's communications director, Craig Oliver: "Hey buddy. Are you guys still on for dinner tomorrow?" Oliver wrote back: "Looking forward to tonight. Is location discreet?" News International executive Will Lewis would join the dinner, first set for Pimlico. But everything about the appointment kept shifting amid the bedlam. The spot was moved to an intimate French restaurant in the upscale neighborhood of Mayfair, not far from Whitehall. The time moved, too. Lewis backed out, leaving just Michel and Oliver.

Bertin texted Michel during dinner. "Another hard core day," she wrote the lobbyist. He replied swiftly (ellipses his):

"Yes . . . mon dieu . . . incredible," he wrote. "Am with Craig now. DC [David Cameron] was very good at PMQ [Prime Minister's Questions]. We need to get through this. You ok? Xx"

On July 7 Michel thanked Oliver for dinner. He didn't hear back.

By that point, opinion had turned against the BSkyB bid. Only a day remained for the public commenting period; more than 130,000 people took advantage of the chance to besiege Hunt's department with emails and messages objecting to News Corp's plans. Michel and his patrons were running out of cards to play.

"They've used their power, in ways we know about and ways that we don't know about," former *Independent* editor in chief Simon Kelner told me at the time. "What we've seen this week is not just the first cracks of the edifice, but you've seen the edifice possibly begin to tumble."

"Politicians have suddenly become a lot braver," Kelner added. "One of the least edifying elements in this phone hacking scandal has been the number of Labour politicians who have spent all their time sucking up to Murdoch. Now they're in opposition, they are denouncing him."

Reliably conservative papers, the *Telegraph* and the *Daily Mail*, had started to take the story seriously. The *Telegraph* reported that the tabloid had hacked the phones of British soldiers and terror victims as well. The story would not stop.

At Wapping, it was beginning to feel like the end of the world. The *News of the World* tabloid had been a presence on the British scene for 168 years. Before Murdoch entered the scene, the paper had paid a call girl more than £20,000 for a salacious story that fatally wounded the government of Prime Minister Harold Macmillan. Under Murdoch six years later, the paper didn't just tell her story. It serialized her memoir in eight parts over two months.

The *News of the World* held onto its role as the leading red-top tabloid. It published just enough reporting about public events so readers knew what was happening in the world. By the 2000s the paper's reporters had so internalized the need to gain scoops that it thought nothing of paying off a cop to get an unlisted mobile number to convince someone with a tangential link to a celebrity or sports star or actor or singer or prince into giving an interview to the paper. The stories weren't quite fabricated but heavily produced by the reporters. Former investigative reporter Graham Johnson catalogues a tawdry line of such stories in his book *Hack*. In one case, he picked up a woman who had become a prostitute patronizing upper-end hotels and decamped with her for the night, solely as a means of writing a story that would embarrass her father, a law lord. The plan went off-kilter when the escort took a shine to him and started to perform a sexual act upon him, one of the few lines that he was not supposed to cross, as it could be used to discredit the paper's reporting in court.

The paper's best-known reporter might well have been Mazher Mahmood, who claimed his reporting had led to the prosecution of more than 250 people. Mahmood often posed as an Arab sheik or some other shadowy figure whose money corrupted prominent people, Sarah, the Duchess of York, and the Pakistani national cricket team among them. The fact that his exposés largely created the scandals he revealed did not faze him: he described himself as "the king of the sting" in the subtitle to a memoir.

As indictments loomed, the Murdochs began the effort to draw a different line, to take a bold stance. The moment required a sacrifice.

NEWS CORP announced the decision with statements reflecting regretful necessity, promising a shift of strategy and outlook. "The *News of the World* is in the business of holding others to account. But it failed when it came to itself," James Murdoch declared in a statement sent to News International employees and shared with government officials and the press.

"*News of the World* and News International failed to get to the bottom of repeated wrongdoing that occurred without conscience or legitimate purpose." The younger Murdoch acknowledged that News International officials had "made statements to Parliament without being in full possession of the facts" and that he personally had not had "a complete picture" when he approved previous out-of-court settlements for Gordon Taylor and the two others. The company would continue full cooperation with police. It would rectify its shortcomings. "We are doing our utmost to fix them, atone for them, and make sure they never happen again."

And he announced the company would kill the paper. Its final edition, on July 10, would carry no ads. Any commercial proceedings would be given to charity.

"Goodbye, Cruel World," the *Telegraph* headlined its front-page story. Rebekah Brooks would stay as News International's CEO. But one of her signature titles would vanish.

"We should see this for what it is," the actor and activist Hugh Grant told the BBC. He called it "a very cynical managerial maneuver" that led to layoffs of hundreds of people while protecting the job of the woman who was editor of *News of the World* even as Milly Dowler's mobile phone messages were being hacked.

Though News International issued the announcement in James's name, everyone spoke as though Rupert Murdoch made the decision himself, as indeed, he had.

"It was done for a straightforward commercial reason: he wanted to make sure he buys BSkyB. He already controls it," said former *Times of London* editor Simon Jenkins. "It was high politics at an almost total moment of national hysteria. He lanced a boil but not enough. None of the executives were sacked."

The company had survived worse. Twenty-one years earlier, as Sky Television was losing about $2 billion a year, News Corp was swimming in debt incurred by the $3 billion *TV Guide* acquisition. Murdoch kept rolling over various loans to keep the company afloat, relying on 146 lenders in all. In October 1990 he called bankers to London and said he wouldn't be able to pay off a $500 million loan, had another $2 billion coming due, and needed to borrow another $600 million. All of them would have to wait to be paid back. One held out: tiny Pittsburgh National Bank, owed only $10 million. A drop in the bucket, in the big picture, that could have kept the company under water for good. It took a personal call from Murdoch himself to the loan officer to persuade the bank from calling in the note. The $10 million—and the empire—was preserved.

With hacking, the company's executives had to shift strategies as they kept losing ground to their critics.

At first, the aim was to protect *News of the World* at all cost by wooing allies and intimidating critics in Parliament and the press, and either holding off, scaring off, or paying off the victims. They did the same to the people who hacked phones on the paper's behalf. But they couldn't save *News of the World*. The next goal was protecting the broadcasting deal to take over BSkyB and past that, Brooks's standing.

But the scandal kept advancing.

15

"THIS ONE": REBEKAH BROOKS

UNDER OTHER CIRCUMSTANCES, REBEKAH BROOKS might well have been considered a victim of hacking. Her first marriage to the soap opera star Ross Kemp imploded in 2005, when she was editor of the *Sun*. Brooks (then Rebekah Wade) was arrested at 4:00 AM on suspicion of having assaulted Kemp but was not charged; she told reporters it was "a silly row that got out of hand." Their spats inspired staffers for her old paper, the *News of the World*, to start hacking repeatedly into messages on their former boss's mobile phone, police later concluded.

Brooks and Kemp had favored Tony Blair's New Labour, and she had befriended Blair, his wife, Cherie, and Gordon and Sarah Brown. The pair split after Kemp's confession of marital infidelity, and Rebekah soon took up with Charlie Brooks, the young Tory leader David Cameron's Eton classmate. Rebekah and her new boyfriend rented homes on the grounds of Blenheim, the Churchill family's historic estate, and later moved to Chipping Norton, where they dined and fraternized with the future prime minister and other leading Tory and media figures, including James and Elisabeth Murdoch and their respective spouses.

In August 2008 then opposition leader Cameron flew on the private plane of Elisabeth's husband, Matthew Freud, the London public relations executive, to the Greek isle of Santorini; Cameron met with the media patriarch and much of his inner circle on his yacht. It was just as important to the young Conservative politician's prospects as Tony Blair's jaunt across the globe to Hayman Island off the coast of Australia had been thirteen years earlier.

Charlie Brooks raised horses, and soon Rebekah was on the fields riding too. Their friends joined in on the fun. In one text to Rebekah Brooks, written in 2009, Cameron wrote, "The horse CB [Charlie Brooks] put me on—fast unpredictable and hard to control—but fun."

In the wake of a key address by Cameron to the Conservative Party, Brooks cheered him on: "brilliant speech. I cried twice. Will love working together." Later, Brooks tutored the next prime minister in the protocol of their modern communiqués: "Occasionally, he would sign them off, LOL—'Lots of love,'" she said, "until I told him it meant 'laugh out loud.' And then he didn't sign them like that anymore." Cameron attended her June 2009 wedding. So did then Prime Minister Gordon Brown. A month later, the Murdochs elevated her to become CEO of News International.

In retrospect, the *Guardian* story in 2009 should have blown away all vestiges of that "line in the sand" walling off the rest of *News of the World* from the specific scandal over the princes. Three days after the *Guardian*'s scoop appeared, Colin Myler called in Neville Thurlbeck and promised him a generous severance package if he agreed to resign. The email "for Neville" detailing transcripts of hacked voice mail messages was too hot for the paper, though Thurlbeck denied wrongdoing.

James Murdoch had told his colleagues in New York there was no cause for concern. Executives at News Corp's headquarters heard the assistant police commissioner John Yates dismiss the *Guardian* story out of hand. That was good enough for them. The board did not formally take up the issue.

More than a year later, in late 2010, I stood next to Brooks outside the glass-paneled meeting rooms of the *Times of London* as she watched Cameron on a TV monitor, waiting for the verdict on which country would get to play host to the World Cup games in 2018 and 2022. She cut a striking figure—initially, it must be said, by her appearance, her pale skin offset by a flowing mane of fiery red hair. Then I was struck by the force of her personality. The UK was a finalist, but thought unlikely to prevail. The set was tuned to Sky News as Cameron and Prince William made impassioned last-minute pitches.

"Just imagine how many papers we could sell if London got the Cup," Brooks said, watching intently. She rolled her eyes as the Swiss president of FIFA, Sepp Blatter, finally announced the games would go to Russia in 2018 and Qatar in 2022, a setback for Cameron and his minister of culture and sport, Jeremy Hunt.

Some executives in Manhattan considered the *New York Times* story in September 2010 to be a wake-up call, raising questions about criminal implications and Brooks's behavior, but James Murdoch insisted hacking could be handled locally. It was a relatively trifling issue, he said, and any involvement from headquarters would be wrongly taken by the company's rivals to mean there was substance to larger accusations.

Rupert Murdoch had one overriding concern: protect Brooks above all. The company's general counsel, Lawrence Jacobs, insisted that the board needed to take charge and to set up an internal investigation. The corporation had to act to satisfy both US and UK authorities that it was rooting out any practices of corruption in its British properties. This could no longer be handled by London. Brooks could not be the focus of defense efforts. Corporate officials in New York had been deceived in 2009 by relying on the assurances of police officials in London who had been compromised by close ties to News Corp's British executives and newsrooms.

But James held New York at bay. His hopes for succession at long last were starting to materialize. He had carried a quiet anger that he had not been designated the future CEO—or even simply promoted to the job—several years earlier. In March 2011, he had been elevated to deputy chief operating officer and chief executive of News Corp's international holdings. The new position formalized his status as the heir apparent. He would move to New York and run the non-American elements of the conglomerate.

And Rupert Murdoch turned elsewhere for legal help. When the *New York Post* had to acknowledge its lead gossip columnist had taken payments from sources and another gossip writer had attempted extortion, the *Post* did not engage in the self-reflection and self-flagellation exhibited by the *New York Times* after the Jayson Blair fabrication and plagiarism scandal. Nor would News Corp do so here.

At his multimillion-pound townhouse on the periphery of Green Park, near Buckingham Palace, in May 2011, a group of senior News Corp officials and lawyers dined at a long table in a session convened by Brooks, then still CEO of News International. Among the guests were Jacobs, Klein, and Brendan Sullivan, a Washington defense attorney who had famously represented Lt. Col. Oliver North during the Iran-Contra hearings and who had been a law partner of Klein's wife. At the dinner, the chairman revealed his own plans. *This is going to be handled by Joel and Brendan*, Murdoch declared. *I will handle the board. Everyone else stay out of it.* Privately, Murdoch had told Klein and Sullivan that they had one mission: to preserve Rebekah Brooks's standing. Klein told others later that that order would be a tall one. To save the Murdochs and to protect the corporate board, she would probably have to go. But he did not press the chairman. Not yet.

At the dinner, Brendan Sullivan declared his faith in Brooks's innocence; indeed, she would soon be entrusted with running the UK company's internal investigation. Attention would be kept away from New York, away from James and especially from Rupert. Sullivan's declaration flew in the face of reality. But Murdoch leaned on Klein more than ever. His chief spokeswoman at the city schools system had just been named Murdoch's chief of staff. Sullivan was a senior partner at his wife's firm.

Klein teamed with News International executive Will Lewis to run News Corp's management and standards committee. For the time being, they would please their client, Murdoch. But they knew a reckoning would confront the company down the line.

Jacobs resigned less than a month after witnessing the rejection of his advice.

EVEN AS James Murdoch shut down *News of the World* in July, he sustained his support for Brooks. "I am satisfied that Rebekah, her leadership of this business and her standard of ethics and her standard of conduct throughout her career are very good," James said, praising her for working "transparently" with police to get to the heart of the matter.

Then James announced he had chosen Brooks herself to lead the company's internal investigation. By the end of the first week of July 2011, Brooks's standing was in considerable doubt. Brooks met with the shell-shocked staff on July 7 to explain the decision to shut down *News of the World*. If she felt personally chastened, it did not show, citing the "onslaught of attacks" the paper had faced since 2006. "You have led the news agenda [the headlines] because of past mistakes, but you have also set the agenda. . . . We don't get that message across."

"This is not exactly the best time in my life, but I'm determined to get vindication for the paper and for people like you," she told them, promising to shield their reputations from what she called a *"Guardian-BBC witch hunt."*

Security guards stood sentinel by the doors; technicians had severed the staff's access to the Internet on their work computers. The newsroom by this point had become a crime scene, lacking only the yellow tape favored by police to declare areas off-bounds.

"By your calling our newspaper toxic, we've all been contaminated by this toxicity," one reporter responded. "There's an arrogance there that you'd think we'd want to work for you there again."

Brooks was apologetic and emphasized her own lack of knowledge of any wrongdoing. "One of the problems, now, is how we dealt with it at the time," Brooks said. In 2006, she said, everyone wrongly defined hacking as an isolated case. The police said so, she noted. News International had believed them. "There's a feeling of a cover-up, our rivals think. Eventually, it will come out why things went wrong and who was responsible. And that will be another very difficult moment in this company's history."

Perhaps mindful of the police, lawyers, and prosecutors poring over emails, documents, and phone records inside the newspaper and in people's homes, no one at the staff meeting articulated the main source of their resentment: like Goodman earlier in his letter of protest at being dismissed for hacking into the princes' phones, reporters and editors believed that their bosses had tolerated, endorsed, and even effectively required these activities. Brooks undercut Murdoch's virtuous declaration that he would dedicate the advertising revenue to charity by telling her staff that the number of companies willing to take out ads had plummeted.

PRIME MINISTER Cameron began edging away from his patrons at News International. On Friday, July 8, 2011, he announced concurrent investigations by police and MPs, and a broad-ranging inquiry into the practices and ethics of the press. (It would be led by Lord Justice Brian Leveson.)

Contrition proved the order of the day. "Because party leaders were so keen to win the support of newspapers, we turned a blind eye to the need to sort [out] this issue, get on top of the bad practices, to change the way our newspapers are regulated," Cameron said. "The people in power knew things weren't right. But they didn't do enough quickly enough—until the full mess of the situation was revealed." Cameron said had he been in Murdoch's position, he would have accepted Brooks's resignation.

News International press aides denied she had made any such offer. Yet behind the scenes, guided by executives in New York, News International eased Brooks from the role she had ostensibly been assigned to oversee the internal inquiries. Stories in the *Guardian* and elsewhere brought a fresh rash of concerns: a report that a senior News International executive, as yet unnamed, had intervened twice to destroy millions of emails dating back to 2005—when the phone hacking of the royals occurred.

Rupert Murdoch flew to London, arriving on the morning of Sunday, July 10. He emerged from a chauffeured sedan carrying the final edition of *News of the World*; "Thank You and Goodbye" read the last headline. It carried the banner: "The World's Greatest Newspaper, 1843–2011."

Murdoch headed to his house in Mayfair and later emerged with Rebekah Brooks, crossing to a meeting at a luxury hotel across the road. Asked by a reporter amid a throng of photographers and cameramen about his priorities now that he was in town, Murdoch answered, "This one," gesturing with his thumb to Brooks, giving public voice to his private instinct.

EACH WEDNESDAY, political junkies in the UK settle around their televisions and computer screens to watch Prime Minister's Questions, the weekly sessions in which the parties joust over questions devised to test the head of the queen's government.

As the second Wednesday of July approached, Cameron's rhetoric was shifting daily, as though an inexorable tide were pulling him to the ground held by his foes. All three parties prepared to join as one to denounce News Corp and force it to abandon the acquisition of BSkyB.

On Monday, July 11, News Corp did something unexpected. It pulled its promise to spin off Sky News so it would not be under direct leadership of News Corp. That concession, made to ease Cabinet approval of the takeover, no longer held. The decision set off a chain of bureaucratic consequences. The British regulatory agency OFT, the Office of Fair Trading, judged that the proposed merger raised questions of media concentration; Jeremy Hunt referred the decision to the Competition Commission. This referral would tie up the decision for months, an outcome that News Corp had been laboring to avoid. Hunt also noted that OfCom, the separate communications regulator, was suddenly reviewing whether News Corp was a "fit and proper" owner of BSkyB at all.

Yet Hunt's seemingly unwelcome referral for review would have the ameliorative effect of delaying consideration to a time when emotions might not run so high and so hot. This process might give politicians a chance to rant against the Murdochs, get it out of their system, and yet allow the deal to be resurrected, Lazarus-like, the following year.

This time the Murdochs blinked. The company's ranking non-Murdoch chief operating officer, Chase Carey, acknowledged reality: the deal for outright ownership of BSkyB had collapsed. He announced News Corp was withdrawing its bid for the company entirely.

Still the public anger did not subside, as fresh developments arrived almost hourly. Police told Prince Charles that he had been targeted for hacking. So had his wife, Camilla, the Duchess of Cornwall. "There needs to be root-and-branch change at this entire organization," Prime Minister Cameron told the House of Commons. "What has happened at this company is disgraceful. It's got to be addressed at every level. And they should stop thinking about mergers when they've got to sort out the mess they've created."

Former prime minister Gordon Brown declared his belief that the *Sunday Times* had misrepresented itself to obtain his private financial records. There were suggestions that turned out to be unproven that the *Sun* paid off hospital workers to secure medical documents confirming that his infant son had a diagnosis of cystic fibrosis, he said. The *Sun* and Rebekah Brooks rejected claims about the story on Brown's child. A parent of a child with a similar condition had, in fact, alerted the paper, Brooks made clear. The parent had said he hoped the Browns would talk about the diagnosis and give some comfort to families in like situations. Brooks had been sensitive to the pain the story would cause, reached out to the Browns, and even received a letter from Sarah Brown thanking her for the care she took in doing so. Several years later, Brooks attended a pajama party to mark Sarah Brown's fortieth birthday with a select group of women friends.

By the summer of 2011, however, the Browns' mood had changed. Standing in the back benches of the House of Commons, consigned there in part, he felt, by the decision of the Murdoch papers to abandon him two years earlier, Brown said he had been punished for challenging the company's plans for consolidation. The scandal, Brown said, was "not the misconduct of a few rogues or a few freelancers but, I have to say, lawbreaking often on an industrial scale, at its worst dependent on links with the British criminal underworld."

Others trained their fire on Brooks as well. Murdoch's chief outside investor, the Saudi prince Al Waleed bin Talal, told the BBC, "For sure, she has to go. You bet she has to go."

Evidence suggested the most fearsome of consequences: seepage to the States. On July 11 the *Mirror* reported that a former New York

City police officer, unnamed, had been approached by reporters for *News of the World*. They offered to pay the ex-cop, now a private investigator, to hack into electronic phone records for people who had been killed in the 9/11 attacks. "The PI said he had to turn the job down. He knew how insensitive such research would be, and how bad it would look." The *Mirror*, it appeared, had not spoken to the unidentified police officer directly, and the third party it quoted was equally anonymous. Yet US lawmakers took the story seriously. Several senators, all Democrats, urged an investigation into whether the Murdoch tabloids had engaged in similar acts in the US.

The liberals were joined by congressman Peter King, chairman of the House Homeland Security Committee, a center-right Republican who generally made common cause with the *New York Post* and Fox News. King wrote to FBI director Robert Mueller: "It is revolting to imagine that members of the media would seek to compromise the integrity of a public official for financial gain in the pursuit of yellow journalism." More than 150 of his constituents had died in the 9/11 attacks.

The FBI should pursue any such offenses aggressively and make sure they were prosecuted to the fullest extent of the law, King wrote: "The 9/11 families have suffered egregiously, but unfortunately they remain vulnerable against such unjustifiable parasitic strains."

Lawyers for News Corp in New York spotted dangers on two fronts. Any prosecution could give grist to those who wanted to challenge the ongoing waivers that the Federal Communications Commission had granted News Corp, including those regulations about owning too many stations in the same town. They barred networks from owning a stake in the production companies that created the television shows on the air and banned "cross-ownership" of newspapers and major TV stations in a single metro area.

At various points, Murdoch circumvented, challenged, and even arguably violated these rules. When Murdoch created a fourth network from the core of Metromedia's television stations, he had to become a naturalized US citizen. The new Fox network did not air a full slate of shows, a technicality that enabled him for a time to sidestep the financial syndication regulations (preventing a network's ownership of TV production companies that create the shows it broadcasts). Later, News Corp won a waiver from the FCC to produce shows it had developed. Murdoch sold the *Chicago Sun-Times* in 1986, after owning it just two years, to acquire a station in that city; he later sold the *Boston Herald* after Senator Ted Kennedy inserted language into a spending bill banning the ownership of a TV station and a newspaper in the same city. (The *Herald* retaliated by publishing every unflattering shot of Kennedy it could find of the senator's shirttails askew, his jowls flapping.) In 2001 the FCC gave Murdoch yet another waiver when he acquired ten television stations held by Chris-Craft, including WWOR, which served New York, despite already owning WNYW and the *New York Post* there. He held on to WWOR after the waiver lapsed.

Those rules, in Murdoch's estimation, stood for the kind of government interference that had complicated his company's growth in Australia, primarily for the benefit of the public broadcasters and the establishment papers that competed with his properties. Lobbyists helped the company skirt such regulations, which the company saw as archaic given the proliferation of digital media, as well as cumbersome.

During the scandalous summer of 2011, regulators might well become less pliant. Under federal law, the possibility of prosecution loomed as well. The 1977 Federal Corrupt Practices Act banned US companies from bribing government officials abroad. Such payments were felonies, though hard to prove. But illegal payments to police officers fell squarely within that definition.

A second provision of the law did not require so complicated a burden of proof. A company whose shares were publicly traded in the US had to register bribes to public officials in publicly filed documents. A failure to do so represented a violation of civil law. In 2008, the

German conglomerate Siemens reached a settlement with the federal government for $800 million to resolve charges that it had paid bribes and kickbacks abroad. (Siemens did not admit having paid bribes.)

In mid-July 2011, News Corp stock dropped more than 11 percent in a week, as major investors proved jittery not just over the fate of the BSkyB acquisition but also the costs of legal implications in the UK. The corporation lifted its expansion of an already planned stock buy-back program to $5 billion from $1.8 billion, a quick boost for the value of shares.

———

SUCH WERE the pressures that coalesced around News Corp by mid-July. Questions were becoming increasingly urgent for Murdoch's closest executives in the US and the UK, Les Hinton atop Dow Jones and the *Wall Street Journal,* and Rebekah Brooks was in the thick of it. Hinton, at worst, was accused of misleading Parliament in assuring lawmakers that such wrongdoing was limited. Brooks was in the thick of it. (The settlements by News International went a long way toward convincing the public of its guilt.)

MPs who had earlier concluded they had been deceived were angered again. On Thursday, July 14, John Whittingdale, the Conservative chairman of the investigating committee before which Brooks and Hinton had previously appeared, told reporters that Brooks had agreed to testify again. But Murdoch father and son had told the committee they were too busy, Whittingdale said, though James offered another day in August.

"It is James Murdoch who has said publicly that executives from the *News of the World* misled [P]arliament in the evidence that they gave to the committee in our previous inquiry," Whittingdale said. "Therefore we are extremely anxious to ask him about that, and we did not feel it was justified to delay until August."

The Parliament's deputy sergeant at arms delivered summonses to the offices of the two Murdochs and Rebekah Brooks at Wapping. It was the first time Parliament had ordered a summons to compel testimony in almost two decades.

By the next day, News Corp stock had fallen an additional 5 percent. Sky's market cap had dropped about 16 percent in just eleven days. Within hours of each other on Friday, July 15, Brooks and Hinton resigned. "I have believed that the right and responsible action has been to lead us through the heat of the crisis," Brooks wrote to News International employees. "However my desire to remain on the bridge has made me a focal point of the debate. This is now detracting attention from all our honest endeavours to fix the problems of the past."

Hinton, too, protested his innocence and ignorance once more. "I believed that the rotten element at the *News of the World* had been eliminated; that important lessons had been learned; and that journalistic integrity was restored," Hinton told his staff. He testified in good faith, if wrongly, but his ignorance was irrelevant: "It is proper for me to resign."

Hinton and Rupert Murdoch exchanged statements of warm appreciation. But Hinton was stunned. "Resignation" was a kind gloss to put on his firing. "All the executives used to have a joke within News Corp: Rupert will be loyal to you right up until the very day when he's not," a former senior official at News Corp told me. Over time Hinton and others understood not to take their ousters personally. You signed up for it.

Brooks's departure was accompanied by a new mechanism for overseeing the internal corporate inquiry. News Corp created a new independent management and standards committee to investigate possible criminal activity and present it to the authorities. The two former assistant US attorneys general already linked to the company—Joel Klein and Viet Dinh—would oversee the review.

But Murdoch also revived a bit of swagger. "The Company has made mistakes," he said. "It is not only receiving appropriate scrutiny but is also responding to unfair attacks by setting the record straight." The Murdochs gave warning: as they prepared to step into the halls of Parliament, they would once more exercise what they felt was their right to determine what constituted fair criticism.

16

"MOST HUMBLE DAY"

————————

THAT SWAGGER DIDN'T LAST FOR long.

Police arrested Rebekah Brooks on July 17, a Sunday, and questioned her on suspicion of involvement in illegally intercepting electronic communications (the hacking into mobile phone voice mails) and corruption (illegally paying police and public officials). She had planned to submit to an arrest two days later, on Tuesday. By this point, however, police had dispensed with all manner of courtesies.

On July 19, the day the Murdochs were to testify, the morning papers were stuffed with reports of a confrontation between Charlie Brooks and security guards at a parking lot near their luxury apartment overlooking the Thames. A passerby had given security guards two briefcases containing a laptop, an iPhone, and a stack of documents, all of which had been retrieved from a plastic sack dumped in a trash bin at the parking lot. What happened next is a matter of some dispute. What is known is that Charlie Brooks did not emerge from the lot with the computer; a spokesman told papers a friend had left it there by accident. Murdoch's tabloids did not display the ferocity of interest that the episode might have engendered had the person involved been someone else.

But that was low farce. The arrest played into a plot with high drama, underscoring the personal ties involved. As Rupert and James Murdoch entered the hearing room in Portcullis House, a modern wing of Parliament, protesters outside chanted, while a pair mocked father and son by donning oversize masks, Rupert denoted by his exaggerated, furrowed brow, James by his high-tech glasses frames.

The hearing room could have been a newish criminal courtroom in any midsize American city, except instead of jurors seated in a box, lawmakers were arrayed in horseshoe fashion, facing the witnesses.

Rupert Murdoch's wife, Wendi Deng, sat behind him, as did Joel Klein. Murdoch had wooed Klein to serve as a chief adviser and to lead the company's push into educational software. Now Murdoch had tapped him to lead internal affairs. He had appeared that day in a show of support for his corporate chairman and to witness the process playing out.

Klein, a slender man with a crown of graying hair and nasal accent reflecting his childhood home of Queens, New York, was nobody's idea of a pushover. Two years earlier, Rupert Murdoch had personally called Klein while he was still chancellor of schools in New York City to suggest he consider coming into the fold. Once Klein left public office, the decision and announcement were swift: he would lead News Corp's revitalized educational division. But as an executive vice president, Klein reported directly to Murdoch in the office of the chairman. Concurrently, Murdoch appointed him to the corporate board. Klein could have become rich at any number of Manhattan law firms, but this arrangement nonetheless rewarded him handsomely. His compensation was worth at least $4.5 million in 2011, his first full year, plus a $1 million signing bonus and $18,000 toward car expenses. The pay bought his legal counsel and loyalty, but Klein did not want to lose his reputation as a lawyer known for tough-minded independence.

Now, Klein's overriding aim was to convince authorities in the US and the UK that the company would tear itself apart to satisfy them of its determination to root out corruption—short of the chairman's office.

The Murdochs had been carefully coached and knew they were addressing different audiences, in testimony broadcast live in the UK and the US. Both men wanted to convey to investors that the fever had broken, that sound management would once more be the order of the day.

Rupert needed to preserve his company's reputation and show contrition and to argue he had no involvement in an operation of such small importance to the company's bottom line. James Murdoch needed to show he was not a callow youth in his father's shadow, but a capable executive who could handle this and other scandals and surprises, a worthy heir to the corporate throne. In short, he needed to salvage his career.

James Murdoch first attempted to read from a prepared statement, as witnesses typically do in congressional hearings in Washington. John Whittingdale told James he could read the statement at the end if adequate time remained. Police removed a group of vocal protesters who leaped up from their seats and started to shout at the Murdochs; Whittingdale then reminded the Murdochs, the committee members, and the public that the committee in 2010 had concluded it was "inconceivable that only one reporter had been involved" in phone hacking and reiterated that "it is also clear that Parliament has been misled."

Whittingdale began by asking what James Murdoch meant when he acknowledged that the company had made statements to Parliament "without being in full possession of the facts." James offered a note of contrition and regret, on behalf of himself, his father, and the employees of News Corp.

Just as he began to explain the context and thrust of his comments, he was interrupted. "Before you get to that, I'd just like to say one sentence," Rupert Murdoch said, reaching out his hand and resting it on his son's arm. "This is the most humble day of my life."

The phrasing of that interjection had been scripted for Murdoch by his advisers, especially his new team of crisis management experts, including senior figures from the giant public relations firm Edelman and Steve Rubenstein of Rubenstein Associates. Several days earlier at One Aldwych Hotel in the heart of London, Murdoch sat perched on the white-fabric chair, his head in hands, repeating his sorrow for the Dowlers. His PR consultants recommended that Murdoch similarly needed to convey his humility once more before Parliament. Yet by interrupting his son at the outset, Murdoch's commanding nature trumped that message of regret and undermined James's standing. He demonstrated that even in crisis, News Corp, a publicly traded company, was propelled by the vision of a single man. And despite Rupert's aspirations for his son, that man wasn't James. If what he said damaged his son's standing or independence, he really didn't care. *His* message would be heard.

THE TWO Murdochs jointly attempted to sketch out a defense, in which the company had relied on the police, the Press Complaints Commission, and outside lawyers hired by News International to perform a thorough review, to tell them what had happened inside their own newsrooms. The police had publicly cleared them. So had the PCC. James said he should have pushed harder to challenge those assumptions. But he said he had been told a thorough inquiry had been conducted and found only limited wrongdoing. The oversight was regrettable, he said. But he left the implication hanging that anyone could have fallen through the same trapdoors.

Labour MP Tom Watson refused to allow James Murdoch to answer for his father. Why, Watson asked Rupert Murdoch, didn't News Corp instantly investigate reports that the paper's reporters bribed police for information?

"I didn't know of it. I'm sorry," the senior Murdoch said. "If I can just say something, and this is not as an excuse, maybe it's an explanation of my laxity: The *News of the World* is less than 1 percent of our company. I employ 53,000 people around the world who are proud, and great and ethical and distinguished people." Yet Murdoch was not known for laxity—he was a notoriously involved CEO, especially when it came to his tabloids.

The younger Murdoch said he had only learned of the seriousness of the problem less than a year before. "As soon as we had that new information at the end of 2010, that indicated to us there was a wider involvement," James Murdoch told MPs, "We acted upon it immediately." He was referring to the lawsuit filed by actress Sienna Miller. The twists and turns of her stormy relationship to fellow film star Jude Law were the stuff that tabloid dreams are made of.

But the year before that "new information" surfaced—in 2009—the *Guardian* exposés indicated that dozens of celebrities and politicians had been targeted illegally by the tabloid and revealed James Murdoch's approval of the secret payment to Gordon Taylor. There were only two interpretations of what had occurred. If they conceded knowing what was going on, they had condoned or intentionally ignored activities that were clearly criminal. James Murdoch in particular confronted the Hobson's choice of managerial incompetence or acquiescence to widespread criminality.

The Conservative MP Louise Mensch was someone who tried over the course of hearings to make the case that hacking was endemic to the British tabloid industry, not simply the Murdoch stable. An author of young adult books who had made a fortune before entering Parliament, she had married the manager of the heavy metal band Metallica and found her own behavior as a twenty-something under scrutiny from critical blogs. As Mensch noted, Piers Morgan, who came up in the Murdoch tabloids and was briefly editor of *News of the World* before he led the rival *Daily Mirror*, had spoken several times cavalierly about phone hacking as a routine practice, though Mensch misstated some of the details.

Yet when Rupert Murdoch appeared, she did not relent. "Is it not the case, sir, that you are the captain of ship?" Mensch asked the older Murdoch. "You are the chief executive officer of News Corp, the global organization."

"A very much larger ship," Rupert Murdoch replied.

"It is a much bigger ship, but you are in charge of it," Mensch said. "And as you said in earlier questions, you do not consider yourself a hands-off chief executive. You work 10 to 12 hours a day. This terrible thing happened on your watch. Have you considered resigning?"

Murdoch said he hadn't. "People I've trusted—I'm saying not who, I don't know what level—have let me down, and I think they behaved disgracefully, betrayed the company and me, and it's for them to pay," he said. "And frankly, I'm the best person to clean this up."

Rupert appeared tired, deflated, even old. Tom Watson emerged as the Murdochs' chief antagonist. "It's revealing in itself what he doesn't know, and what executives chose not to tell him," Watson told James Murdoch, in explaining his focus on the father.

Watson asked Rupert Murdoch, "Did you close the paper down because of the criminality?"

"Yes, we felt ashamed at what had happened and thought we ought to bring it to a close," Murdoch replied. "We had broken our trust with our readers."

That sacrifice did not endure for long. Reporters at rival papers confirmed rumors that a "*Sun on Sunday*" had been under consideration for some time; the printing of a seventh daily edition of the tabloid, the most profitable major paper in the country, would have achieved savings by consolidating staffs anyway. Forty-eight hours before James Murdoch announced the end of the *News of the World*, two domain names were registered with a familiar sound: sunonsunday.co.uk and thesunonsunday.co.uk. Within a few days, News International was identified as the entity holding title to those domains.

The Murdochs were vague about the questions at the heart of the hearings. James Murdoch had not registered that the payment to settle Taylor's hacking complaint indicated any wider problem. James said he had not been told of an email that contained transcripts of voice mail messages of various targets of the tabloid's hacking that carried the legend "for Neville"—Neville Thurlbeck, the paper's chief correspondent. That email indicated that hacking was not an aberration. It was standard operating procedure.

Watson could not believe that James Murdoch could think the enormous payment (for a British case) was reasonable without knowing of the "for Neville" email.

WATSON: "But you paid an astronomical sum and there was no reason to."

JAMES MURDOCH: "There was every reason to settle the case, given the likelihood of losing the case and the damages that we had received counsel would be levied."

In a separate secret settlement in 2010, News International paid one of London's leading public relations executives, Max Clifford, a total exceeding $1 million after he started litigation against News International for mobile phone hacking. Rupert Murdoch said he knew nothing about it. James Murdoch said Rebekah Brooks made the decision to pay Clifford, which he only learned about later.

No party gave the Murdochs any quarter. Tory MP Philip Davies pressed both father and son on the payments. In 2008 News International had lost in a court case filed by the motor racing official Max Mosley after *News of the World* reported he had participated in a Nazi-themed orgy. Mosley *had* taken part in a sex party with several women. But the Nazi theme was said to be an embroidery on the part of Thurlbeck, who could be heard on a tape goading one of the participating women to make a *Sieg heil* salute. As Mosley's father was a noted Nazi sympathizer who had founded the British Union of Fascists, the association was partic-ularly damaging. That was the story on which Thurlbeck was found to have blackmailed a woman into putting her name as author of a fanciful account of the party that he had written.

The questioning briefly gave way to spectacle when Jonathan May-Bowles darted toward Murdoch and attempted to slap him in the face with a platter of shaving cream. One of Murdoch's lawyers stepped forward to block him. Wendi Deng Murdoch, who had played volley-ball competitively as a schoolgirl, leaped above the lawyer and slapped May-Bowles, knocking him, the lawyer, and herself to the ground. "Mr. Murdoch, your wife has a very good left hook," Watson said. Whitting-dale cleared the room of all but the MPs, parliamentary staffers, wit-nesses, their legal team, and the security guards, whose incompetence at allowing the stunt to unfold led to whispers that News Corp's PR advisers had choreographed the event to gain sympathy for the media mogul. The *Telegraph* sent one of its foreign correspondents to profile the middle school instructor in her hometown of Xuzhou who taught Deng Wen Ge (her given name) how to play volleyball.

May-Bowles, a twenty-six-year-old stand-up comic and activist who performed under the name Jonnie Marbles, pleaded guilty later in the month to charges of assault and causing harassment, alarm, and dis-tress. He faced his charges stoically, invoking a familiar phrase: "I'd just like to say that this is the most humble day of my life."

In New York, some executives were questioning whether it was time to coax Murdoch to allow his hired hands to run the company he had worked so hard to build. Chase Carey, notable among report-ers and fellow executives for his handlebar mustache and his evident lack of hunger for the spotlight, had worked for a generation at News Corp helping to guide one division after another. Investors trusted his judgment.

But Murdoch made his verdict on himself clear: he was not ready to yield control of News Corp—especially not to a non-Murdoch.

A NEW legal front was beginning to open in the States. An allegation stated that the actor Jude Law's mobile phone had been hacked when traveling through JFK airport in New York City. Even though the incident involved reporters for Murdoch's British tabloids, and not the *New York Post*, it would show that the tainted practices had jumped the Atlantic. Since the Federal Corrupt Practices Act criminalized payments to government officials abroad, News Corp moved swiftly to hire many top lawyers—among them former US attorney general Michael Mukasey, former US attorney for New York City Mary Jo White, and Mark Mendelsohn, the former top Justice Department official over federal corruption cases involving American companies. "News Corp has pretty much assembled a dream team of all-star foreign corrupt practice litigators," Columbia University legal scholar John Coffee, one of the nation's foremost authorities on corporate governance, told me. "You don't put all that investment into this without having some serious concerns about what might happen." The company established a new "management and standards committee," reporting to Joel Klein, who would in turn report to Viet Dinh, the former assistant US attorney general and News Corp director who had been godfather to one of Lachlan Murdoch's children. The MSC was seen as running damage control. In time, however, it would hand police material damning dozens of News International employees. Klein had to prove to US authorities that the company was being fully cooperative.

Those not in the family—those who were no longer "mates"—no longer exhibited "mateship." The editor, Colin Myler, had seethed over the closing of the *News of the World*. He had been recalled from the *New York Post* to clean up the mess, and yet the company folded the paper under his editorship. "Of course, I didn't close it," Myler said after publishing the paper's final edition several days earlier. "This is not where we wanted to be or deserved to be, but as a final tribute to 7.5 million readers this is for you and the staff." He led more than a hundred staffers, many of them openly weeping, all cheering, out of the cavernous atrium of the *News of the World* offices at Wapping, around the block to a nearby pub.

Many others had aired their grievances behind closed doors. But along with Tom Crone, Myler decided to make a public break. They issued a joint statement: James had known about the "for Neville" email, they said, before approving the big secret payment to Taylor. The younger Murdoch knew that hacking was rife. The Murdochs did not just own the company; Myler and Crone's actions would ensure they owned the scandal too.

17

THE JEWEL
IN THE CROWN

———————

WHEN RUPERT MURDOCH BOUGHT THE Dow Jones Company
in late 2007, he did so to acquire its prized title, the *Wall Street Journal*.
The Dow Jones newswires covered the world of business at a feverish pace, competing with Reuters and Bloomberg for scoops. But the
Journal had global reputation and reach. It was prominent and widely
circulated; it had among the most subscriptions of any paper in the
US. Murdoch, like the other people populating the *Forbes* list of bil-
lionaires, relied on it religiously for news about business, finance, and
the regulations that could affect commerce. The *Journal* became the
jewel in the crown of Murdoch's media empire. He loved owning it.
And yet Murdoch did not much like the *Journal* itself.

Murdoch's first editor at the *Journal*, Marcus Brauchli, had been
installed less than a year before. Compact, fit, smart, with a sly smile
and a deceptive wit, Brauchli had come up through the ranks at the
Journal, making his mark in China and rising within the editing

ranks to win the competition to replace the beloved Paul Steiger as managing editor. (The term "managing editor" for the paper's most senior news executive was a relic, peculiar to the *Journal*, for the job that elsewhere would be editor in chief or executive editor.) Even before getting the top spot, Brauchli had been setting about to modernize the place, energize the paper's digital offerings, and make a greater push globally.

Murdoch had his own ideas. He told Brauchli that readers resented setting aside editions with long pieces to digest later in the week because they felt rebuked by piles of unread papers. The feature called the "A-hed" had been a defining element of the *Journal* for decades—a front-page story that provided a great read about a development that was often of little or no immediate consequence. It was an innovation of the legendary Barney Kilgore, who reinvented the paper amid the chaos of the Great Depression. It was one of two narrative stories placed every day on the front page. The other often generated a behind the scenes look at corporate infighting or malfeasance. Murdoch seemed to suggest that both the A-hed and the daily in-depth piece should disappear.

Moreover, Murdoch had little tolerance for the "paywall" that required people to purchase a digital subscription to get access to the paper's full site. Murdoch wanted anyone anywhere in the world to be able to read *Journal* stories at any time, on any device. *What's the point of doing all this fine journalism if people can't see it?* he wondered. The *Journal*'s paywall was the envy of other newspaper owners, who felt they could not replicate the *Journal*'s value to entrepreneurs and investors. Executives at Dow Jones braced for the loss of revenue.

Early on, at a banquet dinner with bureau chiefs who had traveled to New York from all over the world, the chairman sketched out how he thought a story should be told: in "as few words as possible." Murdoch underscored that these changes originated with him. His pick as publisher, Robert Thomson, told bureau chiefs that some projects celebrated in *Journal*'s newsroom had the "gestational period of a llama." (Eleven-and-a-half months, if you were wondering.) Consequently the *Journal* moved away from stories that deconstructed how business and the markets work—what editors called "how-why-will" stories. Investigative reporting, often strong, still arrived each day, or at least each week, but Thomson put less urgency on it. Thomson saw many reporters on the *Journal* staff as complacent, trapped in a mind-set defined by intellectuals and liberals on the Upper West Side and the *Columbia Journalism Review.*

Thomson's opinions mattered. For though he had been named publisher of the *Journal*, rather than managing editor, it became clear that his editorial vision would guide the paper—which is to say, Murdoch's vision would guide the paper. Thomson even took a second office on the newsroom floor. It was a break in tradition for *Wall Street Journal* publishers. Fighting up a rear-guard and ultimately futile defense, Brauchli made sure it was located in a no-man's land near its sister publication, *Barron's.*

Thomson was born to parents without means in a small town several hours away from Melbourne. He showed verve as a rookie reporter for the Melbourne *Herald*, the paper once run by Murdoch's father, and rose to become a reporter in China for the Associated Press and the *Financial Times*. Lean, with a stoop caused by a severe back ailment, Thomson favored black pants and thin ties, and he adopted a spiky hairstyle. He wrote memos littered with such obscure phrasings that they stumped even the *Journal*'s hyperliterate staff; he twitched at the scent of stories that were intriguing, devoted more to color than exacting precision, though his reporters would later find he could trip them up on the fine points of their stories, too.

Murdoch saw in Thomson a kindred spirit, and it didn't hurt that the younger man had been slighted by a rival. Thomson had been the US editor of the *Financial Times*, but was hired away by Murdoch to be editor of the *Times of London* after being passed over to become the *FT*'s next executive editor. The two men shared a March birthday separated by precisely three decades; they both married Chinese-born women. (Thomson's wife, Wang Ping, was actually a few years older than Wendi Deng Murdoch.) The two families periodically vacationed together, with the Murdoch girls frolicking with the Thomson boys. Murdoch became not just Thomson's employer and mentor, but by some accounts his best friend as well.

In summer 2007, as Murdoch put the final touches on a package to induce the controlling Bancroft family to sell him the *Wall Street Journal* and Dow Jones, he had to address the Bancrofts' notions of editorial independence. Given the paper's tenuous finances, the sale made financial sense but he had to overcome the Bancrofts' pride. "They weren't able to grow the company and lost interest in running it," said Beijing-based reporter Ian Johnson, a Pulitzer Prize–winning chronicler of events in China for the *Journal*. He called the deal a Faustian bargain and campaigned with a small group of reporters against it. The Bancrofts saw their detachment as principled.

To ensure the newspaper's integrity, Murdoch's lawyers created a five-member panel, the Special Committee. It was to be constituted without any existing entanglements with News Corp or the Murdoch family. Chairman Thomas Bray had been a staffer for the *Wall Street Journal*, leaving in 1983, an affiliation that raised no hackles. MIT digital futurist Nicholas Negroponte, another member of the panel, however, had received $2 million from News Corp for the foundation he ran that gives laptops to needy schoolchildren. Those *Journal* reporters who opposed the sale to Murdoch seized on Negroponte's affiliation as a sign the panel would be compromised. The veteran *Journal* reporter E.S. Browning told me at the time, "Murdoch clearly has no intention of creating a board that would be independent. He's going to try to assault it with his lackeys."

The Special Committee also included the former CEO of the Associated Press, the former editor in chief of the *Chicago Tribune*, and a former Republican congresswoman. News Corp expressed confidence that Negroponte had enough independence to act independently. Given that News Corp and Murdoch were functionally the same, reporters and editors put little stock in the statement. But managing editor Marcus Brauchli vouched for Negroponte and the entire Rube Goldberg arrangement. *We can work under Murdoch's system,* he told his staff. *We can work with Murdoch. We need his riches to weather the storms slamming the economy and the industry.*

A similar board established a generation earlier to protect the *Times of London* and the *Sunday Times* proved an occasional bureaucratic irritant to Murdoch and not much more. Questions over the Special Committee's composition passed almost as soon as they surfaced, unnoticed except in journalism circles.

The acquisition of the *Wall Street Journal* went through in late 2007. Murdoch named Les Hinton CEO of Dow Jones. Less than five months later, Hinton told Brauchli that he and Thomson felt he should leave. Brauchli yielded in the face of insurmountable logic: Murdoch, the paper's real editor in chief, wanted him gone. Brauchli consoled himself with a departing payment worth more than $6 million and became executive editor of the *Washington Post.*

The Special Committee had authority to approve the hiring and firing of managing editors. Formally Brauchli's departure was voluntary and did not involve clashes over journalistic integrity, so the switch did not automatically trigger the Special Committee's mandate to act. The members expressed vexation that they were told after the fact. But they approved the appointment of Thomson as managing editor of the paper. Les Hinton slid smoothly into the publisher's seat and, with an apology, publicly defanged the panel charged with defending the paper.

"It was the end of any doubt over who was in charge, and of what Murdoch thought of the old paper," one former *Journal* reporter recalled. To staffers, he said, "the whole special committee just felt like a cynical joke."

By early 2008 the *Wall Street Journal* was under Murdoch's full control. Literate yet accessible, the *Journal* set the standard for reporting business and finance. It was not written to impress the friends of its reporters, as Murdoch believed of the *New York Times*, but for entrepreneurs, Rotarians, investors, ranchers, innovators, and schoolteachers west of the Hudson and east of the Rockies. Yet Murdoch wanted to run the nation's leading general interest newspaper, not its most respected financial publication or "second read" of the morning.

Under Murdoch and Thomson, the *Journal* took a heightened interest in domestic politics and foreign news without explicitly financial components. The paper's daily news metabolism quickened and its tone lightened. Thomson pushed for attention-getting headlines that stretched across the page, for big photographs, for shorter stories, and for reimagined lifestyle sections. The paper reflected that day's news, not waiting until a day or two later to write a lyric assessment. An Associated Press article about mass shootings at Virginia Tech was the top-read story on the paper's website in 2007. The paper had not assigned anyone to cover the story as it broke. Thomson thought that was madness.

The digital age, not just the new owner, dictated major shifts in how the paper operated, concluded Rebecca Blumenstein, a veteran senior editor who flourished under Thomson. "The pace of news changed," she told me. "You have to have a front page now that people feel compelled to read every morning. If people don't feel they have to pay for the *Wall Street Journal*, then they're not going to pay."

Some old hands took these shifts as deliberate steps to unravel Kilgore's legacy and feared, taken together, they would undermine the paper's distinctiveness. One former executive argued that the paper's coverage the day after the Fort Hood shootings in 2009 offered the same kind of breaking news coverage available on any other news site.

"What [the reenvisioned *Journal*] does is reflect Murdoch's intentions, which I think he was clear about from the beginning," said

William Grueskin, who served as the paper's page-one editor, managing editor of WSJ.com, and deputy managing editor for news but left in 2008. "Whether that was a good strategy is, I think, still being sussed out."

Another former editor said the ambition of the place simultaneously weakened. "They don't try to take you inside boardrooms," he claimed. "They simply tell you what happened." Added a former *Journal* executive, "Thomson made the *Journal* more good and less excellent."

Once Thomson was in place as managing editor, however, things began to ease up a bit. Murdoch had already authorized more money to add pages to the front section. Mass layoffs, widely feared, never occurred. Instead, Murdoch repeatedly demonstrated interest in the trade of journalism.

In 2008 Murdoch dropped by the Beijing bureau with little warning, alarming reporters. They were wary of his reputation of appeasing the country's regime. But he had by then largely abandoned his dreams of new fortunes in China. When Murdoch sat in on an interview with a Chinese finance official, his interest was noted by both the Chinese and the Americans. But his interest proved journalistic and political rather than in furthering his own business interests.

And Murdoch charmed staffers, especially researchers and the news clerks on the lowest rungs. The China bureau included many of Murdoch's most lacerating critics. He never mentioned the letter of protest that Johnson and others had signed. Nor did he or Thomson ever punish a single one of them. Murdoch had personally intervened to ensure that Johnson was issued a visa by the authorities to allow him to work there after they had barred him from the country. And during that visit, Murdoch urged the bureau to think big. The year had seen epic stories, such as the deadly Sichuan earthquake that killed tens of thousands of people and a series of protests and riots in Tibet. *The biggest mistake one can make when news breaks is to sit back*, Murdoch said as he addressed the entire bureau. Go check it out. The worst thing that happens is you end up finding a good feature story. It was a rare explicit directive to the *Journal*'s China staff—but also an encouraging one: go find the story.

EVENTUALLY THOMSON decided not to kill Barney Kilgore's beloved A-hed, the front-page lagniappe, though he discarded the *Journal*'s practice of reserving space for a second front-page story that had no particular news peg. So, too, did Murdoch abandon plans to scrap the paywall. The paper tweaked its hybrid "freemium" system, in which some articles were posted outside the paywall, but the general concept survived.

Thomson seemed more dedicated to in-depth, painstaking reporting than his new staff had given him credit for. He didn't like it when reporters devoted a year to a project. That sounded too much like a play for a Pulitzer Prize. But he backed a multiyear project on corporate invasion of online privacy and consistently supported reporting that proved embarrassing to the ruling classes in China.

Among the *Journal*'s proudest traditions was a studied distance from any whiff of partisanship. Staffers for the news pages anxiously monitored headlines, story selection, and placement for signs that the new regime would fulfill their darkest fears—that Murdoch would pull and throw punches to aid favored politicians and causes.

In the minds of several senior editors who privately admitted reservations among themselves, a certain note had been struck by Thomson back on election night 2008. Thomson wanted the headline across the top of the front page to carry the full name of the next president: "Barack Hussein Obama." The *New York Times*, *USA Today*, *Washington Post*, and *Los Angeles Times* did not include the full name in their headlines. And top news editors at the *Journal* beseeched Thomson not to do it. Such a headline would appear to be emphasizing the unlikelihood of the name for a president, its very *otherness*. The conservative controversialist Ann Coulter had uttered the name as frequently as possible in her columns and television appearances to underscore the point: the guy doesn't just have an African father, but he has a Muslim middle name as well! Thomson let it go; the headline did not run.

But within weeks, Thomson named Gerard Baker as his deputy. An alumnus of the *Financial Times* and the *Times of London*, Baker had been the editor of the paper's US operations and a conservative political columnist. Baker was British, charming, literate, and well aware of the repercussions of his praise for Sarah Palin as a serious figure in the fall of 2008 in one of his final columns for the *Times of London*. Baker shared a core conviction with Thomson and Murdoch that most of the news media could be found on the political left. Many current and former reporters and editors for the paper privately agreed.

Baker arrived just as Obama took office, with a firm Democratic majority in both houses of Congress. Thomson and Baker believed newspapers should serve as an oppositional force to the nation's chief executive and wanted to cast the *Journal* more in that image. The paper's new owner and two top editors further believed the *Journal* was populated by liberals and leftists who were blinded to their own bias. Baker told people that Thomson and he wanted to balance that reflexive liberalism. That didn't mean he wanted to replicate Fox News in print. Baker promised instead to guide the paper's coverage right down the middle. The *Journal*'s news side had for years been protected by the asperity of its conservative editorial pages, so its reporters were not subjected to the same ideological scrutiny as those at the *New York Times* or the *Washington Post*. Yet they were proud of their record, saying they believed they provided a fair report each day. Most journalists were prepared to accept or at least accommodate such corrective tweaking. But they were not always sure what to make of the editorial nudges when they occurred.

In the spring of 2009, shortly after Obama's controversial stimulus bill passed Congress, the paper's new top editors ordered up a story reporting that the bill was creating so much uncertainty among companies that it threatened the economic recovery. A command to gather material for the story went out to writers across the paper. The stimulus bill included some $19 billion to encourage adopting the use of electronic medical records. A reporter working on the story told me his sources at big health IT companies said the stimulus had led to an uptick in business for their firms. But that didn't make it into the article. Was that a journalistic choice, an ideological one, or both?

Reporters and editors were surprised by the new senior editors' obsession with the competition. Much of how Thomson and Baker envisioned the *Journal* appeared to be defined in opposition to practices elsewhere, especially the despised *New York Times*. Thomson thought that *Times* chairman and publisher Arthur Sulzberger exemplified passivity. When a December 2009 column by *Times* media critic David Carr cited concerns about the *Journal* editors' conservatism, Thomson called the piece "yet more evidence that the *New York Times* is uncomfortable about the rise of an increasingly successful rival while its own circulation and credibility are in retreat." He revealed that *Times* executive editor Bill Keller had written a letter to a national awards committee (later confirmed as the prestigious Polk Awards) questioning the basis on which *Journal* had won a prize for reporting from China. Thomson added, "Whether it be in the quest for prizes or in the disparagement of competitors, principle is but a bystander at the *New York Times*."

In April 2010 Thomson exacted a minor measure of revenge. The *Journal*'s weekend sections had improved under Thomson, with expanded space for cultural coverage and witty columns on sports. He was within three weeks of the debut of a "Greater New York" section too, competing on local stories for the first time.

The *Journal* published a lifestyle piece that claimed women were attracted to men with sexually ambiguous facial features. The piece was illustrated by a series of photographs of the bottom half of men's faces. One of the "feminine" faces was immediately recognizable, at least in media circles. It belonged to Sulzberger.

Staffers said the idea originated with Thomson. The maneuver would serve as a mind-fuck to Sulzberger, a prank to staffers. But old-timers who cared about the paper's traditions found the stunt contemptible, unworthy of the *Journal*. So did the *Times*. Sulzberger complained about it directly to Thomson a few days later at a dinner honoring foreign correspondents; Thomson deflected the complaint.

"We've been vilified, unjustly so, and often factually incorrectly— most often factually incorrectly, by Fox News," Scott Heekin-Canedy, then president and general manager of the New York Times Company, told me. "This is just another flavor of that."

Not for Thomson the hand-wringing and pants-wetting that he thought afflicted so much of the news business, with the endless whining ("whinging" in Australian and British usage) about the need for transparency and ombudsmen and the two-way conversation with the public. Thomson and Baker would put out a newspaper for Mr. Murdoch that reflected their interests and, they hoped, intrigued readers and impressed advertisers. The tone was set at the top. At an event the next month at the National Press Club, Murdoch called the *Times* "a paper willing to do President Obama's bidding."

Some *Journal* reporters thought some of their peers at the *Times* got away with a degree of voice in their writing that veered into personal views. But skepticism among many *Journal* reporters and many editors toward their own news executives heightened rather than abated. Thomson and Baker took a keen interest in domestic partisan politics, fights with unions specifically, and teacher unions in particular. "Those are stories that both of them knew were important to Mr. Murdoch," a former editor who worked under them said.

A fight in Wisconsin featured all three topics. In early 2011, the newly elected governor, Scott Walker, worked with a Republican-controlled legislature to force greater contributions from union-represented state employees toward their health care and pension costs. It was vital, Walker argued, for the state to close a growing deficit.

Walker contended that the state's fiscal stability also depended on stripping those unions of some decades-old prerogatives: the right to compel state payrolls to deduct and reroute membership dues to union coffers and the right to conduct collective bargaining on behalf of their members for anything other than pay. Showing political finesse in a way that undermined his declaration that his moves were driven by financial need, Walker had exempted unions for police and firefighters, which had supported his campaign.

That proposed shift in the unions' ability to negotiate and compel payments threatened the financial pillars of both organized labor and their Democratic allies. Thomson and Baker watched carefully for pro-labor sympathies to surface in copy from their reporters. When Thomson didn't like the tone of a story, he would Google every person cited in it to learn more about each. If a professor had given money to Democratic candidates, Thomson said, she cannot be cited as a nonpartisan source. "Robert just wants people to be identified for who they are and what they believe," a senior *Journal* editor told me.

"The *Journal* was nudged rightward, partly because Thomson or Murdoch, or both, rightly felt too many journalists are on the left. Lots of us are," another editor involved in some of that coverage said. "On certain stories [the nudge] was more aggressive than others." The question, he said, was whether the remedy for the perceived bias itself weakened or compromised coverage.

In a front-page story on February 23, 2011, by the Washington bureau's Neil King Jr., the first three people quoted directly (other than an allusion to Governor Walker's antiunion sentiments) were all Republicans supportive of Walker's challenge to the unions: Ohio governor John Kasich, new US senator Ron Johnson of Wisconsin, and a state representative from Indiana.

King followed the quotations with this context: "Government figures show that inflation-adjusted per capita income in six right-to-work states increased at a 6.9 percent annual rate over the past 10 years. In contrast, incomes contracted at a 0.5 percent rate in six unionized upper-Midwest states over the same period, as many high-paying automotive and other manufacturing jobs disappeared and foreign automakers concentrated nearly all of their new investment in right-to-work states."

Several colleagues steeped in the details of the story questioned what happened to snarl King's usually straightforward reporting. One reporter asked, "Six right-to-work states? There were twenty-two at the time. Which ones? Why were *they* chosen?"

From another piece, a day later: "The Indiana legislation would have allowed workers at unionized companies to refrain from being part of the union and paying union dues. In the view of many corporations and the Republicans in the Indiana legislature, the bill was a matter of personal freedom and a chance to boost jobs in the state. But Democrats and many union leaders viewed it as an attack on the existence of unions."

That characterization of corporate motivation seemed disingenuous to several reporters at the paper: companies may well have looked at the proposal through the prism of personal freedom or as a means to boost jobs, but they equally wanted to strike at the economic underpinning and resulting political strength of the unions.

"It was often difficult to read between the lines or to know if you were overreacting to requests an editor would make," another reporter said. "Is this a bias an editor is displaying, or is this making the story better?"

To some, the pattern of such nudges evolved into a Rorschach test. "Late at night," a third reporter who often covered politics recalled, "you'd get an email or call saying, 'Gerry would want to rework the story like *this.*'

"Lo and behold, all the quotes from Democratic candidates were gone," this reporter said. "You had two minutes to say, 'It's ok' and make sure they hadn't misspelled a name when they had rewritten it."

Current *Journal* reporters and editors I spoke to said they would not talk publicly by name because they feared for their jobs. Some who had left signed nondisclosure agreements or feared they would need to return, hat in hand, to the *Journal* or News Corp. This was the Faustian bargain described by Ian Johnson: reporters and editors were so thankful their newsroom was spared the waves of layoffs and buyouts affecting their colleagues at places like the *Los Angeles Times*, the *Washington Post*, and even, to a lesser extent, the *New York Times*, that they found it hard to argue on anything but a day-to-day, story-to-story basis. There was a cohort that could not accept working for Murdoch. They decamped for Reuters, Bloomberg News, and the *Times*.

Thomson hated face-to-face confrontation and typically guided coverage through other senior editors, though he could be bullying in emails and conference calls; Baker could be quite charming and subtler but appeared to enjoy the occasional dust-up.

On more than one occasion, Baker told editors that an article could not cite public opinion polls showing that the views of American Catholics on abortion largely mirrored those of the general US population. Polls had consistently shown the same dynamic for years, the editor objected. A reporter involved thought, *It was as though he had simply willed the beliefs of Catholics away.*

Baker was convinced his colleagues were not listening closely enough to what he was trying to say. *Those polls aren't reliably reflecting what Catholics believe,* Baker, himself Catholic, informed his colleague. *By definition, anyone who supports abortion rights cannot receive Communion, which puts you in a specially disadvantaged position as a Catholic. It's different than for most Protestants or Jews.*

In another instance, late at night, Thomson took exception to a story built around a study questioning the viability of the Colorado River because the research had been commissioned by an environmental group. *We have to kill it,* editors were told. The story endured only because Thomson weighed in so late, which meant the paper lacked any other story to fill the hole in the paper's print edition.

Republicans had to be quoted at least as often as Democrats, even if officials in both parties were making the same points. But the reverse was never enforced. When Democratic lawmakers fled Wisconsin and Indiana to deny Republicans a quorum in the two state legislatures, no edicts came down to find other liberals to fill the void of the missing left-of-center voices.

For teachers' unions, the pattern was the same. The editors' antipathy for labor unions, strengthened, for Murdoch, by his fights to open his Wapping plant without union involvement in the 1980s in London, was additionally deepened by their belief that the problem with US education could largely be found in the intransigence of unionized teachers.

Thomson's eye was once caught by an article on the trend of public school districts charging parents extra for honors courses and music classes. Thomson emailed several editors with a scathing note: *This completely leaves out the part where the greedy teachers' unions are driving up the costs of everything.* After some back-and-forth, an editor deftly added a passage about the burden that teacher pensions placed on school districts, which strengthened the story. Thomson had inadvertently emailed the reporter on the story, Stephanie Simon, too. His blast raised her hackles, and she later told colleagues she didn't feel comfortable writing about education issues anymore. Simon left for Reuters in 2012.

As Murdoch spoke about his belief in the need to reform the educational system, in the UK as well as the US, he sided with those who would confront teachers' unions. Some Democrats endorsed that view as well, including Chicago mayor Rahm Emanuel. Murdoch believed in testing students and teachers, in charter schools, in innovative approaches that might rattle some educators.

Teach for America, Michelle Rhee's Students First, homeschooling, and charter school activists—these were considered to be players driven by noble aspirations, arrayed against the greedy teachers' unions. Murdoch had a financial interest in the education field. He was not the first entrepreneur to do so, nor the first media magnate. The Washington Post Company had acquired the Stanley Kaplan educational firm, and in more recent years its profits compensated for the *Post*'s slumping print revenues.

Murdoch had given Joel Klein the assignment to establish News Corp as a player in digital textbooks. He quickly proved that he could make his presence count. The New York school district had two major contracts with Wireless Generation, a for-profit business offering digital curriculums, student assessment, and teacher training. Less than two weeks after News Corp hired Klein, the company acquired Wireless Generation.

There was a lot of money at stake. In June 2011 New York State's Education Department granted a $27 million no-bid contract to Klein and Wireless Generation. But that contract was just to be News Corp's first big dip into far deeper waters. Murdoch had pegged the possible marketplace at nearly $700 billion. The *Journal* trod warily as it reported on this new venture of News Corp. But it soon had another story to cover much closer to home.

18

WSJ: LONDON VERSUS NEW YORK

THE ALLEGATIONS SPILLING FORTH IN almost every broadcast and newspaper in Britain in the summer of 2011 unnerved many reporters and editors at the *Wall Street Journal.* They recognized the story as a test of their journalistic independence from their newspaper's corporate owners and interests, not just their reportorial mettle. The paper reported on all the twists and turns—the accusations, the arrests, the apologies, the demands, the debates. But initially the *Journal* demonstrated little enterprise.

By Thursday, July 14, 2011, the House of Commons Culture, Media, and Sport Committee summoned Rupert and James Murdoch back to London to testify. Reporters at his *Journal* were also calling to pose inconvenient questions about James Murdoch's leadership of the company's British operations. The patriarch telephoned the paper's London bureau chief, Bruce Orwall, to urge reporters to refute "some of the things that have been said in Parliament, some of which are total lies."

News International, Murdoch said, had handled the crisis "extremely well in every way possible," save for some "minor mistakes." James, its executive chairman, had acted "as fast as he could, the moment he could." The *Journal* published the piece, which folded in other developments—including the opening of a federal investigation into whether any phones were hacked on US soil.

The *New York Times*'s Joe Nocera took that article as inspiration to devote a column to what he called the "Fox-ification" of the *Journal*. "The *Journal* was turned into a propaganda vehicle for its owner's conservative views. That's half the definition of Fox-ification," Nocera wrote. "The other half is that Murdoch's media outlets must shill for his business interests. With the *News of the World* scandal, the *Journal* has now shown itself willing to do that, too."

He pointed to Orwall's Murdoch interview as particularly damning. "There was no pushback against any of these statements, even though several of them bordered on the delusional," Nocera wrote. "The *Journal* reporter had either been told not to ask those questions, or instinctively knew that he shouldn't. It is hard to know which is worse." Mea culpa, Nocera wrote. Back in 2007, Nocera had been one of the commentators to declare Rupert Murdoch would be a savior of the *Journal*.

Many news staffers at the *Journal* privately considered Nocera's column terribly unfair. Murdoch hadn't volunteered himself for an interview. He had telephoned to harangue an employee. Orwall leveraged the call into remarks he could put in print, at a time when Murdoch proved an elusive quarry. If anything, Murdoch's own paper allowed him to damage himself by making comments that galled many people following the story.

True, Murdoch could not control how he sounded: when asked what truth there could be found in rumors he would split his newspapers from the rest of the company, or sell them altogether, Murdoch replied, "Pure and total rubbish . . . give it the strongest possible denial you can give." (Not such rubbish, as it turned out.) His journalists saw the paper's publication of those comments as forcing him on the record and, as it happened, allowing him to land blows against himself.

The allegation of "Fox-ified" coverage was particularly nettlesome. The *Journal*'s partnership with NBC's financial cable channel, CNBC, predated Murdoch. Reporters dreaded the looming expiration of that deal in 2012. They feared they would be forced to collaborate with coverage on the Roger Ailes–led Fox Business Network.

Some *Journal* reporters and editors had found Nocera's fears overblown. "Oh, I think all of us, at the time the deal was announced, were anxious what it might mean," said Alan Murray, who was executive editor of the paper's online operations and deputy managing editor under Thomson through late 2012. "What [would] News Corp's control of *The Wall Street Journal* mean? Would it in any way affect the independence of the news department? Would we somehow be forced to carry some other corporate agenda news that News Corp has?"

"But none of that's happened," Murray said.

Yet the taint was edging closer to home, and questions about corporate agendas arose, at least internally, with Les Hinton serving as the connective tissue between Murdoch's holdings on the two sides of the Atlantic. Hinton, the publisher of the *Journal* and CEO of Dow Jones, had been CEO of News International when hacking occurred. Further, Hinton had reassured MPs in testimony that he personally believed the violation of cell phone messages by *News of the World* to be limited to a single case. His words soothed roiling waters at the time. He carried gravitas in the UK; he had even served as the chairman of the enforcement panel of the Press Complaints Commission, an industry-led, self-regulatory body that was intended to field the public's concerns like a state bar or medical association.

In hindsight, Hinton's testimony reads as though it had been carefully couched to help the company smother bad headlines while avoiding legal liability down the line. By 2011 Hinton could duck the heat no longer, despite five decades of service to Murdoch. The chairman delivered the news personally: Hinton had to leave the *Journal*, Dow Jones, and News Corp.

The editorial page of the *Wall Street Journal* shifted into high gear. In a blistering editorial, the *Journal* blamed the tabloid scandal almost exclusively on the failure of police to investigate. And it turned its wrath onto another target: the paper's journalistic rivals. "We also trust that readers can see through the commercial and ideological motives of our competitor-critics," the paper wrote. "The Schadenfreude is so thick you can't cut it with a chainsaw. Especially redolent are lectures about journalistic standards from publications that give Julian Assange and WikiLeaks their moral imprimatur. They want their readers to believe, based on no evidence, that the tabloid excesses of one publication somehow tarnish thousands of other News Corp journalists across the world."

Those remarks were directed squarely at the *Guardian* and the *New York Times*. The liberal British paper had been episodically reporting on the culture of tabloid corruption for eleven years by that point, while in 2010 the *Times* had published its own exposé based in large part on leads provided by the *Guardian*. Murdoch's aides at News Corp called the story a setup: the two papers were colluding to try to damage him.

The *New York Times* piece was particularly damning because it included sources that were on the record. One of them, Sean Hoare, a former *News of the World* reporter who admitted his own actions, was discovered dead at his home the day of the *Journal*'s editorial. Authorities ruled out foul play: His death was later attributed to a drug overdose. But former colleagues said he had been traumatized by the scandal.

Many *Journal* critics refused to believe it, but the paper's news staff and its editorial staff had little or no influence over each other. And no one took the *Journal*'s editorial page editor, Paul Gigot, as a stooge for Murdoch. He had adopted a firm conservative line for the paper well before its takeover by News Corp and, if anything, outflanked Murdoch on his ideological right. Gigot had also pledged to colleagues that he would quit if Murdoch meaningfully interfered to further his business or political interests. Still, the editorial was a remarkable piece of corporate patriotism. It sounded as though it could have sprung from Thomson's mind to the printed page.

The defensiveness in that editorial also was given full voice by the company's supporters and treated seriously by other reputable news organizations. *Washington Post* media reporter Paul Farhi wrote an article that raised the specter of media bias both by Murdoch's publications and by those covering the accusations against News Corp's British journalists, citing "corporate loyalties and entanglements [that] have raised suspicions about news organizations' independence and objectivity."

The *Journal*'s schadenfreude editorial stood out for its incredibly poor sense of timing and judgment and badly misread the mood of the public. Its sister paper, the *Times of London*, struck a tone of remorse, which alienated the editor in chief, James Harding, from his bosses at the paper's corporate headquarters in New York. But the *Journal*'s editorial stance stoked fears of journalists inside the paper that in moments of crisis somehow they would be pressured to serve Murdoch's needs.

The extraordinary circumstances stirred the *Wall Street Journal* special oversight panel to action. On July 25 the committee published a statement in light of the hacking scandal, entitled, "What About the *Journal?*" The Special Committee wrote, "We have found nothing to even hint that the sort of misdeeds alleged in London have somehow crept into Dow Jones." The panel acknowledged that some journalists (presumably inside the paper, but not specified) thought *Journal* reporters should test the honesty of former *Journal* publisher Les Hinton's testimony to British lawmakers. The panel's members said they had repeatedly asked staffers, "Is anybody putting political, ideological, or commercial pressure on you to influence your news judgment?" It concluded, "The broad and consistent answer we get is no."

By and large, that rang true. But that did not reflect life as it was experienced by a dozen *Journal* reporters and editors assigned to cover allegations of criminal activities by various News Corp employees and contractors in the UK. Several reporters and editors had told colleagues of stories that were blocked, stripped of damning detail or context, or just held up in bureaucratic purgatory.

The biggest clash occurred when the investigative reporter Steve Stecklow uncovered a dissonance between the versions of a story on Milly Dowler published in different editions of the *News of the World* on April 14, 2002. At that time, the girl was missing but not yet known to be dead. In the early editions, Stecklow found detailed quotes from voice mail messages included in the article. The final edition of *News of the World* instead carried a lone, passing allusion to a voice mail. No one else appeared to have noted the telling switch.

The reporters and editors who worked on the story with Stecklow thought it was a barn-burner. A reporter for *News of the World* had told the *Journal* that the tabloid had sent eight reporters and photographers to a factory in the British Midlands during Milly Dowler's disappearance in 2002, expecting to find the girl working there. An editor deployed the team based on a message left on her voice mail. The *Journal* learned that the person who sent the reporters north was the paper's chief reporter, Neville Thurlbeck. If true, this incident doubly contradicted News International's claims that everyone thought the hacking was confined to one reporter and a private eye until late 2010. First, Thurlbeck had not been publicly implicated in the hacking of the royals. Second, some *News of the World* editor or company official must have called the news desk and ordered a change in the copy between editions because the paper's hacking was so blatantly revealed in the first version.

To their frustration, the *Journal* reporters couldn't pin down who had intervened (though suspicions focused on Tom Crone). Robert Thomson seized on that omission, saying the article hadn't met the standards expected of the *Journal*. *You guys didn't figure out why the story was changed*, Thomson told his subordinate editors.

The London bureau was led by Bruce Orwall, a journalist well known at his company's headquarters. As the *Journal*'s Hollywood bureau chief, Orwall had edited the front-page story in December 2000 documenting the path Wendi Deng had taken in becoming the third wife of News Corp's billionaire owner.

In July 2011, however, Orwall could be seen holed up in his office engaging in shouting matches via phone with top news executives in New York over the *News of the World* coverage. Orwall had some allies in New York on the story, including Alix Freedman. Freedman was one of the paper's most respected senior editors and a holdover from Paul Steiger's tenure. But Thomson was adamant. The bureau had covered the lead-up to the London Olympics, the royal wedding of Prince William, the European debt crisis, and the tribulations of the euro. None had elicited a fraction of the interest from the top as had the scandal affecting its parent company.

Thomson tried to kill the story several different times. As a fallback strategy, several reporters and editors involved believed, Thomson was intentionally trying to set impossible standards so the story would not see the light of day. Finally Thomson relented. On August 20, 2011, the *Journal* published a front-page piece on the *News of the World* and the telling changes between editions on the Milly Dowler story. In a compromise, the article did not lead with a hard-news approach, but a more anecdotal top. The revelation of the disparity between editions was not disclosed until the ninth paragraph. Still, the story made it to print.

"The fact that [the *Journal* article] did run was good," said one of the paper's journalists involved in the story. "But the process was so painful. If we hadn't fought, Robert would have been happy for us not to run it at all." Freedman left for Reuters the following month.

Covering the parent News Corp under duress was a test of the *Journal*'s mettle in the Murdoch era. When hacking first came up, two years earlier, in July 2009, Rupert Murdoch had been in Sun Valley, Idaho, clustered with other media moguls at their annual deal-making retreat. During an interview by satellite on Fox Business, anchor Stuart Varney gamely and vainly tried to get his boss to address the scandal. Murdoch shut him down. "I'm not talking about that issue at all today," Murdoch quickly said, grimacing. "I'm sorry."

Varney acquiesced swiftly. "No worries, Mr. Chairman. That's fine with me."

In that July 2011 interview with the *Journal*'s Orwall, Rupert Murdoch had blamed outside lawyers at Harbottle & Lewis hired by News Corp for making "a 'major mistake' in underestimating the scope of the problem." In 2007, News International executives including James Murdoch had pointed to the lawyers' review of internal documents to show the company had taken questions of impropriety seriously. When called by members of Parliament, Rupert Murdoch testified on July 20, 2011, that he had been failed by people in whom his executives had put their faith. Murdoch said Les Hinton brought Colin Myler back to London from the *New York Post* to become editor in chief of the *News of the World* specifically "to find out what the hell was going on." Myler, in turn, commissioned Harbottle & Lewis to do just that in 2007.

But as was subsequently becoming clear, the law firm had not been commissioned to conduct a wide-ranging review at all. Instead, it had examined emails that Clive Goodman, the reporter convicted of involvement in hacking in 2006, had exchanged with five editors.

The company limited Harbottle & Lewis's involvement to an assessment of whether Goodman had a strong case for a wrongful termination suit. The law firm's presence was triggered by Goodman's complaint: "This practice [phone-hacking] was widely discussed in the daily editorial conference, until explicit reference to it was banned by the Editor" (at that time, Andrew Coulson).

Hinton had authorized paying Goodman the equivalent of twelve months' salary in an agreement that precluded any employment suit.

The *Journal* reporters didn't have at hand all those details, many of which would be revealed at the inquiry convened weeks later by Lord Justice Brian Leveson. But they showed that News Corp had wrongly presented a human resources defense as a no-nonsense legal review.

Ultimately, the *Wall Street Journal* gave prominent play to both stories: the *News of the World*'s telltale switch in language to mask the hacking done on its behalf, and the sleight of hand in the corporation's public reliance on a narrow document review as a full-fledged internal investigation. MPs cited the voice mail story repeatedly in its final report on the affair. But the *Journal*'s reporters and editors had to fight hard to get those stories in print. And that led them to the question that hovered over the entire process: Why was Thomson involved at all?

Over at the *New York Times*, the top business editor was a former *Journal* editor named Lawrence Ingrassia. He recused himself from all coverage of the tabloid phone hacking scandal because his son had married the daughter of Colin Myler, the final *News of the World* editor. That's what respected news organizations tended to do in such circumstances. Why had Thomson not done the same? Why not assign a senior news executive not in the paper's top chain of command and without ties to the British papers to oversee the reporting?

Journal staffers batted around two answers. Thomson, like Murdoch, had grown up in a completely different newspaper culture. Papers in the Anglo-Aussie tradition took sides, fought for their interests, and were expected to do so.

Additionally, it served the chairman's interests to have his best friend run the show during a crisis. Journalistic propriety be damned. When the cards were down, Mr. Murdoch could rely on his mate to mitigate the damage.

19

"THE ONLY PERSON IN LONDON"

IN SEPTEMBER 2011, DEVELOPMENTS IN London raced ahead of News Corp. Klein and his colleagues embarked on a ruthless cull within the tabloids. Arrests mounted. Bribery and corruption joined mobile phone hacking on the list of allegations. Police swept through reporters' homes in early morning raids. Past courtesies no longer applied. The questions posed the previous April by Murdoch's former *Sunday Times* editor took on added urgency: What did James Murdoch know about hacking, and when did he know it?

Especially dangerous to Murdoch was the resentment of Colin Myler and Tom Crone, who had lost their jobs in July when the Murdochs decided to kill *News of the World*. At the end of the first week of September, the two prepared to take their case public, in front of the cameras at Parliament's Portcullis House, so that all of Britain and the world could hear them attack the man next in line to take over News Corp.

The family, too, had turned on James, in various ways. First Elisabeth and then Rupert told James to step aside. (Rupert changed his mind the next day.) The younger generation's efforts to work in unison to manage the transition from Rupert to the next Murdoch had been shredded. Lachlan had come to London to lend support and counsel but not to reenter the corporate fray. Elisabeth thought James and the newspaper hacks beneath him had led News International to the brink of ruin. *James and Rebekah fucked the company,* Elisabeth was overheard raging at a book party staged by her husband, Matthew Freud, with *Times of London* editor James Harding. Elisabeth wanted James out, perhaps for good. The sale of Elisabeth's production company Shine to News Corp had been accompanied by the plan to appoint her to a seat on News Corp's board of directors. In early August, she announced she would not take it up. James Murdoch's wife, Kathryn Hufschmid, loathed Freud and saw his machinations to position his own wife as the clean Murdoch behind her husband's rift with his sister.

James remained hidden from view amid the company's first quarterly report since the scandal, in early August. The initial questions from investment analysts involved profit margins for News Corp's cable holdings, advertising rates on those channels, the company's appetite for buying back stock (a way to increase the value of each stockholder's shares), what News Corp would do with the $5 billion it set aside to acquire BSkyB, the local TV business, the struggles of Fox Business Network, the prospect of newspaper profits in Australia. One analyst asked Rupert Murdoch whether he might split publishing off from the rest of the company; the chairman again knocked it down in no uncertain terms.

A reporter from Reuters asked, *Would the board support Murdoch's wish for James to succeed him as CEO at some stage in the near future?*

Murdoch hedged. "Well, I hope that the job won't be open in the near future," he said. "Chase [Carey] is my partner. If anything happens to me, I'm sure he will get it immediately, but—if I went under a bus, but Chase and I have full confidence in James. But I think that's all I need to say about it. In the end, the succession is a matter for the Board."

Meanwhile, James Murdoch trod a delicate path. "I acted on the advice of executives and lawyers with incomplete information, and that's a matter of real regret for me," he said in the sole interview he granted. British police officials had exonerated the company: "We now know that was an inadequate investigation, and that is a matter of profound regret for me, as well."

The subject of that investigation continued to haunt News International and its parent company. (In one sign among many, New York State's controller killed News Corp's $27 million educational software contract late that month.) The problem was no longer that a prominent reporter had hired a private investigator to hack into the private voice mails of the royals but that the private investigator, Glenn Mulcaire, had done the job too well and too often for too many masters at *News of the World*.

THE PARLIAMENTARY committee on media reconvened in September 2011. HR executive Daniel Cloke claimed in his testimony that Crone, Hinton, and Myler—basically the paper's entire hierarchy and its corporate bosses—had known of Clive Goodman's 2007 accusations that reporters and editors routinely commissioned phone hacking. But the company had not pursued the larger allegation. The former general counsel for News International, Jonathan Chapman, cited a "feeling of family compassion" at the company, which tempered the impulse to punish those who had committed crimes on the paper's behalf. He described a form of mateship.

As Crone and Myler addressed the committee, however, they felt bound by no such kinship. Instead, they told a relatively simple story:

things were going south. They had told James the risks. James Murdoch had received the email from Julian Pike and Tom Crone, who told him about the "for Neville" email. Crone and Myler met with Murdoch to make sure he understood the stakes, and he authorized them to settle the lawsuit swiftly and silently for anything up to about £500,000. The News International executives had minimized the importance of the meeting in earlier testimony. Now it was the hinge on which their testimony swung.

"If it all went public with Mr. Taylor, we were at risk of four other litigants coming straight in on top of us, with enormous cost," Crone testified. "If we have to pay way over the odds for Mr. Taylor, especially if there is a confidentiality clause . . . that is a good course of action. If it is £415,000 or £425,000 to settle one case, thereby avoiding being sued by four other people who might have similarly high demands and huge legal costs, that is the right decision to take from my point of view."

News International kept much of the British media legal establishment on retainer at one time or another but had agreed to waive lawyer-client privilege over past conduct of the cases, part of its effort to demonstrate to American and British authorities its willingness to cooperate. The waiver of legal privilege meant all those deliberations were now cascading into public view.

In their testimony, Crone and Myler often sidestepped questions to stick to their main and most damaging point: "There was no ambiguity about the significance of that document [the 'for Neville' email] and what options there were for the company to take," Myler said. Given their earlier, contradictory testimony, the two men had trouble convincing parliamentary committee members to rely on their account, especially of James Murdoch's state of mind. Conservative MP Louise Mensch turned to Crone: "I have to say, sir, that your evidence has really been as clear as mud."

JAMES MURDOCH'S status remained clouded as the date of News Corp's annual shareholder conference neared. The event was scheduled for Los Angeles in mid-October on the Fox Studio lots at the 476-seat Darryl F. Zanuck Theater—a secluded spot on a site controlled by the company. Protesters would have a much tougher time disrupting the meeting than they would in New York's Upper West Side, where the meetings were usually held. Security was tight.

Along with James's leadership, Rupert's acumen had been called into question too. External analysts looked at a trail of misdeeds and misjudgments—from the acquisition of Elisabeth Murdoch's Shine for a very generous price, to the $2.8 billion write-down of the *Wall Street Journal*, to the purchase of MySpace and its fire-sale disposal a few short years later.

"We have consistently given Mr. Murdoch's board an F since they first incorporated in the US, and that's only because there's no lower grade," Nell Minow of GMI Ratings, a firm that assesses integrity in corporate governance, said ahead of the company's annual meeting. Amid the hacking revelations, Murdoch's leadership is "a big, big mess," she said. "Rupert Murdoch went to testify before Parliament and he said, at the same time, 'I didn't know this was going on' and 'I'm the guy to fix it.' Those are two incompatible statements. Anybody who is swayed by that is not paying attention."

"If you had this happen in a normal company, in theory, the board would have required the CEO to resign," said Laura Martin, senior media analyst for the investment bank Needham and Company. But she said investors believed News Corp's shares would rise more with Murdoch steering the ship than someone new.

At the shareholders' meeting at the theater tucked at the back of Fox Studios, Rupert Murdoch carried himself with a confidence laced with bravado. He started his address by calling News Corp's history "the stuff of legend."

"The company has been the subject of both understandable scrutiny and unfair attack," Murdoch said. But his voice was not the only one that shareholders heard. Union critics who held News Corp shares gave Labour MP Tom Watson their proxy, and in the process gave him a soapbox from which to speak. "I think I've got a duty to bring that to the shareholders' attention, because, after all, they are also responsible for what this company does," Watson said. "And I think the board have let them down." The board was stacked with Murdoch's children, former executives, political allies, and current or former business partners. The Murdoch family trust held about two-fifths of all voting shares, which gave it near control of all stockholder decisions. Like almost everyone else who came into Rupert Murdoch's orbit, the board members found it difficult to distinguish between the interests of the family and the company.

At the session, Watson informed Murdoch and shareholders there would be a new front on the parliamentary inquiry he was helping to direct: email and computer hacking. The company paid more than $5 million that day to the Dowlers, much of it earmarked for a charity of their choice, to settle their claim against the company.

The day proved arduous for Rupert Murdoch. Officials from institutional investors such as the California state pension fund demanded that he separate the roles of chairman and CEO. Murdoch became testy, cutting off his former Australian editor turned corporate activist Stephen Mayne: "Stephen, I'd hate to call you a liar, but you're wrong." To a representative from the Church of England, Murdoch snapped, "Your investments haven't been that great, but go ahead." Why the Church of England invested in a company that had topless girls on the third page of its most profitable publication every day was a separate question. Perhaps it showed the modernity, or the erosion of standards, of British institutions. Perhaps it merely underscored the ubiquity of Murdoch's presence in British commerce.

Rupert Murdoch easily enough won reelection to his corporate board. Saudi prince Al Waleed bin Talal had promised to cast the 7 percent of voting shares he held following the Murdoch line. (Murdoch had invested News Corp money in Waleed's Saudi media enterprises.) Yet the day proved an embarrassment. James Murdoch lost nearly 35 percent of the vote for reappointment to the board—a majority of all non-Murdoch votes cast. Lachlan, who had never run the British enterprises, lost a third of the vote.

AT THE outset of November, just days before appearing yet again before the parliamentary committee, James stepped down from the boards within News International that ran the two tabloids (News Group Newspapers) and the *Times of London* and the *Sunday Times* (Times Newspapers Ltd). He was disengaging from the UK.

Lawmakers on the parliamentary committee investigating *News of the World* experienced something out of the movie *Groundhog Day*. In 2010 the committee unsatisfyingly concluded that News International had suffered from "collective amnesia." On November 11, 2011, one question dominated the conversation: was James Murdoch a fool or a knave?

He did learn of the "for Neville" email, the younger Murdoch admitted to the MPs, before authorizing Crone to pay enough money to make Gordon Taylor's complaint disappear. But he had only understood half the email's import. Crone and Myler told him it contained transcripts. They never called it the "for Neville" note, nor did they mention Thurlbeck at all, he said. By Murdoch's account, he knew only that the transcripts proved the existence of a second specific instance of hacking, not that it was commonplace at his paper. Myler should have told him more. The lawyers failed him. The police gave him false assurance. He never received the outside lawyer's doomsday assessment of the culture of criminality alive in the newsroom.

"If there was a mistake or a shift that we need to focus on, it was the tendency for a period of time to react to criticism or allegations as being hostile or motivated commercially or politically," Murdoch testified. "What we did not necessarily do was reflect as dispassionately as we might have, among all the din and clamor that surrounds a large business such as this."

Watson baited Murdoch amid the exchange. "Are you familiar with the word mafia?"

MURDOCH: "Yes, Mr. Watson."

"Have you ever heard the term *omertà*? It is the mafia term for the code of silence."

"I am not an aficionado of such things," Murdoch replied.

"Would you agree that it means a group of people who are bound together by secrecy, who together pursue their group's business objectives with no regard for the law, using intimidation, corruption, and general criminality?"

"Absolutely not," Murdoch said. "Frankly, I think that that is offensive and it is not true."

Watson then reminded him of the bill of particulars in the hands of police and prosecutors: "There are allegations of phone-hacking, computer-hacking, conspiring to pervert the course of justice and perjury facing this company and all this happened without your knowledge. Mr. Murdoch, you must be the first mafia boss in history who didn't know he was running a criminal enterprise."

Watson had gone a step too far. But other MPs, including Conservatives, also took tough shots. Watson's Labour colleague Paul Farrelly challenged James Murdoch's competence. *Why hadn't he asked to read the lawyer's reports? Why would he authorize such big payments? Why did he fail to realize that the hacking of Gordon Taylor's phone meant the illegal practice stretched beyond coverage of the royals? Why did he not take the* Guardian's *2009 report on the Taylor settlement seriously?*

"So even at that stage in the middle of 2009 as the executive chairman of News International," Farrelly asked, "you are possibly the only person in London who still thinks that there is [only] one rogue reporter and one private detective?"

More odious developments surfaced before the cameras. The public learned of the private eyes following the lawyers and MPs. Every MP on the House of Commons committee conducting the investigations in 2009 and 2010 had also been followed by private investigators seeking dirt. Murdoch apologized profusely.

The committee could not land the knockout punch. Then again, James Murdoch could not make the bleeding stop.

The MPs were not the only ones investigating News International's behavior. Prime Minister Cameron had created an inquiry to be run by Lord Justice Brian Leveson. The judge and his lead interrogator, attorney Robert Jay, were taking a hard look at the press's relationship with police, politicians, and power. As they did so, additional disclosures came to light.

At the outset of 2012, the *Times of London* admitted that in order to disclose in print the identity of an anonymous police blogger known as "Nightjack," it had hacked his email. In court, lawyers for the newspaper had deceived the judge, maintaining that the reporter deduced his identity from publicly available information. Meanwhile, the *Sunday Times* acknowledged subjecting Gordon Brown to "blagging," a broad term encompassing deception by journalists to obtain information illegally. The *Guardian* had earlier posted audio of a con man posing as a lawyer to persuade Brown's attorneys to hand over private terms about the sale price of Brown's flat. The paper's editor, John Witherow, confirmed that incident, but also said one of his employees had impersonated Brown in a call to Abbey National Bank in order to get confidential financial figures. In the middle of February, police arrested a handful of employees at the *Sun* on suspicion of bribing police officers and military personnel for information.

Later that month, Rupert Murdoch returned to London to oversee the printing of the first edition of the *Sun on Sunday*, the new tabloid to replace *News of the World*. The paper felt distinct from the one it replaced. The first *Sun on Sunday* was light on scandal, heavy on sports, inspiration, celebrity gossip (but not *too* mean), and a scattering of politics and world affairs.

Murdoch beamed for the cameras. The new publication was a welcome distraction that would restore some of the advertising and circulation revenue lost when he shut down the *News of the World*. James was nowhere to be seen.

Only twenty-four hours later, one of the most senior police officials at Scotland Yard testified that *Sun* journalists had made illegal payments to a broad swath of public officials in a half-dozen or more government agencies. "It reveals a network of corrupted officials," deputy assistant police commissioner Sue Akers testified before Judge Leveson. "There also appears to have been a culture at the *Sun* of illegal payments, and systems have been created to facilitate those payments whilst hiding the identity of the officials receiving the money."

The cancer at News Corp's British holdings had metastasized.

20

AILES SEEKS
A LEGACY

LIKE RUPERT MURDOCH, ROGER AILES insisted he had no
time for people who obsessed on status such as college pedigrees, big
journalism awards, or invitations to fancy, high-powered dinners on
Manhattan's Upper East Side. Periodically he would register his disdain for such attributes while attending fancy, high-powered dinners
on Manhattan's Upper East Side.

By 2011 Roger knew what kind of mark he had made at Fox News,
an organization shaped in his own image, a concoction of show business, populist conservative politics, pugilism, and reporting. But there
was the question of legacy—what would endure.

Ailes's channel had helped conservatives push news coverage to
the right. Fox made the news business, especially television news,
brasher, more opinionated, and splashier. It brought local television
news judgments and Hollywood sensibilities into the national and

political arenas. MSNBC had found profit for the first time by bank-
ing hard left, but that was no rebuke of Fox; it was an homage.

Ailes had subtly steered his channel to shift with the times. To
harness anti-Obama sentiment, he had dropped the outmatched liberal Alan Colmes from *Hannity & Colmes*, added Glenn Beck, and
created Fox Nation, a red-meat, red-state online offshoot for those
who found the Fox News website too evenhanded. Yet in the summer
of 2010, Ailes decided to create another brand on the web that might
prove more welcoming to the nation's quickest growing demographic:
Hispanics.

He turned to Francisco Cortes for help. A Bronx native of Puerto
Rican descent, Cortes started at Fox after a stint in the US Army as
one of the first enrollees in the Ailes Apprenticeship. Ailes wanted to
create a new Fox-friendly pipeline of young African American, Asian,
and Latino journalists to help stock the newsroom with a diverse crew
trained in the Fox way. He decided to create a new website called
Fox News Latino, aimed largely at English-speaking Hispanics. The
site incorporated pieces from freelancers and a dozen staffers with
the aggregation of news coverage from other sources, particularly in
Latin America.

Ailes agreed with Ronald Reagan's aphorism that Latinos' faith,
whether Catholic or evangelical, their patriotism, their service in the
armed forces, and their aspirations to become small business owners made many Hispanics potential conservative converts, despite
strong affinities for Democrats at the ballot box. Ailes believed the
site served an important purpose on business, journalistic, and ideological grounds.

Latinos make up one-sixth of the nation's population, but accounted
for more than half of the country's population growth between 2000
and 2010. What was considered left or liberal on Fox News represented mainstream views for a site aimed at Latinos—even a site with

the Fox brand. Ailes's relatively low-cost initiative paid off. Hispanic activists praised Fox News Latino even as they attacked coverage on Fox News. The site beat the similar ventures from the Huffington Post and NBC News to the punch.

Periodically, Fox News Latino journalists influence the news channel's coverage, at least around the edges. Fox News Latino's Bryan Llenas appeared on Fox News to describe the results of a poll on Latino views commissioned by the website in the early stages of the 2012 elections. Llenas noted that Hispanic voters cared more about the economy than immigration, but said that the latter issue defined their moral compass. "Eighty-five percent support undocumented workers working in this country," Llenas told the anchor, Rick Folbaum. "If you ask them whether they prefer the word 'illegal' versus 'undocumented,' a majority of them believe that the term 'illegal immigrant' is offensive."

Latinos represented the future of ratings. Glenn Beck did, too, at least for the near term. But Beck came with conspiracy theories, wild-eyed accusations, and predictions of doom. His ratings declined throughout 2010 and protests from such liberal groups as Color of Change led hundreds of advertisers to peel away. Some of the remaining advertisers peddled gold for hoarding and seeds for staple crops, as though civilization was on the verge of collapse. Beck liked talking about religion, often apocalyptically, at great length. Ailes felt that was the kiss of death on cable television. Each man had a clear vision for the kind of show he wanted on the air. They just didn't match up.

The chairman had always minted the stars. Fox News was the star. O'Reilly was perhaps the network's one untouchable figure. But no one could be bigger than Fox News itself, a fact seemingly lost on Beck. He not only had a radio show but created his own production company, Mercury Radio Arts, through which he performs in a traveling concert show. In August 2011, Beck staged a rally on the same day and spot as Martin Luther King Jr.'s "I Have a Dream" speech, forty-seven years earlier. He created the Blaze, a conservative news and aggregation site modeled after the liberal Huffington Post. His colleagues at Fox wondered whether any of that would have been possible but for Fox. Ailes's aides privately characterized Beck as a demagogue, a perpetual motion machine producing one bad headline after another. Beck's loyalists whispered that Ailes was a control freak, stifling his continued rise after Beck had demonstrated that you could get prime-time ratings at 5:00 PM eastern time—well before most people had returned from work on the East Coast.

In the spring of 2011 Ailes took steps to remove Beck from the air. A carefully orchestrated joint interview with the Associated Press allowed Ailes and Beck to present a relatively unified front. Beck said he had asked Ailes for a reduced role at Fox that did not include his daily evening show. "Half the headlines say he's been canceled," Ailes told the AP. "The other half say he quit. We're pretty happy with both of them." Fox News executive Joel Cheatwood would follow Beck to his production company, Mercury Arts. The announcement included the promise that Mercury Arts would continue to develop projects for Fox News and its digital platforms. Neither side believed that promise would be fulfilled.

On his show the next evening, Beck showed flashes of his trademark humor—along with his trademark ego. "There's a lot more important news than, 'What's the big fat chunky guy doing for his future?'" Beck told viewers. "When I took this job, I didn't take it because it was going to be a career for me." He then proceeded to compare himself to Paul Revere.

Beck's coworkers thought he was a deranged business genius. For his new online channel, Blaze TV, Beck followed his instincts: the first broadcast was beamed from Jerusalem, where he encouraged Israelis to live with hope. Why they needed his encouragement was not clear. He built up his own video channel and news service, and it earned him tens of millions of dollars a year. He later sought to place it on cable systems throughout the country.

Ailes and Bill Shine, Fox's programming chief, created a tempo-rary show to fill Beck's slot called *The Five*. It was built around four conservative voices and one liberal—four attractive people under fifty and one guy in his mid-sixties. The odd man out in each grouping was Bob Beckel, who managed Democratic presidential nominee Walter Mondale's landslide loss in 1984 and got caught up in personal scandal afterward. He was not outmatched in bombast, but Beckel presented an intemperate and outmoded face of liberalism on the channel.

The show flourished and stuck around. Ailes surprised even himself with its success.

———————

THAT SAME spring, Ailes's emotional investment in Fox was being tested. Ailes was paid $5 million a year, plus a bonus of $1.25 million at the end of the fiscal year, plus a "high end special bonus" of $8 million that he would undoubtedly receive. Fox's ratings allowed network executives to squeeze extra money not just from advertisers but from cable system providers as contracts to carry Fox for their subscribers expired. News Corp would annually grant Ailes extra shares worth another $4 million (give or take) once Fox Business Network broke even and additional stock if it started hitting some profit targets. He traveled to all business-related events on a company-paid private jet. News Corp paid for Ailes's security detail too. Over time, the pack-age could exceed $20 million a year. But Ailes told associates he was still just a hired hand. Rupert Murdoch underscored Ailes's status by refusing to grant him a meaningful stake in the company that came with a vote.

Far from New York, a woman well versed in the ways of politics and power traveled thousands of miles for a private conversation bearing a greeting from Ailes. Kathleen T. McFarland, "KT" on the air, was a Fox News analyst and a former aide on national security and military matters in three different Republican administrations. McFarland also ran unsuccessfully for the Republican Party nomination for US Senate in New York in 2006. In April 2011 she met with Gen. David Petraeus, then overseeing American military strategy in Afghanistan, for an off-the-record conversation at his offices in Kabul. She sought his assessment of operations there in her role as a commentator and columnist. Toward the end of the ninety-minute session, she told Petraeus she had a message from her boss. Ailes had his mind on a big prize: the White House. Ailes had little confidence in Mitt Romney for the 2012 race. *The Republican field needs shaking up*, Ailes thought. *Petraeus could be a good addition to the mix.*

The ambitious general could see where McFarland was going and headed her off: "I'm not running." Petraeus and McFarland joked nervously about the presence of his aides. "Everybody at Fox loves you," McFarland said and then detoured to ask Petraeus what he'd like Fox to change about its coverage of the war in Afghanistan.

But the Fox analyst doubled back to the message she said she was carrying for Ailes. "I'm not runnin'," Petraeus repeated, laughing. McFarland said Ailes advised him to stay in government only if Obama named him chairman of Joint Chiefs of Staff of the Armed Services. "If you're offered anything else, don't take it," she said. "Resign in six months and run for president." Ailes would run his campaign. At no point did Petraeus indicate surprise. "Rupert's been after me, as well," the general replied. He then turned to his cohort of aides. "You all have really got to shut your mouths," Petraeus told them.

McFarland moved to reassure him: "I'm only reporting this back to Roger. And that's our deal." Petraeus said he was interested in only two jobs: chairman of the joint chiefs and another that he would not specify. "That has to be off the record," he said. He repeated that he would never run for the White House. "If I ever ran, I'd take [Ailes] up on his offer," Petraeus said, and added a revelation of his own: "He said he would quit Fox." Ailes had promised to bankroll his run, Petraeus said, before correcting himself. "That must have been Murdoch." McFarland quickly agreed. "I think the one who's bankrolling it is the big boss," she said.

By the end of the month, Obama had nominated the general to become director of the Central Intelligence Agency. When Bob Woodward of the *Washington Post* revealed the exchange and posted the audio online much later, Ailes said he had been joking. McFarland took the fall: "I know now that Roger was joking, but at the time, I wasn't sure."

MITT ROMNEY was the front-runner among Republicans from the outset, the guy "up next," as Bob Dole had been in 1996, and John McCain in 2008. He had 1950s good looks, fairly strong name recognition from his 2008 bid, and a seemingly bottomless bottom line. But no matter how strongly he professed his conservative beliefs, even calling himself "a severe conservative," Romney failed to stir passion in the core Republican primary voter.

Romney appeared on many conservative radio talk shows but routinely shut out reporters on the trail, preferring to deliver carefully honed messages at tightly controlled forums. In one four-week period that fall, Romney did no interviews with the national press corps. The *New York Times* magazine and *Time* magazine did cover stories on Romney without any help from the candidate.

Ailes had confidence in none of the alternatives to Romney, not Herman Cain, Rick Perry, or even network alums Newt Gingrich and Rick Santorum. Still, Fox gave credulous treatment to all of them and even to sideshows such as Donald Trump. Fox treated him more kindly than his own network, NBC, which aired his show *Celebrity Apprentice.* Trump was the ultimate in empty calories and Ailes knew he could not beat Obama. But Ailes let it ride.

When Gingrich surged, Romney met privately with Fox News executives, and subsequently surfaced several times on the network. Then he sat down with Fox's Bret Baier, who asked: "How can voters trust what they hear from you today is what you will believe if you win the White House?" On key issues—climate change, abortion, immigration, gay rights—Romney had advocated a variety of contradictory positions, including some held by the Obama administration.

"Well, Bret, your list is just not accurate," Romney replied, grimacing. "So, one, we'll have to be better informed." Baier pressed him again, prompting Romney to accuse Fox of taking talking points from commercials paid for by Democrats. It was all downhill from there.

One common belief outside the network, especially among its detractors, held that Fox intended to dictate a winner for 2012—the "Fox primary," one critic dubbed it. It was an imprecise assessment. Fox News was appealing to conservative viewers and voters by rigorously refereeing the internal party fight in which there was no clear-cut crowd pleaser. In an earlier era, party bosses had performed that role in smoke-filled rooms. After primaries were established, the political press corps—the boys and girls on the buses and airplanes—played that part. But in the Republican field, Ailes's Fox News dwarfed all media players.

Santorum received a boost from the top Fox pundit of all. Rupert Murdoch fired up a personal Twitter account on New Year's Eve 2011. Among his inaugural political missives of the 2012 cycle: "Can't resist this tweet, but all Iowans [should] think about Rick Santorum. Only candidate with genuine big vision for country." Romney was thought to have won the Iowa caucuses in a close vote. Days later, however, Santorum was declared the victor following a party recount. It would not be enough to give him enduring momentum. He would hold his former employers at Fox responsible for failing to give him sufficiently fulsome coverage. So, for that matter, did Gingrich. Romney, for his part, told Ailes point-blank that Fox favored Gingrich and Santorum over him. If Ailes had granted one of the Republicans favored status, the candidate didn't know it.

OVER THE months Ailes reconciled himself to Romney's ascension. In May, *Fox & Friends* broadcast a four-minute segment that was like a political hit piece on Obama, contrasting his aspirational 2008 themes of hope and change with discordant music and images of a dystopian America. After an angry call from White House press secretary Jay Carney, Fox removed the video from its website and Bill Shine said it was not "authorized" by senior executives. The network did not issue an apology; it rarely did. Instead, the issue was addressed internally. The same instinct played out in a different way when Fox News wrongly reported that the US Supreme Court had overturned the president's health care overhaul, on constitutional grounds. CNN also misreported the decision—the result of journalists for both networks failing to read past the second page of the ruling. Fox gave viewers the correct outcome more quickly than did CNN. But CNN posted a correction and an apology. Fox said it had gotten the story right, as the ruling declared Obamacare unconstitutional on page two and resurrected it on page three.

AS THE general election reached full steam, Fox executives believed Obama was getting a pass on important issues that would have bedeviled George W. Bush, including the death of Americans at the US consulate in Benghazi. The network devoted extensive coverage to the issue, replaying the footage of the consulate ablaze in the days before the election. Anchors and pundits said other news outlets were failing to give adequate attention to the administration's failure to secure their diplomats' safety. The network was providing balance to the bias it identified in others.

In the week before Election Day, the so-called Superstorm Sandy devastated parts of New Jersey and New York State. After the storm, however, New Jersey governor Chris Christie accepted the warm embrace of the federal government, literally, in the person of President Obama. Christie, a Republican, praised the president, who promised and delivered immediate financial support and much needed personnel. Christie took to Fox News to explain why he welcomed the active aid from a Democratic White House just days ahead of the election.

"Right now I'm much more concerned about preventing any other loss of life, getting people to safe places. And then we'll worry about the election," Christie said. "I've spoken to the president three times yesterday. He's been incredibly supportive and helpful to our state. And not once did he bring up the election."

Steve Doocy, the host of *Fox & Friends*, nudged Christie to offer a photo opportunity for Romney: "Is there any possibility that Governor Romney may go to New Jersey to tour some of the damage with you?"

"I have no idea. Nor am I the least bit concerned or interested," said Christie, as caustic as ever. "I could care less about any of that stuff. I have a job to do. I've got 2.4 million people out of power. I've got devastation on the shore. I've got floods in the northern part of my state. If you think right now I give a damn about presidential politics, then you don't know me."

Romney's partisans privately groused that Christie was doing what was best for his own future political prospects, both in New Jersey, a blue state, and in his mind for a possible presidential bid four years later. But Christie was striking a partnership of convenience that would pay off for the state. At times, Christie exhibited the giddiness of a kid. He expressed delight to be flying on a presidential helicopter. Obama further rewarded him a few days later with a call from his musical hero, Asbury Park's Bruce Springsteen, from Air Force One. Springsteen had been performing at Obama events in Ohio.

Rupert Murdoch paid close attention. His papers and Fox News had supported Christie as he rose from top federal prosecutor to governor to a national political prospect. Romney had come close to selecting Christie as his running mate, although, according to a friend of Ailes, Murdoch and Ailes met with Romney and made it clear that conservatives—and they—would not take him seriously unless he picked Congressman Paul Ryan of Wisconsin. Romney's choice of Ryan earned him widespread praise from the *New York Post*, the *Wall Street Journal* editorial page, and Fox News programs.

On November 3, the Saturday before Election Day, Murdoch took to Twitter to praise New York mayor Mike Bloomberg and Christie for their handling of the storm damage but added, "Can't blame Christie for being on the front page of every paper palling up with O [meaning Obama] but misleading." A bit later on, Murdoch tweeted that Christie "was first Republican gov to support Romney, and has worked tirelessly for him[.] Help to remind." Murdoch was telling Christie to let voters know that his support belonged to Romney.

As a mark of respect, if not deference, Christie telephoned Murdoch to explain he would seek help for residents wherever he could get it. Murdoch bluntly told Christie he might irreparably damage his chances for higher office if he did not reiterate his support for Romney. He told the New Jersey governor exactly what he had to do to retain credibility in meaningful conservative circles.

The next morning, at a press conference covered by national cable news channels, Christie reiterated his loyalty for Romney.

Typos, misspellings, and the occasional gaffe mark the Twitter feed as Murdoch's own, not one commandeered by PR advisers. Murdoch was doing his part for the Romney camp, letting Twitter followers know he expected the Republican to win, despite polls to the contrary. "Monolithic media will spend next three days pushing Obama, but final outcome far from certain," he wrote on November 3. "Early voting patterns look very different."

THE NEXT DAY: "Seems slight edge to Obama, but Romney seeing small late surge. Many state polls look unreliable."

His statement seemed to encompass polls commissioned by his own properties. Those conducted by the *Wall Street Journal* in partnership with NBC News and rival surveys paid for by Fox News also showed fairly constant margins in favor of the president, in the swing states as well as nationally. But Fox's programs relied heavily on a rotation of other conservative pollsters, pundits, and public opinion gurus. They strayed beyond analysis into promises of a Romney resurgence.

Former George W. Bush strategist Karl Rove was Fox's leading analyst. He also had the run of the opinion pages of the *Wall Street Journal*. On October 4, his column in the *Journal* was headlined: "Can We Believe the Presidential Polls?"

"Mr. Bush was hitting the vital 50 [percent] mark in almost half the polls (unlike Mr. Obama) and had a lead over Mr. Kerry twice as large as the one Mr. Obama now holds over Mr. Romney," Rove wrote. "So why was the 2004 race 'a dead heat' while many commentators today say Mr. Obama is the clear favorite? The reality is that 2012 is a horse race and will remain so. An incumbent below 50 percent is in grave danger. On Election Day he'll usually receive less than his final poll number."

A chief force behind American Crossroads, a new form of political action committee that took money from anonymous donors, Rove helped raise hundreds of millions of dollars for Republican candidates across the country. But despite his strategic role in the race he remained a nearly constant presence as an analyst on Fox. The polls, he warned viewers, are "endowed by the media with a scientific precision they simply don't have." On October 9, David Paleologos, director of the Suffolk University Political Research Center, told Fox viewers that Romney was cresting. "In places like North Carolina, Virginia, and Florida we've already painted those red," Paleologos told Bill O'Reilly. "We're not polling any of those states again. We're focusing on the remaining states." (Obama would win Virginia and Florida.)

On October 15 Dick Morris, the former adviser to Democratic president Bill Clinton and Republican Senate majority leader Trent Lott, weighed in. "If Romney simply continues to be the same man that he was two weeks ago . . . this momentum will continue. And I told you nine months ago, and I've said for the last nine months, and I say it again tonight, this election will be a landslide for Romney."

Other conservatives made the same case elsewhere. The *New York Times* poll aggregator, Nate Silver of the blog 538, came in for particular derision for promising near black-and-white certainty in a world defined by gray-hued margins of error. Silver's twist was to predict not just the national vote and state-by-state breakdowns (with accompanying Electoral College scenarios) but also the degree of certainty any given candidate would prevail. Given Silver's openly liberal outlook, the *Times* took a gamble that his methodology would hold up. If not, the newspaper would be criticized for having tilted its coverage.

On November 1, Dick Morris offered the Fox audience a vision for what would happen. "It is not neck and neck, it's a few laps. I think that Romney is going to win by 5 to 10 points in the popular vote. I think he's going to win the electoral vote by something like 310, 300 to 220, 230." Morris continued, "I think he's going to carry—and this isn't just [a] guess, it's based on the latest polling—I think he's going to carry New Hampshire, Ohio, Iowa, plus, of course, Florida, Colorado and Virginia. And then I think he's got—he's going to carry Pennsylvania. I think he's got a good shot at carrying Wisconsin, an outside chance at Michigan and Minnesota." (Not one of those predictions held just five days later.)

On the day before the election Newt Gingrich offered his prediction on Fox News: "My personal guess is you'll see a Romney landslide, 53 percent-plus in the electoral, in the popular vote, 300 electoral votes plus. And we may come very close to capturing control of the Senate in that context."

That same night Morris doubled down: "We're going to win 325 electoral votes. We're going to win the popular vote by 5 points or more. . . . There's about a seven-point margin between the enthusiasm of Democrats and that of the Republicans."

Election Day would prove to be a shock for viewers who had relied primarily on Fox News for their political coverage.

———————

AILES HAD thought hard enough about his legacy that he had arranged to write a memoir with Jim Pinkerton, the former White House aide under presidents Ronald Reagan and George H.W. Bush who had become a columnist and Fox News media critic. But he never quite found the time. Gabriel Sherman, a reporter for *New York* magazine, wrote a cover story on Ailes and signed a book contract to write an unauthorized biography. He interviewed Fox journalists, followed Ailes to public events around the country, and even wrote about the Putnam County, New York, newspaper that Ailes owns and operates with his wife, Elizabeth Tilson Ailes.

Andrea Tantaros, co-host of Fox's *The Five*, called Sherman a "stalker," a "harasser," and a "Soros puppet"—that last epithet a reference to his affiliation with the New America Foundation, which has received donations from George Soros and his son Jonathan. (As it happens, Pinkerton had also been a fellow at the New America Foundation.) To handle the competing narrative of his life, Ailes instead granted generous access to Zev Chafets, a magazine writer and former *New York Daily News* columnist who had written a favorable biography of Rush Limbaugh. Chafets said he had adopted Fox's mantra as his own: "I report. You decide." His authorized biography, which Ailes did not review before publication, came out in March 2013.

Fox commentators such as Patrick Caddell blasted Sherman; a writer for Breitbart News questioned his mental well-being; while another media blogger asked Sherman to comment on whether he took prescription pills. An outfit in Scottsdale, Arizona, with no relationship to Sherman or his publisher bought a bunch of domain addresses that incorporated the author's name and the planned title of his book. It began to look to some Fox watchers like a campaign.

What Ailes really wanted for his final hurrah at Fox was less a memoir than an equity stake. He wanted more than just additional shares of News Corp stock, and he wanted his payday to dwarf what other major media executives received. One Ailes associate said the Fox News chief was obsessed with the pay of David Zaslav of Discovery Communications. According to Discovery's 2012 filings with federal regulators, Zaslav was paid $3 million in salary and another $4.84 million as a cash bonus (of a possible $5 million maximum bonus). And he was granted "long-term incentive compensation" in stock worth $23.9 million in fair market value. The tidy package amounted to more than $36 million for the year. Much to Ailes's chagrin, Rupert Murdoch wasn't about to pay him that much.

That chafed Ailes. So in early 2012 he talked to Newsmax CEO Christopher Ruddy, whose conservative news outfit had established a highly profitable network of newsletters and a magazine from its opinion and news website. Ruddy had built up offices in West Palm Beach, Florida, as well as in midtown Manhattan, just seven blocks from News Corp. He had hopes of creating a television channel for the brand too. *Come on board*, Ruddy told Ailes. Ruddy promised him a $25 million a year salary and equity, holding out the promise of a payday worth hundreds of millions.

Ailes was tempted. But he was aging and had health issues—not just his weight and hemophilia but arthritis and others too. A start-up might be exciting but also exhausting. And he had little inclination to relinquish control at Fox. He had never groomed a successor who could guide Fox after he left or a new generation of prime-time stars either, with the possible exception of Megyn Kelly. The network's big names were stable but aging. Over the years, some executives had internally speculated the next stage of Fox's development might demand a manager rather than an all-consuming visionary like Ailes. It is a mark of his force of personality that people at Fox typically wondered whom Ailes would recommend to succeed him (if he had reached such a conclusion, he did not share it with others), rather than whom the Murdochs would want.

In late October, Fox announced that Ailes had signed a four-year contract extension that would take him through June 2017, past his seventy-seventh birthday. The network and News Corp leaked that he had received a big raise.

———

ON ELECTION night Fox analysts and reporters rightly noted that 2012 had not inspired the kind of captivating campaign that Obama ginned up for victory in 2008. At the start of the night, the Fox News chairman warned commentators participating in his channel's election coverage: "If things don't go your way tonight, don't go out there looking like someone ran over your dog." Yet the coverage on Fox proved largely dour and depressive. "President Obama will win because he ran a good campaign," political anchor Bret Baier said early in the evening. "He will not win because of the state of the economy."

Even the Democratic and liberal analysts on Fox were largely reduced to talking about electoral tactics and the unresolved gridlock ahead. Viewers would find it hard to believe that the final tally showed Obama had won by nearly four percentage points in the popular vote. Several pundits, including Bill O'Reilly and Stephen Hayes, circled back to Superstorm Sandy as a stroke of good fortune for the incumbent. "While Governor Romney was talking about bipartisanship," Brit Hume said, "the president gave an image to Americans on television of him practicing it. That's pretty strong medicine."

O'Reilly said Republicans had failed to grapple with the changing demographic face of the American electorate. But there was a thread of melancholy woven into his analysis. The day of the traditional white American was done, he said. The US was becoming more like Western Europe, he went on, as Americans wanted others to bear their every burden—turning President John F. Kennedy's famed admonition on its head. O'Reilly ascribed Obama's victory to the desire for handouts, especially among people of color, though O'Reilly very explicitly said such indolence cut across racial lines. (In so doing, intentionally or not, he echoed a Murdoch tweet of November 3: "Just look at European welfare state and broken countries. Some want US to follow, others not. Why can't we debate civilly?")

Fox analyst and host Dana Perino, the former George W. Bush press secretary, noted that women favored Obama heavily, suggesting that Democrats used abortion to scare them into entering voting booths. Fox's coverage revealed little about the forces behind the election but a great deal about the coming clash within the Republican Party: whether Mitt Romney had been too moderate to win or had failed to connect with the minorities making up an increasing number of US voters.

Once the Fox News Decision Desk put Ohio in Obama's win column, giving the White House to the president, *Fox News Sunday* anchor Chris Wallace announced that officials with the Romney campaign had called to argue the margin was too small to make such a projection. Correspondents on other networks reported similar complaints a bit later. Karl Rove took up the Romney cause on the air and vigorously attacked his own network's analysis—to the point where anchor Megyn Kelly called out, "That was awkward!" Late in the evening, Rove returned to the air and contended the margin of

Obama's lead was small and a significant fraction of ballots cast had yet to be tallied.

Kelly asked Rove, "Is this just math that you do as a Republican to make yourself feel better, or is this real?" Ailes later said he had called Michael Clemente, a senior Fox News executive, and ordered the cameras be kept on Rove. The confrontation was great television. Kelly ultimately strode down the hallways of Fox News to the number-crunchers running the desk to have them explain their projections. She owned the studio that night, shushing Wallace and even darting over to brush some lint off Joe Trippi's shoulders. Yet she couldn't convince Rove, who reviewed counties he thought were still in play, at one point adding, "and then there are cats and dogs elsewhere that add up to another 120,000 votes." Rove learned the lessons of the 2000 elections all too well.

By the end, having lost the argument and the night, Rove declared that President Obama's victory carried little weight. He had "blown the last two years—he's played small ball," Rove said around 12:40 AM on Wednesday. "This does not bode well for the future. . . . He may have won the battle but lost the war." Dick Morris, who had confidently predicted a Romney landslide, did not appear on air.

Seconds shy of 2:00 AM Eastern Time, Kelly and Baier found a glimmer of grace to offer the reelected president's victory speech. And then Baier noted: "Hard to believe, but Iowa Caucus is 1,154 days away."

AS HE watched returns on election night, Ailes told Chafets that illegal immigrants can no longer be treated with hostility. They cannot be called illegal aliens any more. The following morning, he lectured his senior staff about it on a conference call. Within twenty-four hours, Sean Hannity announced to viewers that his thinking had "evolved" on immigration reform. Things had to change.

The assault against what became known as the conservative media cocoon began swiftly. "Unreal," George W. Bush's former chief strategist, Matthew Dowd, tweeted later that Wednesday. "Nearly every piece of data for last 3 weeks pointed to Romney loss. Ray Charles could have seen it coming." Hume had offered the closest his network's viewers would receive to a fair-minded note of warning from a non-Democrat. "The state polls portray Obama ahead. And there are a lot of them." But even he had called the race a tie a few weeks ahead of the election.

Conservatives had taken it on faith that Democratic voter turnout would replicate the deflated levels of 2010, and not the much higher levels of 2008. And Republican professionals had trashed polling altogether. One aspiring conservative Virginia political consultant set up a blog promising to "unskew" the polls—readjusting them to what he thought they should look like. The polls were the newest front in the all-out war on journalistic bias.

Prominent Republicans angled for cabinet posts just days ahead of the election, convinced the Republican ticket would win. Romney did not draft a concession speech, which is customary, because he was so confident about the outcome. And then the votes started coming in.

"Because I had a rooting interest in the other side, that view was strengthened and amplified by what I wanted to happen, which I freely confess," said *New York Post* columnist John Podhoretz, also the editor of conservative *Commentary* magazine and a cultural critic for the conservative *Weekly Standard*. "People don't ordinarily cast a skeptical eye on data and information that supports their opinions. They're happy to take it."

"The conservative followership has been fleeced, exploited and lied to by the conservative entertainment complex," former George W. Bush speechwriter David Frum said on MSNBC's *Morning Joe*.

Dick Morris explained himself. "There was a period of time," he told Sean Hannity, "when the Romney campaign was falling apart.

People were not optimistic; nobody thought there was a chance of victory. And I felt it was my duty at that point to go out and say what I said."

Morris said he believed what he told viewers, but he betrayed his true intent: not as a network consultant to inform the audience but to rally the Romney campaign. (Fox blurred his motivations further by typically presenting him as a former Clinton adviser—though he had cast his lot with Republicans for more than a decade.) Ailes fired Morris from Fox after the election and kept Rove off the air for a few days. Sarah Palin's contract was allowed to lapse, unmourned in Fox's corporate suites. But the people who replaced them were just as partisan.

Jon Huntsman Sr., a chemical company billionaire and father of the former Utah governor and failed Republican presidential candidate, took Fox to task during an interview on the channel itself. "I just think the Republican Party was misled by Dick Morris and Karl Rove and these folks," Huntsman told Fox's Neil Cavuto. "I am an avid Fox News fan, but, you know, Intrade and . . . [the *New York Times*'s] Nate Silver—and all these polling services had it right, except Fox. And they lulled us to sleep."

Huntsman said he wasn't criticizing the network—in part because he viewed it as "entertainment."

Huntsman's categorization of Fox—as entertainment—was being adopted by its corporate owners too.

21

GOODCO VERSUS SHITCO

BY FEBRUARY 2012 NEWS INTERNATIONAL'S containment strategy had crumbled. The effort to contain scrutiny to a single reporter and investigator had failed. So had attempts to limit attention to a single newspaper and to protect Rebekah Brooks. Anyone without the last name Murdoch was expendable.

In the UK, the plan was to allow the *Sun* to thrive, standing apart from its tarnished sister tabloid. By mid-February 2012, however, police had arrested nine *Sun* reporters and editors on suspicion of having bribed a breathtaking array of government and law enforcement officials. Even worse, from the standpoint of many of Murdoch's British journalists, fellow News Corp employees working under Joel Klein and Will Lewis had volunteered the evidence allegedly implicating them. Over the next year, the company sought to blunt the search for more damaging information. In late January 2012, Dinah Rose, a British lawyer for News International, conceded the company's responsibilty but said there was nothing more to find. "We accept we are the villains," she told the judge as the company settled the cases of three dozen hacking victims. "We have the horns and the tails." But, she attested, the company's compliance was complete. There was no need to chase phantoms.

The High Court judge, Geoffrey Vos, expressed little confidence in that profession of good faith by News International and its executives. The company had deleted millions of emails, removed key evidence from servers, even dismantled its own reporters' computers. "They are to be treated as deliberate destroyers of evidence," Vos said in court. "I have been shown a number of emails which are confidential. Suffice it to say they show a rather startling approach." In court, News International admitted that senior executives and directors of its tabloid unit "knew about the wrongdoing and sought to conceal it by deliberately deceiving investigators and destroying evidence."

The collaboration with authorities came at a cost. Inside News International's newsrooms, Will Lewis was quickly losing whatever respect he had built up in his years as an editor at various British papers. His was a grim task, to be sure, but one he embraced. Boyish and canny, Lewis had been a respected journalist and a brilliant corporate player at the *Financial Times* and, until a falling out, inside the *Telegraph* newspapers as well while editor in chief. Widespread suspicions emerged that he had orchestrated the leak of the *Telegraph*'s damning tape of cabinet minister Vince Cable trashing Murdoch. The tapes were first publicly released by Lewis's friend, Robert Peston of the BBC, rather than by the *Telegraph* itself, a blot on the paper's reporting. When directly asked at the Leveson Inquiry, Lewis declined to answer whether had played a role in the release of Cable's remarks.

Lewis was also playing to a New York audience rather than one in London. He had been the one pouring tea for the Dowlers in that July 2011 meeting at which Rupert Murdoch so assiduously apologized. Lewis hitched himself to Klein, and they labored to forestall punitive federal action against the company under the Foreign Corrupt Practices

Act. Full disclosure to Scotland Yard in the UK and the feds in the US promised the best path. As an anonymous but conveniently knowledgeable source told Lewis's old paper, the *Telegraph*, the arrests at the *Sun* are "a mark of the absolute determination of News Corporation to drain the swamp."

Staffers at the *Sun*, however, were on the brink of revolt as Klein's team directed police to key emails, notebooks, and phone records. Some of those arrested held the paper's most-senior positions, including a deputy editor, the chief reporter, the chief foreign correspondent, and the news editor. Trevor Kavanagh, the *Sun*'s associate editor, who was a columnist and occasional Murdoch dining companion, spoke out twice on BBC radio. "The newsroom is full of people who feel deeply unhappy about the way that their colleagues, who they've worked alongside for sometimes decades, and who they respect and admire as supremely professional operators, have ended up being arrested, searched, put on police bail and suspended from their duties," Kavanagh said. He called the investigation a witch-hunt but saved special contempt for News Corp's role. "Certain parts of the company are actually boasting that they're sending information to the police, which has put these people I've just described into police cells."

Rupert Murdoch flew to London to quell the Wapping Rebellion. He promised to keep the arrested *Sun* employees on staff until any conviction. In a private meeting with several *Sun* journalists who had been arrested, Murdoch signaled they retained his affinity. "I don't know of anybody that did anything that wasn't being done across Fleet Street and wasn't the culture. We're being picked on, I think," Murdoch said, his remarks captured by digital recorders hidden by more than one of the *Sun* journalists present and later leaked to *Private Eye* and *Exaro News*. "We're talking about payments for news tips from cops. That's been going on for a hundred years, absolutely. . . . It was the culture of Fleet Street." He said that he may have panicked: "We might have gone too far in protecting ourselves." Murdoch then announced the creation of the *Sun on Sunday,* promising to reclaim the most profitable day of the week and holding out the prospect of more jobs to boot. His pledges reduced internal pressures but did little to stave off further revelations.

On February 27, 2012, the Leveson judicial inquiry released emails from 2006 suggesting Rebekah Brooks knew that Glenn Mulcaire had been paid more than one million pounds to hack into cell phones for *News of the World.* Two days later, James Murdoch resigned from News International.

The company presented the resignation as a long-planned move to allow him to take up a more global portfolio at the company. But in Britain his credibility was spent. It did not help that Prime Minister David Cameron found himself on foreign soil again fielding questions from reporters about News Corp. He had addressed the Milly Dowler revelations from Kabul back in July 2011; more than six months later, at a press conference in Brussels about the flagging economy of the European Union, Cameron once again attempted damage control.

Rebekah Brooks had been given a retired police horse, Raisa, by the top brass of the Metropolitan Police in 2008, a gift that appeared to violate Scotland Yard's policies on handling former workhorses. Reporters for the *Telegraph* who had learned about Raisa had badgered 10 Downing Street's press shop for days asking whether Cameron had ever ridden the horse. The questions were swatted aside for days as absurd.

From Belgium came Cameron's tortured admission that yes, in fact, he had ridden the retired horse given to Brooks by the Metropolitan Police. He started by apologizing for any confusion that had emerged and emphasizing his ties with Charlie Brooks rather than Rebekah: "He's a good friend, and he's a neighbor in the constituency," Cameron said.

"Before the election, yes, I did go riding with him," Cameron admitted. "He has a number of different horses and, yes, one of them was this former police horse, Raisa, which I did ride." The closely knit Murdoch press, senior police executives, and the nation's leading politicians were captured in a single canter. Such untimely reminders of coziness gave heartburn to executives in Wapping and in Manhattan. The Murdochs vastly preferred being the target of a punch than of a punch line. They knew how to fight back.

———

DURING THIS time, Rupert Murdoch's British papers were creating mischief for Cameron, whom Murdoch considered weak; undercover reporters for the *Sunday Times* captured a Tory fund-raiser as he seemed to be promising "premier league" access to the prime minister for donors who gave more than £200,000. The fund-raiser had to resign, and Cameron was forced into a series of embarrassing admissions about his meetings with donors. Meanwhile, the *Sun* kicked off what would become a two-month campaign against a consumption tax on pasties, a sort of Cornish calzone. It was a minor element of a much broader bill, but Chancellor George Osborne ultimately folded in the face of the tabloid's relentless coverage.

In New York, News Corp executives quietly girded for more bad headlines as they sold a division called NDS, a satellite TV encryption company vital to Sky TV's enterprises in the UK and elsewhere. News Corp acquired the Israeli start-up in 1992, later taking the company public and making nearly $2 billion in 2008 when selling its stake down from 67 percent to just under half. News Corp retained, as was its frequent practice, effective control. James Murdoch served on its board, as well he might: NDS served as BSkyB's chief smartcard vendor. Instead of repeatedly replacing the pricey boxes that sat above or below television sets, News Corp invested in NDS smartcard technology. The cards themselves were cheap and their technological protections could be continually updated.

In March the technology giant Cisco reached an agreement to buy the company for $5 billion from News Corp and its investment partner. NDS was about to receive some very unwelcome attention. The BBC-TV investigative show *Panorama* had teamed up with a senior correspondent at the *Australian Financial Review,* Neil Chenoweth, who had previously written a critical biography of Murdoch. (The *AFR* is owned by Fairfax Media, Murdoch's largest newspaper rival in Australia.) Chenoweth had obtained 14,000 emails involving NDS contractors and computer pirates and used them to piece together what he concluded was a multiyear and multifaceted plot to sabotage the company's competitors. News Corp had derailed a related lawsuit filed by the French media conglomerate Vivendi, which had accused News Corp of intercepting its smartcard phones. Another lawsuit was decided in News Corp's favor. But in late March 2012, *AFR* and BBC's *Panorama* each presented a hard-hitting report within eighteen hours, in which they mined familiar veins. Computer hackers accused former police officers working for NDS of encouraging criminal behavior. The two news organizations posted the emails for the public to sort through. That was intended both as an experiment in "crowd-sourcing" further reporting and as a way to strengthen their case to British authorities that the full emails should be made public.

News Corp officials took the stories as intentionally hostile acts. Rupert Murdoch angrily posted tweets against "old toffs and right-wingers." "Seems every competitor and enemy piling on with lies and libels," he tweeted. "So bad, easy to hit back hard[,] which preparing." He had given fair warning. The company's various divisions struck back in unison against Chenoweth, the *Australian Financial Review,* and the BBC. In Australia, News Ltd CEO Kim Williams accused Chenoweth of relying on stolen emails and said the journalist had "manipulated and often misunderstood" the facts. Williams challenged the *Australian Financial Review* to "put up or shut up"—to hand over evidence of wrongdoing to the Australian federal police proving its allegations, as though publishing were not itself an act of revelation. News Corp chief operating officer Chase Carey charged that *"Panorama* presented manipulated and mischaracterized emails to produce unfair and baseless accusations."

Lawyers for News Corp wrote letters cautioning other British and Australian publications not to rely on the BBC and *Australian Financial Review* reports for their coverage. In New York, a News Corp official privately denigrated the investigative pieces to me as wildly overheated: Technology companies often relied on computer hackers to monitor and even test their own shortcomings and those of their competitors without engaging in harmful or criminal activity. I thought the BBC and *AFR* made a fairly persuasive case from the documents they had obtained and presented, though I was open to its refutation. Absent firm proof contradicting the arguments, and given the unreliability of the company's past denials involving operations in the UK, I asked the official, how can you and News Corp reasonably expect the benefit of the doubt? The News Corp official had no answer.

Meanwhile, leaks had confirmed that OfCom had stepped up its review of whether News Corp was a "fit and proper" controlling owner of BSkyB. In early April, James Murdoch stepped down as nonexecutive chairman of BSkyB too. His retreat from the UK was nearly complete. Two days later, on April 5, Sky News admitted that it had hacked into the emails of a man who had faked his own death. It had also illegally obtained access to the emails of a suspected pedophile. The managing editor of the cable news channel had approved both seemingly illegal acts.

It was a straight flush. The five most important Murdoch news outlets in the UK either conceded breaking the law or faced credible accusations of criminal activity.

ON APRIL 25, 2012, Rupert Murdoch took his turn at the Leveson Inquiry. He had prepared in arduous rehearsals with Joel Klein and the company's new general counsel, Gerson Zweifach, who, like Brendan Sullivan, was also from Williams & Connolly. Murdoch would not be the out-of-touch octogenarian badgered by MPs the previous July. Murdoch calmly apologized for not keeping a more careful eye on *News of the World.* "I have to admit that some newspapers are closer to my heart than others. But I also have to say that I failed," Murdoch said.

Despite that admission, the media mogul denied any personal culpability and defended both James Murdoch and Rebekah Brooks, saying other British company officials had executed a cover-up. That admission did not seem scripted; it caused Zweifach to shoot up from his chair to catch Murdoch's eye. Judge Leveson immediately rebuked the lawyer, ordering him to sit down. At another moment, Murdoch took a shot at *Daily Mail* editor Paul Dacre, while explaining that his lawyers had expressly told him not to do so.

At key moments, Murdoch interrupted, challenged, even jabbed his questioner, lawyer Robert Jay, if only to yield respectfully when Judge Leveson intervened. At times, Murdoch seemed to relish the testimony. But he looked alone sitting at the table, without even James to intercede, as he flipped through thick binders of evidence while parrying Jay's attacks. No one had been able to tie Murdoch directly to hacking or even to corruption. For Leveson, the key question remained the undue influence, or even occasional control, Murdoch exercised over British cabinets and hence public policy. As Jay kept circling the riddle of whether Murdoch pursued his ideological beliefs or his business interests, Murdoch professed humility. He explained why he rebuked *Sun* editor Kelvin MacKenzie for the jubilant April 1992 front-page headline ("It's the Sun Wot Won It!") after Conservative prime minister John Major beat Labour's Neil Kinnock. "We don't have that kind of power," Murdoch demurred.

The extraordinary lengths to which politicians went to court him—Blair flying to an island off Australia, Gordon Brown to Idaho, Aussie prime ministers to New York, David Cameron to a Greek isle—were unnecessary, Murdoch said: "If any politician wanted my opinions on major matters, they only had to read the editorials in the *Sun*." Murdoch portrayed these encounters as completely mundane, as though he had bumped into a neighbor at the supermarket.

Murdoch's papers may have helped elect or at least anoint a string of winners in the UK—Thatcher, Major, Blair, Cameron—and helped topple an Australian prime minister in the 1970s (and would be poised to do so again). But Murdoch claimed his influence on politics and policy was vastly overstated. As Jay drilled down more deeply, the media mogul declared it was illogical to think financial imperatives drove his editorial stances. If they did, he said, he would have stuck by the Conservatives at every election, like the *Telegraph*. The Tories were better for business.

Under Blair, Jay pointed out, Labour softened its stance on media ownership, labor unions, the euro, and other policies dear to Murdoch's heart. Lance Price, a former press aide to Blair, called Murdoch effectively a cabinet member—indeed, one of only three people other than Blair whose opinion counted in making government policy. Murdoch insisted that he was "oblivious" to the commercial advantages of one politician holding office over another and had neither requested nor received any business favors from politicians, including Thatcher and Blair. "I've never asked a Prime Minister for anything." But Murdoch did not need to do anything so "cack-handed," Jay said, sending American reporters scurrying to online dictionaries. When Murdoch wanted to know more about the Italian government's sentiment toward News Corp's efforts to acquire a television network in that country from Silvio Berlusconi, Blair called Premier Romano Prodi to learn more.

And Jay challenged Murdoch's memory and his word, with documentation of a luncheon he attended with Thatcher in early 1981 as he sought to take over the *Times* newspapers. Although he had maintained he had never ever spoken to Thatcher about the matter, a senior aide to Thatcher had taken notes, filing a memo titled, "Commercial—in Confidence." At the lunch, requested by Murdoch, he explained his plans to cut costs paid to the unionized labor force. (The *Times* had been losing money but the *Sunday Times* was projected to be profitable the following year, a point Murdoch did not make at the lunch.) Murdoch did not ask Thatcher to avoid tying up his bid in endless regulatory reviews. He did not do anything so "cack-handed." One of Thatcher's aides, Woodrow Wyatt, wrote a note saying that he had told Murdoch that government supported the bill needed for his acquisition of the *Times* newspapers. "Margaret is very keen on preserving your position. She knows how much she depends on your support. Likewise you depend on hers in this matter."

Thatcher's trade minister, John Biffen, approved the bid, and the government did not refer the decision to a commission that reviewed mergers and corporate consolidation. Murdoch's bid, on the merits, may well have been the best the previous owners could have secured. But none of the other suitors received a private audience with the prime minister to set out his case.

Former prime minister John Major later alleged, under oath, that Murdoch had not asked but demanded at a private dinner in early 1997 that he retreat from the integration of the country's political and economic destiny with Europe. Murdoch set the shift as a condition of his newspapers' support. Major refused and Murdoch's papers switched to Labour.

Murdoch also had expansive discourses with Tony Blair over the euro, which the prime minister was eager to join and Murdoch opposed. Blair needed only to have read the editorials of the *Sun*, as Murdoch said, to learn the news executive's stance. But Murdoch expressed his opposition in person, also at Chequers. Blair did not change his government's position. But he did agree to schedule a referendum so British voters could weigh in on whether to adopt the common European currency, just as the *Sun* had demanded. It served as a break on momentum toward the euro—and a sign Blair was willing to bend to acknowledge Murdoch's wishes.

At the Leveson Inquiry, Murdoch said he never asked David Cameron to reduce the amount of money the BBC received from mandatory fees on all television owners. But in denying that he made any request to Cameron, Rupert Murdoch seemed to concede he had raised the other topic with his predecessors.

"I'd been through that with previous prime ministers and it didn't matter what they said, they all hated the BBC and they all gave it whatever it wanted," Murdoch said. Cameron's cabinet froze the BBC license fee for six years amid the recession; the broadcaster's budget was to be cut 16 percent.

Around and around Robert Jay and Rupert Murdoch went, in front of Justice Leveson. Thinking he was out of hearing of others in the room, Murdoch turned to his lawyers during a break and spat out, "Let's get this fucking thing over with today." The questioning continued into the next day. Murdoch became more contrary.

Murdoch savored settling scores. He suggested that a pecuniary motive drove the former *Sunday Times* editor and ex-Sky chairman Andrew Neil: "Mr. Neil seems to have found it very profitable to get up and spread lies about me, but that's his business," Murdoch said. Former *Sun* editor David Yelland's contention that most News Corp editors wake up in the morning wondering what Murdoch would think of the day's news inspired a curt rebuttal: "I think you should take it in the context of Mr. Yelland's very strange autobiography, when he said he was drunk all the time he was at the *Sun*."

While Murdoch said he bore corporate responsibility for any criminal actions in his newsrooms, he assumed no personal culpability for creating a culture that allowed it, even cultivated it. He, too, was a victim, he testified.

LESS THAN a week later, Murdoch's antagonists in Parliament had their revenge. Led by John Whittingdale, the Parliamentary Committee on Culture, Media, and Sport unanimously found that it had been misled in previous testimony by Les Hinton, by Tom Crone, and by Colin Myler. On a partisan split—the Labour and Liberal Democrat members against the Conservatives—the committee declared itself to be "astonished" by James Murdoch's incuriosity as an executive. MP Tom Watson read aloud the majority's further conclusions. "We found News Corp carried out an extensive cover-up of its rampant law-breaking," Watson said. "Its most senior executives repeatedly misled Parliament. . . . In the view of the majority of committee members, Rupert Murdoch is not fit to run an international company like BSkyB."

Watson chose his phrasing carefully. The law required the TV regulator OfCom to determine whether the owner of a broadcaster was a "fit and proper" proprietor. The Murdochs did not really believe that OfCom would yank their authority to control BSkyB. But Watson and his allies on the committee had just handed the agency cover to do so if it wanted. On the other hand, the split vote allowed the corporation's executives in the UK and the US to portray the MPs denunciation as driven by partisan politics.

Yet the ghost of the *News of the World* caught a break the following week. Testifying before the Leveson Inquiry, a lawyer for the Metropolitan Police said forensic engineers could not establish that reporters for the tabloid had intentionally erased Milly Dowler's voice mail messages or whether a software program for the cell phone provider had automatically erased them. Old editors and reporters for the *News of the World* defiantly emerged on Twitter and in print to throw that misstep back in the paper's face. The scandal never would have gained steam without that part of the story, they said.

They were wrong, of course. The dead girl sufficed. The *Guardian*'s Nick Davies and others believed they had reported even that element of the story accurately. But the *Guardian* and its fellow crusaders had to retreat on that point, and it put them temporarily on the defensive.

ONE FACT had become clear to Rupert Murdoch: it was time to disarm the critics by changing the subject. For years investors and analysts had told News Corp's investment relations staffers that the entertainment business would be worth far more standing alone from the publishing side—the newspapers. Lachlan, Elisabeth, and others in the family had pushed a split for years. The newspapers had a constituency of one, even among Murdochs: Rupert himself. The previous summer, Murdoch had rejected the very idea of a split. "Pure and total rubbish," he had told Bruce Orwall, the *Wall Street Journal*'s London bureau chief.

But he now agreed to sever the newspaper side from the entertainment side of News Corp. The move carried enormous implications. The entertainment side would be flush with profit engines, especially Fox News and the share of BSkyB, but also cable channel FX, more than two dozen local American television stations, and Fox Sports, as well as Sky's various international channels in India, Latin America, and the Fox movie studios (previously 20th Century Fox). Operating in their own freestanding corporation would be the company's far less profitable newspapers, HarperCollins books, Joel Klein's education division, the major marketing division, and the Australian television properties. Rupert Murdoch promised to serve as chairman for both new companies, and as CEO of the entertainment wing. The division was modeled to an extent on the split of Viacom, the entertainment conglomerate, into two companies—CBS and Viacom, both run by Sumner Redstone.

The split represented a reckoning. For years, the *New York Post* had lost money hand over fist. The *Wall Street Journal*'s value had dropped by half. The *Times of London* was awash in red ink. Murdoch's Australian papers, though still dominant, suffered severe circulation losses. "I think the basic newspaper business is like an ice cube," said investor Don Yacktman, melting fast. Yacktman is president and cofounder of Yacktman Asset Management, which holds roughly 5 percent of all News Corp voting shares.

Murdoch had fought for so many years to avoid this outcome. At his direct instigation, Jesse Angelo created the digital tablet publication *The Daily* as a $35 million experiment, as though he were operating Bell Labs, trying to figure out a profitable model publication that had no print counterpart and lived exclusively on the iPad and later the Android and similar devices. The *Journal* and Dow Jones eked out a profit, but the margins were small. The financial news services of Bloomberg and Thomson Reuters had pummeled the Dow Jones newswires nearly into submission. The *Journal* had been insulated by profits from Fox News, BSkyB, FX, Avatar, and *The Simpsons*. Now the *Wall Street Journal* would be responsible for helping keep its sister publications afloat.

For now, the rump group of newspapers and associated companies would be called the "New News Corp"; the entertainment division, including Fox News and the Fox Business Network, would be called the "Fox Group." Inside the *Wall Street Journal*, the companies were rechristened almost instantly: "ShitCo" and "GoodCo." No one had any trouble figuring out which was which.

22

"WE ARE JUDGED BY OUR ACTS"

RUPERT MURDOCH structured the split of his companies around the geography of his holdings and the psychology of his children. ShitCo, the publishing half, included all the newspapers, the book publisher HarperCollins, and the new educational division, Amplify. It also encompassed News Corp's Australian television holdings, which were significant and growing. The company had never attained the television profile in Australia that it achieved in the UK or the US. But it paid $2.2 billion to roughly double its stakes in FoxTel, the nation's leading private cable and satellite television provider, and in Fox Sports Australia. Together, the two pay-TV providers presented many of Australia's most popular programs. They would be included in the new News Corp to consolidate the distant country's properties and to give the papers a financial boost.

The chairman principally designed the deal, however, to appeal to Lachlan. Rupert Murdoch hoped that in this crucible of crisis he could forge stronger ties to his elder son. Lachlan could manage the new company, hire professionals to run it, and be the king of commercial media in Australia over its most-read and most-influential publications. Rupert promised that the new publishing company would be created debt free—he would infuse it with more than $2.5 billion in cash to offer some running space and some scratch for acquiring more properties. Rupert would be the chairman, for now. Lachlan could be CEO, head of his own venture, thousands of miles away from his father and boss.

The *Sun* remained the largest circulation paper in the UK, and its new sibling *Sun on Sunday* regained much, though not all, of what was lost when *News of the World* was shuttered. Thanks to Murdoch's reversal of his plans to drop the paywall, the *Wall Street Journal* had the largest paid circulation in the US, a combination of digital and print subscribers. The papers endured as dominant titles. These, too, would fall under Lachlan. The new News Corp would still command respect and attention. Presumably Lachlan would become chairman of the new company once his father relinquished control. Presumably his father would one day actually relinquish control.

The rump company dominated a financially ailing field. News Corp's newspapers were not by and large conjuring up promising solutions on digital platforms. Murdoch had scrapped the digital-only *The Daily*, a midmarket tablet publication that had struggled to find an audience willing to pay. Murdoch's *New York Post* had been lapped online by the British *Daily Mail*, which had a livelier and more addictive website. Murdoch's *Times of London* and *Sunday Times* were gaining modest traction behind a severe paywall. The Australian papers shared the sharp drops in circulation endemic to the industry in the English-speaking world. Despite the endowment that Murdoch offered, and the hope that Klein's Amplify might someday help subsidize the new News Corp, the company might not solve the newspaper industry's seemingly existential challenges any quicker than anyone else. Doom mongers wondered if Murdoch's new print media company was no more than News Corpse.

Rupert Murdoch also could not will his first pick to accept the CEO job. Lachlan left News Corp driven by his anger toward Roger Ailes and then-president Peter Chernin for trying to marginalize him, mixed with a feeling that his father had betrayed him. Those emotions had not abated. One friend characterized Lachlan's mind-set this way: *If you don't have that belief in me as an executive, fuck you. I'll have that belief in myself.* Seven years later, Lachlan still harbored hard feelings toward News Corp, toward the whole pit of corporate intriguers, even toward his father for failing to protect him. Lachlan's affections were for Australia, not for newspapers or corporate politicking.

Rupert Murdoch still wanted them all back in: Lachlan, Elisabeth, even James. James hoped his father would last long enough to give him time to write his next chapter. Elisabeth continued to run Shine as part of News Corp but stayed off the corporate board. Soon enough, she would distance herself from the family in a very public way.

———————

IN THE summer of 2012, anticipation built within the British media industry as a third Murdoch would take the lectern in Edinburgh to deliver the MacTaggart Lecture. Elisabeth joked about the honor being "a massive pain in the ass," saying she struggled to shape what to say, especially as the first woman in seventeen years to give the talk. "The committee may be less than keen on women, but by God, you do love a Murdoch," she said to laughter.

Elisabeth Murdoch spoke purposefully, her words chosen carefully. Her father had cited Adam Smith while her brother had relied on Charles Darwin, the two intellectual champions, respectively, of the free market (in the economy) and the survival of the fittest (in biological evolution). She took inspiration from a more recent source. "I am firmly with Dennis Potter when he said the job of television is to make hearts pound," she said.

The reference astounded those in the crowd who knew Potter's history. Britain's pre-eminent television script writer, Potter made his mark with dark humor and lacerating cultural criticism. He had also attacked her father from that very perch in 1993 as one of "the nastiest people besmirching our once-fair land," and as "a drivel-merchant, global huckster and so-to-speak media psychopath, Rupert Murdoch . . . Hannibal the Cannibal."

"There is no one person more responsible for the pollution of what was already a fairly polluted press," Potter said the next year, in his final interview before he died. "The pollution of the British press is an important part of the pollution of British political life, and it's an important part of the cynicism and misperception of our own realities that is destroying so much of our own political discourse."

Elisabeth used the MacTaggart address to reject the values attributed to her father and her brother James. Citing Potter's kindred spirit, Elisabeth said, "I was determined to jump in and start making television that changed the world." She sketched out her career, in and out of the Murdoch stable, but argued that Shine belonged in the camp of independent British producers, defined in opposition to the major Hollywood studio market, despite its corporate siblings at Fox Studios.

She also rebutted her brother's 2009 assault on the BBC and his claim that only profit guaranteed independence. "James was right that if you remove profit, then independence is massively challenged. But I think that he left something out: the reason his statement sat so uncomfortably is that profit without purpose is a recipe for disaster." As a society, "we have become trapped in our rhetoric," she said, with society a stand-in for her family and her family's company. "Independence from regulation and the freedom we need to innovate and grow is only democratically viable when we accept that we have a responsibility to each other and not just to our bottom line. Profit must be our servant, not our master."

Elisabeth was declaring herself to be a different kind of media executive—a different kind of Murdoch. Elisabeth's challenge to James was much like her grandmother Dame Elisabeth's quiet retort to Rupert. The debate was playing out in the new generation. "In the same way that we have allowed our priorities to be confused between purpose and profit," the younger Elisabeth Murdoch said in Edinburgh, "we seem to have got the emphasis wrong between building a community and selling a commodity." And so attendees, along with News Corp shareholders and Wall Street and British financial analysts, heard her express support for the BBC's mandatory licensing fee. She was waging peace. Sky, ITV, and BBC needed one another to thrive for a healthy British television and media landscape, she said.

Elisabeth Murdoch had prepared for months, walking through the implications of her remarks with her husband, Matthew Freud. James's camp felt Elisabeth had abandoned her brother. She repudiated the values that the present-day corporation embodied. It was an audacious audition. Elisabeth expressed her anger at what her father and her brother had done. And she hinted that she was willing to come in from the cold, but only on her own terms.

THE BBC that Elisabeth Murdoch had praised had turned its investigative scrutiny onto News International repeatedly over the previous two years, focusing on phone hacking, satellite TV pirates, bribery, surveillance, and political intimidation. The news stories had taken on an increasingly sharp edge as the reporting of the *Guardian*, the *New York Times*, and the *Independent* gave the broadcaster space and confidence to pursue its leads.

The BBC lost its nerve, however, when it came to reporting on itself. The previous year had marked the death of one of the network's most lauded and peculiar figures, Jimmy Savile. The self-congratulatory disc jockey and children's TV host with the startling blond hair had been celebrated in a year-end tribute that marveled at his push for pop music and the fund-raising he did for children's charities. He drove a Rolls Royce, wore flashy jewelry and jogging suits, and adopted a zany affect, whipping kids (and off camera, some of their parents) into a frenzy.

Following his death, the BBC's investigative unit at the show *Newsnight* was preparing a story alleging that Savile had raped some of the children who appeared on his shows decades earlier. But the show's editor killed the story. The *Newsnight* staff erupted into civil war. Hundreds of women surfaced to accuse the dead star of preying on them as teens. Some men said Savile violated them, too, when they were boys. ITV broadcast a documentary on Savile. The BBC reeled. Executives for the program, the news division, and the entire broadcasting corporation were shunted aside or lost their jobs. MPs hauled BBC officials and its chairman, Murdoch's old antagonist Chris (now Lord) Patten, to testify at parliamentary hearings. The allegations against Savile implicated an era of sexual entitlement by famous figures at the BBC and elsewhere. Britain's most esteemed institutions had turned a collective blind eye. Even the National Health Service was implicated, as Savile had been given the run of a hospital for which he had raised money; women said he raped them there when they were young.

Bad publicity ensuing from the story could damage the *New York Times*, which had announced that the BBC's former top executive, Mark Thompson, would become its CEO in November. Murdoch taunted his rivals, tweeting on October 14, "Saville [sic]-BBC story [has a] long way to run. BBC [is by] far the biggest, most powerful organization in UK." Other tweeters suggested more powerful organizations: the Church of England, the British Navy, even News Corp.

Not surprisingly, Murdoch's papers covered the story vigorously. The *Sun* published semilurid headlines with each new allegation against Savile and his alleged fellow predators. The *Times of London* soberly dissected the BBC's unconvincing explanation of its failure to respond to early accusations against its star and of its decision to shelve its documentary. Yet News International officials believed that if they pushed the matter too hard, the BBC's defenders could claim they were trying to undermine a rival. Such calculations were themselves another consequence of the hacking scandal: they kept the papers' thirst for blood in check.

WHEN JUDGE Leveson came out with his final report, Fleet Street braced for the worst. Editors and executives indicated they could accept some additional restrictions on the press. Politicians met with press representatives, hacking victims, and their families. Prime Minister Cameron, for example, invited in Hugh Grant, Charlotte Church, and the former television crime-show host Jacqui Hames. Murdoch could not control himself, tweeting, "Told UK's Cameron receiving scumbag celebrities pushing for even more privacy laws. Trust the toffs! Transparency under attack." Cameron and Grant were upper-class Oxford graduates, elites striking deals behind closed doors. Murdoch (Worcester College, Oxford, Class of 1952) followed up with tweeted digs at Grant for his liaison with a prostitute in Los Angeles years earlier and for fathering a child out of wedlock; Murdoch apologized for wrongly claiming Grant had played no role in the child's life. But he was otherwise unrepentant. The private lives of the famous were fair game for his tweets as much as his newspapers.

Leveson's report dismantled layers of rationalizations, built over decades, for systematic abuses. Despite a system of self-regulation, he noted, the press had ignored its obligations "to respect the truth, to obey the law, and to uphold the rights and liberties of individuals." The pursuit of the story has too often, he wrote, "caused real hardship and, on occasion, wreaked havoc with the lives of innocent people."

Leveson argued that the industry required a tighter form of self-regulation, infused with a touch of legal compulsion. The new structure needed to offer people who believed they had been wronged in the press the means for fair-minded arbitration of complaints. Publishers that refused to submit to the regulator would be far more likely to have to pay for legal costs, even if they prevailed in court.

The proposed solutions created a fresh batch of problems. Would the supposedly "light touch" by lawmakers remain all that light when another press scandal flared? If editors passing judgment on their brethren seemed incestuous, would it be any better for political appointees to do so? In the US, the Federal Communications Commission had the increasingly anachronistic task of holding radio and broadcast television stations responsible for airing obscene language and sexually explicit imagery. The growth of cable, satellite, and Internet-based video services made regulation of content on purely broadcast outlets seem quaint, though such material clearly reached tens of millions of children watching old-fashioned television stations through the day. Typically such decisions had little to do with the journalism offered by those stations, however, as federal officials had long since abandoned monitoring political coverage for balance and all but given up adjudicating challenges to the veracity of programming. The remedy for poor speech was more of it, and the US was awash in opinionated fare on radio, cable news, the Internet, and, from the former members of the audience, on social media platforms. Leveson's report acknowledged that new media landscape but focused directly on the press anyway. A blogger could base his website in the West Indies, as did Paul Staines, a British conservative libertarian whose gossipy posts caused fits for both Tory and Labour politicians, and thereby sidestep press regulations. So could, presumably, an American magazine that did not circulate print editions in the UK but sold digital subscriptions there. A lot of wrinkles had to be worked out. Leveson used government involvement as a last-ditch threat: if the press did not create a credible form of self-regulation, he would try to get OfCom designated as the official regulator for the press as well as television.

Labour and Liberal Democratic politicians vied to embrace the proposals. David Cameron expressed doubts. He opposed creating new government involvement in press affairs. His former allies at the Murdoch papers and some of their competitors, such as the *Daily Mail*, the *Telegraph*, and the *Spectator*, voiced skepticism bordering on contempt for Leveson's plan. As the weeks passed, the specter of state influence sparked a backlash, especially among publications that were not implicated in widespread abuses. In March 2013, after several rounds of negotiations between newspaper executives and the government collapsed, Cameron pushed a plan with a royal charter. The self-regulatory arrangement, which would be enshrined in law by Parliament, would take away the industry's veto over appointments to the panel that would enforce the press code, yet ensure that most members had strong journalistic ties. The proposal made some reformers recoil. The *Guardian*'s Rusbridger, who previously said greater regulation was inevitable, argued that the newspaper industry deserved a year to deliver its best shot at a workable solution before the government intervened.

Press executives, politicians, and victim advocates expended extraordinary effort to outfit the earlier, nearly worthless system "with teeth." But the problem went beyond the flaws in the processes of various regulators. Leveson proposed a serious shift in the relationship between the state and the press at the heart of one of the world's leading democracies simply because the shadow cast by one news outfit was so great that police, prosecutors, and politicians could not imagine enforcing the law against the criminal activities of its journalists.

The most direct, albeit radical solution, as media analyst Claire Enders argued before Leveson, would be to limit the size and reach of major media companies. Her plan's appeal lay in its logic and simplicity. Such an approach would have required major government interference in the workings of private industry. And it would have been reasonably seen as targeting News Corp, rendering its takeover of BSkyB or any other significant acquisition in Britain off-limits, even in the future. Labour leader Ed Miliband advocated that path before Leveson but not in Parliament.

Murdoch had dodged the big bullet.

IN CHINA, where Murdoch once had great ambitions for News Corp, the stakes could not have been higher. In early 2012, a British reporter poached by Thomson for the *Wall Street Journal* from the *Times of London*, Jeremy Page, had pieced together a story about a possible cover-up involving a murdered British businessman, the wife of a powerful Chinese politician, and a Chinese police chief seeking sanctuary in the British embassy. "It involved a certain amount of risk to publish something like that," said Rebecca Blumenstein, a senior *Journal* editor overseeing the story. After she and others carefully edited the article, Blumenstein turned to Thomson, handing him a copy. Thomson's eyes widened as he pored through it. He did not cite any concerns about News Corp's vast Chinese business interests, which included not just the paper but the company's blockbuster films. He said simply, "Are we confident about the sourcing?"

Two weeks later, Chinese officials confirmed the outlines of the *Journal* piece, an endorsement accompanied by the regime's decision to shut down access to the paper's Chinese language site inside China. David Barboza of the *New York Times* later revealed corruption involving the family of the Chinese premier, Wen Jiabao. When the

Times website was shut down and fifty-five of its computers hacked, the newspaper publicly denounced Chinese retaliation. The *Journal* carried itself much more quietly, only to find the *Times* rewarded months later with a Pulitzer Prize for Barboza's reports, one of four it won in 2013. The *Journal* won a Pulitzer, too—for the opinion columns of contrarian conservative Bret Stephens. The newsroom had been once again shut out of the most revered awards in print journalism. Those at the *Journal* who respected Thomson thought judges at the Pulitzers were once again punishing the paper's reporters and editors for the sin of working for a publication owned by Rupert Murdoch.

They found solace elsewhere. "Some of the initial concerns about the values of the *Journal*—in that it would turn into a business version of the *New York Post*—have proven to be unfounded," said William Grueskin, a former senior news executive for the paper. "The *Journal*'s news has continued to be pretty much on a straight and narrow path, though I think it has a very different focus."

In September 2012, Murdoch returned to Australia for one of his periodic visits. He liked addressing the troops, in this case at the annual awards for News Ltd. "We must not take, whatever we do, our foot off the gas when it comes to our newspapers," Murdoch said at Sydney's State Theatre, a charming jumble of art deco, Gothic, and Italianate touches. "Print will be with us for many, many years. But we must also provide our readers with the greatest news experience possible on other platforms. Where others hesitate in the face of disruptive technologies, we see opportunity and will charge forward."

In the US, Murdoch's gaze turned westward. Most of the major assets of Fox Group outside Fox News—were based in Hollywood. The Tribune Co. was exiting a bankruptcy and eager to shed its newspaper properties, including some of the most storied papers in the country. Murdoch wanted to add the *Los Angeles Times* to his newspaper portfolio, so he could own the most influential publication based in the world's entertainment capital. The sister *Chicago*

Tribune held a mild appeal as well. Tribune preferred selling its newspaper unit to a single buyer, both for the ease of the transaction and also because it had some partnerships with other publishers that would be damaged by unraveling the chain. But given rules preventing ownership of a major paper and multiple television stations in the same market, and Fox's two LA TV stations, Murdoch wasn't fully convinced he could get such a deal past federal regulators at the FCC anyway. "It won't get through with the Democratic administration in place," Murdoch told the *Los Angeles Times*. The public interest media lawyer and Murdoch-watcher Andrew Schwartzman did not think the possibility of a Murdoch-owned *Los Angeles Times* was so far-fetched. "This is a strategy of deciding what you want to do, figuring out a mechanism that will ultimately get you there, and then proceeding based on a bet that the regulators will change to accommodate what it is that you're trying to do," Schwartzman said. Murdoch, he said, "has repeatedly won such bets." One of the key owners of Tribune was the investment firm Angelo, Gordon & Co. Its cofounder, John Angelo, is the father of James Murdoch's friend and fellow executive Jesse Angelo.

In December, Rupert Murdoch announced that he would kill off the tablet-only *The Daily* to appease investors and to protect the American publication Murdoch truly loved—the *New York Post*. Angelo, who had served as *The Daily*'s sole editor, would return to the *Post*, this time as publisher. The *Post*'s tone and metabolism would stay the same. Yet for the first time, every Murdoch publication had to justify its existence. Unlike the *Sun* or *Sydney Daily Telegraph*, both of which were losing circulation, the *Post* did not dominate its market and had been losing money at an accelerating rate. Angelo knew the numbers previously, more or less. But he found looking at the books as the top business executive a jarring experience. *Holy shit*, Angelo told a friend. *That's a lot of money to lose.* (He would later serve as editor, too.)

Murdoch would remain chairman and CEO of the sleeker and investor-friendly Fox Group, the media and entertainment conglomerate including Fox News, Fox Studios, Fox Sports, and the like. To assure investors that they should hold onto their new News Corp stock, Fox Group (later rechristened 21st Century Fox) would assume any costs stemming from the hacking scandals. The tab had reached several hundred million dollars by the end of 2012 and was likely to grow. Chase Carey would remain chief operating officer, the number one non-Murdoch. James Murdoch would stay on as deputy chief operating officer and would await his chance to succeed his father. He was among a very small number of people who thought that possible.

Despite his father's wishes, Lachlan Murdoch refused to return to the new News Corp, no matter how snugly the structure would fit into his Sydney-based life. He knew he would be CEO in name only. His father would *always* want to run the papers, know what was happening, scan the revenue lines, scour for daily gossip. There was room for only one Murdoch in that alignment. Subsequently Rupert Murdoch rewarded a surrogate son, appointing Thomson to lead News Corp, as he had elevated a surrogate daughter, Rebekah Brooks, at News International.

Thomson leapfrogged his boss, Lex Fenwick, the publisher of the *Wall Street Journal* and the CEO of Dow Jones, to lead the entire corporation. The CEO of the reconstituted News Corp, holding sway over the most influential and widely read newspapers in the US, the UK, and Australia, would be a news executive with only a few months of pure business-side experience. Thomson had the boss's full trust and a seemingly Sisyphean task, promising investors "relentless" cost-cutting at the papers accompanied by digital innovation that would prove, he promised, their salvation.

Thomson's appointment had consequences elsewhere in the empire. Some associates thought Joel Klein was disappointed that he had not been named CEO. If so, he never said so publicly, soldiering on as chief of his new technology-based education venture. His legal strategy seemed to have worked. The US Justice Department could have made a criminal case against News Corp under the Federal Corrupt Practices Act for the bribes funneled to British cops. But the Brits were aggressively pursuing those cases. News Corp's cooperation with law enforcement agencies was reasonably strong, and prosecutors and regulators prepared a nine-figure settlement that would be announced after the split. That was a huge relief at corporate headquarters.

Tom Mockridge, brought in from Sky Italia to steady News International as its CEO, could not abide being passed over as News Corp's new CEO. He quit and would later emerge as the new CEO for Virgin Media's expanded pay-TV play in the UK. Murdoch's earlier nemesis, John Malone of Liberty Media, had just bought Sir Richard Branson's controlling stake in Virgin Media. The appointment involved an element of revenge for both Mockridge and his new boss.

Rebekah Brooks was set to face trial in fall 2013 on charges of phone hacking, bribing public officials, and concealing computers and documents from police in July 2011. She was to be alongside several former colleagues, including Andy Coulson, Ian Edmondson, and the private investigator Glenn Mulcaire, who was to stand trial on separate charges. Additionally, Brooks was set to face criminal charges for perversion of the course of justice, along with her husband, Charlie, her former secretary, and the former security chief for News International. She, like her co-defendants, disputed all charges.

In Parliament, Labour MP Tom Watson wrote a book about his fight against News International, *Dial M for Murdoch*, and advanced back up his party's hierarchy. Louise Mensch resigned her seat, moved to New York City to be closer to her husband, and became a columnist for Murdoch's *Sun* tabloid.

James Harding, editor of the *Times of London*, left the paper after being told News Corp wanted someone else in the job. He had been the youngest and one of the most popular editors in the paper's history. His paper had admitted a single case of email hacking that had not been approved ahead of time by editors or lawyers. But Murdoch and other executives could not forgive his tough editorial line against hacking and the British parent company. Murdoch told Leveson he could not believe Harding had not bought the disks that had the MP expense records on them—handing that scoop to the *Daily Telegraph*. Harding had thought paying for the story was dishonorable. Murdoch thought getting beaten was. Harding later became BBC news chief. Will Lewis came to New York to work on strategic issues for News Corp.

Thomson's deputy, Gerard Baker, succeeded Thomson as managing editor at the *Journal* and editor in chief of the Dow Jones Newswires. Murdoch strode into the *Journal* newsroom with Thomson for the announcement, all three men clad in nearly identical dark striped suits and collared white shirts without a tie, as the chairman doused his new editor with a bottle of high-end champagne. A significant number of his journalists anticipated Baker's tenure with apprehension, given his record. Instead, at least in the first six months, he proved a pleasant surprise, tapping Blumenstein and a few other American editors with roots in the paper's pre-Murdoch era as his top deputies. Baker was well aware of his reputation. He showed a light touch at the start.

At a dinner held by the British-American Business Association in February 2013, former *Time* magazine managing editor Walter Isaacson launched into effusive praise for Baker and the *Journal*. *After what you have done in the last four years*, Isaacson said, *the* Wall Street Journal *today is the best newspaper that I have ever seen in my lifetime.* New York Times Co. CEO Mark Thompson sat in the crowd stoically as Isaacson said those words. It was a funny thing: The head of the new News Corp would be Australian. The managing editor of the *Wall Street Journal* was British. The *New York Post* was still run by an untamable Aussie. The *New York Times* had turned to an ex-BBC executive and frequent Murdoch critic for its CEO. And the *New York Daily News* was edited by Colin Myler, the Brit who had run newsrooms at Murdoch's *Sun* and *News of the World*.

By 2013, New York's newspaper scene was effectively defined by, and in reaction to, the World of Murdoch.

RUPERT MURDOCH had counted on his mother as a touchstone, a reminder of his Australian roots and a handy one-liner to ward off any suggestion he was getting too old for the job. *Well, my mum's ninety,* Murdoch would say, in later years shifting the age to one hundred, *and she still gets about.* Finally, in December 2012, at the age of 102, Dame Elisabeth died. Her death occasioned a state funeral. Prime Minister Julia Gillard, never favored by Murdoch, did not attend. She would later fall, replaced by Labor's Kevin Rudd. The tributes poured in, from Murdoch's own roster of commentators and critics and old political allies, but also from foundation presidents, university officials, hospital directors, museum docents, and the like. For Dame Elisabeth's memorial, mourners packed St. Paul's, the Anglican cathedral in downtown Melbourne, just a block north of the Yarra River and close by so many of the cultural institutions that she had patronized and championed over the years. Huge television screens were set up outside the church for the throngs who wanted to watch the tributes to this great Australian figure.

She was hardly a saint to her son, though. *She was tough,* he told people. The service was broadcast nationally. Murdoch paid loving tribute: "Today I wish to speak to the extraordinary accomplishments of this exceptional woman. On its own, that would be a formidable task. It is made even more daunting by the obligation of a grateful son, to do a justice to a mother whose love gave me more than I could ever hope to repay."

Elisabeth Greene Murdoch made clear she was devoted first and foremost to Keith Murdoch—and that her love for their children was an expression of her love for him. Since their aging father would not be the family disciplinarian, she took on that task too. "Just let me say that Mum assumed that role with none of the angst or self-doubt that consumes so many modern parents," Dame Elisabeth's son said to laughter. "I still remember, vividly, the good smacking I got for pulling my big sister Helen's pigtails."

Murdoch's mother gave him an indirect smacking once again, decades later, during a nationally televised documentary by telling an interviewer that she assessed success and failure differently than her son did. Money couldn't be the point, she said. Murdoch told those who had come to pay their respects that Dame Elisabeth was a woman who disdained finery and preferred pursuing charity by stealth. "However you came to know her, what you remember is the strength of character that defined Elisabeth Murdoch's life," Rupert said. "It was formed by the credo she learned so many decades ago at the Clyde School: We are judged by our acts."

We are judged by our acts. Dame Elisabeth lived long enough to see her son's full ascent. Keith Murdoch died when Rupert was just twenty-one, at the tail end of his studies at Oxford. The pudgy-faced son burned with a desire to demonstrate he could make his mark in the same field as his father.

Dame Elisabeth watched closely what followed. She saw Rupert establish a new paper of quality for the coverage of purely national issues. In the 1980s she saw him forswear his Aussie citizenship so he could hold onto his American television stations. She had followed his career as he and his editors sought to create the most influential news organization in Australian, English, and American politics. He had proved a worthy entrepreneur as he scorned government models for how things should work. All along, Rupert had acted to acquire more properties, shedding those that had become inconvenient, as he built the most powerful media empire in the English-speaking world. Dame Elisabeth had seen it career out of control in the UK, half a world away, where all the corner-cutting and deal-making and law-breaking of his tabloids finally came to a shuddering stop and gave credence to Murdoch's critics.

None of that gave Murdoch his due as an innovator and a patron of public service in journalism. His largess had sustained the *Times of London*, which would not have been viable on its own. The value of the *Wall Street Journal* had been written down by more than half since its acquisition, but Murdoch did not back away from it.

Murdoch's patronage always came at a price. News Corp was a publicly traded company in name only. Whatever title anyone else held, Murdoch was the proprietor. Murdoch's Manhattan office is on the eighth floor of News Corp's headquarters. His office is on the right. On the left, a visitor will see a bank of desks filled with Murdoch's assistants. On the wall nearby is an oil painting on a bronze background of a newspaper folded in half. The paper's flag, the insignia on top of the front page, bears the legend *The Herald*. Editors who work with Murdoch and have a sense of history think that has to be an allusion to his father's paper, the Melbourne *Herald*, which Keith Murdoch was unable to retain in the weeks leading up to his death. Rupert had acquired it and more than 150 newspapers besides. His mother had seen all that over the decades and wondered why he needed more. She saw a nation of citizens. He saw markets populated by consumers. Rupert Murdoch loved and understood his mother. But they engaged with the world around them very differently. He wanted to explode entrenched models, harness fresh technologies to draw in new customers, and then build some more.

Murdoch was accompanied to the memorial service by his wife, Wendi Deng, and their two young daughters. Lachlan was there, with his wife, the actress and model Sarah Murdoch. James and Elisabeth did not attend.

Rupert still cared about the banished Rebekah Brooks. Her scandals became his disgrace. Her tenure was like the economy in the first decade of the 2000s: disaster masquerading as runaway success. Yet he had ensured a generous payout: a severance package worth $17.6 million. In April 2013, Brooks was spotted in Australia yachting and relaxing with the Murdochs. That same month, police in London announced they had discovered hundreds more cases of phone hacking than had been suspected previously. Investigators had initially looked at the now-closed tabloid's news desk for the same reason that Willie Sutton was said to have robbed banks: that's where the money was. Reviewing the news desk records, police found fastidiously ordered accounting. The new charges involved the features desk, which police claimed had engaged in more subterfuge to cloak the purpose of the expenditures. That had taken more time for police to penetrate.

In her final years, Dame Elisabeth watched as her son and grandson allowed an apparently criminal culture to take root at the family's two most profitable newspapers. In spring 2013, the company agreed to pay $135 million to settle the grievances of a dissident group of shareholders, led by a union-controlled bank and other institutional investors. The settlement was a small price to pay to make the lawsuit go away.

Through all this the market cap of the company—its value as determined by the worth of all its shares—had risen by 50 percent since the announcement of the split, to the impressive peak of $73 billion. The value of Murdoch's shares in the company had climbed to about $10 billion.

People invariably compared Murdoch to William Randolph Hearst, the American media baron of an earlier age who inspired the great movie *Citizen Kane*. That seems too limited a comparison. Perhaps he was more like the nation's early oil barons who controlled new terrain and pock-marked the countryside in drilling—a man unlikely to ask for permission *or* forgiveness, who provided millions of Americans with a product they came to view as indispensable.

Murdoch similarly could not have accumulated his fortunes without our help. We are all, as consumers of media, involved and even responsible for the creation of Murdoch's World—those of us who pick up his tabloids at the newsstand, enjoy the cable news wars, subscribe to his prestigious papers, watch a ballgame on TV, buy tickets to a movie, even those of us who are News Corp investors through pension funds or mutual funds. We make up the market that he sought to create and feed. He played us, as much as he played everyone else. And we have rewarded him handsomely for it.

Speaking to investors in New York City, Rupert Murdoch cast the corporate split in personal terms. "I have been given an extraordinary opportunity most people never get in their lifetime: the chance to do it all over again." He would soon dispatch the *Post*'s Col Allan back to Sydney and swapped editors at the *Sun*, too. But his declaration carried more than one meaning. Two weeks later, Murdoch filed for divorce from his third wife, Wendi Deng Murdoch.

This union, his lawyers wrote carefully, had "broken down irretrievably for a period of more than six months." As the years progressed, Wendi had socialized separately from Rupert, enjoying a California lifestyle, circulating with Hollywood, Australian, and Chinese movie stars, and developing some outside ventures. Rumors that she had been romantically involved with several prominent entrepreneurs and other figures had reached Rupert's ears. As long as she didn't embarrass him, he did not care to learn more, one former aide said. In this case, an aide to Tony Blair even felt compelled to deny to the *Hollywood Reporter* that the former prime minister had ever had an affair with Deng Murdoch.

Yet the move in June 2013 to obtain a formal divorce marked yet another wrecked personal relationship, the latest in the line. His mother gone, his children alienated and angry, Murdoch turned his attention back to his business—and not his entire business, but particularly his newspapers. Though he was formally the CEO as well as chairman of the new 21st Century Fox, and only chairman of the new News Corp, Chase Carey would run the Fox entertainment and television company capably. The decades-old names of News International and

News Limited vanished, replaced, respectively, by the brands News UK and News Corp Australia. Rupert would once more lead a company with the newspapers at its core taking up, with Robert Thomson as his lieutenant, the seemingly impossible challenge of how to make newspapers profitable. He wanted to prove the naysayers wrong.

Murdoch has never convincingly shown any capacity for self-reflection. He reaches a fork in the road, chooses a path, and sets off. Another person in his position who absorbed the revelations about the way the company operated might have decided to step down to give the company a fresh start. Someone with a different psychological makeup might have wondered what he had done to create a culture that had so completely severed any connection the people running his British tabloids had with the people they covered and served. But if Murdoch ever had such doubts, he showed no sign of them.

In his eighty-second year of life, disgraced and denounced as "unfit" to lead a major media company by the British Parliament, isolated from his family and challenged by financial forces besetting the entire newspaper business, Murdoch was undaunted. His media enterprise counted many millions as customers and yet had an audience of one.

His father, Keith Murdoch, the absent role model whose memory he always sought to uphold, had made his name by writing about an ill-advised attack in a thankless cause. A century later, Keith Rupert Murdoch was preparing for combat on forbidding terrain, far from loved ones, in the name of his own fading empire, in his case a commonwealth of newspapers.

ACKNOWLEDGMENTS

I HAVE been blessed with friends, colleagues, and family who have squandered no end of time to keep me on course in the researching and writing of this book.

The idea of writing one originated with Jeremy Schaap, who argued that I should translate my years of reporting on Fox News and the cable news industry into a more expansive treatment. In early July 2011, I watched a remarkable press conference taking place in Kabul, Afghanistan, where the British prime minister was forced to answer questions about whether the Murdochs were fit owners of the largest pay television provider in the UK. *Murdoch's World* stems from the stories that ensued and is also based on additional reporting specifically for this project, which broadened the scope of my interest.

Many current and former executives at News Corp's headquarters as well as officials and journalists at its various constituent news organizations sat patiently for interviews, answered late night queries, and offered key guidance. As the Murdoch family and News Corp formally discouraged them from participating, I cannot thank most of them by name, but I am appreciative nonetheless.

Others who spoke on the record to me provided information and insight that were crucial to various elements of my reporting and this book, and I am grateful to them all. Among the many are Tim Arango, Paul Barry, Nick Boles, Rebecca Blumenstein, Chris Bryant, Ken Chandler, Zev Chafets, Neil Chenoweth, James Chessell, John Coffee, Damien Collins, Charles Elson, Paul Farrelly, David Gordon, Roy

Greenslade, Brit Hume, Andrew Jaspan, Simon Jenkins, Ian Johnson, Simon Kelner, Thomas Keneally, Bill Keller, Mark Lewis, Kelvin MacKenzie, Robert Manne, Stephen Mayne, Paul McMullan, Louise Mensch, Anne Schroeder Mullins, Andrew Neil, Freya Petersen, Alan Rusbridger, Graeme Samuel, Vivian Schiller, Mark Stephens, Tom Watson, Ellen Weiss, Juan Williams, and Michael Wolff. Thanks also to Geraldo Rivera, a daily inspiration to journalists everywhere.

My NPR colleague in London, Phil Reeves, was my partner on the hacking scandal and a key guide to the ways of Fleet Street, back-stopped by our producer Stewart Willy. The support of NPR has been outstanding, especially from my editors Laura Bertran and Stu Seidel, even as we have ventured into sensitive areas. NPR's Margaret Low Smith, Kinsey Wilson, and Gary Knell have also been particularly sup-portive. The occasional frantic query to NPR's resourceful reference librarians always yielded a swift, patient, and comprehensive answer.

Murdoch's World would not have come together had it not been for my agent, Robert Guinsler of Sterling Lord Literistic, and the team at PublicAffairs. My editor, Clive Priddle, tamed an enormously compli-cated tale spanning four continents and more than five decades with a literate touch and a welcome sense of irreverence. Melissa Raymond kept the process moving apace. Emily Lavelle planned the book's launch with the precision of NASA. The encouragement of Peter Os-nos throughout meant a great deal to me.

Chuck Salter, Isaac Kramnick, Kelly McBride, Mike Pesca, Lisa Pollak, Robert Smith, Robert Tashjian, John Hassel, and Sam Zarifi served as vital sounding boards. Max Folkenflik and Margaret Mc-Gerity kindly opened their law offices to me, enabling me to complete my writing away from home and newsroom. Glenn Altschuler and Michael Ollove gave much-needed scrutiny to various drafts of my manuscript. John McIntyre provided a scrupulous copyedit.

My parents, Robert and Vivian Folkenflik, the most dedicated edu-cators and most intelligent writers I have ever met, made painstaking suggestions which vastly improved this book. And it would not have been possible to complete the book without the love and support of my wife, Jesse, and the joy of our daughter, Viola. I may have been writing *Murdoch's World*, but I live wholeheartedly in theirs.

David Folkenflik
Laguna Beach, California
July 30, 2013

SELECTED BIBLIOGRAPHY

Calder, Iain. *The Untold Story: My Twenty Years Running the National Enquirer.* Miramax, 2004.

Chafets, Zev. *Roger Ailes Off Screen.* Sentinel HC, 2013.

Chenoweth, Neil. *Murdoch's Pirates.* Allen & Unwin, 2012.

———. *Rupert Murdoch: The Untold Story of the World's Greatest Media Wizard.* Crown Business, 2002.

Chippindale, Peter, and Chris Horrie. *Stick It Up Your Punter!: The Uncut Story of the Sun Newspaper.* 2nd ed. Pocket Books, 1999.

Collins, Scott. *Crazy Like a Fox.* Portfolio, 2004.

Dover, Bruce. *Rupert Murdoch's China Adventures: How the World's Most Powerful Media Mogul Lost a Fortune and Found a Wife.* Tuttle Publishing, 2008.

Ellison, Sarah. *War at the Wall Street Journal.* Houghton Mifflin Harcourt, 2010.

Evans, Harold. *Good Times, Bad Times.* Atheneum, 1984.

———. *My Paper Chase.* Little, Brown, 2009.

Ghemawat, Pankaj. *Games Businesses Play.* MIT Press, 1997.

Jenkins, Simon. *The Market for Glory.* Faber & Faber, 1987.

Johnson, Graham. *Hack: Sex, Drugs, and Scandal from Inside the Tabloid Jungle.* Simon & Schuster, 2012.

Keneally, Thomas. *Australians: Eureka to the Diggers.* Allen & Unwin, 2012.

———. *A Commonwealth of Thieves: The Improbable Birth of Australia.* Nan A. Talese, 2006.

Kiernan, Thomas. *Citizen Murdoch.* Dodd Mead, 1986.

Leigh, David, and Luke Harding. *Wikileaks: Inside Julian Assange's War on Secrecy.* PublicAffairs, 2011.

Leveson Inquiry. Documents and Final Report. LevesonInquiry.org.uk.

Mahmood, Mazher. *Confessions of a Fake Sheik: The King of the Sting Reveals All.* HarperCollins, 2008.

Manne, Robert. *Bad News.* Quarterly Essay, 2011.

McKnight, David. *Rupert Murdoch: An Investigation of Power.* Allen & Unwin, 2012.

Milbank, Dana. *Tears of a Clown: Glenn Beck and the Teabagging of America.* Doubleday, 2010.

Morgan, Piers. *The Insider: The Private Diaries of a Scandalous Decade.* Ebury Press, 2005.

News International and Phone-hacking. Eleventh Report, House of Commons, Culture, Media, and Sport Committee, May 1, 2012. http://www.publications.parliament.uk/pa/cm201012/cmselect/cmcumeds/903/903i.pdf.

Nissenson, Marilyn. *The Lady Upstairs: Dorothy Schiff and the New York Post.* St. Martin's Press, 2007.

O'Shea, James. *The Deal from Hell: How Moguls and Wall Street Plundered Great American Newspapers.* PublicAffairs, 2011.

Price, Lance. *The Spin Doctor's Diary: Inside Number 10 with New Labour.* Hodder & Stoughton, 2005.

———. *Where Power Lies: Prime Ministers v. the Media.* Simon & Schuster, 2000.

Shawcross, William. *Murdoch: The Making of a Media Empire.* Touchstone Books, 1997.

Tifft, Susan E., and Alex S. Jones. *The Patriarch: The Rise and Fall of the Bingham Dynasty.* Summit Books, 1991.

———. *The Trust: The Private and Powerful Family Behind the New York Times.* Little, Brown, 1999.

Tofel, Richard J. *Restless Genius: Barney Kilgore, the Wall Street Journal, and the Invention of Modern Journalism.* St. Martin's Press, 2009.

Watson, Tom, and Martin Hickman. *Dial M for Murdoch.* Allen Lane, 2012.

Williams, Juan. *Muzzled: The Assault on Honest Debate.* Crown, 2011.

Wolff, Michael. *The Man Who Owns the News.* Bodley Head, 2008.

NOTES

Chapter 1

Page 1   *The man at the center of the maelstrom:* The account of the meeting between Rupert Murdoch and the Dowler family in this chapter is based in significant part on my interviews with two sources who had a contemporaneous knowledge of the events that occurred, plus ensuing public statements and testimony.

Page 1   *He was tanned and reasonably fit:* From photographs and video taken that day. For example, from the *Independent:* www.independent.co.uk /news/uk/crime/rupert-murdoch-pays-dowlers-3m-for-phone-hacking -2357471.html.

Page 1   *the luxury hotel One Aldwych:* Author's visit to hotel in November 2011.

Page 2   *His company served millions of readers and viewers on five continents:* List of News Corp assets contained in company's 2011 10K Annual Report: http://investor.newscorp.com/secfiling.cfm?filingID=1193125–11–221637.

Page 2   *an imposing presence, and an impassive expression:* July 15, 2011. Video footage of Dowler family lawyer Mark Lewis making a press statement after meeting with Murdoch, www.youtube.com/watch ?v=HE0agejrdIA.

Page 2   *She was a saxophone fan:* Dowler family home video released by Surrey police in 2008, as posted online by the *Telegraph:* www.telegraph .co.uk/news/uknews/crime/8505692/Milly-Dowler-police-video.html.

Page 2   *dressed in classic British school uniform:* Much of this reconstruction is based on Colette McBeth, "Court Sees CCTV Footage of Milly Dowler's Last Journey," BBC News, May 11, 2011, www.bbc.co.uk/news /uk-13367711.

Page 3   *For most of 2002, Milly's parents and sister had no idea:* Ben Taylor, "Nightmare for Milly's Sister," *Daily Mail* (UK), www.dailymail.co.uk /news/article-109162/Nightmare-Millys-sister.html.

Page 3   *poring through Milly's journal writings:* Caroline Gammell, "Levi Bellfield Trial: Pornography Made Milly Dowler's Father First Suspect," *Telegraph,* May 16, 2011.

Page 3   *Milly's bones were found months later:* "Bones Gave No Clues to Milly Dowler Killing," *Sun,* June 14, 2011.

Page 3   *The Dowlers' pain and anger were heightened*: Nick Davies and Amelia Hill, "Missing Milly Dowler's Voicemail Was Hacked by News of the World," *Guardian*, July 4, 2011, as well as subsequent coverage that month in the British press.

Page 3   *people working for Murdoch's* News of the World: Shenai Raif, "Hackers Jailed for Royal Tap," *Daily Mirror*, January 27, 2007.

Page 4   *Murdoch controlled roughly 40 percent*: "Murdoch Sells Voting Shares in News Corp. Worth About $40 Million," *Dow Jones Business News*, February 15, 2013. Other elements of this paragraph about Murdoch's holdings and his aspirations for his family are based on my interviews with current and former executives for News Corp in the US, UK, and Australia.

Page 4   *What to do about the CEO of Murdoch's British properties:* Jon Ungoed-Thomas, "Cracks in the Titan," *Sunday Times*, July 17, 2011, supplemented by my contemporaneous interviews with a News International official and a News Corp official.

Page 5   *the company's $14 billion takeover:* David Folkenflik, "It's the End of the 'World' but the Story Isn't Over," *Weekend Edition Sunday*, July 10, 2011, and similar coverage elsewhere.

Page 5   *Everyone at that meeting with the Dowlers knew:* Exchange between Murdoch and the Dowlers is based on my interviews with two people who had contemporaneous knowledge of the meeting. Additionally, public statements from Dowler family lawyer Mark Lewis on July 15, 2011, as above.

Page 6   *an echo of old battles:* Shawcross, *Murdoch*, pp. 20–29.

Page 6   *New allegations claimed that his reporters:* "Phone Hacking: 9/11 Victims 'May Have Had Mobiles Tapped by News of the World Reporters,'" *Daily Mirror*, July 11, 2011.

Page 7   *Gemma Dowler spoke directly to Murdoch:* Sally Dowler, testimony at Leveson Inquiry, November 21, 2011, p. 11.

Page 7   *blinking into the July sunlight:* "History for London, United Kingdom," Friday, July 15, 2011, www.wunderground.com/history /airport/EGLL/2011/7/15/DailyHistory.html?req_city=NA&req_state =NA&req_statename=NA.

Page 7   *Murdoch was confronted:* Shown in footage contained in David Bowden, "Milly Dowler Family Set for 2 Million Pound Hacking Payout," Sky News, September 19, 2011.

Chapter 2

Page 9   *the idea of Australia:* Multiple current and former Murdoch editors, executives, and confidants, interview by author.

Page 9   *Robert Thomson, born in a small town:* Mark Baker, "Rupert Has Got a Crush on You," *The Age*, March 23, 2013; several current and former Thomson colleagues, interviews by author.

Page 9   *Col Allan, from the tiny agrarian town:* Lloyd Grove, "Rupe's Attack Dog Gets Bitten, Keeps Barking," *New York Magazine*, September 10, 2007.

Page 9   *The British-born Les Hinton:* James Robinson, "Les Hinton: Murdoch Consigliere Who Smoothed Waters After Goodman Case," *Guardian*, July 8, 2009.

Page 10   *David Hill, an Aussie who ran sports:* Joe Flint, "Fox Sports' David Hill Superimposes His Will on TV," *Los Angeles Times*, March 25, 2010.

Page 10   *"The story of our company is the stuff of legend":* David Folkenflik, "Murdoch Confronts Critics at News Corp Meeting," *All Things Considered*, October 21, 2011.

Page 10   *"Adelaide is irrelevant":* Graeme Samuel, interview by author, Melbourne.

Page 10   *An infant born in Melbourne:* Information taken from institutional websites, including Newscorp.com, Newsspace.com.au, various not-for-profit organizations in Australia.

Page 11   *Stephen Mayne, formerly an editor:* Description of Mayne derived from author's interviews of Stephen Mayne; a former News Corp official; and an associate of Lachlan Murdoch. All subsequent Mayne quotes in this chapter are taken from author's interviews with Mayne.

Page 11   *much of what his father had written didn't stand up:* Shawcross, *Murdoch*, pp. 21–22.

Page 12   *The son adopted radical leftist politics:* Shawcross, *Murdoch*, pp. 32, 38.

Page 12   *publicity manager of the Cherwell:* Chris Baraniuk, "Who Guards the Guardians," *Oxford Today*, October 15, 2012.

Page 13   *"I don't know of any son of any prominent media family":* Dynasties: The Murdochs, ABC (Australia), 2001. Subsequent quotes from Dame Elisabeth are also derived from this documentary.

Page 13   *He married young and had a daughter:* Kiernan, *Citizen Murdoch*, pp. 55–56, 81–82.

Page 14   *News Corp was granted waterfront property:* Paola Totaro, "Auditor Attacks Showground Deal for Murdoch," *Sydney Morning Herald*, December 9, 1997.

Page 15   *"He's a big, bad bastard":* Paul Keating to Tony Blair, July 16, 1995, from Alistair Campbell's diaries, as cited by Leveson Inquiry lead lawyer Robert Jay in question to Blair. From Leveson transcripts, May 28, 2012, Blair testimony, pp. 60–61.

Page 15   *"I don't want to pretend this is a guy":* Andrew Jaspan, interviews by author, for this and subsequent quotations.

Page 15   *John Hartigan, then CEO and chairman of News Ltd:* Leigh Sales, interview, July 14, 2011, ABC (Australia), www.abc.net.au/7.30/content/2011/s3269880.htm.

Page 16   *he informed Hartigan it was time:* Andrew Crook, "Farewell Big Harto: News Ltd CEO John Hartigan Resigns," Crikey.com.au, November 9, 2011.

Page 16   *"Long time in newspapers":* Tom Baxter, interview by author.

Page 16   *beachside community of Albert Park:* Author, visit to Albert Park; Kate MacFadyen, interview by author.

Page 17 *Between six and seven of every ten copies:* Figures from the Audit Bureau of Circulation and Roy Morgan Research for 2011 as cited in Wendy Bacon, *Sceptical Climate: Media Coverage of Climate Change in Australia,* Australian Centre for Independent Journalism, 2011, p. 23.

Page 17 *"he's the bloke they have to please":* Paul Barry, interview by author. (Subsequent Barry quotations taken from this interview.)

Page 17 *"It's a pretty clear stranglehold":* Monica Attard, interview by author.

Page 18 *Rupert Murdoch addressed the nature of media ownership:* Murdoch, BBC interview, 1968, http://youtu.be/wtcq8RDDPFU?t=2m.

Page 19 *"Most [Australian] Labor politicians hated Rupert":* Former senior News Corp executive, interview by author; Tony Wright, "Politicians of All Stripes Beat a Path to Murdoch's Door," *The Age,* July 16, 2011.

Page 19 *"by far the most detailed paper":* Robert Manne, interview by author.

Page 19 *"Here is Australia's first truly national newspaper":* Copy of full July 1964 mission statement provided to author by News Ltd, as reproduced, with permission: www.npr.org/assets/news/2012/04/05/australian.pdf.

Page 21 *Murdoch believed that the avid backing:* Philip Dorling, "Whitlam Radical, Fraser Arrogant, Hawke Moderate: Secret Cables Reveal Murdoch Insights," *Sydney Morning Herald,* May 20, 2013.

Page 21 *the* Australian *sets the tone:* Numerous Australian journalists, both for Murdoch and non-Murdoch titles, interviews by author.

Page 21 *"someone's probably not going to edit":* James Chessell, interview by author, for this and subsequent Chessell quotations.

Page 22 *he took direct aim at the* Australian*:* Manne, *Bad News.*

Page 23 *The paper commissioned a full book review:* Matthew Ricketson, "Forensic Critique of a Paper of Influence," *Australian,* September 24, 2011.

Page 23 *the newspaper fired back:* Headlines in the *Australian* included "Conspiracy Theories May Be Less Laughable If Manne Got Out More"; "Bad News: The Diary of a Murdoch Hater"; "Manne Allows Ideology to Cloud His Judgments"; "A Critic Untroubled by Facts Who Seeks to Silence Dissent"; and "Manne Throws Truth Overboard."

Chapter 3

The discussion of newspapers at the beginning of this chapter is influenced by my interviews in recent years with many editors who previously worked for or competed with Murdoch's News International, including former *Sun* editor Kelvin MacKenzie, former *Sunday Times* (UK) editor Andrew Neil, former *Times of London* editor Simon Jenkins, former *Independent* editor Simon Kelner, former *News of the World* deputy features editor Paul McMullan, former *Sunday Herald* editor (and senior editor at the *Times of London*) Andrew Jaspan, *Times of London/Sunday Times* head of digital Tom Whitwell, *Sunday Times* executive editor Tristan Davies, former assistant *Sun* editor Roy Greenslade, former chief executive of the *Economist* and ITN David Gordon, *Guardian* editor in chief Alan Rusbridger, and former *Guardian* director of digital content Emily Bell, among others. In addition, my thinking was shaped by less formal conversations with a dozen other British journalists, by my interviews with eight members of Parliament, by my reading of various British papers, and by the testimony of the editors of various British newspaper titles before the Leveson judicial inquiry.

Page 24 *"xenophobic, bloody-minded, ruthless"*: Roy Greenslade, "A New Britain, a New Kind of Newspaper," *Guardian*, February 25, 2004.

Page 24 *"Stick it Up Your Junta!"*: As cited in Chippindale and Horrie, *Stick It Up Your Punter!*, p. 136.

Page 25 *stands in the Hillsborough soccer stadium in Sheffield collapsed:* Chippindale and Horrie, *Stick It Up Your Punter!*, pp. 345–348.

Page 25 *The reporter on the story, Harry Arnold:* "Sun Reporter Harry Arnold's Hillsborough Headline Regret," BBC.co.uk, September 7, 2012, www.bbc.co.uk/news/uk-england-south-yorkshire-19507065.

Page 25 *comedian had eaten a woman's hamster*: Max Clifford, witness statement to Leveson Inquiry, February 9, 2012.

Page 26 *"always been in the gutter"*: Kelvin MacKenzie on BBC Two's *Daily Politics* show, December 8, 2011.

Page 26 *MacKenzie boasted:* Kelvin MacKenzie, interview by author.

Page 26 *"If any politician wanted my opinion"*: Rupert Murdoch, testimony before Leveson Inquiry, April 25, 2012, morning session.

Page 27 *in a previous generation*: See, for example, Tifft and Jones, *The Patriarch;* and *The Trust.*

Page 27 *"I find American newspapers boring—and biblical"*: Simon Jenkins, interview by author.

Page 28 *Murdoch sketched out his philosophy:* Rupert Murdoch, MacTaggart Lecture, Edinburgh International Television Festival, August 25, 1989, p. 4, www.geitf.co.uk/sites/default/files/geitf/GEITF_MacTaggart_1989 _Rupert_Murdoch.pdf.

Page 28 *Prince Charles, by then married . . . telephoned his girlfriend:* Michelle Green, "Bugged and Bedeviled," *People*, February 1, 1993.

Page 29 *the prince's sexual banter:* Paul McMullan, interview by author.

Page 29 *the British press faces tight regulations:* British media lawyers David Hooper and Mark Stephens, interview by author; *Guardian* editor Alan Rusbridger, interviews by author.

Page 29 *could obtain so-called super-injunctions:* Roy Greenslade, "Law Is Badly in Need of Reform as Celebrities Hide Secrets," *London Evening Standard*, April 20, 2011.

Page 29 *McMullan snorted at the idea:* Paul McMullan, interview by author.

Page 29 *"anything that the public is interested in is in the public interest"*: Paul McMullan, testimony to Leveson Inquiry, November 29, 2011, pp. 39–40.

Page 29 *"Privacy is for paedos"*: McMullan, testimony to Leveson Inquiry, November 29, 2011, p. 91.

Page 30 *One of McMullan's infamous scoops:* McMullan, interview by author.

Page 30 *McMullan showed undue modesty:* McMullan gave a fuller account to the Leveson Inquiry, p. 93.

Page 31 *"Do you just stick your fingers in your ears":* McMullan, interview by author.

Page 31 *Johnson later claimed that he had "blackmailed":* Joshua Haddow, "Confessions of a Tabloid Terrorist," *Vice* (UK), www.vice.com/en_uk /read/confessions-of-a-tabloid-terrorist-hack-graham-johnson-q-and-a.

Page 31 *"the editors start shouting":* McMullan, interview by author.

Page 31 *"The tone was buccaneering":* David Gordon, interview by author.

Page 31 *Murdoch's cadre of Australians imported . . . "mateship":* This section is based on David Folkenflik's interviews with Andrew Jaspan, who worked for and against Murdoch in the UK and competed against Murdoch in Australia; a former News Corp executive; former *New York Post* editor and publisher Ken Chandler; and Australian historian and novelist Thomas Keneally.

Page 32 *traces the origins of mateship:* Keneally, email exchange and conversation with author.

Page 32 *the carnage of Gallipoli:* Keneally, email exchange with author.

Page 32 *Associated R &R Films Pty Ltd:* As cited in Wolff, *Man Who Owns the News,* p. 63.

Page 32 *Mateship can take the form of a favor:* Andrew Jaspan, interview by author.

Page 33 *invited to spend a boozy night:* Freya Petersen, email interview by author.

Page 34 *tapped his mate Dunleavy:* Shawcross, *Murdoch,* pp. 196–197.

Page 34 *In her entry in* Who's Who*:* Geoffrey Levy, "Rebekah Brooks, the Schmoozer Hated by Murdoch's Wife and Daughter," *Daily Mail,* July 17, 2011.

Page 34 *Brooks had prepared particularly well:* Piers Morgan, *Insider,* pp. 39, 50.

Page 35 *"name and shame" approach:* "Police Criticize Paedophile 'Name And Shame,'" BBC News, July 30, 2000; "Innocent Man Branded Child Abuser," BBC News, August 3, 2000.

Page 35 *eighty-three convicted sex offenders:* Matt Born, "Paper Drops Paedophile Campaign," *Telegraph,* August 5, 2000.

Page 35 *handing over a mobile phone from the paper:* Mark Stephens, lawyer for Sara Payne, interview by author.

Page 35 *Dr. Yvette Cloete returned to her home:* Brendan O'Neill, "Whispering Game," BBC News, February 16, 2006.

Page 35 *A mob chased a family:* "Mob Violence at Home of 'Paedophile,'" *Telegraph,* August 4, 2000; "Police Condemn 'Paedophile' Attacks," BBC News, August 7, 2000; "Families Flee Paedophile Protests," BBC News, August 9, 2000; Dave Hill, "After the Purge," *Guardian,* February 5, 2001.

Page 36 *Bryant clad only in briefs:* Simon Walters, "Posing in His Y-Fronts for a Website Called Gaydar, the MP Who Helped Scrap Ban on Gay Sex in Public," *Mail on Sunday,* November 30, 2003; Richard Littlejohn, "No, I'm the Only Gay in the Valleys," *Sun,* December 2, 2003; "Blair's Attack Poodle Says Pants to the Lot of You," *Sunday Times,* December 7, 2003.

Page 36 *"Shouldn't you be on Clapham Common?"* Chris Bryant MP, interview by author.

Page 37 *Some of the older reporters hired private investigators:* As cited by Graham Johnson in *Hack*, Kindle edition, location 2905 of 5126.

Chapter 4

Page 38 *On a subfreezing morning:* Author's attendance during tour, as reflected in David Folkenflik, "With Headline Bus Tour, 'New York Post' Takes Manhattan," *All Things Considered*, March 19, 2013. Various *Post* headlines as indicated in text of chapter.

Page 39 *Murdoch had broken into the American market:* Julie Domel, "Rupert Murdoch's 1973 Purchase of E-N," *San Antonio Express-News*, July 29, 2011.

Page 40 *This world welcomed Ken Chandler:* Ken Chandler, interview by author. Subsequent Chandler quotations from this chapter are also derived from that interview.

Page 40 *Murdoch . . . promised in writing that he would keep faith:* Nissenson, *Lady Upstairs*, p. 403.

Page 41 *Murdoch deployed:* Interviews by author with Chandler; and additionally a former senior *Post* editor; and a former midlevel *Post* editor; also as cited in Kiernan, *Citizen Murdoch*, pp. 208–209.

Page 41 *how to take down Geraldine Ferraro:* As cited in Kiernan, *Citizen Murdoch*, pp. 289–290, invoking the reporting of Geoffrey Stokes in the (Murdoch-owned) *Village Voice* on Dunleavy memo.

Page 41 *didn't think much of a woman:* As cited in Kiernan, *Citizen Murdoch*, p. 290.

Page 43 *"What would Rupert think about this?":* Viv Groskop, "David Yelland: 'Rupert Murdoch Is a Closet Liberal,'" *Evening Standard*, March 29, 2010.

Page 43 *making the conservative case for war:* Julia Day, "Murdoch Praises Blair's 'Courage'," *Guardian*, February 11, 2003.

Page 44 *Murdoch called British prime minister Tony Blair:* "Rupert Murdoch Pressured Tony Blair over Iraq, Says Alastair Campbell," Nicholas Watt, *Guardian*, June 15, 2012.

Page 44 *Every now and then he'd invite a reporter up:* Former *New York Post* reporter Tim Arango, interview by author.

Page 44 *periodically urinating in a sink:* As cited in Lloyd Grove, "Rupe's Attack Dog Gets Bitten, Keeps Barking," *New York Magazine*, September 10, 2007.

Page 44 *the tail that wagged the dog:* As cited in Corky Siemaszko, "For Sale: Page Six," *New York Daily News*, May 19, 2007.

Page 45 *it emerged in the Aussie press:* For example, Glenn Milne, "Rudd Admits to U.S. Strip Club Visit," *Sydney Daily Telegraph*, August 19, 2007; "Strip Club Outing Will Hurt Me, Rudd says," ABC (Australia), August 19, 2007.

Page 45 *Sandra Guzman, a Latina journalist:* Allegations and quotations taken from original complaint in *Sandra Guzman v. News Corp et al.*

09-CV-9323. Admissions by *Post* editors on Steve Dunleavy's remarks to Robert George taken from depositions attached to the case.

Page 46 *the* Post *endorsed her for Senate:* As cited in "Pataki's the One," editorial, *New York Post,* November 6, 2004.

Page 46 *Ruddy was speaking warmly:* Chris Ruddy, "Bill Clinton Interview: Hillary Will Make the Decisions," NewsMax, October 31, 2007; Chris Ruddy, interview by author.

Page 46 *yet the* New York Post *endorsed Barack Obama:* "Post Endorses Barack Obama," editorial, *New York Post,* January 30, 2008.

Page 47 *Fox News chairman Roger Ailes interceded:* David Carr and Tim Arango, "A Fox Chief at the Pinnacle of Media and Politics," *New York Times,* January 9, 2010.

Page 47 *Elisabeth Murdoch ... had raised money:* Andrew Porter, "Elisabeth Murdoch Hosts Barack Obama Fundraiser," *Telegraph,* May 14, 2008.

Page 47 *the* Post *reverted to form:* "New York Post Endorses John McCain," editorial, *New York Post,* September 8, 2008.

Page 47 Post *cartoonist Sean Delonas drew a chimpanzee:* "They'll have to find someone else to write the next stimulus bill," Sean Delonas, editorial cartoon, *New York Post,* February 18, 2009.

Page 47 *In an editorial headlined: New York Post,* "That Cartoon," February 20, 2009.

Page 47 *Allan also released a statement:* Nico Pitney, "New York Post Defends Cartoon, Slams Al Sharpton," Huffington Post, February 21, 2009.

Page 48 *Murdoch issued his own apology:* "Rupert Murdoch Apologizes for Chimp Cartoon," CNN.com, February 24, 2009.

Page 48 *"I don't understand the history":* Allan's testimony as presented in *Guzman v. News Corp. et al.*

Page 48 *Among Allan's critics:* Michael Wolff, interview by author. Former News Corp executive Gary Ginsberg told the author he did not remember the episode and otherwise declined to comment on it.

Page 49 *Deng's story was one of astonishing ambition:* John Lippman, Leslie Chang, and Robert Frank, "Rupert Murdoch's Wife Wendi Wields Influence at News Corp," *Wall Street Journal,* November 1, 2000.

Page 49 *a Chinese Becky Sharp:* Eric Ellis, "Wendi Deng Murdoch," *The Monthly* (Australia), June 2007.

Page 49 *The divorce settlement was reported to have cost $1.7 billion:* For example, Paola Totaro, "The Reluctant Son: Lachlan Murdoch and News Corp," *Monthly,* March 2012; Amy Chozick, "After 14 Years, Murdoch Files for Divorce from Third Wife," *New York Times,* June 14, 2013.

Page 49 *in reality she settled:* Author's interview with former senior News Corp executive, which accords with reporting by earlier Murdoch biographers Michael Wolff and Neil Chenoweth.

Page 49 The Man Who Owns the News *received scant coverage:* Database searches show no articles containing "Michael Wolff" or "*The Man Who Owns the News*" in any News Corp newspaper in the US or the UK in the period surrounding the publication of the book. The *Australian* published a laudatory review by Stephen Loosley, "Making Murdoch," on November 29, 2008. The paper also published a less flattering feature column calling the book gossip.

Page 49 *the gossip website Cityfile:* Cityfile.com is now defunct, but the article is cited in Owen Thomas, "Victoria Floethe, the New Media Ingenue," February 26, 2009, http://gawker.com/5161010/victoria-floethe-the-new-media-ingenue. Not all observers credited Wolff's explanation for the coverage of his personal life. Foster Kamen, then of the *Village Voice*, wrote skeptically of Wolff's claims that the *Post* planted the story of his affair in blogs to give it cover: Kamen, "Shut Down: Michael Wolff's Rupert Murdoch /City File/Page Six Conspiracy Theory: Shut It Down!" http://blogs.village voice.com/runninscared/2010/05/michael_wolffs.php. Through public relations representatives, Col Allan and other *Post* executives would not comment for this book.

Page 49 *a younger colleague:* Accounts of Wolff's interactions with *Post* reporters amid his marital travails drawn from Wolff, interview by author; and from Victoria Floethe, "How I Became the Femme Fatale of New York Gossip," *Spectator*, April 1, 2009.

Page 49 *another cartoon by Delonas:* "Oh, Mr. Wolff, your books are so moral and ethical. I hope your wife appreciates them," Sean Delonas, cartoon, *New York Post*, March 3, 2009.

Page 49–50 *the* Post *published seven pieces . . . the* Post's *articles stopped cold:* Database searches by author.

Chapter 5

Page 51 *Murdoch acquired six television stations:* Daniel Rosenheim and Charles Storch, "Murdoch Group to Buy Metromedia," *Chicago Tribune*, May 7, 1985.

Page 51 *bought out Marvin Davis's stake:* Background on deals drawn from Mark Seal, "The Man Who Ate Hollywood," *Vanity Fair*, November 2005.

Page 52 *Steve Dunleavy:* Description of Dunleavy and ensuing events inspired in part by Marc Fisher, "The King of Sleaze," *GQ*, April 1990; Ken Chandler, interview by author; Freya Petersen, interview by author. Also, Shawcross, *Murdoch*, p. 54.

Page 52 *"I hope it wasn't his writing foot"; the gunman was not the Son of Sam:* Jonathan Mahler, "What Rupert Wrought," *New York Magazine*, May 21, 2005.

Page 52 *"television was considered a foul little business":* Tom Shales, "Fox's Ridiculous 'Reporters,'" *Washington Post*, July 30, 1988.

Page 53 *"We're a network now":* Steve Wulf, "Outfoxed," *Sports Illustrated*, December 27, 1993.

Page 53 *Neil told me:* Andrew Neil, interview by author.

Page 54 *MSNBC launched at about the same time:* Characterizations based on author's interviews with MSNBC president Phil Griffin, former NBC News president Steve Capus, and former executives Rick Kaplan and Erik Sorenson, among others.

Page 54 *"I'll tell you what television didn't do":* Ailes, interview in *Esquire*, December 2010, www.esquire.com/blogs/politics/roger-ailes-interview -5039254#ixzz2N9vteIqL.

Page 55 *"Cable news punches above its weight":* Former Fox News vice president for news David Rhodes, interview by author, for "TV Network Expands Bloomberg News' Horizon," *All Things Considered,* December 8, 2010.

Page 56 *On the first day:* Some description of the Fox network's debut drawn from John Carmody, "The TV Column," *Washington Post,* October 7, 1996.

Page 56 *One of the most important new faces of Fox:* Material on Brit Hume derived from several author interviews with Hume; David Folkenflik, "The Voice of Reason," *Baltimore Sun,* June 2, 2003; and Folkenflik, "Brit Hume to Step Down as Fox News Anchor," *All Things Considered,* November 6, 2008.

Page 58 *Time Warner's refusal to welcome Fox:* Harry Berkowitz, "Plug Is Pulled," *Newsday,* October 12, 1996; Clifford J. Levy, "Lobbying at Murdoch Gala Ignited New York Cable Clash," *New York Times,* October 13, 1996; Joel Siegel, Greg B. Smith, and Jere Hester, "Clobbered in Cable War," *New York Daily News,* November 7, 1996.

Page 58 *"Fox was the recipient of special advocacy":* Portions of Judge Denise Cote's decision ran in the *New York Times* on November 7, 1996, under the headline: "Excerpts from Ruling."

Page 59 *Children of such prominent Democratic families:* Chafets, *Roger Ailes,* pp. 147–152.

Chapter 6

The events described in this chapter are based on the author's personal experiences and observations, extensive interviews over a period of years about disparate episodes, and interviews conducted purely for the purpose of this book. The chapter draws on interviews with five former Fox News public relations staffers, one current Fox News executive, one former Fox News executive, and two associates of Fox News CEO Roger Ailes. In addition, it draws on a formal interview and an informal conversation I had with Ailes. All the events portrayed in this chapter that did not involve the author rely on accounts from at least two sources with contemporaneous knowledge of what occurred. Ailes declined to be interviewed for this book, through his chief publicity executive, Brian Lewis, who also declined to participate, citing Murdoch's position on the book.

Page 61 *On Election Day 2000:* David Folkenflik, contemporaneous notes and recollections; conversations with former editors at *Baltimore Sun.*

Page 62 *I called Fox in trying to sort out:* The account of Geraldo Rivera's "friendly fire" misadventures in Afghanistan is drawn from my reporting of the time and my contemporaneous notes. David Folkenflik, "War News from Rivera Seems off the Mark," *Baltimore Sun,* December 6, 2001; Folkenflik, "Reports of War Draw Fire to Fox," *Baltimore Sun,* December 15, 2001; Folkenflik, "Fox News Calls Rivera's Report an Honest Mistake," *Baltimore Sun,* December 27, 2001.

Page 63 *Fox PR people had taken some protective steps:* David Bauder, "Gun-toting Geraldo Rivera Sparks Debate on Role of Journalists in War," Associated Press, December 11, 2001. (AP stories posted in the later "BC" cycle, such as this article and the next Bauder piece cited, typically run in the next morning's newspapers.)

Page 64 *"Pretty pathetic placement":* David Folkenflik, notes of Briganti voice mail message.

Page 64 *a tepid statement to the Associated Press:* David Bauder, "Fox: Rivera Made 'Honest Mistake' in Reporting Friendly Fire Incident," Associated Press, December 26, 2001. Appearing on the *O'Reilly Factor* on January 3, 2002, Rivera briefly alluded to the episode without correcting it: "I made an honest mistake and a really weak-kneed, back-stabbing, sweaty-palmed reporter from a minor newspaper used it . . . as a platform to attack me."

Page 64 *landed me on Fox's blacklist:* Contemporaneous conversations with Fox News staffers and other media reporters who told me they had been informed of my status.

Page 64 *"Irena's doghouse":* Three former Fox News staffers independently volunteered that term. That said, the existence of Briganti's list was fully encouraged by Lewis.

Page 65 *Fox News adopted a pro-war tenor:* Cavuto mockery and the Fox News ticker taunts against antiwar protesters contained in David Folkenflik, "Fox Defends Its 'Patriotic' Coverage," *Baltimore Sun*, April 2, 2003.

Page 65 *"a fresh coat of paint on an outhouse":* Matt Kempner, "Zahn on Ratings Roll," *Atlanta Journal Constitution*, September 25, 2002.

Page 65 *"I could have put a dead raccoon on the air":* Bill Carter, "Fox News Fires a Star Host over a CNN Bid," *New York Times*, September 6, 2001.

Page 65 *I noticed that Fox News had fallen into the habit:* David Folkenflik, "The Fox News Wishing Well," NPR.org, May 9, 2005, www.npr.org/templates /story/story.php?storyId=4638852. Similarly, David Bauder, "Watch Your Back When Fox News Wishes Well," Associated Press, July 23, 2006.

Page 66 *Laurie Dhue, a Fox anchor who had complained:* The events involving Dhue and the Radio and Television Correspondents' dinner are based on the author's interviews with Anne Schroeder Mullins, then a gossip reporter for the *Washington Post*, a staffer for Fox News, and, in one aspect, a third person present at the event.

Page 66 *"Fox News babes were in high spirits":* Anne Schroeder, Names and Faces column, *Washington Post*, April 8, 2005.

Page 67 *On the blogs, the fight was particularly fierce:* Four former Fox News employees told me of these practices.

Page 68 *suddenly blazing eyes:* My memorable encounter with Roger Ailes at New York's Metropolitan Museum of Art took place at the launch party for the Fox Business Network on October 24, 2007.

Page 70 *Matthew Flamm . . . was sandbagged:* The description of the Matthew Flamm episode is based on my interviews with three people aware of Flamm's thinking at the time plus a former Fox News staffer with knowledge of the network's response to his coverage.

Page 70 *They want to copy the success that MSNBC has had:* From Matthew Flamm, "Fox News Eyes O'Reilly for Election Night," Crainsnyc.com, posted February 29, 2008. Source not identified in original item.

Page 71 *TVNewser posted a punishing item:* Chris Ariens, "Hume, Not O'Reilly, Will Anchor FNC's Election Night," TVNewser.com, posted February 29, 2008.

Page 71 *A second-tier site, Big Head DC:* "Crain's Reporter Has an Omelet Worth of Misinformation on His Face Today," BigHeadDC.com, posted February 29, 2008. The site no longer exists, but the page can be retrieved at this web address: http://web.archive.org/web/20080302094947/http:// www.bigheaddc.com.

Page 71 *What the hell had happened?:* Author's separate interviews with three people with contemporaneous knowledge of Flamm's actions.

Page 71 *To salt the wound:* Compare distorted image of Flamm viewable on Big Head DC posting to image on earlier FishbowlNY.com item: www .mediabistro.com/fishbowlny/files/original/Photo_110305_009.jpg.

Page 72 *Timothy Arango, then a media reporter:* This episode is based on my interview with Tim Arango of the *New York Times* and a separate interview with a former Fox News staffer with contemporaneous knowledge.

Page 72 *Arango's story, headlined "Back in the Game":* Tim Arango, "CNN Back in the Game with U.S. Presidential Race," *New York Times,* March 5, 2008.

Page 72 *unbylined story on Jossip:* "Did *NYT* Media Reporter Tim Arango Just Get out of Rehab?" Jossip, March 5, 2008. The website Jossip no longer exists, but the posting can be accessed at this URL: http://web .archive.org/web/20080710104234/http://www.jossip.com/did-nyt-media -reporter-tim-arango-just-get-out-of-rehab-20080305.

Page 73 *Bill Keller . . . emailed Arango a note:* Tim Arango, interview by author; Bill Keller, email interview by author.

Page 73 *another* Times *media reporter, Jacques Steinberg:* Jacques Steinberg, "Fox News Finds Its Rivals Closing In," *New York Times,* June 28, 2008.

Page 73 *Steve Doocy and Brian Kilmeade . . . went after Steinberg:* Simon Maloy, "Fox News Airs Altered Photos of *NY Times* Reporters," Media Matters, July 2, 2008. The liberal media watchdog Media Matters carries an extensive online database of coverage it criticizes, especially on Fox: http://mediamatters.org/research/2008/07/02/fox-news-airs -altered-photos-of-ny-times-report/143921.

Page 73 New York Times *media columnist David Carr accused Fox News:* David Carr, "When Fox News Is the Story," *New York Times,* July 7, 2008.

Page 73 *Fox pulled back:* One current and one former Fox News staffer, interviews by author, as well as interviews with executives at other media outlets.

Chapter 7

Page 75 *unnamed Clinton operatives:* "CNN Debunks False Report About Obama," CNN, January 23, 2007. The CNN report was one of several by major news organizations to refute convincingly such claims.

Page 75 *citing ties to William Ayres:* Jim Rutenberg, "Obama's Personal Ties Are Subject of Program on Fox News Channel," *New York Times,* October 6, 2008.

Page 76 *Obama denounced:* Scott Shane, "Obama and '60s Bomber: A Look into Crossed Paths," *New York Times,* October 3, 2008.

Page 76 *Murdoch brokered a meeting:* This account is substantially drawn from Wolff, *Man Who Owns the News,* Kindle edition, location 5811–12; also Wolff, "Tuesdays with Rupert," *Vanity Fair,* October 2008; supplemented by author's interview with former News Corp executive.

Page 76 *an interview with Fox's top-rated figure: O'Reilly Factor,* September 4, 2008.

Page 77 *Hume told me he had lost his enthusiasm:* Author's interviews for this and subsequent Hume quotations.

Page 77 *"a weak and piteous thing":* Andrew O'Hehir, "I Watched Fox News for Five Hours Last Night," Salon.com, November 6, 2008.

Page 77 *Fox News mapped out a strategy:* Bill Shine, interview by author; David Folkenflik, "Fox News Thrives in Age of Obama," *All Things Considered,* March 23, 2009.

Page 78 *Sammon . . . "engaged in . . . mischievous speculation":* Bill Sammon, interview by author. The issue arose after a speech Sammon gave to a Hillsdale College alumni cruise was reported in a Media Matters posting: Eric Hananoki, "Cruise Ship Confession: Top Fox News Official Admits Lying On-Air About Obama," Media Matters, March 29, 2011.

Page 79 *Beck brooded about whether FEMA:* For a classic example involving FEMA and conspiracy theories about concentration camps, see *Beck,* March 3, 2009.

Page 79 *"much more like the Founding Fathers":* This and subsequent quotations by Glenn Beck obtained from interview by author.

Page 79 *Shepard Smith, a maverick figure:* This section is influenced by author's interview with Smith; two former Fox News staffers; and two current Fox News executives. The section also draws on David Folkenflik, "Fox's Shep Smith Keeps Opinions to Himself," *Morning Edition,* October 21, 2008; and Sherry Ricchiardi, "The Anti-Anchor," *American Journalism Review,* December 2009–January 2010.

Page 80 *He liked to rattle O'Reilly:* Former Fox News producer Joe Muto, interview by author.

Page 80 *found a consistent formula:* Author's analysis of six months' worth of "all-star panels" on *Special Report,* August 2010 through January 2011.

Page 81 *"you should not be able to remove rats":* Glenn Beck on *Beck,* September 9, 2009.

Page 81 *"Rats could attack us in the sewer":* James Rosen, *Special Report with Bret Baier,* September 9, 2009.

Page 81 *relevant passage from Sunstein's article:* Cass R. Sunstein, "The Rights of Animals: A Very Short Primer," *University of Chicago Law & Economics,* August 2002.

Page 82 *"the biggest bunch of crybabies"*: Chris Wallace, *O'Reilly Factor*, September 21, 2009.

Page 82 *Feinberg announced that salaries:* Robert Schmidt and Ian Katz, "Feinberg Wants All Companies to Adopt Pay-Cut Model," Bloomberg News, October 22, 2009.

Page 82 *White House and Treasury press officials conferred:* These urgent exchanges were captured in emails obtained by the conservative legal watchdog Judicial Watch. Press release: "Documents Show Obama White House Attacked, Excluded Fox News Channel." Documents are viewable here: www.judicialwatch.org/press-room/press-releases/documents-show -obama-white-house-attacked-excluded-fox-news-channel; Chafets, *Roger Ailes*, p. 198, on Ailes calling other network Washington executives reminding them of First Amendment overtones, that Treasury could next shut out their news organizations.

Page 83 *"We see Fox right now as the source"*: Anita Dunn, interview by author; David Folkenflik, "Obama Administration Takes on Fox News," *All Things Considered*, October 14, 2009.

Page 84 *other news outlets had bathed the president:* Michael Clemente, interview by author.

Page 84 *One of the New Black Panthers brandished:* David Folkenflik, "Conservative Media Stokes New Black Panther Story," *All Things Considered*, July 20, 2010. Includes author's interview with Mark Potok.

Page 85 *Adams rekindled the story:* J. Christian Adams, interview by NPR's Michel Martin, *Tell Me More*, July 13, 2010.

Page 85 *Fox's Kelly . . . devoted forty-five segments:* "Report: Fox News Has Hyped Phony New Black Panthers Scandal at Least 95 Times," Media Matters, July 16, 2010.

Page 85 *the late conservative blogger Andrew Breitbart:* Andrew Breitbart, interview by author.

Page 85 *Still, Linda Chavez:* Ben Smith, "A Conservative Dismisses Right Wing Black Panther 'Fantasies,'" Politico, July 17, 2010.

Page 86 *Kelly told Powers more than once:* Kirsten Powers on *America Live* with Megyn Kelly, July 13, 2010.

Page 86 *On returning from maternity leave:* Megyn Kelly with radio host Mike Gallagher, *America Live*, August 9, 2011.

Page 86 *Kelly also stood up for the right of Chaz Bono:* As reflected in a posting from liberal group Think Progress on September 14, 2011: "Megyn Kelly Debunks Gay-Bashing Psychiatrist's 'Dancing with the Stars' Theories."

Page 86 *a billowing atomic mushroom cloud:* Frank James, "Fox News Gives Obama Mushroom Cloud Treatment," Two-Way blog, NPR.org, April 7, 2010; "Fox News: We Shouldn't Have Linked Obama-Mushroom Cloud," David Folkenflik, Two-Way blog, April 9, 2010; Jay Wallace, interview by author.

Page 87 *Shirley Sherrod, an African American regional agriculture official:* CNN wire staff, "Vilsack, White House Apologize to Former USDA Official," July 21, 2010.

Page 87 *the policy was observed for little more than a week:* Fox News producer Joe Muto, interview by author.
Page 87 *the Pew Research Center released a poll:* "Growing Number of Americans Say Obama Is a Muslim," Pew Research Center, August 18, 2010, www
.pewforum.org/Politics-and-Elections/Growing-Number-of-Americans
-Say-Obama-is-a-Muslim.aspx; "CNN Investigation: Obama Born in This
Country," CNN, April 25, 2010.

Chapter 8

The characterization of the recent political past in Australia in this chapter
is based in significant part on interviews with a dozen Australians who are
thoughtful observers of the scene, including journalists, lawyers, and corporate
figures. I have also drawn on articles in the *Australian,* the *Monthly,* the ABC
(Australia), Crickey.com.au, the Melbourne *Herald Sun,* the *Conversation,* the
Sydney Morning Herald, and *The Age.* This chapter was initially inspired
by the reporting I did in late 2011 and early 2012 for my NPR story "How
Murdoch's Aussie Papers Cover Climate Change," *All Things Considered,*
April 6, 2012. The Australian academic and journalist David McKnight also
devoted a chapter to related topics in his 2012 book, *Rupert Murdoch: An In-
vestigation of Power.*
Page 89 *Clive Hamilton . . . identified twelve figures:* The following Hamilton quotations were taken from "The Dirty Politics of Climate Change," a
speech he delivered on February 20, 2006, on behalf of the Climate Change
and Business Conference, www.tai.org.au/documents/downloads/WP84.pdf.
Page 90 *the Liberal Party of Prime Minister John Howard:* Angus Grigg,
"The Player," *Australian Financial Review Magazine,* September 29,
2006.
Page 90 *only . . . Indonesia . . . exports more coal:* World Coal Association,
www.worldcoal.org/resources/coal-statistics.
Page 91 *One episode stood out:* "A Climate of Confusion," *Australian,* January
16, 2006.
Page 91 *significant funding from the family of his younger sister:* Paul Barry,
"The Power Index: Rich Crusaders No. 6," Crickey.com.au, March 7, 2012.
Page 92 *At the Beacon Theater in New York City:* "Rupert Murdoch's Speech
on Carbon Neutrality," text of Murdoch speech, *Australian,* May 10, 2007.
Page 92 *James Murdoch's wife, Kathryn:* Environmental Defense Fund and
Clinton Foundation websites; EDF official, interview by author.
Page 92 *The elder Murdoch had been won over:* Marc Gunther, "Rupert
Murdoch's Climate Crusade," *Fortune,* August 27, 2007. My description of
the efforts of each News Corp division is partially drawn from this account
and from the corporation's own videos and statements at gei.newscorp.
com. Blair's presence at the Pebble Beach retreat had been previously dis-
closed, as in Gaby Hinsliff, "The PM, the Mogul, and the Secret Agenda,"
Observer (UK), July 22, 2006.

Page 93 *"Global warming is a crime for which we are all guilty"*: Kiefer Sutherland's appearance on News Corp promotional tape no longer available, but previously accessed on company's global energy initiative website: http://gei.newscorp.com/video/2008/07/24-climate-change-psa.html.

Page 93 *Asa Wahlquist . . . said she fought with editors:* "Audio Backs Tweets in Editor's Defamation Row," ABC (Australia), November 29, 2010. Audio available at www.abc.net.au/news/2010–11–29/audio-backs-tweets-in-editors-defamation-row/2355368.

Page 94 *a study examining how her country's newspapers handled:* Bacon, *Sceptical Climate*, www.acij.uts.edu.au/pdfs/sceptical-climate-part1.pdf. Other figures and insights taken from that study are cited in the body of this chapter. Additional quotations in this chapter drawn from author's interview with Bacon.

Page 96 *disclosures to an environmental group:* Carbon Disclosure Project, www.cdproject.net/en-US/Results/Pages/leadership-index.aspx.

Page 96 *Ailes said soberly, looking at the camera:* News Corp Global Energy Initiative website. Ailes appears for about thirty-six seconds in http://gei.newscorp.com/video/2008/06/global-energy-initiative-intro.html. By late 2004, the consensus of researchers in the field was captured by Naomi Oreskes, "Beyond the Ivory Tower: The Scientific Consensus on Climate Change," *Science*, December 3, 2004, www.sciencemag.org/content/306/5702/1686.full#affiliation. Fox did execute a special on global warming presenting that consensus a year later, *The Heat Is On: The Case of Global Warming*, hosted by Rick Folbaum, Fox News Channel, November 13, 2005. But the following spring, some doubt was cast in another special: *Global Warming: The Debate Continues*, hosted by David Asman, Fox News Channel, May 21, 2006.

Page 97 *Hart found Fox far more likely than its competitors:* "Market Influences on Climate Change Frames in CNN and Fox News Climate Change Broadcasts," P.S. Hart, 2008. Paper presented at the International Communication Association Annual Meeting, Montreal, Quebec, Canada.

Page 97 *Fox was far more likely to cover global warming:* Lauren Feldman et al., "Climate on Cable: The Nature and Impact of Global Warming Coverage on Fox News, CNN, and MSNBC," *International Journal of Press/Politics*, 2011.

Page 98 *"Given the controversy over the veracity of climate change data":* Ben Dimiero, "FoxLeaks: Fox Boss Ordered Staff to Cast Doubt on Climate Science," Media Matters, December 15, 2010.

Page 98 *an overwhelming imbalance in Fox's coverage:* Aaron Huertas and Dena Adler, "Is News Corp Failing Science? Representations of Climate Science on Fox News Channel and in the *Wall Street Journal* Editorial Page," Union of Concerned Scientists, September 2012.

Page 98 *The day before I met Professor Bacon:* "Sixteen Concerned Scientists: No Need to Panic About Global Warming," *Wall Street Journal*, January 27, 2012. The paper also received sharp rebuttals from scholars: Kevin Trenberth et al., "Check with Climate Scientists for Views on Climate,"

Wall Street Journal, letter to the editor, February 1, 2012; William D. Nordhaus, "Why the Global Warming Skeptics Are Wrong," *New York Review of Books,* March 22, 2012.

Page 99 *"obviously there is doubt":* Matthew Thompson, "News Ltd Carbon Coverage Campaigning Not Reporting; New Report + News Response," *Conversation,* December 1, 2011.

Page 99 *Bacon's work made the cut:* "History's Headliners," *Australian,* December 9, 1999. The article listed the top 100 "historic people, stories, books, and events" that defined twentieth-century Australian journalism. Bacon was listed for her work at the *National Times* in the mid-1980s with several other "talented, aggressive reporters."

Page 99 *Manne wrote a lengthy critique:* Robert Manne, interview by author.

Page 100 *calling competing newspapers . . . "propagandists":* Andrew Bolt, "Feeling Burned over a Cause for Concern," *Herald Sun,* April 16, 2008.

Page 100 *"News Ltd was to become a 'green' company":* Former News Corp executive; Robert Manne; Andrew Jaspan; Monica Attard, interviews by author.

Page 100 *Dame Elisabeth Murdoch . . . signed a letter:* Michael Gordon, "Climate Crusader: Dame Elisabeth Murdoch Joins Public Campaign for a Price on Carbon," *The Age* (Melbourne), June 15, 2011.

Page 101 *Piers Akerman of News Corp's* Sydney Daily Telegraph: Piers Akerman on *The Insiders* on ABC (Australia), June 19, 2011.

Page 101 *"Greens and their crazy cronies":* As cited in "Climate Criticism Allowed," *Sydney Daily Telegraph,* July 5, 2012; Adjudication no. 1542 by Australian Press Council. John Newton/*Sydney Daily Telegraph,* July 5, 2012.

Page 101 *"Climate change very slow but real":* Rupert Murdoch, Twitter feed, @rupertmurdoch: https://twitter.com/rupertmurdoch/status/223097 765427818496.

Chapter 9

The reporting that informs Chapter 9 was influenced by multiple interviews and less-formal conversations with Juan Williams. I was additionally aided by conversations with NPR senior Washington editor Ron Elving, NPR correspondent and Fox News analyst Mara Liasson, former NPR senior vice president for news Ellen Weiss, former NPR CEO Vivian Schiller, and *Fox News Sunday* host Chris Wallace, as well as several NPR board members and member station general managers and NPR producers and editors who spoke on condition they were not named. An earlier interview I conducted with Roger Ailes also helped me understand how he looks at the role that reporters for other news outlets play for Fox when they are paid to appear as the network's analysts.

Page 103 *the facts did not match the legend:* David Folkenflik, "Marshall May Not Have Tried to Enroll in UM Law School," *Baltimore Sun,* August 20, 1995. The late Carl T. Rowan; Juan Williams, interviews by author.

Page 104 *women at the* Washington Post: Howard Kurtz, "Post Reporter Williams Apologizes for 'Inappropriate' Verbal Conduct," *Washington Post*, November 2, 1991.

Page 104 *I profiled Williams:* David Folkenflik, "Juan Williams Fills Two Roles," *Baltimore Sun*, April 25, 2001.

Page 104 *some of those colleagues:* The following paragraphs draw on the author's interviews with Juan Williams and five NPR colleagues.

Page 105 *Williams seemed at his most empathetic:* Juan Williams, "President Bush, Part 1: The Interview," *All Things Considered*, January 29, 2007.

Page 105 *Many listeners . . . believed he had veered:* "Letters: Overplaying Bush," *All Things Considered*, February 1, 2007.

Page 106 *Scott Simon occasionally weighed in:* Scott Simon, "Even Pacifists Must Support This War," op-ed, *Wall Street Journal*, October 11, 2001.

Page 106 *Williams backed the Bush administration's stance:* Juan Williams, "Don't Mourn *Brown v. Board of Education*," op-ed, *New York Times*, June 29, 2007.

Page 106 *NPR turned down the offer:* Howard Kurtz, "NPR Rebuffs White House on Bush Talk," *Washington Post*, September 25, 2007. Irena Briganti's quotation is also from Kurtz's article.

Page 107 *an expectation among many of NPR's liberal listeners:* Author's personal experience.

Page 107 *commentators had raised rumors:* Roger Stone, interview by Geraldo Rivera, Fox News, June 1, 2008; others, such as Bob Beckel, spoke of a "shoe going to drop" involving Michelle Obama explaining why Hillary Clinton stayed in the Democratic primary past the point of mathematical hopes of prevailing.

Page 107 *"Stokely Carmichael in a designer dress":* Juan Williams, *O'Reilly Factor*, January 26, 2009.

Page 107 *"not out of the realm of mainstream political discourse":* Alicia Shepard, "Juan Williams, NPR, and Fox," NPR Ombudsman column, February 11, 2009, NPR.org.

Page 108 *NPR had repeatedly asked Fox to stop identifying Williams:* One NPR editor; one NPR public relations staffer; and two Fox News public relations staffers, interview by author.

Page 108 *He could not believe the angst:* Juan Williams's concerns derived from author's multiple conversations and interviews with Williams.

Page 108 *NPR executives had their own concerns:* Reservations from NPR leadership derived from author's interviews with multiple NPR executives, political editors, and show editors both before and after his termination by the network.

Page 108 *On an episode of ABC's Chat show* The View: Bill O'Reilly, *The View*, October 14, 2010.

Page 108 *received an attaboy from Williams:* Juan Williams, *O'Reilly Factor*, October 18, 2010.

Page 108 *Weiss terminated Williams's contract early:* David Folkenflik, "NPR Ends Juan Williams's Contract after Muslim Remarks," NPR.org, October 21,

2010; Folkenflik, "NPR Dismisses News Analyst Juan Williams," *All Things Considered;* stories in ensuing days about the unfolding crisis for the network.

Chapter 10

Page 110 *Vivian Schiller, speaking to the Atlanta Press Club:* As reported in David Folkenflik, "Fox News Gives Juan Williams $2 Million Contract," *Morning Edition,* October 22, 2010.

Page 111 *Glenn Beck used Williams's termination:* All quotations from Beck, Baier, and other Fox News personalities are taken from footage and transcripts of Fox News programs on the night of October 21, 2010, including *Beck, Special Report, O'Reilly Factor,* and *Hannity.*

Page 112 *Octavia Nasr was forced out for a tweet:* Keach Hagey, "CNN's Firing of Octavia Nasr Protested," Politico, July 8, 2010, among others.

Page 112 *Rick Sanchez also had been dumped by the network:* "Rick Sanchez Fired from CNN," Huffington Post, October 1, 2010, among others.

Page 113 *"When is somebody giving his or her opinion?":* Barbara Walters, *The View,* ABC, October 21, 2010.

Page 113 *NewsBusters revived comments:* Nina Totenberg, *Inside Washington,* July 8, 1995, www.youtube.com/watch?v=7msrF1V4NeY; Totenberg, interview by author; David Folkenflik, "Totenberg on Helms Comment: 'It Was a Stupid Remark,'" NPR.org, October 26, 2010.

Page 113 *Jesse Watters . . . confronted Schiller:* Watters, *O'Reilly Factor,* October 25, 2010.

Page 113 *News Corp had become a participant:* See, for example, Keach Hagey, "Fox Parent's Donation Causes a Stir," Politico, August 17, 2010; Jim Rutenberg, "With Another $1 Million Donation, Murdoch Expands His Political Sphere," *New York Times,* October 1, 2010.

Page 114 *"Roger [Ailes] may not have given the Tea Party life":* Chris Ruddy, interview by author; Ruddy made similar remarks in Gabriel Sherman, "The Elephant in the Green Room," *New York Magazine,* May 22, 2011.

Page 114 *Officials at some NPR member stations:* Author interviews with fifteen member station officials.

Page 114 *"will never forgive NPR":* Chris Wallace, interview by author.

Page 114 *"Are you kidding me, NPR?"* Jon Stewart, *The Daily Show,* October 25, 2010.

Page 114 *Murdoch's son-in-law, Matthew Freud:* David Carr and Tim Arango, "A Fox Chief at the Pinnacle of Media and Politics," *New York Times,* January 10, 2010.

Page 114 *Roger Ailes shot back that Freud "needs to see a psychiatrist":* Joe Flint, "Roger Ailes Says He's Not Going Anywhere, and News Corp's Chase Carey Concurs," *Los Angeles Times,* January 13, 2010.

Page 115 *Ailes attacked once again:* Howard Kurtz, "Fox News Chief Blasts NPR 'Nazis,'" Daily Beast, November 17, 2010.

Page 115 *fit neatly with the extreme rhetoric:* As did others, I catalogued some of Beck's invocations of Nazis in describing the Obama White House and other liberals in David Folkenflik, "Fox News Nazi Rhetoric Starts at the Top," *All Things Considered,* November 19, 2010.

Page 115 *evoked elements of anti-Semitic slurs:* Deborah Lipstadt, interview by author. Subsequent quotations from Lipstadt are derived from that interview.

Page 116 *Milbank found Beck had referred: Washington Post* columnist Dana Milbank has written extensively about Beck's rhetoric in his book *Tears of a Clown.*

Page 116 *Ailes ultimately apologized:* Alex Welprin, "Roger Ailes Apologizes to ADL for Calling NPR Officials Nazis," TVNewser.com, November 18, 2010.

Page 116 *In a subsequent book,* Muzzled: Juan Williams, *Muzzled.* Quotations drawn from author's interview with Williams. David Folkenflik, "In *Muzzled,* Juan Williams Tells His Side of the Story," *All Things Considered,* July 27, 2011.

Page 117 *The record tends to belie his perception:* Williams's previous book *Enough* was featured in a lengthy interview with Steve Inskeep: "Juan Williams on African-American Victimhood," *Morning Edition,* August 7, 2006.

Page 118 *Weiss resigned:* David Folkenflik, "NPR V.P. Resigns, CEO Rebuked Over Williams' Firing," *Morning Edition,* January 7, 2011.

Page 118 *Schiller was ousted a few months later:* David Folkenflik, "Vivian Schiller, CEO of NPR, Steps Down," *Morning Edition,* March 9, 2011. The original thirteen-minute excerpt of tapes: Matthew Boyle, "NPR Executives Caught on Tape Bashing Conservatives and Tea Party, Touting Liberals," *Daily Caller,* March 8, 2011. Glenn Beck's conservative news site, the Blaze, compared the tapes and showed them to be a distortion of how the two-hour lunch had played out: Scott Baker, "Does Raw Video of NPR Expose Reveal Questionable Editing and Tactics?" the Blaze, March 10, 2011. I reviewed the tapes with colleagues and outside experts for an additional analysis for *Morning Edition* that reached the same conclusion: "Key Elements of NPR Gotcha Video Taken Out of Context," *Morning Edition,* March 14, 2011.

Chapter 11

Page 119 *"crocked by a ten-year-old"* Clive Goodman, "Black Adder," *News of the World,* November 6, 2005.

Page 120 *Mulcaire told a sideline reporter:* Contemporaneous video of Mulcaire's goal and sideline video: www.youtube.com/watch?v=K8826wD -XLE; "Glenn Mulcaire: Awful Bloke, Decent Footballer," *New Statesman,* July 6, 2011.

Page 120 *the time was right:* Peter Burden, "'NoW' Hacker Had Beans to Spill and a Crust to Earn," *Independent,* July 19, 2011.

Page 120 *had adopted a bit of cloak and dagger:* Michael Silverleaf QC, letter to Tom Crone, June 3, 2008, published as attachment JCP 20–26 in written evidence to House Select Committee on Culture, Media, and Sport inquiry on News International and Hacking (henceforth CMS report).

Page 120 *a surprisingly easy task:* Author's interview with Mark Stephens, lawyer for multiple targets of cell phone mail hacking.

Page 121 *police turned up more than 11,000 pages:* James Robinson, "Phone Hacking: Met to Pass Glenn Mulcaire Papers to Litigants," *Guardian,* June 27, 2011.

Page 121 *he had done nothing wrong:* "Full Text of Clive Goodman's Letter to News International," *Independent,* August 16, 2011.

Page 122 *the first in a pair of payments: News International and Phone-Hacking,* Eleventh Report from House of Commons Committee on Culture, Media, and Sport, April 30, 2012, part 3.

Page 122 *outside lawyers had done an extensive review:* Les Hinton, testimony before House of Commons Committee on Culture, Media, and Sport, September 15, 2009.

Page 123 *"We like being pirates":* As cited in Lloyd Grove, "Rupe's Attack Dog Gets Bitten, Keeps Barking," *New York Magazine,* September 10, 2007.

Page 123 *"We're like a pirate ship":* Senior *Wall Street Journal* news executive, interview by author.

Page 123 *On the parent corporation's board:* News Corp annual report 2011; News Corp website, section on corporate governance, www.newscorp.com /corp_gov/bod.html.

Page 124 *far from the corridors of power:* Nick Davies, interview by author; this interview formed the basis of Folkenflik, "Guardian Reporter Rocks Murdoch Empire," *All Things Considered,* July 11, 2011. Subsequent Davies quotes also from author's interviews of Lewis.

Page 125 *Working in parallel to Nick Davies:* Mark Lewis, interview by author; this interview formed the basis of David Folkenflik, "Lawyer Follows News Corp, Hacking to U.S.," *All Things Considered,* April 12, 2012. Subsequent Lewis quotations are derived from author's interviews unless otherwise noted.

Page 126 *Painstakingly annotated documents sat undisturbed:* Don Van Natta Jr., Jo Becker, and Graham Bowley, "Tabloid Hack on Royals, and Beyond," *New York Times Magazine,* September 5, 2010.

Page 126 News of the World *had agreed to pay: News of the World* memorandum of contract with "Paul Williams," unsigned, dated February 4, 2005, CMS report attachment JCP 27. This account is supplemented by information disclosed in the Linklaters letter on behalf of News Corp Management and Standards Committee to John Whittingdale MP, August 15, 2011; Crone, email to Myler, May 24, 2008; transcript of Pike notes of call with Colin Myler, May 27, 2008, CMS report, attachment JCP7.

Page 126 *Mark Lewis demanded documents:* Mark Lewis, interview by author.

Page 127 *Myler wasn't happy—it was a mess:* Transcript of Pike notes of call with Colin Myler.

Page 127 *first true corporate reckoning:* Silverleaf, letter, June 3, 2008.

Page 128 *Under British law:* British lawyers, interviews by author. The characterization draws on Theodore Eisenberg and Geoffrey P. Miller, "The English Versus the American Rule on Attorney Fees: An Empirical Study of Public Company Contracts," *Cornell Law Review,* January 2013.

Page 128 *"drew a line in the sand":* Julian Pike, record of attendance, June 3, 2008, CMS report, JCP 8.

Page 128 *"wanted to be vindicated or be rich":* Pike, record of attendance, June 6, 2008, CMS report, JCP 11.

Page 128 *"it is as bad as we feared":* Colin Myler, email to James Murdoch, June 7, 2008, contained in Linklaters letter to Whittingdale, December 12, 2011.

Page 128 *"no worries":* James Murdoch, email reply, June 7, 2008, contained in Linklaters letter, as above.

Page 128 *James Murdoch waved Crone and Myler:* Tom Crone and Colin Myler, testimony to CMS, September 6, 2011; James Murdoch, testimony to CMS, November 11, 2011.

Page 128 *sick of the drip, drip, drip:* Transcript of Julian Pike notes of call with Tom Crone, June 10, 2008, CMS report, JCP 13. "CM was moving towards telling Taylor to fuck off—on the end of drip drip—do a deal."

Page 129 *Murdoch approved payments:* James Murdoch, testimony to CMS, July 19, 2011.

Page 129 *It took Nick Davies until July 2009:* Nick Davies, "Murdoch Papers Paid £1m to Gag Phone-Hacking Victims," *Guardian,* July 8, 2009.

Page 129 *announced he had conducted a review:* Statement by Assistant Commissioner John Yates, July 9, 2009.

Page 129 *News International put out a slashing statement:* News International Statement on *Guardian* article, News Corp, July 10, 2009.

Page 130 *Jonathan Rees, a private investigator:* Nick Davies and Vikram Dodd, "Murder Trial Collapse Exposes News of the World Links to Police Corruption," *Guardian,* March 11, 2011.

Page 130 *Rusbridger sent warnings:* This section is drawn from Alan Rusbridger, interviews by author; and *Guardian* reports.

Page 130 *Rusbridger urged Bill Keller:* Alan Rusbridger; Bill Keller, interview by author.

Page 131 *whose reporters developed their own reporting:* Don Van Atta Jr., Jo Becker, and Graham Bowley, "Tabloid Hack Attack!" *New York Times Magazine,* September 5, 2010.

Page 131 *filed a complaint:* Letter from *News of the World* managing editor Bill Akass to *New York Times* public editor Arthur S. Brisbane, September 17, 2010, as reproduced in "Public Editor's Journal," September 18, 2010.

Page 131 *Lewis and his clients had overstated their case:* David Hooper, interview by author.

Page 132 *she had warned the head of the parliamentary panel:* "Statement by Baroness Buscombe, Chairman of the Press Complaints Commission, on New Evidence in the Phone Message Hacking Episode," remarks at Society of Editors Annual Conference in Stansted, November 15, 2009.

Page 132 *Buscombe apologized the next year:* Prior statement, updated July 2010.

Page 132 *reporters and private eyes were assigned:* Letter from Tom Crone to House of Commons Select Committee on Culture, Media, and Sport, December 1, 2011; author's interviews of Mark Lewis and Tom Watson MP; Nick Davies, "News of the World hired Investigators to Spy on Hacking Victims' Lawyers," *Guardian*, November 7, 2011.

Page 133 *News International established a fund:* James Robinson, "News of the World Phone Hacking Victims Get Apology from Murdoch," *Guardian*, April 8, 2011.

Page 133 *revelations raised the questions from Watergate:* Andrew Neil, interview by author.

Page 134 *enjoyed sauntering through newsrooms:* Three former News Corp newspaper editors, interviews by author.

Page 134 *some of them would go awry:* Representatives of institutional investors in News Corp, including CalPers and Amalgamated Bank, interviews by author; outside corporate governance analysts, including Nell Minow, interviews by author.

Page 134 *wrote down the value of the* Wall Street Journal *and Dow Jones:* Felix Gillette, "Rupert Murdoch, News Corp, Dodge Phone Hacking Ruin," Bloomberg Businessweek, April 18, 2013.

Page 135 *Elizabeth Murdoch walked off with more than $200 million:* News Corp Annual Report 2011, p. 14.

Page 135 *News Corp sold the social media website MySpace:* "Specific Media Acquires MySpace from News Corporation," News Corp press release, June 29, 2011; Dawn C. Chmielewski and Jessica Guynn, "News Corp Sells MySpace for $35 Million," *Los Angeles Times*, June 30, 2011.

Page 135 *Rupert Murdoch wanted to invest $28 million:* Matthew Cranston, "Cowley's Cunning: How We Got $9m out of Canberra," *Australian Financial Review*, September 24, 2011; "Why News Corp. Invested $30 Million in Cow and Chicken Farms," *Business Insider*, December 6, 2012.

Page 136 *Elisabeth suggested Fox import:* Wolff, *Man Who Owns the News*, Kindle edition, location 1737.

Page 136 *Fox News . . . profits standing at roughly $900 million a year:* Estimates from SNL Kagan for 2011, as cited in "State of the Media 2013," the Pew Research Center's Project for Excellence on Journalism, March 18, 2013.

Page 136 *jurors took just seven hours:* Caroline Davies, "Milly Dowler Murder: Levi Bellfield Convicted," *Guardian*, June 23, 2011.

Page 137 *a series of grievous wrongs:* Nick Davies and Amelia Hill, "News of the World Hacked Milly Dowler's Phone During Police Hunt," *Guardian*, July 4, 2011.

Page 138 *"Prime Minister, if I could ask you":* Transcript of press conference in Kabul, Prime Minister's Office, July 5, 2011.

Page 138 *"an obsession of one newspaper":* House of Commons Official Report, House of Commons debates, July 6, 2011.

Page 138 *offered little protection:* "300 Alleged Phone Hacking Victims: Phone Hacking: The Victims and Possible Victims," BBCNews.co.uk, May 15, 2012; Lisa O'Carroll, "From Prince Charles to Milly Dowler," *Guardian*, November 29, 2012.

Page 139 *"a dispassionate sociopathic act":* Steve Coogan, written statement to Leveson Inquiry, posted November 22, 2011.

Page 140 *in commerce he accepted the rules:* Author search of IMDB and Amazon .com databases.

Chapter 12

This account of the creation of Sky and the takeover of British Satellite Broadcasting to form BSkyB draws on many previous accounts, especially Sky's corporate history: http://corporate.sky.com/about_sky/timeline; Pearson's corporate history: www.pearson.com/about-us/our-history.html; Chenoweth, *Rupert Murdoch: The Untold Story of the World's Greatest Media Wizard*; Ghemawat, *Games Businesses Play*, chapter 7, "Entry and Deterrence: British Satellite Broadcasting and Sky."

Page 141 *its first radio transmission in 1922:* Caroline Crampton, "Ninety Years of BBC Radio: Listening Back Through Time," *New Statesman*, November 14, 2011.

Page 142 *"He basically stole a march on them":* David Gordon, interview by author.

Page 143 *the succession games Rupert Murdoch played:* Author interviews with associate of Lachlan Murdoch and two former News Corp executives; accounts of family dynamics in Shawcross, *Murdoch;* and Wolff, *Man Who Owns the News*.

Page 144 *tossed the five-year-old Rupert:* Chenoweth, *Rupert Murdoch*, pp. 36–37.

Page 144 *Elisabeth Murdoch worked at News Corp's basic cable channel:* Sarah Ellison, "The Rules of Succession," *Vanity Fair*, December 2011.

Page 144 *"the management trainee":* Emiliya Mychasuk and Peter Fray, "The Sky's the Limit," *Sydney Morning Herald*, November 8, 2003.

Page 144 *"She's ambitious, she's aggressive":* Ali Cromie, "Liz Murdoch, Caught in the Death Star," *BRW* magazine, December 3, 1999.

Page 145 *He had been a gawky youth:* Author interviews with Halla Timon, childhood friend of James Murdoch, and two Harvard College classmates; Jon Rees, "A New Star Is Burning Bright in Asia's Sky," *Scotsman*, January 22, 2001.

Page 145 *A photographer for the rival* Sydney Morning Herald: "A Chip Off the Old Block?" BBCNews.co.uk, November 4, 2003.

Page 145 *the wedding toast of his college friend:* John Koblin, "Jesse Angelo: Rupert Murdoch's Main Man," *Women's Wear Daily*, February 3, 2011.

Page 146 *Newspapers had to give away their articles for free:* A former senior editor at a News Corp newspaper, interview by author.

Page 146 *His father had been consistently blocked:* James McGregor, former Dow Jones China CEO, interview by author; China Central Television consultant Jim Laurie, interview by author; Dover, *Rupert Murdoch's China Adventures.*

Page 147 *all three children of Rupert and Anna:* This account of family dynamics based on author's interviews with one current News Corp executive, three former News Corp executives, and one associate of Lachlan Murdoch. Useful detail can be found in Wolff, *The Man Who Owns the News.*

Page 147 *young Grace and Chloe would share:* "A Conversation with Rupert Murdoch," *Charlie Rose Show,* July 20, 2006.

Page 147 *gave each of the six children $160 million:* Andrew Edgecliffe-Johnson, "Rupert Murdoch Files for Divorce," *Financial Times,* June 13, 2013.

Page 147 *James Murdoch traveled to Edinburgh:* James Murdoch, "The Absence of Trust," 2009 MacTaggart Lecture, www.geitf.co.uk/sites/default /files/geitf/GEITF_MacTaggart_2009_James_Murdoch.pdf.

Page 147 *the James MacTaggart for whom the event had been named:* Matt Wells, "Who Was James MacTaggart?" *Guardian,* August 21, 2005.

Page 148 *He spoke presciently:* Rupert Murdoch, 1989 MacTaggart Lecture, www. geitf.co.uk/sites/default/files/geitf/GEITF_MacTaggart_1989_Rupert _Murdoch.pdf.

Page 148 *leading public officials:* Correspondence from Murdoch aides to Sununu and other White House officials, George H.W. Bush Presidential Library.

Page 149 *"in hindsight, I regret":* Rupert Murdoch testimony, Leveson Inquiry, April 25, 2012, morning session, p. 94.

Page 149 *the first decade of the twenty-first century:* Description of BSkyB's financial standing drawn from BSkyB 2009 Annual Report; "BSkyB Profits from High Definition Services," BBC.co.uk, July 29, 2010; News Corp 2011 annual report.

Page 150 *convinced Rupert Murdoch to shift his support:* "Labour's Lost It," *Sun,* September 29, 2009; Stephen Brook and Patrick Wintour, "*Sun* Turns Its Back on Labour," *Guardian,* September 29, 2009.

Page 150 *Tory stars embodied British privilege:* Andy McSmith, "George Osborne: A Silver Spoon for the Golden Boy," *Independent,* June 19, 2010; Elizabeth Day, "George Osborne: From the Bullingdon Club to the Heart of Government," *Observer,* October 1, 2011.

Page 151 *The tabloids feasted:* Keith Gladdis and Sara Nuwar, "Parties with a Cocaine-Snorting Dominatrix," *News of the World,* October 16, 2005; "Tories' Fate Is in Your Hands," editorial, *News of the World,* October 16, 2005. John Bingham, "George Osborne: Tabloid 'Spoiler' That Took on Life of Its Own," *Telegraph,* September 12, 2011; Matthew Holehouse, "George Osborne Allegations: Andy Coulson's 'Favourable' Editorial," *Telegraph,* September 12, 2011.

Page 151 *the two men discussed "politics and policy":* Leveson Inquiry, exhibit KRM29.

Page 151 *Osborne told Cameron that they wanted:* James Chapman and Tim Shipman, "I Knew That Hiring Coulson Was Risky, Admits Osborne," *Daily Mail,* June 11, 2012.

Page 151 *"Have we any Tories coming to KRM party?" . . . "I will encourage":* Leveson Inquiry, exhibit FM21.

Page 152 *Cameron dispatched Jeremy Hunt:* David Leigh and Vikram Dodd, "Jeremy Hunt Visited News Corp in US as Murdochs Considered BSkyB Bid," *Guardian,* April 25, 2012.

Page 152 *James Murdoch invited Cameron to drinks:* Leveson Inquiry, exhibit JRJM 10.

Page 152 *"in return for Rupert Murdoch's support":* Simon Kelner, interview by author.

Page 153 *News International had additionally extracted promises:* George Eaton, "The Murdoch-Cameron Deal," *New Statesman,* October 1, 2009.

Page 153 *Kelner's* Independent *ran a marketing campaign:* Simon Kelner, interview by author; contemporaneous coverage.

Page 153 *four months after Cameron's camp took power:* Leveson Inquiry, exhibit FM 81.

Page 154 *code-named Rubicon:* See emails in Leveson Inquiry, exhibit RMB 1, for example, Rebekah Brooks to Frederic Michel, June 27, 2011, "when is the rubicon statement"; Michel's reply: "Hunt will be making references to phone-hacking in his statement on Rubicon this week. . . ."

Page 154 *Mark Thompson . . . joined other media executives:* "Mark Thompson Expresses 'Regret' over Sky Letter," BBCNews.co.uk, November 8, 2010.

Page 154 *an independent analysis from Claire Enders:* Leveson Inquiry, annex 2 to submission by Claire Enders.

Page 154 *News Corp officials countered:* Internal News Corp documents filed to Leveson Inquiry, exhibit VC 1–2, p. 66 ("Possible Acquisition by News Corporation of British Sky Broadcasting Group Plc./ Preliminary Briefing by News Corporation to the Department of Business, Innovation and Skills and the Office of Communications").

Page 155 *Hunt and Michel kibbitzed back and forth:* Leveson Inquiry, exhibit FM 8: text message Michel to Hunt, August 28, 2010.

Page 155 *"a very useful meeting":* Frederic Michel, questions from Robert Jay, Leveson Inquiry, May 24, 2012, transcript, p. 65.

Page 155 *Michel also lined up government officials:* Leveson Inquiry, exhibit FM 12, Frederic Michel text to Lena Pietsch, communications director to deputy prime minister Nick Clegg, January 13, 2011: "James could do the energy/environment event on 28th feb or 1st march: would that work for Nick? We are very keen to have him there."

Page 156 *"I would like to be able to show it":* Leveson Inquiry, exhibit FM 2, Fred Michel, email, October 7, 2010.

Page 156 *"There is real unease in Libdem ranks":* Leveson Inquiry, exhibit KRM 18, Michel, email to Matthew Anderson, October 8, 2010.

Page 156 *"What did you have in mind":* Leveson Inquiry, exhibit FM 3, Giles Wilkes, email to Michel, November 8, 2010.

Page 156 *"Hi daddy!":* Leveson Inquiry, exhibit FM 8, Michel text to Hunt, November 9, 2010.

Page 156 *Hunt then received direct legal advice:* "'I Just Heard James Murdoch Out,' Says Jeremy Hunt," *Telegraph,* May 31, 2012.

Page 156 *"You must be fucking joking":* Leveson Inquiry, schedule of emails between James Murdoch and Frederic Michel relevant to KRM 18; James Murdoch, email to Michel, November 15, 2010.

Page 157 *"James Murdoch is pretty furious":* Leveson Inquiry, exhibit AS 7, "Fortnightly Update 19 November 2010." This memo is the source for subsequent quotations as well.

Page 157 *James Murdoch and his family had joined the Camerons:* Leveson Inquiry, exhibit JRJM 9.

Page 158 *"UK Authorities have assumed that News exercises material influence":* From "Possible Acquisition by News Corporation of British Sky Broadcasting Group Plc./ Preliminary Briefing by News Corporation to the Department of Business, Innovation and Skills and the Office of Communications," as cited above.

Page 158 *actually undercover reporters for the* Telegraph: Robert Winnett, "Vince Cable: I Have Declared War on Rupert Murdoch," *Telegraph*, December 21, 2010.

Page 158 *"Just OfCom to go!":* Leveson Inquiry, exhibit JH 16, Jeremy Hunt, text to Frederic Michel, December 21, 2010. Subsequent text messages between Hunt and Osborne from same exhibit, sent on same day.

Page 159 *the younger Murdoch dined with the Camerons:* Leveson Inquiry, exhibit JRJM 9.

Page 159 *the fresh face Conservatives wanted to put forward:* Richard Wray, "Jeremy Hunt: Ambitious Entrepreneur Still Has Much to Prove," *Guardian*, May 17, 2010.

Page 160 *"the look of an estate agent":* Alan Bennett, "Diary," *London Review of Books*, January 3, 2013.

Page 160 *Just before Christmas . . . Ian Edmondson:* Vikram Dodd, James Robinson, and Nicholas Watt, "Met Police Reopen Investigation into Phone Hacking at News of the World," *Guardian*, January 26, 2011.

Page 160 *According to Michel's minutes:* Leveson Inquiry, exhibit JRJM 5.

Page 161 *Michel texted Gabby Bertin:* Leveson Inquiry, exhibit FM 12.

Page 161 *allowing News Corp to arrange its ducks in a row:* Michel emails cited in David Leigh and Nick Davies, "Jeremy Hunt and the Murdochs: How Minister Oiled Wheels of BSkyB Bid," *Guardian*, April 24, 2012.

Page 162 *"This is the second job":* As cited in "In Quotes: Coulson Steps Down," BBCNews.co.uk, January 21, 2011.

Page 162 *"might be best to wait":* Susan Beeby, email, cited in "Text Trail: Inside Jeremy Hunt's iPhone," *Independent*, June 1, 2012.

Page 162 *Coulson dined with him at Chequers:* "Andy Coulson Stayed with Cameron at Chequers After Resigning over Hacking Scandal," *Daily Mail*, July 15, 2011. Also source for Craig Oliver's email to Hunt concerning view that James Murdoch would "pull a fast one."

Page 163 *"You were great" . . . "Merci":* Leveson Inquiry, exhibit FM 8.

Page 163 *the murder case . . . fell apart:* Nick Davies and Vikram Dodd, "Murder Trial Collapse Exposes News of the World Links to Police Corruption," *Guardian*, March 11, 2011.

Page 163 *News International admitted phone hacking:* James Robinson, "News of the World Phone Hacking Victims Get Apology from Murdoch," *Guardian,* April 8, 2011.

Chapter 13

Page 165 *Bryant asked Brooks whether her newspaper:* Chris Bryant MP questioning Rebekah Wade (later Brooks) and Andrew Coulson amid hearings on privacy and the press, March 11, 2003, House of Commons Select Committee on Culture, Media, and Sport.

Page 166 *"We have paid the police":* House of Commons Select Committee on Culture Media, and Sport, examination of witnesses, March 11, 2003.

Page 166 *"Do you declare how much, if any":* News International and Phone-Hacking, Eleventh Report from House of Commons Committee on Culture, Media, and Sport, April 30, 2012, part 3.

Page 167 *"We do not pay for interviews": Ethical Journalism: A Handbook of Values and Practices for the News and Editorial Departments,* the New York Times Co.; *Los Angeles Times Ethics Guidelines; NPR Ethics Handbook; BBC Editorial Guidelines.*

Page 167 *the* Telegraph *paid the equivalent:* "Daily Telegraph Paid £100k for MPs' Expenses Scoop," *Press Gazette,* September 25, 2009.

Page 168 *Networks evaded their own rules:* David Folkenflik, "ABC News Under Fire for Payment to Murder Suspect," *All Things Considered,* March 19, 2010.

Page 168 *he had an impeccable source:* Calder, *Untold Story,* pp. 254–255.

Page 169 *"It was almost industry standard":* Paul McMullan, interview by author.

Page 169 *These highly trusted police officials:* Mark Hughes, "Royal Protection Officers 'Were Paid for Information,' News International Emails Show," *Telegraph,* July 12, 2011.

Page 169 *Alex Marunchak . . . paid translator:* Tom Watson MP, interview by author; "NoW journalist Worked as Translator for Met," BBC Channel 4 News, July 18, 2011.

Page 169 *Neville Thurlbeck, had been an unpaid police informant:* Chris Greenwood, "News of the World Hacking Suspect Neville Thurlbeck 'Was Police Informant,'" *Daily Mail,* July 19, 2011.

Page 170 *proved that Lord Jeffrey Archer . . . had perjured himself:* "Archer Jailed for Perjury," BBC News, July 19, 2001; personal biography, Neville Thurlbeck.com.

Page 170 *Caught on video pleasuring himself:* Peter Burden, "Neville 'Onan the Barbarian' Thurlbeck—Not Hard at Work," www.peterburden.net /archives/900.

Page 170 *blackmailed women who had taken part in a sex party:* Neville Thurlbeck, testimony to Leveson Inquiry, December 12, 2011, morning session.

Page 170 *John Lyndon of the Surrey police wrote in a private note:* DCI John Macdonald, witness statement to Leveson Inquiry, quoting Lyndon's contemporaneous notes from April 23, 2002.

Page 171 *the* Times of London *reported police had been given evidence*: Sean O'Neill and Roland Watson, "Hacking: Coulson Authorized Payments to Police for Stories," *Times of London*, July 6, 2011.

Page 171 *Sir Paul Stephenson . . . disclosed:* Statement from Sir Paul Stephenson, Metropolitan Police Commissioner, July 6, 2011.

Page 171 *members of Parliament bluntly questioned Hayman:* Andy Hayman, testimony before House of Commons Select Committee on Home Affairs, July 12, 2011.

Page 172 *real money never changed hands:* Roy Greenslade, interview by author.

Page 173 *After a review of the past inquiry:* Statement by Assistant Commissioner John Yates, July 9, 2009.

Page 173 *Andy Hayman chimed in with supportive columns:* Andrew Hayman, "News of the World Investigation Was No Half-Hearted Affair," *Times of London*, July 12, 2009; Hayman's column also ran in *News of the World*.

Page 173 *Prescott had been repeatedly told:* "John Prescott on News of the World Phone Hacking Payout," *Hull Daily Mail*, January 19, 2012.

Page 174 *Yates clung to the justification:* Nick Davies, "Phone Hacking: Met Police Put on Spot by Ignored Leads and Discreet Omissions," *Guardian*, September 5, 2010.

Page 174 *repeatedly dined with editors:* Nick McDermott and Michael Seamark, "Time to Call In Those Bottles of Champagne," *Daily Mail*, March 1, 2012.

Page 174 *The* News of the World *felt it had an inside line:* Lucy Panton, witness statement, Leveson Inquiry, April 3, 2012.

Page 175 *"Bit of advice, plse":* "Investigation into the Involvement and Actions of Assistant Commissioner John Yates in the Recruitment Process of the Daughter of Neil Wallis," Independent Police Complaints Commission, April 12, 2012.

Page 175 *"stories that came from police force employees":* Paul McMullan, interview by author.

Page 176 *the* Sun*'s black tie affair at the five-star Savoy Hotel:* Jenna Sloan, "PM Told Me He Was Busy. I Said, 'Do You Have to Shoot Off?'" *Sun*, July 9, 2011.

Page 176 *Andy Coulson . . . was arrested on charges:* Sandra Laville, "Andy Coulson Arrested over Phone Hacking Allegations," *Guardian*, July 8, 2011.

Page 176 *a luxury spa and retreat:* Nick McDermott and Michael Seamark, "Time to Call In Those Bottles of Champagne," *Daily Mail*, March 1, 2012.

Chapter 14

The history of the *News of the World* and the *Sun* under Murdoch set forth in this section is greatly informed by interviews with such former Murdoch editors as Ken Chandler, Roy Greenslade, Andrew Jaspan, Simon Jenkins, Kelvin MacKenzie, and Andrew Neil; by Leveson testimony from various past

Murdoch editors; by statements by Rupert Murdoch in documentaries and other settings; and by such books as Shawcross, *Murdoch;* Wolff, *The Man Who Owns the News;* and Chippindale and Horrie, *Stick It Up Your Punter!*

Page 177 *"David was in great form":* Leveson Inquiry, exhibit FM 13.

Page 177 *Cameron saw Rupert Murdoch twice more:* Leveson Inquiry, exhibit KRM 27.

Page 177 *Rebekah Brooks had emailed Michel:* Leveson Inquiry, exhibit FM 6.

Page 178 *Michel was puffing up his role:* An entire exhibit of evidence compared emails Michel sent quoting statements supposedly from culture minister Jeremy Hunt that had been conveyed in emails and text messages by his special adviser, Adam Smith. Leveson Inquiry, exhibit FM 1.

Page 178 *Michel texted Hunt:* Leveson Inquiry, exhibit FM 8.

Page 178 *companies withdrew their ads:* Laura Smith-Spark, "Firms Reconsider Ad Deals over Newspaper Hacking Scandal," CNN.com, July 7, 2011; "Ad Pressure Eases as NOTW Calls It a Day," *Grocer,* July 9, 2011.

Page 178 *memo assuring staffers:* "Full Text of Rebekah Brooks' Email to News International Staff," *New Statesman,* July 5, 2011.

Page 179 *Cameron told MPs in the House of Commons:* House of Commons, Oral Answers to Questions (Commonly called Prime Minister's Questions), July 6, 2011.

Page 180 *Tory MP Zac Goldsmith said:* House of Commons Official Report, House of Commons debates, July 6, 2011.

Page 180 *a dissonant vote of support:* "Statement from Rupert Murdoch, Chairman and Chief Executive Officer, News Corporation," press release, July 6, 2011.

Page 180 *"These were not the actions of a 'rogue'":* Edward Miliband, in House of Commons, Oral Answers to Questions, July 6, 2011.

Page 181 *Both Bertin and Michel ended their texts:* Leveson Inquiry, exhibit FM 14, for this and subsequent texts between Fred Michel and Gabby Bertin.

Page 181 *"Hey buddy. Are you guys still on for dinner":* Leveson Inquiry, exhibit FM 13, for this and subsequent texts between Fred Michel and Craig Oliver.

Page 181 *"They've used their power":* Simon Kelner, interview by author.

Page 182 *The* Telegraph *reported that the tabloid had hacked:* Duncan Gardham, "News of the World: Bereaved Relatives of 7/7 Victims Had Phones Hacked," *Telegraph,* July 5, 2011.

Page 182 *he picked up a woman who had become a prostitute:* Johnson, *Hack,* Kindle edition, Locations 2532–2771.

Page 183 *his exposés largely created the scandals he revealed:* Mahmood, *Confessions of a Fake Sheik.*

Page 183 *he announced the company would kill the paper:* "James Murdoch, Deputy Chief Operating Officer, News Corporation, and Chairman, News International, Statement on News of the World," press release, July 7, 2011.

Page 183 *the* Telegraph *headlined its front-page story:* "Goodbye, Cruel World," *Telegraph,* July 8, 2011.

Page 184 *"We should see this for what it is":* Hugh Grant, *BBC Question Time,* July 7, 2011.

Page 184 *"a straightforward commercial reason":* Author's interview with Simon Jenkins.

Page 184 *News Corp was swimming in debt:* Shawcross, *Murdoch,* p. 360. Australian financial investigative journalist Neil Chenoweth provides a different gloss in his book *Rupert Murdoch* on pp. 83–86. Drawing in part on the work of another Australian newspaper reporter, he makes a strong circumstantial case that the loan Murdoch so coveted was not to cover the company's debts but to pay off Murdoch family debt stemming from a private investment in a newspaper company in Queensland, Australia. If true, the mixture of corporate and personal ends that Chenoweth's account strongly suggests reflects an early episode where the corporation's fate hinged on decisions taken to benefit the family's private interests.

Page 184 *the company's executives had to shift strategies:* Author's interviews with Andrew Neil and a former News Corp executive.

Chapter 15

Page 186 *Brooks (then Rebekah Wade) was arrested:* "Kemp's Wife Wade Plays Down Row," BBC News, November 4, 2005.

Page 186 *befriended Blair, his wife, Cherie:* Peter Oborne, "The Great Murdoch Conspiracy," *Telegraph,* July 14, 2011.

Page 186 *Rebekah soon took up:* Roy Greenslade, "Rebekah's World: Lunch in Venice, Dinner at Wiltons, Weekends with the Oxfordshire Set," *Guardian,* June 5, 2009; Andy McSmith, "Behind Murdoch's Throne: The Story of Rebekah Brooks," *Independent,* July 6, 2011.

Page 187 *Cameron flew on the private plane:* Rupert Murdoch, testimony, Leveson Inquiry, April 25, 2012, afternoon session.

Page 187 *"fast unpredictable and hard to control":* Simon Walters, "Cameron's Horseplay Texts with Rebekah Brooks," *Mail on Sunday,* November 3, 2012.

Page 187 *"brilliant speech. I cried twice":* That and subsequent text message cited read as part of testimony of Rebekah Brooks before the Leveson Inquiry, May 11, 2012, morning session.

Page 187 *Colin Myler called in Neville Thurlbeck:* Neville Thurlbeck, letter to John Whittingdale MP, November 11, 2011.

Page 187 *no cause for concern . . . good enough for them:* Two former News Corp executives, interview by author.

Page 188 *she watched Cameron on a TV monitor:* This scene is drawn from a visit to the *Times of London* newsroom by the author in December 2010.

Page 188 *Rupert Murdoch had one overriding concern:* Two people with contemporaneous knowledge of Murdoch's intent, interview by author.

Page 189 *a quiet anger:* Three former News Corp officials, interview by author.

Page 189 *the Post did not engage in the self-reflection:* An associate of Rupert Murdoch, interview by author.

Page 189 *multimillion-pound townhouse:* Much of this passage is informed by Greg Farrell et al., "Dinner at Rupert's," Bloomberg Businessweek, February 9, 2012. It is supplemented by author's interviews with two people having contemporaneous knowledge of the event and the company's legal strategy.

Page 190 *"I am satisfied that Rebekah":* "James Murdoch, Deputy Chief Operating Officer, News Corporation, and Chairman, News International, Statement on News of the World," press release, July 7, 2011.

Page 190 *"onslaught of attacks":* "Audio of Brooks Meeting NOTW Staff," Sky News, July 9, 2011, serves as the source of her remarks, and those of reporters, at that session.

Page 192 *Contrition proved the order of the day:* "David Cameron's Statement on Phone Hacking: The Full Text," *Guardian,* July 8, 2011.

Page 192 *eased Brooks from the role:* News Corp executive, interview by author.

Page 192 *to destroy millions of emails:* Nick Davies and Amelia Hill, "Phone Hacking: Police Probe Suspected Deletion of Emails by NI Executive," *Guardian,* July 8, 2011.

Page 192 *Rupert Murdoch flew to London:* "Thank You and Goodbye: Last Ever News of the World Goes to Print," *Daily Mail,* July 10, 2011.

Page 192 *"This one," gesturing with his thumb:* Lisa O'Carroll, "Rebekah Brooks: Where It All Went Wrong," *Guardian,* July 15, 2011.

Page 193 *News Corp . . . pulled its promise:* "News Corporation Withdraws Proposed Undertakings in Lieu of Reference with Respect to Its Proposed Acquisition of BSkyB," press release, July 11, 2011.

Page 193 *Hunt referred the decision:* Hunt's decision as reproduced in Leveson Inquiry, exhibit KRM 17.

Page 193 *the Murdochs blinked:* "News Corporation Withdraws Proposed Offer for British Sky Broadcasting Group PLC," press release, July 13, 2011.

Page 194 *"root-and-branch":* Cameron, addressing House of Commons. As quoted in David Folkenflik, "Murdoch Withdraws Bid for BSkyB," *All Things Considered,* July 13, 2011.

Page 194 *Gordon Brown declared:* "Gordon Brown Attacks News International Tactics," BBCNews.com, July 12, 2011; "Gordon Brown Condemns NI 'Lawbreakers,'" *Independent,* July 13, 2011.

Page 194 *the Saudi prince Al Waleed bin Talal:* "News Corp Major Shareholder Has No Plans to Sell Stake," BBC News, July 14, 2011.

Page 194 *seepage to the States:* David Collins and Tom McTague, "She's My No. 1," *Daily Mirror,* July 11, 2011.

Page 195 *King wrote to FBI director:* "King Demands Investigation into Claims of Hacking of 9/11 Victims," press release, July 13, 2011.

Page 195 *lawyers for News Corp:* Two News Corp officials and two lawyers familiar with the case, interview by author.

Page 196 *Ted Kennedy inserted language . . . the* Herald *retaliated:* Former *Boston Herald* publisher Ken Chandler and two former Kennedy aides, interview by author.

Page 196 *the FCC gave Murdoch yet another waiver:* David Andelman, "FCC Poised to Let Murdoch Buy Ch. 9," *New York Daily News,* July 21, 2001; Andrew Jay Schwartzman, interview by author.

Page 196 *the possibility of prosecution:* This passage is informed by the insight on the Federal Corrupt Practices Act gained by author's interviews with John Coffee, director of Columbia University law school's Center on Corporate Governance; Alexandra Wrage, president of corporate compliance firm Trace; and Charles Elson, director of the University of Delaware's Center for Corporate Governance, among others.

Page 197 *an already planned stock buy-back program:* "News Corporation Announces Stock Repurchase Program of $5 Billion," News Corp press release, July 12, 2011.

Page 197 *MPs . . . were angered again:* Video of John Whittingdale MP statement to reporters, as reproduced at "John Whittingdale: 'Rupert Murdoch Has Been Summoned,'" Telegraph.co.uk, July 14, 2011.

Page 198 *Brooks and Hinton resigned:* "A Message from Rebekah Brooks on Her Departure from News International," News Corp press release, July 15, 2011; "A Message from James Murdoch on Issues at News International," News Corp press release, July 15, 2011; "Les Hinton, Chief Executive Officer of Dow Jones & Company and Publisher of the *Wall Street Journal*, Resigns from Company," News Corp press release, July 15, 2011; "A Note from Rupert Murdoch Regarding the Resignation of Les Hinton," News Corp press release, July 15, 2011.

Page 198 *"a joke within News Corp":* Former News Corp executive, interview by author.

Chapter 16

Page 200 *Police arrested Rebekah Brooks:* "Rebekah Brooks Arrested by Hacking Police," BBC News, July 17, 2011; Helen Lewis, "The Intriguing Timing of Rebekah Brooks' Arrest," *New Statesman*, July 17, 2011.

Page 200 *a confrontation between Charlie Brooks and security guards:* Amelia Hill, "Police Examine Bag in Bin Found Near Rebekah Brooks' Home," *Guardian*, July 18, 2011; Sam Greenhill, "Brooks and Mystery of Dumped Bag," *Daily Mail*, July 19, 2011; Paul Sonne, "Brooks' Husband's Laptop Found in Garage," *Wall Street Journal*, July 19, 2011; Martin Evans, "Phone Hacking: Brooks' Husband Denies Cover Up After Bag Found Near Flat," *Telegraph*, July 20, 2011.

Page 201 *Rupert Murdoch had personally called Klein:* Joel Klein, interview by author; David Folkenflik, "News Corp Education Tablet: For the Love of Learning?" *Morning Edition*, March 18, 2013.

Page 201 *His compensation was worth:* Klein's compensation taken from News Corp filing with the US Securities and Exchange Commission, Form 10-Q (Quarterly Report), filed May 5, 2011.

Page 202 *he needed to salvage his career:* Two former News Corp executives and former *Sunday Times* editor and Sky executive Andrew Neil, interviews by author.

Page 202 *James Murdoch first attempted:* Rupert Murdoch and James Murdoch, testimony, House of Commons Select Committee on Culture, Media, and Sport, July 19, 2011. Video: www.parliamentlive.tv/Main/Player.aspx

?meetingId=8910&st=14:35:25. All subsequent quotations from the two Murdochs and the MPs questioning them at that hearing contained in this chapter can be found there as well.

Page 203 *new team of crisis management experts:* Ian Burrell, "Team Murdoch: The Men Coaching Rupert for his Date with MPs," *Independent,* July 18, 2011; Paul Thomasch, "Murdoch Turns to PR Elite for Crisis Control," Reuters, July 19, 2011.

Page 204 *Louise Mensch was someone:* Louise Mensch MP, interview by author.

Page 204 *who came up in the Murdoch tabloids:* David Folkenflik, "CNN's Morgan Under Pressure Amid Hacking Scandal," *All Things Considered,* August 5, 2011.

Page 205 *Tom Watson emerged:* Tom Watson MP, interview by author; Jon Bernstein, "The Politics Interview: Tom Watson," *New Statesman,* September 28, 2011.

Page 205 *a "Sun on Sunday" had been under consideration:* Lara O'Reilly, "Sun on Sunday Set for Launch Following NOTW Closure," *Marketing Week,* July 8, 2011.

Page 206 *separate secret settlement:* Nick Davies and Rob Evans, "Max Clifford Drops News of the World Phone Hacking Action in £1 Million Deal," *Guardian,* March 9, 2010.

Page 207 *middle school instructor:* David Eimer, "Meet the Man Who Taught Wendi Deng the 'Spike' That Saved Husband Rupert Murdoch from a Foam Pie," *Telegraph,* July 23, 2011.

Page 207 *Deng Wen Ge (her given name):* Eric Ellis, "Wendi Deng Murdoch," *The Monthly* (Australia), June 2007.

Page 207 *twenty-six-year-old stand-up comic:* Mimi Turner, "Murdoch Pie Man Convicted: 'Most Humble Day of My Life,'" *Hollywood Reporter, July* 29, 2011.

Page 208 *News Corp moved swiftly:* Patricia Hurtado and Tom Schoenberg, "News Corp Independent Directors Hire Debevoise Law Firm," Bloomberg News, July 19, 2011; "Management and Standards Committee Publishes Terms of Reference," News Corp press release, July 21, 2011.

Page 208 *"pretty much assembled a dream team":* John Coffee, interview by author.

Page 208 *Colin Myler, had seethed:* Michael Rundle, "Watch: News of the World Editor Colin Myler Leads Out Staff After Final Edition Published," Huffington Post, July 9, 2011.

Page 209 *along with Tom Crone, Myler decided to make a public break:* Lisa O'Carroll and Patrick Wintour, "James Murdoch Misled MPs, Say Former NOTW Editor and Lawyer," *Guardian,* July 21, 2011.

Chapter 17

Chapters 17–18, which describe events that took place within the *Wall Street Journal,* are based on interviews conducted by the author with more than two dozen current and former *Journal* (and Dow Jones) executives, editors, and reporters as well as several people at competing newspapers. Many of those who chose to speak with me did so on condition that I not name them directly. A smaller number were interviewed on the record by name. Many who worked at the *Journal* said they could not speak by name because the *Journal* had not authorized them to do so. Others who now work elsewhere said they might have to work at the *Journal* or Dow Jones again in the future and did not want to poison relations with the *Journal's* leadership. Their widely shared concern was a testament to their concern over retribution and their belief that, whatever their misgivings, Murdoch's News Corp has provided a haven for reporters amid tumultuous financial times for the industry.

Richard Tofel's *Restless Genius* provides invaluable insight into the paper's storied past, while Sarah Ellison's *War at the Wall Street Journal* offers a compelling account of the courtship that led to Murdoch's acquisition of the paper. Wolff's *Man Who Owns the News* is a particularly entertaining and revealing earlier look at the family and its dynamics by an author who had exceptional access to the Murdochs and their inner circle in the lead-up to the purchase of Dow Jones.

Page 210 *Murdoch did not much like the* Journal *itself:* Three former *Journal* editors and two current *Journal* editors, interview by author.

Page 210 *Murdoch's first editor . . . Marcus Brauchli:* This account of Brauchli and his tenure at the newspaper is based on the author's interviews with seven current and former *Wall Street Journal* editors and two former *Journal* executives.

Page 211 *an innovation of the legendary Barney Kilgore:* Tofel, *Restless Genius*, pp. 119–120; Barry Newman, "What Is an A-Hed?" *Wall Street Journal*, November 3, 2010.

Page 211 *had little tolerance for the "paywall":* Senior *Wall Street Journal* editor; former *Wall Street Journal* editor, interview by author; Eric Pooley, "Exclusive: Rupert Murdoch Speaks," *Time*, June 28, 2007.

Page 211 *"as few words as possible":* Ellison, *War*, p. 188.

Page 212 *"gestational period of a llama":* A senior *Journal* editor and a former *Journal* reporter, interview by author.

Page 212 *Thomson saw . . . the* Journal *staff as complacent:* This account of Thomson's views on the newspaper is based on the author's interviews with seven current and former *Journal* editors who worked for the newspaper during all or part of his tenure as managing editor.

Page 212 *Thomson . . . showed verve as a rookie reporter:* This characterization of Thomson's background and career, up to and including the *Journal*, draws on interviews with three colleagues who worked closely with him at the *Journal* and the *Times of London*. Physical description of Thomson is informed by author's personal observation. Also Mark Baker, "Rupert Has Got a Crush on You," *The Age*, March 23, 2013.

Page 213 *He called the deal a Faustian bargain:* Ian Johnson, interview by author.

Page 213 *campaigned with a small group of reporters:* Richard Perez-Peña, "Murdoch's Arrival Worries Journal Employees," *New York Times*, July 19, 2007; two *Wall Street Journal* reporters, interview by author.

Page 213 *the Special Committee . . . was to be constituted:* Thomas Bray, interview by author.

Page 213 *"Murdoch clearly has no intention":* E.S. Browning, interview by author.

Page 214 *"felt like a cynical joke":* Former *Journal* reporter, interview by author.

Page 215 *wanted to run the nation's leading general interest newspaper:* Five current and former *Wall Street Journal* editors, interview by author; Eric Pooley, "Excusive: Rupert Murdoch Speaks," *Time*, June 28, 2007.

Page 215 *the top-read story on the paper's website:* Senior *Wall Street Journal* news executive and public relations official for the newspaper, interviews by author.

Page 215 *"The pace of news changed":* Wall Street Journal deputy editor in chief Rebecca Blumenstein, interview by author.

Page 215 *the day after the Fort Hood shootings:* Former *Wall Street Journal* executive, interview by author.

Page 215 *"reflect Murdoch's intentions":* Former *Journal* senior news executive William Grueskin, interview by author.

Page 216 *"They don't try to take you inside boardrooms":* Former senior *Journal* news executive, interview by author.

Page 216 *"more good and less excellent":* Former *Wall Street Journal* executive, interview by author.

Page 216 *began to ease up a bit:* This description of Thomson and Murdoch's shifts relies on author's interviews with four *Journal* editors at the time.

Page 216 *The biggest mistake one can make: Journal* editor, interview by author.

Page 217 *So, too, did Murdoch abandon plans to scrap the paywall:* David Carr, "For Murdoch, It's Try, Try Again," *New York Times*, August 9, 2009.

Page 217 *"Barack Hussein Obama":* Former senior *Wall Street Journal* editor, interview by author.

Page 218 *Baker was British, charming, literate:* Author's observations supplemented by characterizations made by several senior *Journal* editors.

Page 218 *his praise for Sarah Palin:* Gerard Baker, "Go West, Towards the Future of Conservatism," *Times of London*, September 5, 2008.

Page 218 *believed the Journal was populated by liberals and leftists:* Twelve current and former editors and reporters, including five to whom Thomson and Baker directly conveyed their thinking, interviews by author.

Page 219 *that didn't make it into the article:* Former *Journal* reporter involved with that article, interview by author; Elizabeth Williamson et al., "Stimulus Confusion Frustrates Business," *Wall Street Journal*, April 20, 2009.

Page 219 Times *media critic David Carr cited concerns:* David Carr, "Under Murdoch, Tilting Rightward at the Journal," *New York Times*, December 13, 2009.

Page 219 *"yet more evidence that the* New York Times": John Koblin, "Robert Thomson Takes Swing at David Carr, Bill Keller," *Observer*, December 14, 2009.

Page 220 *sexually ambiguous facial features:* Jena Pincott, "Why Women Don't Want Masculine Men," *Wall Street Journal,* March 27, 2010; Michael Wolff, "Murdoch to Sulzberger: You Are a Girlie Man," VanityFair.com, March 27, 2010; three senior *Wall Street Journal* journalists, interviews by author.

Page 220 *Sulzberger complained about it directly:* John Koblin, "Battle of the Barons!" *Observer,* April 14, 2010.

Page 220 *"We've been vilified, unjustly so":* Scott Heekin-Canedy, interview by author.

Page 220 *"a paper willing to do President Obama's bidding":* Rupert Murdoch, remarks on the *Kalb Report* at the National Press Club in Washington, DC, April 6, 2010.

Page 220 *skepticism . . . heightened rather than abated:* This section is based on the author's interviews with seven current and former reporters and editors for the *Journal.*

Page 221 *"Robert just wants people":* Senior *Journal* editor, interview by author.

Page 221 *"The* Journal *was nudged rightward":* Former *Journal* editor, interview by author.

Page 221 *In a front-page story on February 23, 2011:* Neil King Jr., "It's Crunch Time for Organized Labor," *Wall Street Journal,* February 23, 2011.

Page 222 *"Six right-to-work states":* Reporter who covered related matters for the *Journal* at the time, interview by author.

Page 222 *From another piece, a day later:* Thomas M. Burton, Amy Merrick, and Douglas Belkin, "GOP Retreats on Indiana Labor Law," *Wall Street Journal,* February 24, 2011; critique drawn from author's interviews with several reporters for the newspaper.

Page 222 *"It was often difficult to read between the lines":* Former *Wall Street Journal* reporter, interview by author.

Page 223 *"'Gerry would want to rework the story like this'":* A *Wall Street Journal* reporter who often covered politics, interview by author.

Page 223 *Those polls aren't reliably reflecting:* Account of Baker's exchanges with editors derived from author's interview with two *Journal* editors and one reporter.

Page 224 *Thomson took exception to a story:* A reporter with contemporaneous knowledge about the story, interview by author.

Page 224 *This completely leaves out the part:* Three current or former reporters aware of episode contemporaneously, interviews by author.

Page 225 *There was a lot of money at stake:* Rachel Monahan, "Rupert Murdoch Given $27 Million No-Bid Contract From State Department of Education," *New York Daily News,* July 31, 2011.

Page 225 *Murdoch had pegged the possible marketplace:* Calvin Reid, "News Corp's Joel Klein Outlines Plans for Amplify Education Unit," *Publishers Weekly,* December 5, 2012.

Chapter 18

Page 226 *The patriarch telephoned the paper's London bureau chief:* Bruce Orwall, "In Interview, Murdoch Defends News Corp," *Wall Street Journal,* July 14, 2011; Bruce Orwall et al., "Murdoch Defiant as FBI Acts—U.S. to Probe 9/11 Claim; News Corp CEO to Face U.K. Panel," *Wall Street Journal,* July 15, 2011.

Page 227 *what he called the "Fox-ification" of the* Journal*:* Joe Nocera, "The Journal Becomes Fox-ified," *New York Times,* July 15, 2011. Nocera's earlier, pro-Murdoch column: "Promises and Desires," *New York Times,* June 2, 2007.

Page 227 *privately considered Nocera's column terribly unfair:* One former editor, two current editors, and one reporter still at the paper, interviews by author.

Page 228 *The allegation . . . was particularly nettlesome:* Two senior editors, two former senior editors, and four reporters for the *Journal,* interview by author.

Page 228 *"anxious what it might mean":* Former *Journal* deputy managing editor Alan Murray, interviews by author.

Page 229 *reads as though it had been carefully couched:* Les Hinton, answers to questions from House of Commons Select Committee on Culture, Media, and Sports, September 15, 2009.

Page 229 *In a blistering editorial:* "News and Its Critics," *Wall Street Journal,* July 18, 2011.

Page 229 *the* Times *had published its own exposé:* *Guardian* editor Alan Rusbridger and former *New York Times* executive editor Bill Keller, interviews by author.

Page 230 *Gigot had also pledged to colleagues:* Two former *Journal* editors, interviews by author.

Page 230 *Farhi . . . raised the specter of media bias:* Paul Farhi, "Murdoch, Rivals Alike Face Questions About Coverage of Hacking Scandal," *Washington Post,* July 17, 2011.

Page 230 *the* Times *of London . . . struck a tone of remorse:* See, for example, "Tuesday's Test: Rupert and James Murdoch Are Right to Give Evidence to Parliament, for the Press Must Be Accountable," editorial, *Times of London,* July 15, 2011. The piece begins with the memorable line: "The 'Dear John' letters sent to Parliament by Rupert and James Murdoch yesterday were a serious mistake."

Page 230 *the committee published a statement:* "What About the Journal? A Report from the Special Committee," *Wall Street Journal,* July 25, 2011.

Page 231 *did not reflect life as it was experienced:* This passage is based on the author's interviews with four *Wall Street Journal* staffers.

Page 231 *investigative reporter Steve Stecklow uncovered a dissonance:* Steve Stecklow et al., "Tabloid's Pursuit of Missing Girl Led to Its Own Demise Years Later," *Wall Street Journal,* August 20, 2011.

Page 231 *thought it was a barn-burner:* This passage on the *Journal*'s Milly Dowler voice mail story is based on author's interviews with five current and former *Wall Street Journal* journalists with knowledge of events as they unfolded.

Page 232 *Orwall had edited the front-page story:* John Lippman, Leslie Chang, and Robert Frank, "Rupert Murdoch's Wife Wendi Wields Influence at News Corp," *Wall Street Journal,* November 1, 2000.

Page 232 *Orwall could be seen holed up in his office:* One current and one former *Wall Street Journal* journalist, interviews by author.

Page 233 *"the process was so painful":* Wall Street Journal journalist with involvement in these events, interview by author.

Page 233 *Stuart Varney gamely and vainly tried:* Rupert Murdoch and Stuart Varney, *Varney & Co.,* July 9, 2009.

Page 233 *he had been failed by people:* Rupert Murdoch, testimony before Select Committee on Culture, Media, and Sport, July 19, 2011.

Page 234 *The law firm's presence was triggered by Goodman's complaint:* As reproduced in the *Independent,* "Full Text of Clive Goodman's Letter to News International," August 16, 2011.

Page 234 *sleight of hand in the corporation's public reliance:* Paul Sonne, Jeanne Whalen, and Bruce Orwall, "New Issues Emerge for News Corp. in Britain," *Wall Street Journal,* August 17, 2011.

Page 234 *[Ingrassia] recused himself from all coverage:* Author's email exchange with *New York Times* spokeswoman Eileen Murphy.

Chapter 19

Page 236 *prepared to take their case public:* Tom Crone, letter to John Whittingdale MP, chairman of the House of Commons Select Committee on Culture, Media, and Sport, August 6, 2011; Colin Myler, letter to Whittingdale, August 10, 2011. Both letters are included in *News International and Phone-Hacking,* April 30, 2012, the Culture, Media, and Sport Committee's eleventh report.

Page 237 *The younger generation's efforts to work in unison:* Author's interviews with two former News Corp officials and a confidant of one of the adult Murdoch children; Sarah Ellison, "The Rules of Succession," *Vanity Fair,* December 1, 2011.

Page 237 *James and Rebekah fucked the company:* Michael Wolff, tweet, as cited in Jamie Doward and Lisa O'Connell, "Murdochs in 'Family Fallout' over Crisis," *Guardian,* July 16, 2011.

Page 237 *James remained hidden from view:* News Corp earnings call, August 11, 2011, http://seekingalpha.com/article/286535-news-management-discusses-q4-2011-results-earnings-call-transcript?part=single.

Page 238 *"that's a matter of real regret":* James Murdoch, interview by Tom Bradbury, July 8, 2011.

Page 238 *In one sign among many:* Sharon Otterman, "Subsidiary of News Corp Loses Deal for State," *New York Times,* August 29, 2011.

Page 238 *Chapman . . . cited a "feeling of family compassion":* Jonathan Chapman, testimony to CMS, September 6, 2011.

Page 238 *As Crone and Myler addressed the committee:* Tom Crone and Colin Myler, testimony to CMS, September 6, 2011.

Page 240 *"given Mr. Murdoch's board an F":* Neal Minow, interview by author.

Page 240 *"If you had this happen in a normal company":* Laura Martin, interview by author.

Page 240 *confidence laced with bravado:* Rupert Murdoch, address to News Corp annual shareholders meeting, Fox Studios, Los Angeles, October 21, 2011. Subsequent quotations and exchanges with shareholders at the meeting taken from same event.

Page 241 *"I think I've got a duty":* Tom Watson MP, interview by author.

Page 241 *board members found it difficult to distinguish:* Two former News Corp executives, interviews by author.

Page 241 *The day proved arduous:* Amy Chozick and Michael J. De La Merced, "Murdoch's Sons Rebuked by News Corp. Shareholders," *New York Times*, October 24, 2011.

Page 242 *was James Murdoch a fool or a knave?* James Murdoch, testimony to CMS, November 11, 2011. Murdoch's remarks to MPs are drawn from that session as well.

Page 244 *The public learned of the private eyes:* Louise Mensch MP, remarks during James Murdoch testimony; Crone, letter to Whittingdale, December 1, 2011; author's interview with Lewis.

Page 244 *the identity of an anonymous police blogger:* Ben Webster, "The Times and the Nightjack Case," *Times of London*, January 19, 2012; David Allen Green, "Why the Hacking of NightJack Matters," *New Statesman*, January 20, 2012.

Page 244 *the* Sunday Times *acknowledged . . . "blagging":* John Witherow, testimony at Leveson Inquiry, January 17, 2012; "Leveson Inquiry: The Sunday Times 'Blagged Gordon Brown,'" *Telegraph*, January 17, 2012.

Page 244 *In the middle of February:* David Batty, "Senior Sun Journalists Arrested in Police Payments Probe," *Guardian*, February 11, 2012.

Page 245 *Rupert Murdoch returned to London:* "Rupert Murdoch Says Sun on Sunday 'to Launch Soon' and Lifts Suspensions," *Sun*, February 20, 2012.

Page 245 *"a network of corrupted officials":* Deputy assistant police commissioner Sue Akers, testimony to Leveson Inquiry, February 27, 2012.

Chapter 20

Page 246 *fancy, high-powered dinners:* Former Fox News executive, interview by author.

Page 247 *He turned to Francisco Cortes for help:* Francisco Cortes, interview by author; David Folkenflik, "How Fox Pioneered a Formula for Latino News," *All Things Considered*, August 8, 2012. Additional background drawn from Eliza Gray, "Roger Ailes' Border War," *New Republic*, February 11, 2013.

Page 247 *accounted for more than half of the country's population growth:* Sharon R. Ennis, Merays Rios-Vargas, and Nora G. Albert, "The Hispanic

Population: 2010," part of US Census Bureau report, "2010 Census Briefs," May 2011, www.census.gov/prod/cen2010/briefs/c2010br-04.pdf.

Page 248 *a poll on Latino views:* Carolyn Salazar, "Almost Half of Latino Voters Find 'Illegal Immigrant' Offensive, Says Poll," Fox News Latino, March 8, 2012.

Page 248 *"Eighty-five percent support undocumented workers":* Bryan Llenas, interview by Rick Folbaum, *Fox News Live,* March 9, 2012.

Page 248 *The chairman had always minted the stars:* The background on Beck's tenure at Fox News is informed by author's interviews with Glenn Beck, Bill Shine, and several other journalists at the network.

Page 249 *Ailes took steps to remove Beck:* The depiction of Beck's departure is based on the author's interviews with two Fox News executives, one Ailes associate, and two Beck associates.

Page 249 *A carefully orchestrated joint interview:* David Bauder, "Fox News Channel Ending Glenn Beck's Daily Show Later This Year," Associated Press, April 6, 2011.

Page 249 *flashes of his trademark humor: Beck,* April 6, 2011.

Page 249 *a deranged business genius:* Author's interviews with a current Fox News executive, a former Fox News producer, and a former Fox executive.

Page 250 *Ailes was paid:* Compensation figures for Roger Ailes taken from News Corp's "Form 10-Q Quarterly Report," filed with the US Securities and Exchange Commission on February 2, 2009.

Page 250 *still just a hired hand:* Author's interviews with four people to whom Ailes expressed this sentiment.

Page 251 *she told Petraeus she had a message:* This remarkable exchange was captured and posted online by the *Washington Post.* Material in this passage is drawn from Bob Woodward, "Fox News Chief's Failed Attempt to Enlist Petraeus as Presidential Candidate," *Washington Post,* December 3, 2012; "Transcript: Kathleen T. McFarland Talks with Gen. David Petraeus," *Washington Post,* December 3, 2012.

Page 251 *The Republican field needs shaking up:* Ailes shared his thinking about the presidential field with Howard Kurtz, "Secret Tape: Ailes Tried to Entice Petraeus to Run," Daily Beast, December 4, 2012.

Page 252 *Romney did no interviews:* List of Romney media appearances and interviews between October 11 and November 11, 2011, provided to author by Romney campaign.

Page 253 *Romney met privately with Fox News executives:* Friend of Ailes, interview by author.

Page 253 *Then he sat down with Fox's Bret Baier:* Romney, interview by Bret Baier, Fox News *Special Report,* November 29, 2011.

Page 253 *the "Fox primary":* Walter Shapiro, "The Idiot Box," *New Republic,* September 14, 2011.

Page 253 *"Can't resist this tweet":* Rupert Murdoch Twitter account, @rupert murdoch, January 2, 2012.

Page 253 *hold his former employers at Fox responsible:* Zev Chafets, "Exclusive Excerpt: Roger Ailes Off Camera," VanityFair.com, March 2013.

Page 253 *So, for that matter, did Gingrich:* Scott Conroy, "Gingrich Charges Fox News with Pro-Romney Bias," Real Clear Politics, April 11, 2012. "Were Murdoch and News Corp Anti-Gingrich?" the4thEstate.net, May 3, 2012; "News Corp Not Only Media Corporation Hostile to Gingrich," the4thEstate.net, May 15, 2012.

Page 254 *like a political hit piece:* Dylan Byers, "Fox Releases 4-Minute Attack on Obama," Politico, May 30, 2012.

Page 254 *Fox removed the video:* Jeremy W. Peters, "Enemies and Allies for 'Friends,'" *New York Times*, June 20, 2012.

Page 254 *CNN posted a correction and an apology:* Jane Mayer, "The Health Care Ruling That Wasn't," *New Yorker*, June 28, 2012.

Page 254 *Fox said it had gotten the story right:* Bill Hemmer, Fox News rolling coverage of the Supreme Court ruling, June 28, 2012.

Page 255 *Christie took to Fox News:* Chris Christie, interview on *Fox & Friends*, October 30, 2012.

Page 255 *Obama further rewarded him:* Matt Katz, "Christie Makes a Friend Named Bruce Springsteen," *Philadelphia Inquirer*, November 5, 2012.

Page 256 *Murdoch and Ailes met with Romney:* A friend of Ailes, interview by author.

Page 256 *"Can't blame Christie":* Rupert Murdoch, Twitter feed, November 3, 2012.

Page 256 *"first Republican gov to support Romney":* Rupert Murdoch, Twitter feed, November 3, 2012.

Page 256 *As a mark of respect:* Michael Barbaro, "After Obama, Christie Wants a G.O.P. Hug," *New York Times*, November 19, 2012.

Page 256 *"Monolithic media will spend next three days":* Rupert Murdoch, Twitter feed, November 3, 2012.

Page 257 *"Romney seeing small late surge":* Rupert Murdoch, Twitter feed, November 4, 2012.

Page 257 *his column in the* Journal: Karl Rove, "Can We Believe the Presidential Polls?" *Wall Street Journal*, October 4, 2012.

Page 258 *"we've already painted those red":* David Paleologos, interview, *O'Reilly Factor*, October 9, 2012.

Page 258 *"this momentum will continue":* Dick Morris, interview, *Hannity*, October 15, 2012.

Page 258 *the* Times *took a gamble: New York Times* editor, interview by author.

Page 258 *offered the Fox audience a vision: Dick* Morris, interview, *On the Record with Greta Van Susteren*, November 1, 2012.

Page 258 *"My personal guess":* Newt Gingrich, interview, *On the Record with Greta Van Susteren*, November 5, 2012.

Page 259 *"about a seven-point margin":* Dick Morris, interview, *Hannity*, November 5, 2012.

Page 259 *arranged to write a memoir:* Bill Keller, "Murdoch's Pride is America's Poison," *New York Times*, May 5, 2012.

Page 260 *whether he took prescription pills:* Eddie Scarry of FishbowlDC, email to Gabriel Sherman, May 7, 2013. Sherman provided the email to the author.

Page 260 *bought a bunch of domain addresses:* Erik Wemple, "Roger Ailes Biography Sparks an Internet Shopping Spree," WashingtonPost.com, January 25, 2013.

Page 260 *obsessed with the pay of David Zaslav:* Author's interview with two Ailes associates for this account of his flirtation with Newsmax.

Page 260 *he was aging and had health issues:* Chafets, *Roger Ailes*, p. 234.

Page 260 *He had never groomed a successor:* Two former News Corp officials, interview by author. Ailes told Zev Chafets that he had indeed made plans for his succession but was keeping them secret. However, the job, strictly speaking, is not Ailes's to bestow.

Page 261 *Ailes had signed a four-year contract extension:* Sam Thielman, "Roger Ailes Renews News Corp. Contract," *Adweek*, October 19, 2012.

Page 261 *"looking like someone ran over your dog":* Ailes, quoted in Gabriel Sherman, "How Karl Rove Fought with Fox News over the Ohio Call," *New York Magazine*, November 7, 2012.

Page 262 *"That's pretty strong medicine":* Brit Hume, remarks on Fox News channel's election night coverage, November 6, 2012. Subsequent statements from Fox News anchors and pundits in this section—Bill O'Reilly, Dana Perino, Bret Baier, Chris Wallace, Megyn Kelly, and Karl Rove—are also taken from that Fox News broadcast, stretching from Tuesday evening through early morning Wednesday, unless otherwise noted.

Page 262 *"Just look at European welfare state":* Rupert Murdoch, Twitter feed, November 3, 2012.

Page 263 *Ailes later said he had called Michael Clemente:* Chris Ariens, "Roger Ailes on Election Night: 'Rove was wrong. He backed down. Our guys were right,'" TVNewser, November 16, 2012.

Page 263 *illegal immigrants can no longer be treated with hostility:* Chafets, *Roger Ailes*, pp. 244–245.

Page 264 *"Nearly every piece of data":* Matthew Dowd, Twitter feed, November 8, 2012.

Page 264 *Hume had offered the closest:* Brit Hume, Fox News election night coverage, November 6, 2012.

Page 264 *a blog promising to "unskew" the polls:* Dean Chambers, interview by author.

Page 264 *Romney did not draft a concession speech:* Byron York, "In Boston, Stunned Romney Supporters Struggle to Explain Defeat," *Washington Examiner*, November 7, 2012.

Page 264 *"strengthened and amplified by what I wanted to happen":* John Podhoretz, interview by author.

Page 264 *"The conservative followership has been fleeced":* David Frum, *Morning Joe*, November 9, 2012.

Page 264 *Morris explained himself:* Dick Morris, *Hannity*, November 12, 2012.

Page 265 *Ailes fired Morris . . . and kept Rove off the air:* Gabriel Sherman, "Fox News Puts Karl Rove on the Bench," *New York Magazine*, December 4, 2012.

Page 265 *Jon Huntsman Sr. . . . took Fox to task:* Jon Huntsman Sr., interview, *Your World with Neil Cavuto*, November 16, 2012.

Chapter 21

Page 266 *the plan was to allow the* Sun *to thrive:* One News International executive and two knowledgeable former News Corp executives, interviews by author.

Page 267 *"We have the horns and the tails":* Jane Croft and Ben Fenton, "Hacking Victims Say News Group Destroyed Evidence," *Financial Times,* January 19, 2012; Erik Larson, "News Corp. Must Search Laptops After 'Startling' E-mails," Bloomberg News, January 23, 2012. Judge Vos's comments also drawn from these articles.

Page 267 *Lewis was quickly losing:* Two News Corp executives, interviews by author.

Page 267 *Lewis declined to answer:* William Lewis, testimony to Leveson Inquiry, January 10, 2012, afternoon session.

Page 267 *they labored to forestall punitive federal action:* Two current News Corp executives and one former News Corp executive, interviews by author; Sarah Ellison, "Murdoch's Civil War," *Vanity Fair,* June 2012.

Page 268 *"drain the swamp":* David Barrett, Robert Mendick, and Patrick Sawer, "Sun Executives Arrested over Illegal Police Payments," *Telegraph,* January 28, 2012.

Page 268 *Trevor Kavanagh . . . spoke out twice:* Kavanagh, interview, BBC Radio 5 *Live;* Radio 4 *World at One,* February 13, 2012.

Page 268 *called the investigation a witch-hunt:* Trevor Kavanagh, "This Witch-Hunt Has Put Us Behind Ex-Soviet States on Press Freedom," *Sun,* February 13, 2012.

Page 268 *Murdoch signaled they retained his affinity:* "Street of Shame: Sun hacks have Murdoch taped," *Private Eye,* Issue 1342, June 28, 2013.

Page 269 *emails from 2006 suggesting Rebekah Brooks knew:* Rick Dewsbury, "Rebekah Brooks Knew in 2006 About Widespread Phone Hacking at News of the World—After Being Tipped Off by Police," *Daily Mail,* February 28, 2012.

Page 269 *The company presented [James's] resignation:* News Corp executive, interview by author; "James Murdoch Steps Down as Executive Chairman, News International to Focus on Expanding International TV Businesses," News Corp press release, February 29, 2012.

Page 269 *once again attempted damage control:* Tom Harper, "I've Looked After Horses All My Life and We Gave It Back in Good Condition," *Independent,* February 29, 2012.

Page 269 *Reporters for the* Telegraph *. . . badgered 10 Downing Street:* See, for example, Gordon Raynor, "Rebekah Brooks and the Police Gift Horse," *Telegraph,* February 29, 2012; Martin Evans, "'Gift Horse' to Brooks Surprised Me, Says Scotland Yard Chief," *Telegraph,* March 1, 2012; Christopher Hope, "Cameron Silent on Rides with Raisa," *Telegraph,* March 1, 2012; Hope, "Tale of the Police Horse and the Chipping Norton Set That Grew Legs," *Telegraph,* March 1, 2012; Hope, "Horsegate: I Did Ride Brooks's Police Horse Raisa, Says David Cameron," *Telegraph,* March 2, 2012.

Page 269 *"He's a good friend, and he's a neighbor":* Christopher Hope, "At Last, Cameron Talks Some Horse Sense," *Telegraph,* March 3, 2012.

Page 270 *Tory fund-raiser promising "premier league" access:* "Tory Charges £250,000 to Meet PM," *Sunday Times,* March 25, 2012.

Page 270 *a two-month campaign against a consumption tax:* Tom Newton Dunn and Steve Hawker, "Pasty La Vista, Taxman," *Sun,* May 29, 2012.

Page 270 *quietly girded for more bad headlines:* "News Corp and the Permira Funds Sign Agreement to Sell NDS Group Ltd," News Corp press release, March 15, 2012.

Page 270 *a satellite TV encryption company vital to Sky TV's enterprises:* This passage is based on author's interviews with News Corp official; a News International spokeswoman; Neil Chenoweth; Mark Lewis; and correspondence between News Corp and the *Australian Financial Review.*

Page 271 Panorama *had teamed up:* "Murdoch's TV Pirates," BBC 1 *Panorama,* April 2, 2012.

Page 271 *Chenoweth had obtained 14,000 emails:* Neil Chenoweth, "Pay Piracy Hits News," *Australian Financial Review,* March 28, 2012, and subsequent articles in the *AFR.*

Page 271 *derailed a related lawsuit:* Richard Verrier, "Canal Plus Sues NDS Group," *Los Angeles Times,* March 13, 2002; "Vivendi to Sell Unit to News Corp," Bloomberg News as reposted on LosAngelesTimes.com, June 10, 2002; "BSkyB Eyes Expansion into Europe," Bloomberg News, republished by *Investment Week,* August 26, 2003.

Page 271 *"old toffs and right-wingers" . . . "lies and libels . . . easy to hit back hard":* Rupert Murdoch, Twitter account, March 28, 2012.

Page 271 *accused Chenoweth of relying on stolen emails:* Darren Davidson, "News to AFR: Put Up or Shut Up over Piracy Allegations," *Australian,* April 2, 2012.

Page 271 "Panorama *presented manipulated":* "Statement from Chase Carey, President and Chief Operating Officer, News Corporation Regarding Misrepresentation of NDS by the BBC's *Panorama,*" News Corp press release, March 28, 2012; Dr. Abe Peled and NDS issued six statements and letters to refute the BBC and the *Australian Financial Review* in six successive days starting on March 28, 2012, http://nds.com/Media_Center /Press_Releases.

Page 272 *Lawyers for News Corp wrote letters cautioning:* Mark Hughes, "BBC to Make Fresh Claims of Murdoch Firm Law-Breaking," *Telegraph,* March 24, 2012.

Page 272 *a News Corp official:* News Corp official, interview by author.

Page 272 *OfCom had stepped up its review:* Elizabeth Rigby, Salamander Davoudi, and Andrew Edgecliffe-Johnson, "Challenge to Murdoch Grip on BSkyB," *Financial Times,* March 8, 2012.

Page 272 *His retreat from the UK was nearly complete:* "Statement from Rupert Murdoch, Chairman and CEO of News Corporation, and Chase Carey, President and Chief Operating Officer, News Corporation Regarding James Murdoch's Decision to Step Down as Chairman of BSkyB," News Corp press release, April 3, 2012.

Page 272 *Sky News admitted that it had hacked:* Dan Sabbagh, Nick Davies, and Robert Booth, "Sky News Admits Hacking Emails of 'Canoe Man,'" *Guardian,* April 5, 2012; Lilly Vitorovich, "Sky News Says Emails Were Hacked in 'Public Interest,'" *Wall Street Journal,* April 5, 2012.

Page 273 *Murdoch seemed to relish the testimony:* Rupert Murdoch, testimony to Leveson Inquiry, April 26, 2012, morning session. Murdoch's ensuing quotations and events are drawn from Murdoch's testimony on April 25 and 26 before the inquiry, as cited in the text.

Page 274 *called Murdoch effectively a cabinet member:* Price, *Spin Doctor's Diary,* p. xii.

Page 275 *a senior aide to Thatcher had taken notes:* "Prime Minister: Rupert Murdoch Lunch," memo by Bernard Ingham, January 5, 1981, www.margaret thatcher.org/document/FA5DB3D8544A461DACEDF181801765AE.pdf.

Page 275 *"Margaret is very keen":* Woodrow Wyatt note cited by Robert Jay in Leveson Inquiry, Rupert Murdoch testimony, April 25, 2012, morning session.

Page 275 *John Major later alleged, under oath:* John Major, testimony before Leveson Inquiry, June 12, 2012.

Page 276 *the broadcaster's budget was to be cut:* Harry Phibbs, "Budget Cuts Will Give the BBC a Taste of the Real World," *Daily Mail,* October 19, 2010; James Robinson and Mark Sweney, "BBC Budget Cut by 16 Percent in Spending Review, George Osborne Confirms," *Guardian,* October 20, 2010.

Page 276 *"get this fucking thing over with":* Murdoch, as overheard by *Guardian* media reporter Dan Sabbagh, cited in Nick Davies, "Rupert Murdoch Gives More Away Than Planned at Leveson," *Guardian,* April 25, 2012.

Page 277 *Tom Watson read aloud:* "Murdoch 'Not Fit to Run' International Company," BBC News, May 1, 2012.

Page 277 *driven by partisan politics:* "News Corporation Statement of UK's Parliamentary Select Committee of Culture, Media, and Sport's News of the World Report," News Corp press release, May 1, 2012. It includes this assessment: "News Corporation regrets that the Select Committee's analysis of the factual record was followed by some commentary that we, and indeed several members of the committee, consider unjustified and highly partisan. These remarks divided the members along party lines."

Page 277 *the ghost of the* News of the World *caught a break:* John Macdonald, witness statement, Leveson Inquiry, May 8, 2012; Martin Evans, "Leveson Inquiry: Milly Dowler's Phone Was Hacked but Messages May Not Have Been Deliberately Deleted," *Telegraph,* May 9, 2012.

Page 278 *he now agreed to sever the newspaper side:* "News Corporation Announces Intent to Pursue Separation of Businesses to Enhance Strategic Alignment and Increase Operational Flexibility," News Corp press release, June 28, 2012; three News Corp officials, interviews by author.

Page 279 *The split represented a reckoning:* Author's interview with a senior Murdoch newspaper editor, a former News Corp executive, and an adviser to one of the adult Murdoch children. Much of the history, particularly from the perspective of Murdoch critics, is recounted in News Corp Shareholder Derivative Litigation, C.A. no. 6285-VCN, Delaware State Court of Chancery, Verified Third Amended Consolidated Shareholder Derivative Complaint.

Page 279 *"newspaper business is like an ice cube":* Don Yacktman, interview by author.

Page 279 The Daily *as a $35 million experiment:* "Murdoch Debuts Daily iPad Paper," *All Things Considered,* February 2, 2011.

Page 279 *Now the* Wall Street Journal *would be responsible:* Senior *Wall Street Journal* executive, interview by author.

Page 279 *"ShitCo" and "GoodCo":* Former *Wall Street Journal* executives, interviews by author.

Chapter 22

Page 280 *the geography of his holdings and the psychology of his children:* The account of Rupert Murdoch's motivations and Lachlan's reactions in this passage are derived from author's interviews with current and former News Corp executives and friends of Lachlan Murdoch.

Page 280 *it paid $2.2 billion:* Elysse Morgan, "Packer Agrees to Consolidated Media Sale," ABC News (Australia), September 7, 2012.

Page 282 *If you don't have that belief:* Friend of Lachlan Murdoch, interview by author.

Page 282 *Rupert Murdoch still wanted them all:* News Corp executive and former News Corp executive, interview by author.

Page 282 *"a massive pain in the ass":* This quotation from Elisabeth Murdoch and others in this section are taken from her address at the James MacTaggart Memorial Lecture, Edinburgh Television Festival, 2012.

Page 283 *"the nastiest people besmirching":* Dennis Potter, James MacTaggart Memorial Lecture, August 27, 1993.

Page 283 *"the pollution of what was already a fairly polluted press":* Dennis Potter, interview by Melvyn Bragg, BBC Channel 4, April 5, 1994.

Page 285 *the show's editor killed the story:* Dan Sabbagh and Josh Halliday, "Jimmy Savile: Newsnight Staff Were Furious After Abuse Report Dropped," *Guardian,* October 1, 2012.

Page 285 *ITV broadcast a documentary:* "The Other Side of Jimmy Savile," ITV *Exposure,* October 3, 2012.

Page 285 *Murdoch's old antagonist Chris (now Lord) Patten:* Lord Patten, testimony to Commons Select Committee for Culture, Media, and Sport, November 27, 2012.

Page 285 *could damage the* New York Times*:* David Folkenflik, "Mark Thompson Takes Over at New York Times Co.," *Morning Edition,* November 15, 2012.

Page 285 *"Saville [sic]-BBC story long way to run":* Rupert Murdoch, Twitter feed, October 14, 2012.

Page 286 *if they pushed the matter too hard:* News Corp editor, interview by author.

Page 286 *invited in Hugh Grant, Charlotte Church:* "Charlotte Church's Media Regulation Hope After David Cameron Meeting," BBC News, October 9, 2012.

Page 286 *"Cameron receiving scumbag celebrities":* Rupert Murdoch, Twitter feed, October 13, 2012.

Page 286 *his liaison with a prostitute:* John Hiscock, "Hugh Grant on Prostitution Charge," *Telegraph,* June 28, 1995.

Page 286 *wrongly claiming Grant had played no role:* Lara Gould and Ben Ellery, "About a Boy! Hugh Grant Has Second Child with 'Fab Mum' Tinglan Hong," *Mail on Sunday,* February 17, 2013.

Page 286 *Murdoch apologized . . . but was otherwise unrepentant:* Cahal Milmo, "Murdoch Says Sorry to Grant over 'Love Child' Remark," *Independent,* October 19, 2012.

Page 286 *Leveson's report dismantled layers of rationalizations: Report of the Leveson Inquiry into Culture, Practices, and Ethics of the Press,* November 29, 2012.

Page 287 *A blogger could base his website in the West Indies:* Paul Staines, "Bring On the Press Police," Wall Street Journal Online, November 27, 2012.

Page 288 *Cameron expressed doubts:* Michael Holden and Kate Holton, "Britain's Cameron Rejects Press Law After Hacking Scandal," Reuters, November 29, 2012.

Page 288 *Cameron pushed a plan with a royal charter:* Fraser Nelson, "Why the Spectator said 'No' to David Cameron's Royal Charter for Regulation of the Press," *Spectator,* March 19, 2013; Alan Rusbridger, "We Need Reform AND a Free Press. This Will Require Both Time and Openness," *Guardian,* March 25, 2013; "UK Urged to Reconsider Post-Leveson Media Proposals," letter to Prime Minister David Cameron from the Committee to Protect Journalists, April 2, 2013.

Page 289 *as media analyst Claire Enders argued:* Claire Enders/Enders Analysis, submission to Leveson Inquiry, July 17, 2012; also Annex 1 and Annex 2 to Enders's submission.

Page 289 *Ed Miliband advocated that path:* Dan Sabbagh, Lisa O'Carroll, and John Plunkett, "Murdoch's Share of the Newspaper Market Is Too Big, Says Miliband," *Guardian,* June 12, 2012.

Page 289 *story about a possible cover-up:* A series of stories about Bo Xilai by Jeremy Page of the *Wall Street Journal* is nicely captured in "Bo Xilai: Inside the Scandal: A WSJ Documentary," WSJ Digital Network, June 29, 2012.

Page 289 *"It involved a certain amount of risk":* Rebecca Blumenstein, interview by author.

Page 289 *the* Times *website was shut down:* Author's interviews with Lawrence Ingrassia, assistant managing editor of the *New York Times,* and Richard Bejtlich, chief security officer for the Mandiant consulting firm.

Page 290 *the Pulitzers were once again punishing:* Two *Wall Street Journal* editors, interview by author.

Page 290 *"proven to be unfounded":* William Grueskin, interview by author.

Page 290 *"We must not take . . . our foot off the gas":* Nick Leys, "Murdoch Affirms 'Papers Here for Years to Come,'" *Australian,* September 24, 2012.

Page 290 *a charming jumble:* The history of the State Theatre in Sydney is set out on its website, www.statetheatre.com.au/HistoryGallery.aspx.

Page 290 *Murdoch's gaze turned westward:* Author's interviews with one News Corp official; two former Tribune Co. officials; and one Tribune Co. official; Meg James, "Rupert Murdoch, Other Potential Buyers Eye L.A. Times," *Los Angeles Times,* October 19, 2012.

Page 291 *"It won't get through":* Meg James and Nicole Sperling, "Rupert Murdoch Says Los Angeles Times Purchase Not a Sure Thing," *Los Angeles Times,* January 14, 2013.

Page 291 *"a strategy of deciding what you want":* Andrew Jay Schwartzman, interview by author.

Page 291 *in hopes of appeasing investors:* A News Corp executive and a News Corp newspaper editor, interviews by author.

Page 291 *Holy shit, Angelo told a friend:* Two of Angelo's associates, interviews by author.

Page 292 *Fox Group . . . would assume any costs:* News Corp executive, interview by author.

Page 292 *Lachlan Murdoch refused to return:* An associate of Lachlan Murdoch and a former News Corp official, interview by author.

Page 292 *"relentless" cost-cutting:* "News Corp Promises 'Relentless' Cuts at Newspapers," Reuters, May 28, 2013.

Page 292 *thought Joel Klein was disappointed:* Former News Corp professional, interview by author.

Page 293 *legal strategy seemed to have worked:* Lawyer familiar with federal investigation into News Corp's potential Federal Corrupt Practices Act violations, interview by author.

Page 293 *Tom Mockridge . . . could not abide:* Andrew Edgecliffe-Johnson and Emily Steel, "Murdoch's UK Newspaper Chief Resigns," *Financial Times,* December 2, 2012; Maisie McCabe, "Liberty Global Hires Tom Mockridge to Run Virgin Media," *MediaWeek,* May 8, 2013.

Page 293 *Rebekah Brooks was set to face trial:* Lisa Carroll, "Rebekah Brooks Trial to Start in September at Old Bailey," *Guardian,* June 7, 2013.

Page 293 *Labour MP Tom Watson wrote a book*: Watson and Hickman, *Dial M for Murdoch.*

Page 293 *Louise Mensch resigned her seat:* "Louise Mensch to Quit as an MP, Triggering Corby By-election," BBC News, August 6, 2012.

Page 293 *James Harding . . . left the paper:* Peter Jukes, "Bad Times at The Times: James Harding Steps Down," Daily Beast, December 13, 2012; Ben Webster, "Harding to Stand Down as Editor of The Times," *Times of London,* December 13, 2012; "James Harding Named as Director of BBC News," BBC News, April 16, 2013.

Page 294 *Murdoch thought getting beaten was:* Rupert Murdoch, testimony to Leveson Inquiry, April 25, 2012, morning session.

Page 294 *Gerard Baker . . . succeeded Thomson:* "Gerard Baker Named Top Editor for Dow Jones, Wall Street Journal," Dow Jones press release, December 3, 2012.

Page 294 *the chairman doused his new editor:* From Twitter feed photo of Kathryn Lurie, an online editor at the *Wall Street Journal*, December 3, 2012.

Page 294 *anticipated Baker's tenure . . . a light touch:* Six current *Journal* editors and reporters, interview by author.

Page 294 *former* Time *magazine managing editor Walter Isaacson:* Author's email exchange with Walter Isaacson; author's interview with *Wall Street Journal* senior editor.

Page 295 *my mum's ninety, Murdoch would say:* Former senior News Corp official, interview by author.

Page 295 *mourners packed St. Paul's:* This account is informed by press reports, including Andrew Rule, "An Exceptional Life Celebrated," *Herald Sun*, December 19, 2012; and Karl Quinn, "A Life of Strong Love and Quiet Generosity," *The Age*, December 19, 2012.

Page 295 *"Today I wish to speak to the extraordinary accomplishments":* "Dame Elisabeth: A Life Lived Always in Full Bloom," eulogy by Rupert Murdoch, republished in the Melbourne *Herald Sun*, December 19, 2012. All quotes pulled from transcript and checked against video of the event.

Page 297 *an oil painting on a bronze background:* Former senior News Corp newspaper editor, interview by author.

Page 298 *Brooks was spotted in Australia:* Amanda Perthen, "The Sun Shines on Rebekah . . . for Now: Ex-tabloid Editor Sips Beer on Sydney Yacht with the Murdochs Ahead of Trial," *Daily Mail*, April 13, 2013.

Page 298 *features desk . . . had taken more time for police to penetrate:* Mark Stephens, interview by author. Stephens is an attorney for many cell phone hacking victims and was, himself, the victim of cell phone hacking.

Page 298 *the company agreed to pay $135 million:* News Corporation Derivative Litigation Settlement, April 22, 2013.

Page 299 *"do it all over again":* Darren Davidson, "'Chance to Do It All Over Again,' Rupert Murdoch Says of Company's Historic Split," *Australian*, May 30, 2013.

Page 299 *filed for divorce:* Andrew Edgecliffe-Johnson, "Rupert Murdoch Files for Divorce," *Financial Times*, June 13, 2013.

Page 299 *he did not care to learn more:* Former News Corp executive, interview by author.

Page 299 *an aide to Tony Blair felt compelled to deny:* Stuart Kemp, "Rupert Murdoch Divorce: Tony Blair's Spokesperson Denies Rumors of Affair with Tony Blair," *Hollywood Reporter*, June 14, 2013.

Page 299 *News International and News Limited vanished:* "News International renamed News UK," News UK press release, June 26, 2013; "News Ltd set for a name change," Australian Associated Press, as posted on SBS.com.au, June 26, 2013.

Page 299 *Murdoch has never convincingly shown any capacity for self-reflection:* Four former News Corp executives, interviews by author.

INDEX

Award-winning journalist DAVID FOLKENFLIK has been NPR's media correspondent since 2004. He previously covered media and politics for the *Baltimore Sun* and edited the 2011 book, *Page One: Inside The New York Times and the Future of Journalism.* He has covered Murdoch and News Corp extensively and has been a frequent commentator on the hacking scandal in both the United States and the United Kingdom. Folkenflik lives with his wife, the radio producer Jesse Baker, and their daughter in New York City.

PublicAffairs is a publishing house founded in 1997. It is a tribute to the standards, values, and flair of three persons who have served as mentors to countless reporters, writers, editors, and book people of all kinds, including me.

I. F. STONE, proprietor of *I. F. Stone's Weekly*, combined a commitment to the First Amendment with entrepreneurial zeal and reporting skill and became one of the great independent journalists in American history. At the age of eighty, Izzy published *The Trial of Socrates*, which was a national bestseller. He wrote the book after he taught himself ancient Greek.

BENJAMIN C. BRADLEE was for nearly thirty years the charismatic editorial leader of *The Washington Post*. It was Ben who gave the *Post* the range and courage to pursue such historic issues as Watergate. He supported his reporters with a tenacity that made them fearless and it is no accident that so many became authors of influential, best-selling books.

ROBERT L. BERNSTEIN, the chief executive of Random House for more than a quarter century, guided one of the nation's premier publishing houses. Bob was personally responsible for many books of political dissent and argument that challenged tyranny around the globe. He is also the founder and longtime chair of Human Rights Watch, one of the most respected human rights organizations in the world.

•   •   •

For fifty years, the banner of Public Affairs Press was carried by its owner Morris B. Schnapper, who published Gandhi, Nasser, Toynbee, Truman, and about 1,500 other authors. In 1983, Schnapper was described by *The Washington Post* as "a redoubtable gadfly." His legacy will endure in the books to come.

Peter Osnos, *Founder and Editor-at-Large*